NEON GENESIS EVANGELION

THE SHINJI IKARI RAISING P

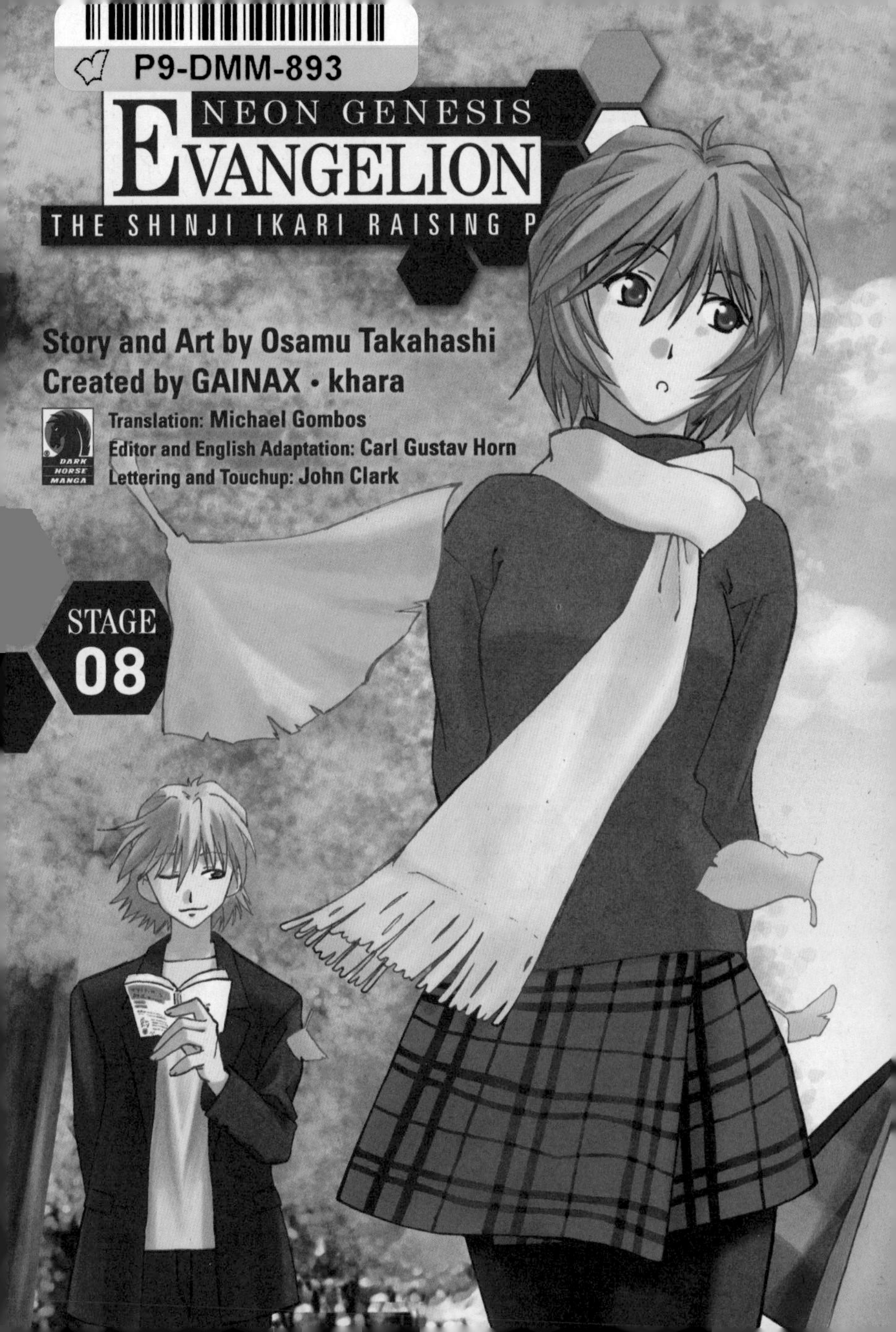

Story and Art by Osamu Takahashi
Created by GAINAX • khara

Translation: Michael Gombos
Editor and English Adaptation: Carl Gustav Horn
Lettering and Touchup: John Clark

DARK HORSE MANGA

STAGE 08

NEON GENESIS EVANGELION
THE SHINJI IKARI RAISING PROJECT

CONTENTS

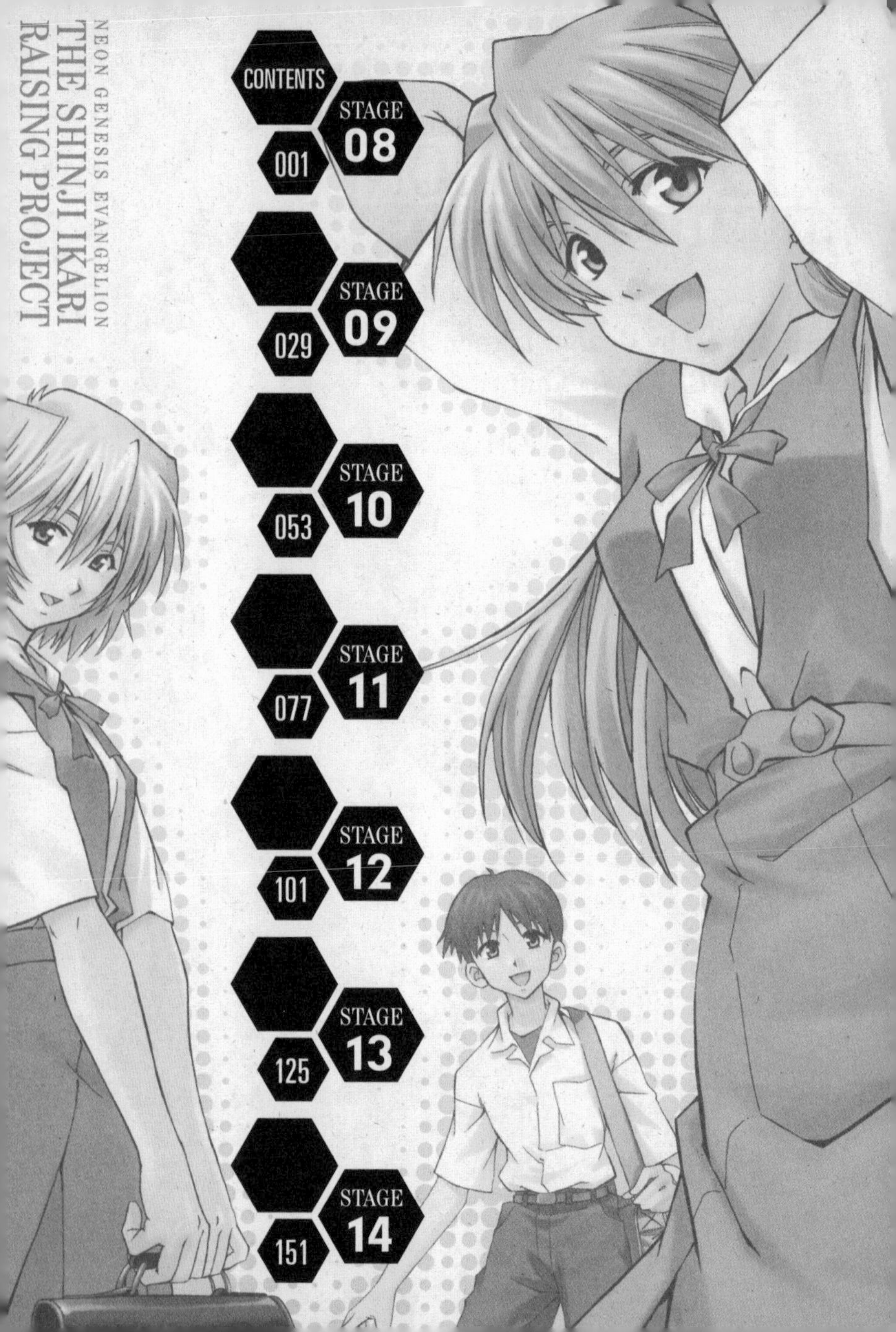

STOP!

止まれ

THIS IS THE BACK OF THE BOOK!

This manga collection is translated into English, but arranged in right-to-left reading format to maintain the artwork's visual orientation as originally drawn and published in Japan. If you've never read comics this way before, take a look at the diagram below to give yourself an idea of how to go about it. Basically, you'll be starting in the upper-right-hand corner, and will read each word balloon and panel moving right to left. It may take a little getting used to, but you should get the hang of it very quickly. Have fun! If this is the millionth manga you've read this way, never mind.

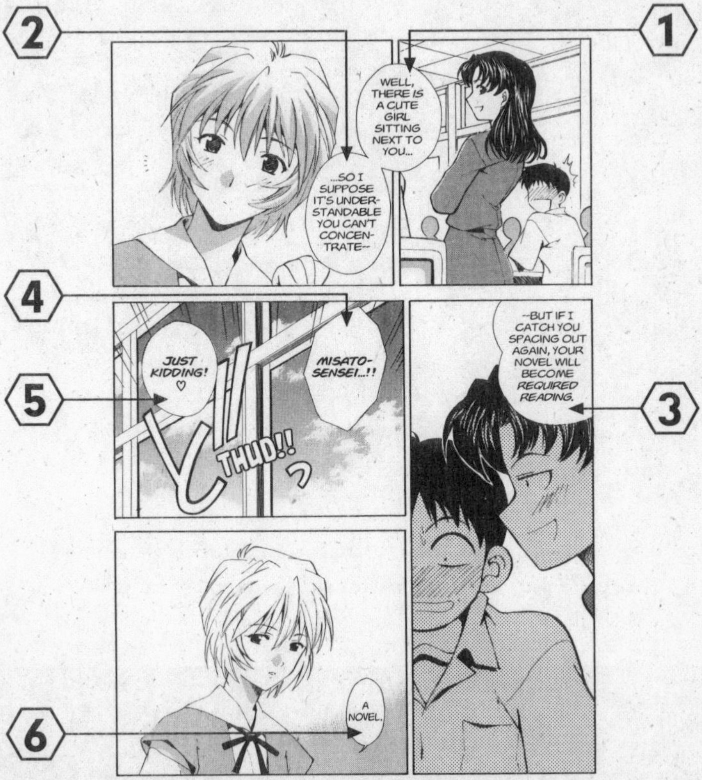

1
WELL, THERE IS A CUTE GIRL SITTING NEXT TO YOU...
2
...SO I SUPPOSE IT'S UNDERSTANDABLE YOU CAN'T CONCENTRATE--
3
--BUT IF I CATCH YOU SPACING OUT AGAIN, YOUR NOVEL WILL BECOME REQUIRED READING.
4
MISATO-SENSEI...!!
5
JUST KIDDING! ♡
THUD!!
6
A NOVEL.

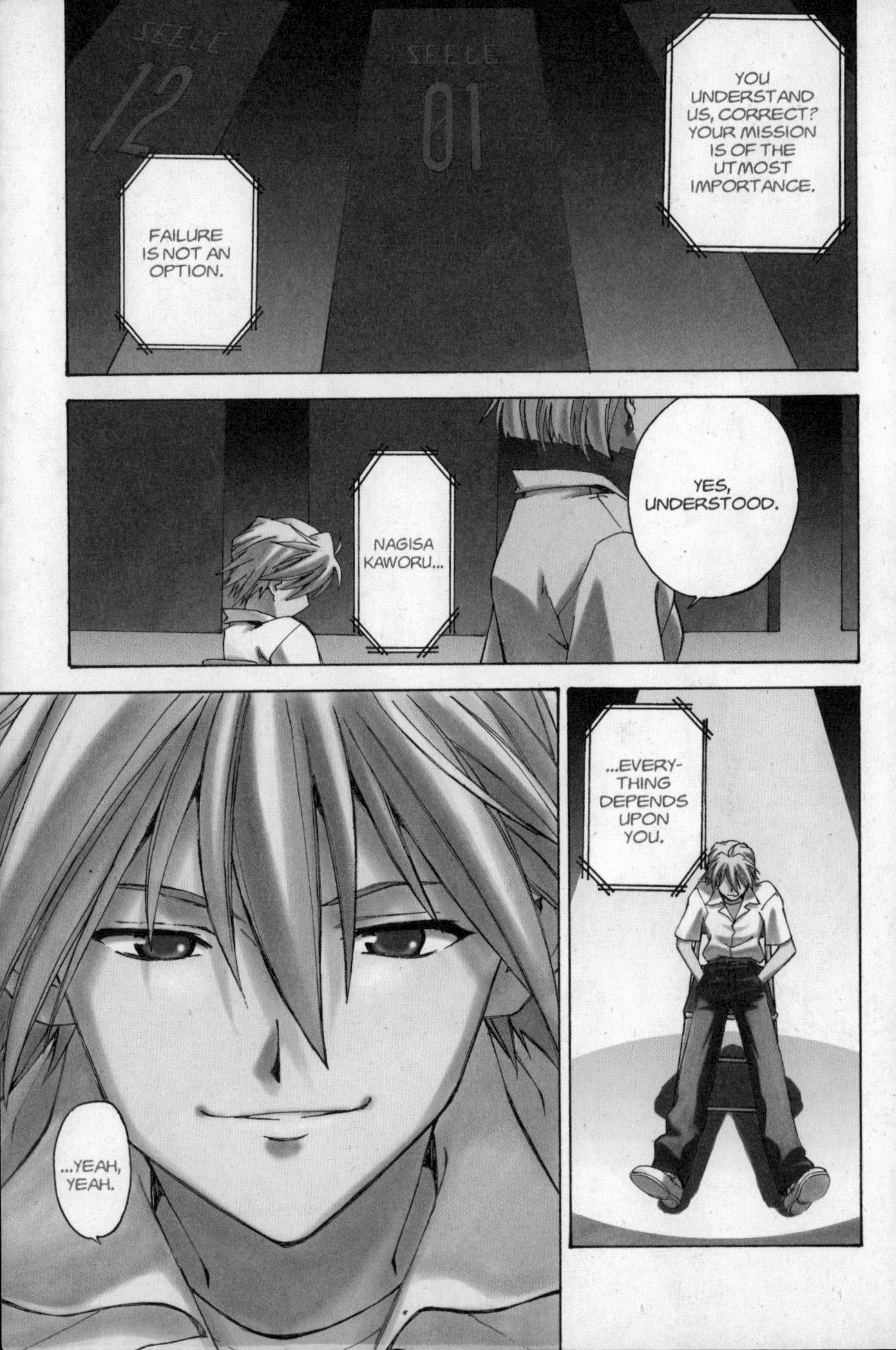
SEELE 01
YOU UNDERSTAND US, CORRECT? YOUR MISSION IS OF THE UTMOST IMPORTANCE.
SEELE 12
FAILURE IS NOT AN OPTION.
YES, UNDERSTOOD.
NAGISA KAWORU...
...EVERY-THING DEPENDS UPON YOU.
...YEAH, YEAH.

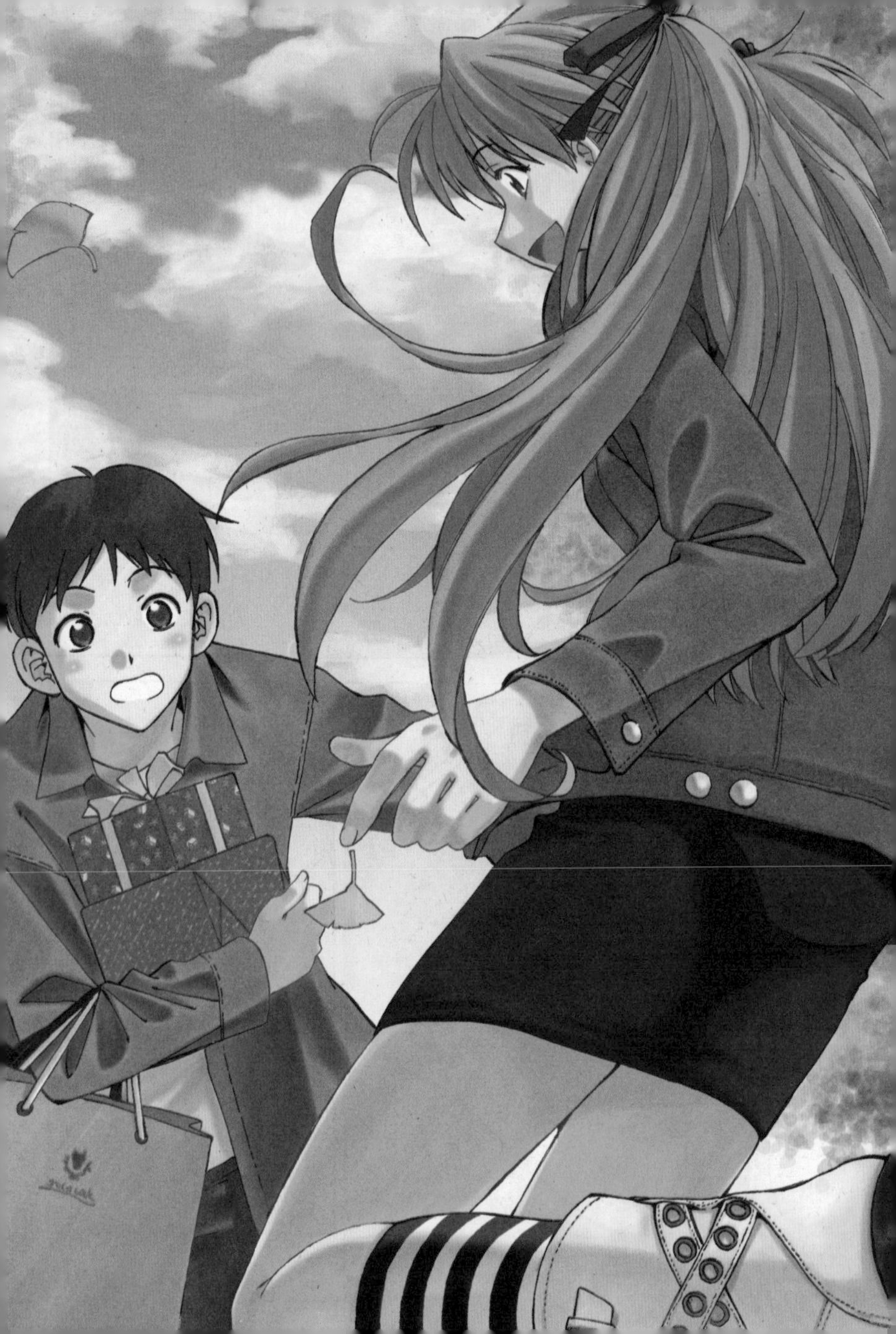

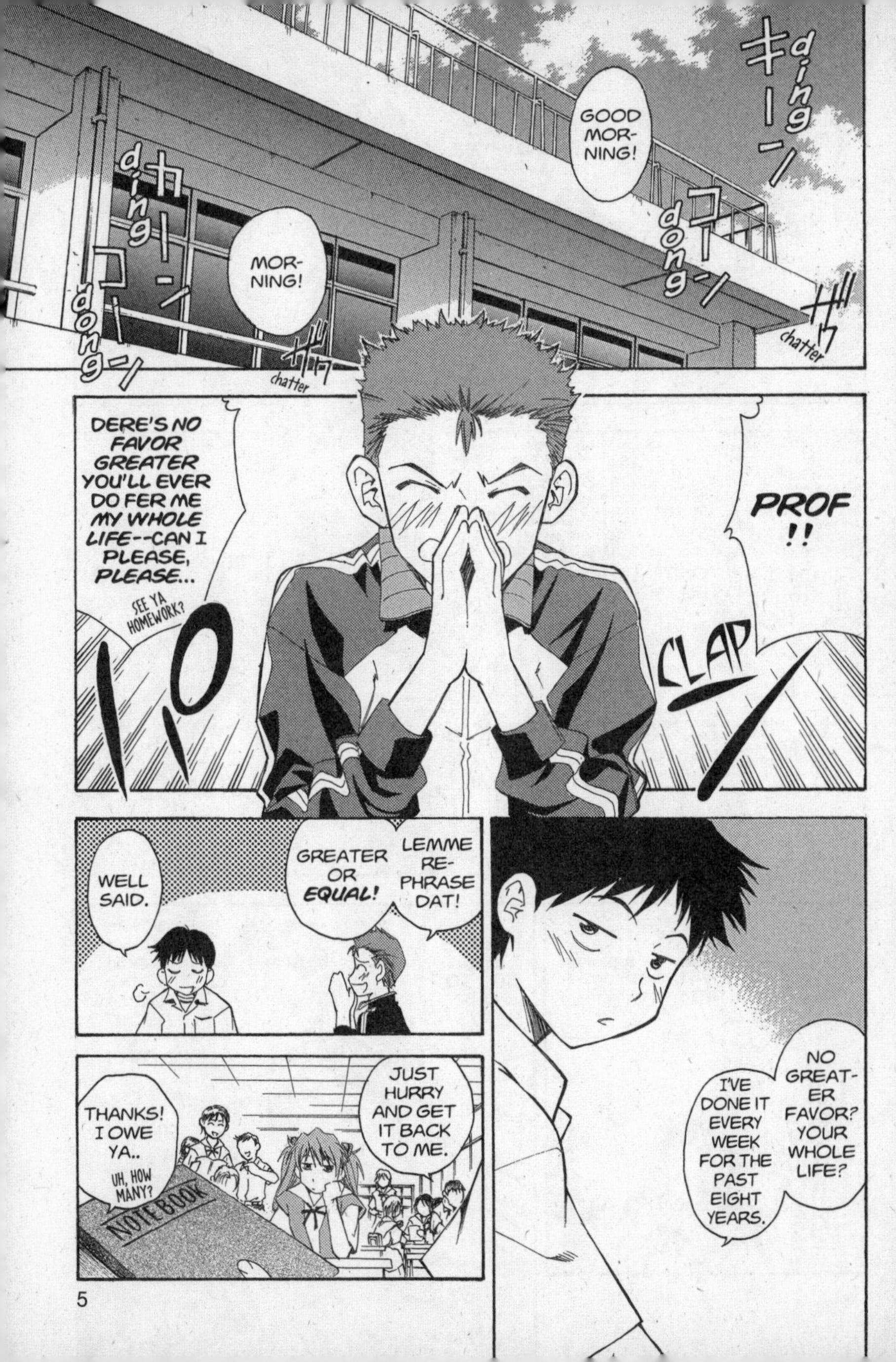
ding
dong
chatter
GOOD MOR-NING!
MOR-NING!
ding
dong
chatter
PROF !!
CLAP
DERE'S NO FAVOR GREATER YOU'LL EVER DO FER ME MY WHOLE LIFE--CAN I PLEASE, PLEASE...
SEE YA HOMEWORK?
NO GREATER-ER FAVOR? YOUR WHOLE LIFE?
I'VE DONE IT EVERY WEEK FOR THE PAST EIGHT YEARS.
LEMME RE-PHRASE DAT!
GREATER OR EQUAL!
WELL SAID.
JUST HURRY AND GET IT BACK TO ME.
THANKS! I OWE YA..
UH, HOW MANY?
NOTEBOOK

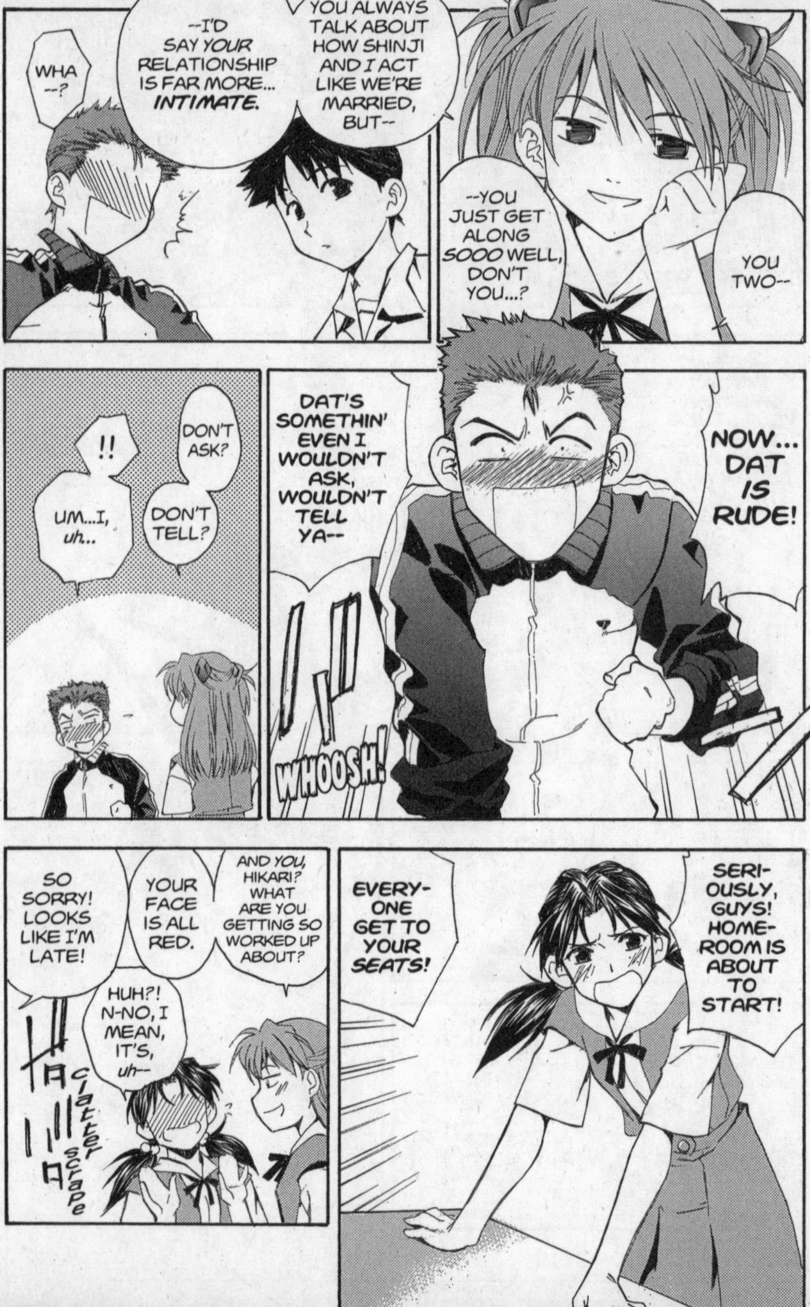
YOU TWO--
--YOU JUST GET ALONG SOOO WELL, DON'T YOU...?
YOU ALWAYS TALK ABOUT HOW SHINJI AND I ACT LIKE WE'RE MARRIED, BUT--
--I'D SAY YOUR RELATIONSHIP IS FAR MORE... INTIMATE.
WHA --?
NOW... DAT IS RUDE!
DAT'S SOMETHIN' EVEN I WOULDN'T ASK, WOULDN'T TELL YA--
WHOOSH!
DON'T ASK?
!!
DON'T TELL?
UM...I, uh...
SERI-OUSLY, GUYS! HOME-ROOM IS ABOUT TO START!
EVERY-ONE GET TO YOUR SEATS!
AND YOU, HIKARI? WHAT ARE YOU GETTING SO WORKED UP ABOUT?
YOUR FACE IS ALL RED.
SO SORRY! LOOKS LIKE I'M LATE!
HUH?! N-NO, I MEAN, IT'S, uh--
clatter
scrape

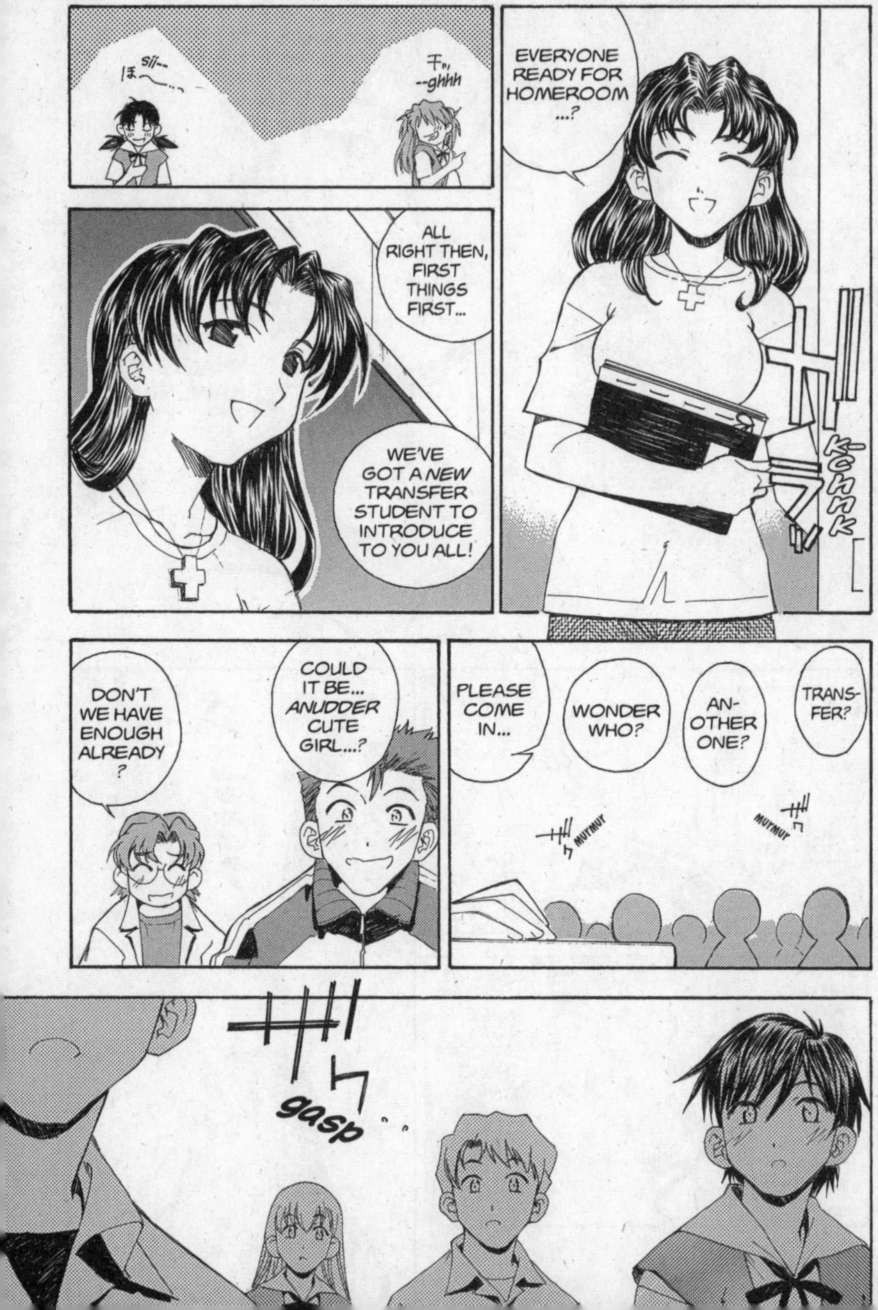
EVERYONE READY FOR HOMEROOM ...?
K-CHNK
チッ
--ghhh
ほ〜...
sii--
ALL RIGHT THEN, FIRST THINGS FIRST...
WE'VE GOT A *NEW* TRANSFER STUDENT TO INTRODUCE TO YOU ALL!
TRANS-FER?
AN-OTHER ONE?
WONDER WHO?
PLEASE COME IN...
MUYMUY
MUYMUY
COULD IT BE... *ANUDDER* CUTE GIRL...?
DON'T WE HAVE ENOUGH ALREADY ?
gasp

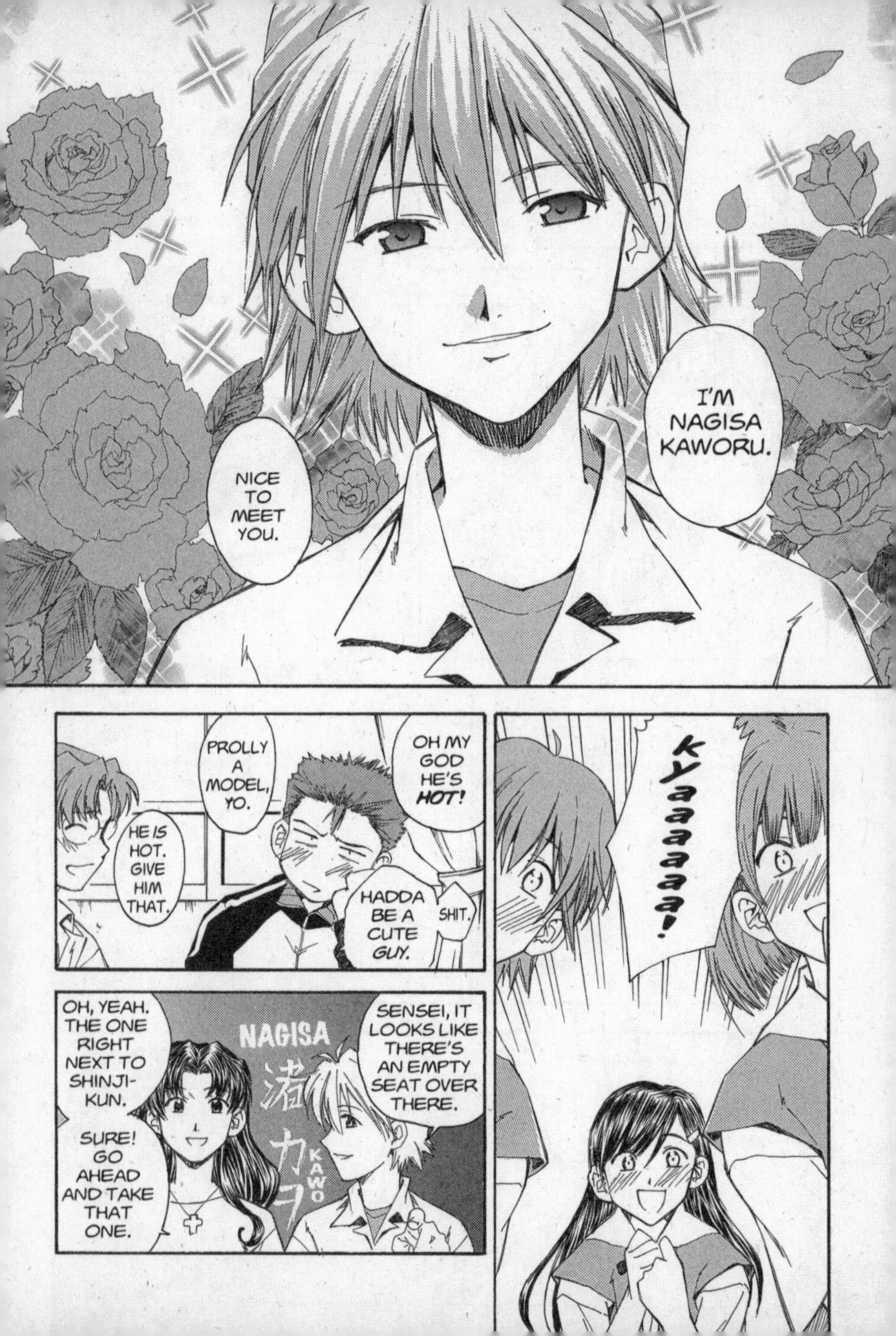
I'M NAGISA KAWORU.
NICE TO MEET YOU.
KYaaaaaaaa!
OH MY GOD HE'S *HOT*!
PROLLY A MODEL, YO.
SHIT.
HADDA BE A CUTE *GUY*.
HE *IS* HOT. GIVE HIM THAT.
SENSEI, IT LOOKS LIKE THERE'S AN EMPTY SEAT OVER THERE.
NAGISA 渚 カヲ KAWO
OH, YEAH. THE ONE RIGHT NEXT TO SHINJI-KUN.
SURE! GO AHEAD AND TAKE THAT ONE.

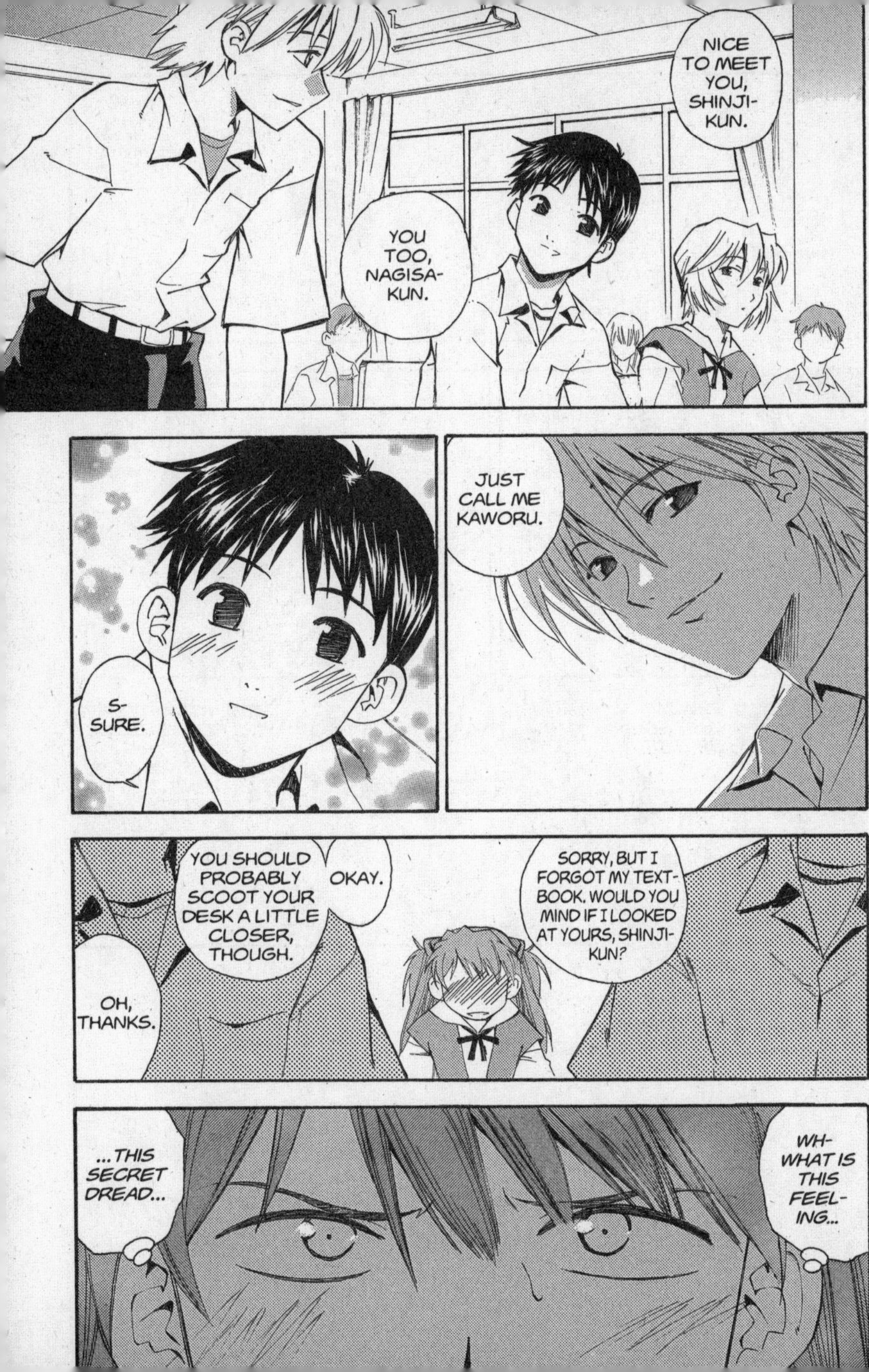
NICE TO MEET YOU, SHINJI-KUN.
YOU TOO, NAGISA-KUN.
JUST CALL ME KAWORU.
S-SURE.
SORRY, BUT I FORGOT MY TEXT-BOOK. WOULD YOU MIND IF I LOOKED AT YOURS, SHINJI-KUN?
OKAY.
YOU SHOULD PROBABLY SCOOT YOUR DESK A LITTLE CLOSER, THOUGH.
OH, THANKS.
WH-WHAT IS THIS FEEL-ING...
...THIS SECRET DREAD...

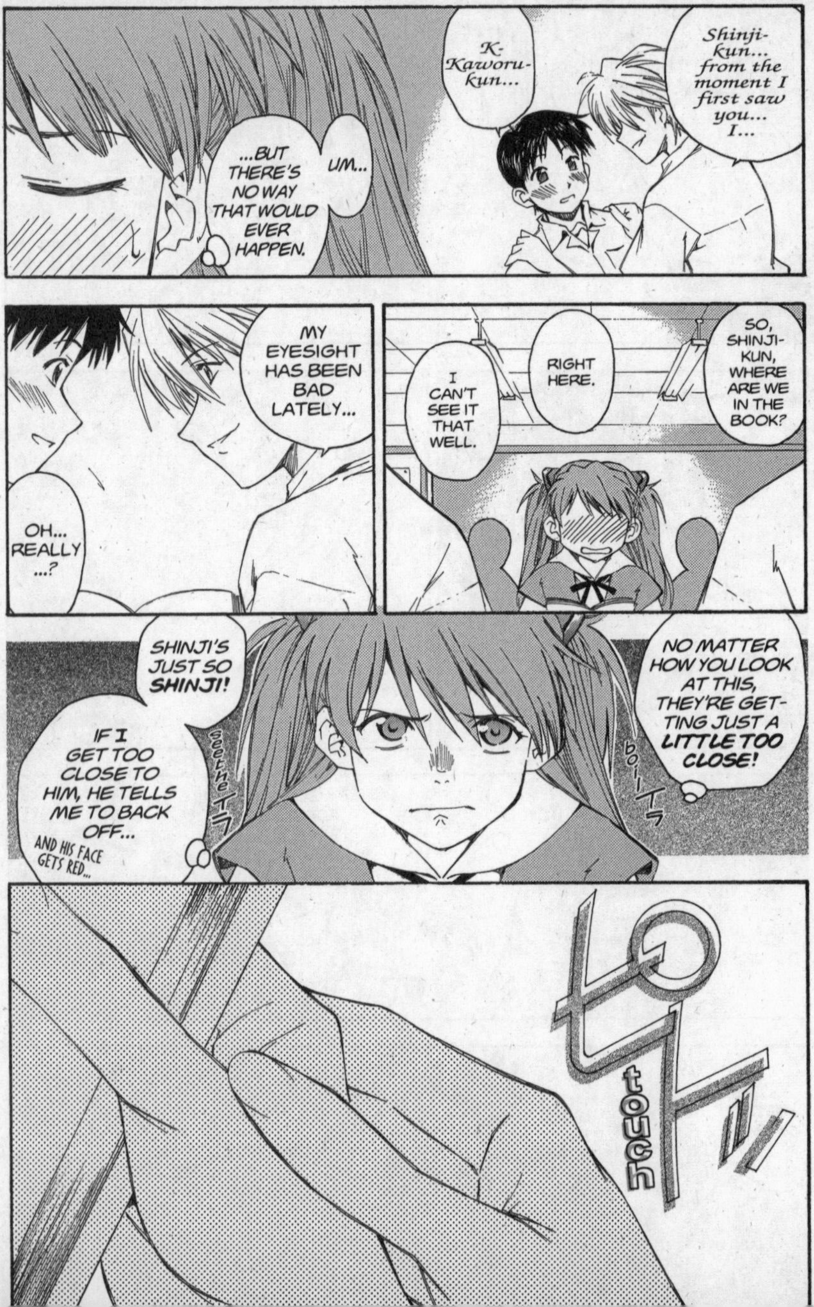
Shinji-kun... from the moment I first saw you... I...
K-Kaworu-kun...
UM...
...BUT THERE'S NO WAY THAT WOULD EVER HAPPEN.
SO, SHINJI-KUN, WHERE ARE WE IN THE BOOK?
RIGHT HERE.
I CAN'T SEE IT THAT WELL.
MY EYESIGHT HAS BEEN BAD LATELY...
OH... REALLY ...?
NO MATTER HOW YOU LOOK AT THIS, THEY'RE GETTING JUST A LITTLE TOO CLOSE!
boil
SHINJI'S JUST SO SHINJI!
seethe
IF I GET TOO CLOSE TO HIM, HE TELLS ME TO BACK OFF...
AND HIS FACE GETS RED...
touch

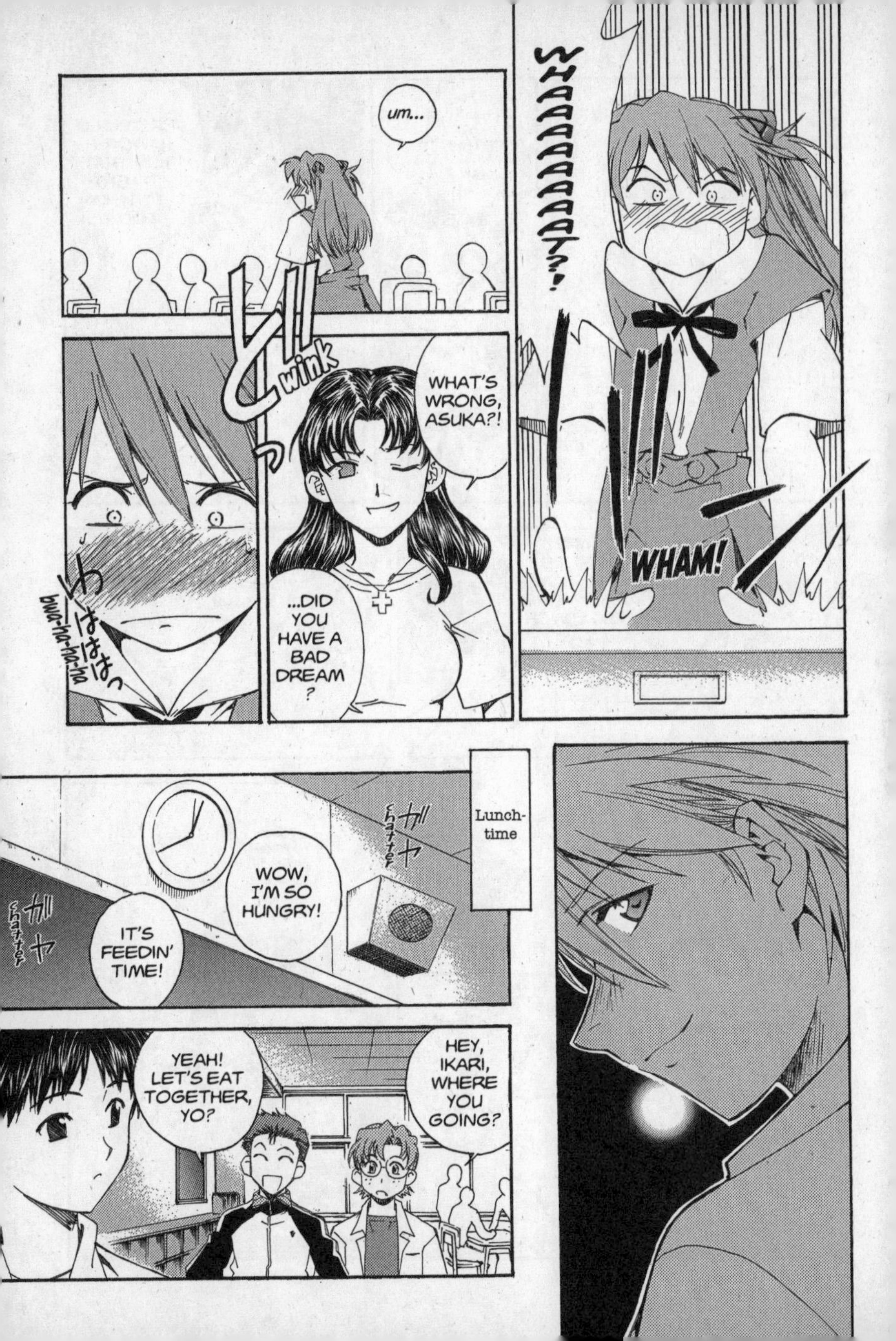
WHAAAAAAAAAT?!
WHAM!
um...
WHAT'S WRONG, ASUKA?!
...DID YOU HAVE A BAD DREAM?
wink
bwa-ha-ha-ha
Lunch-time
ガヤ chatter
WOW, I'M SO HUNGRY!
IT'S FEEDIN' TIME!
ガヤ chatter
HEY, IKARI, WHERE YOU GOING?
YEAH! LET'S EAT TOGETHER, YO?

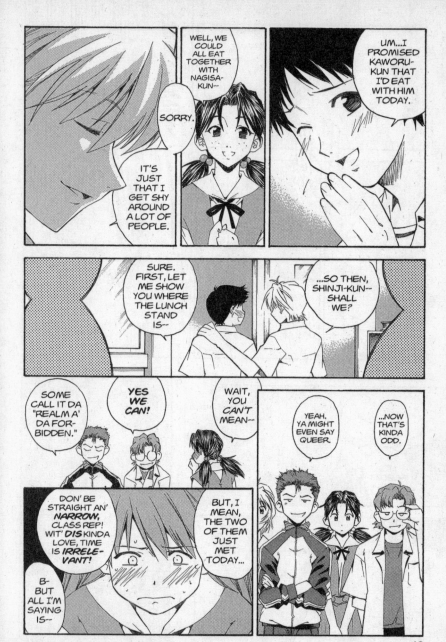

UM...I PROMISED KAWORU-KUN THAT I'D EAT WITH HIM TODAY.
WELL, WE COULD ALL EAT TOGETHER WITH NAGISA-KUN--
SORRY.
IT'S JUST THAT I GET SHY AROUND A LOT OF PEOPLE.
...SO THEN, SHINJI-KUN-- SHALL WE?
SURE. FIRST, LET ME SHOW YOU WHERE THE LUNCH STAND IS--
...NOW THAT'S KINDA ODD.
YEAH. YA MIGHT EVEN SAY QUEER.
WAIT, YOU *CAN'T* MEAN--
YES WE CAN!
SOME CALL IT DA "REALM A' DA FOR-BIDDEN."
BUT, I MEAN, THE TWO OF THEM JUST MET TODAY...
DON' BE STRAIGHT AN' ***NARROW,*** CLASS REP! WIT' ***DIS*** KINDA LOVE, TIME IS ***IRRELE-VANT!***
B-BUT ALL I'M SAYING IS--

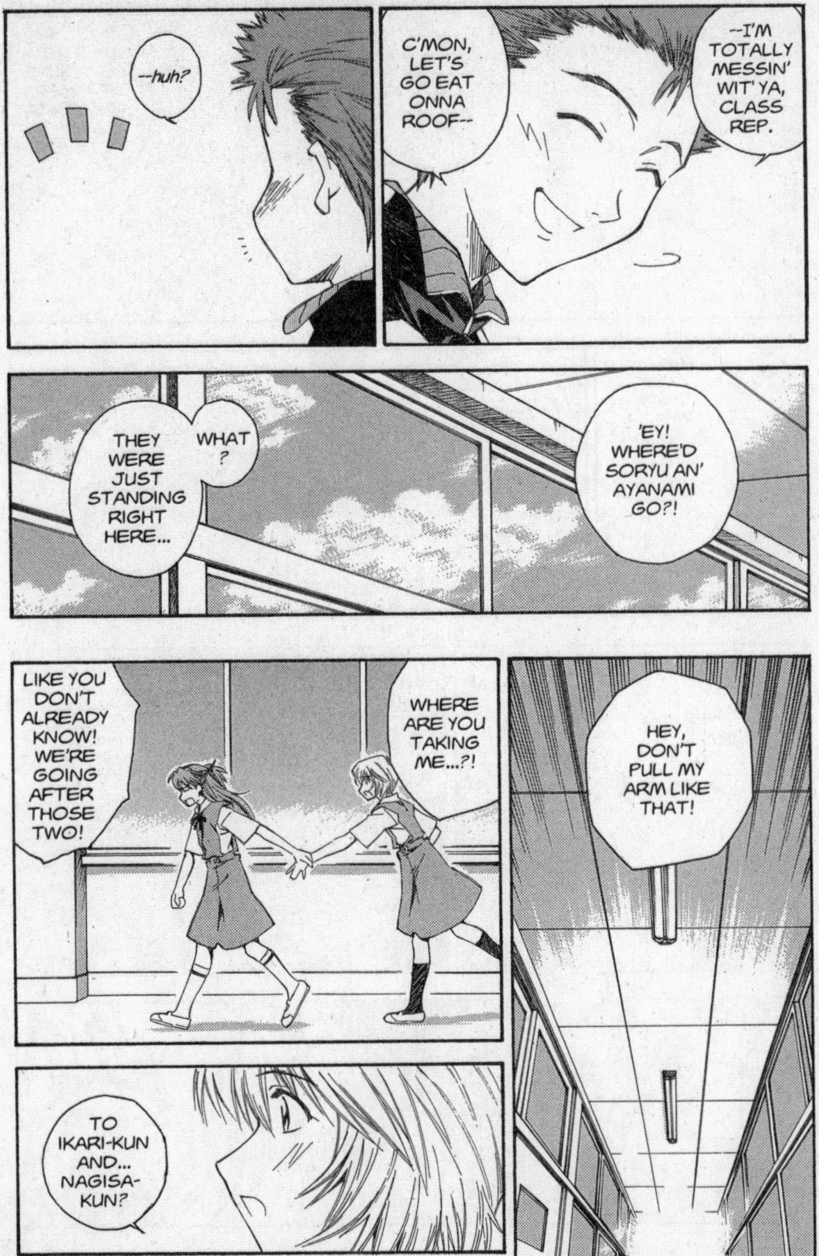
--I'M TOTALLY MESSIN' WIT' YA, CLASS REP.
C'MON, LET'S GO EAT ONNA ROOF--
--huh?
'EY! WHERE'D SORYU AN' AYANAMI GO?!
WHAT?
THEY WERE JUST STANDING RIGHT HERE...
HEY, DON'T PULL MY ARM LIKE THAT!
WHERE ARE YOU TAKING ME...?!
LIKE YOU DON'T ALREADY KNOW! WE'RE GOING AFTER THOSE TWO!
TO IKARI-KUN AND... NAGISA-KUN?

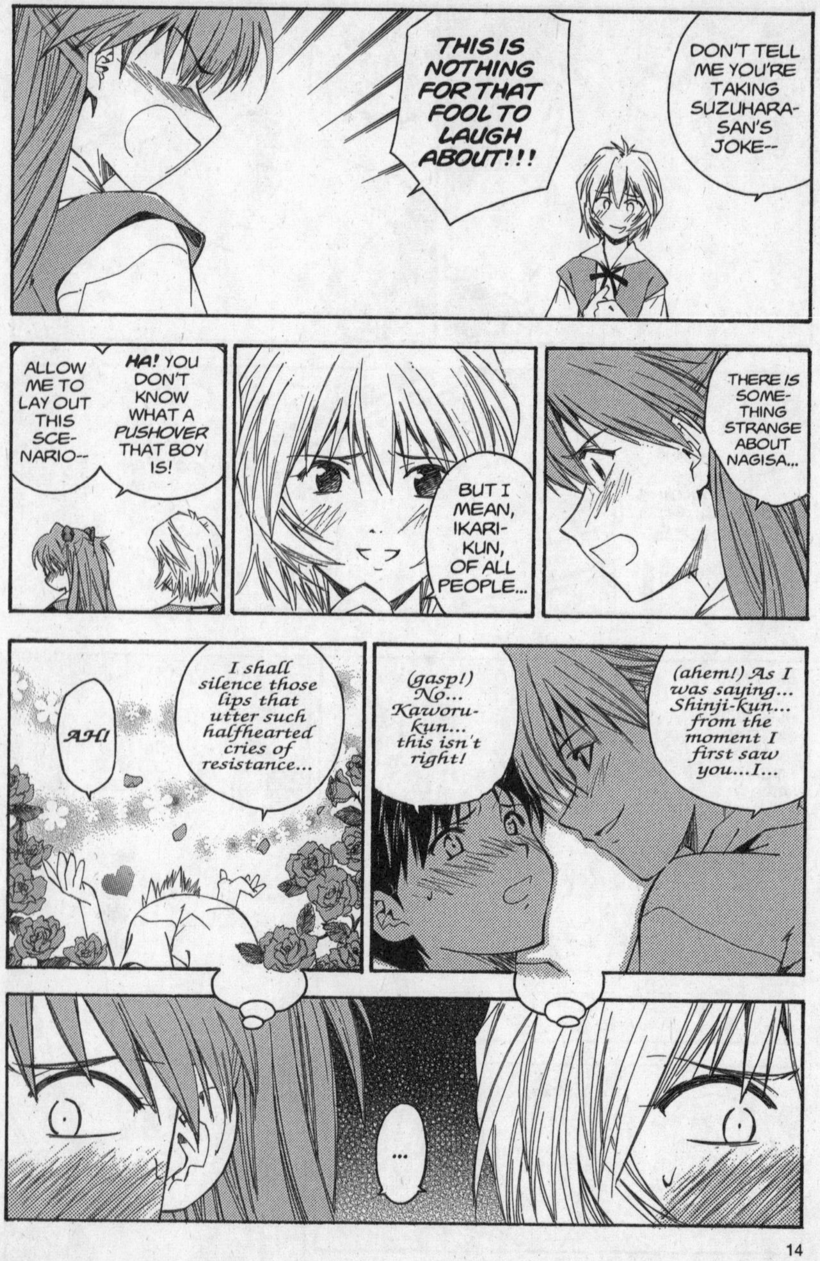

DON'T TELL ME YOU'RE TAKING SUZUHARA-SAN'S JOKE--
THIS IS NOTHING FOR THAT FOOL TO LAUGH ABOUT!!!
THERE IS SOMETHING STRANGE ABOUT NAGISA...
BUT I MEAN, IKARI-KUN, OF ALL PEOPLE...
HA! YOU DON'T KNOW WHAT A PUSHOVER THAT BOY IS!
ALLOW ME TO LAY OUT THIS SCENARIO--
(ahem!) As I was saying... Shinji-kun... from the moment I first saw you...I...
(gasp!) No... Kaworu-kun... this isn't right!
I shall silence those lips that utter such halfhearted cries of resistance...
AH!
...

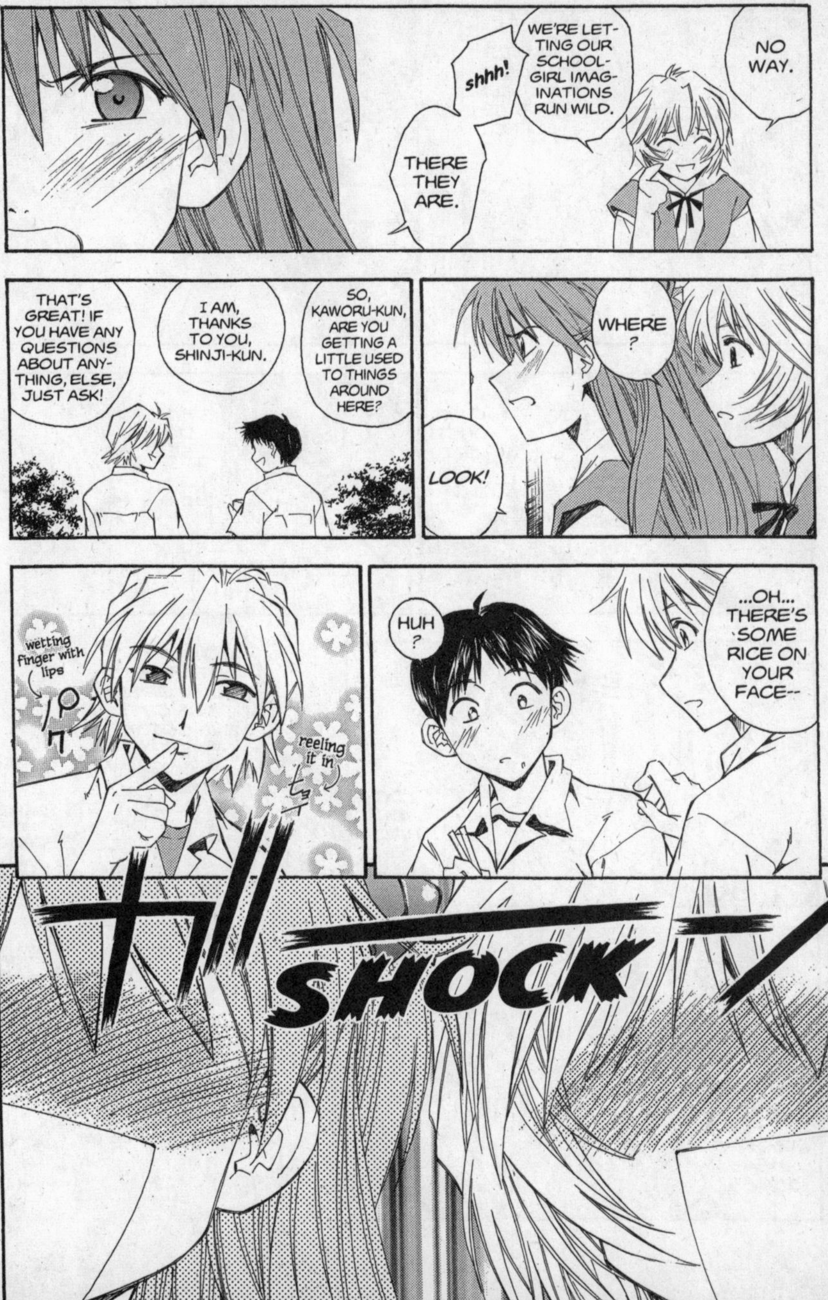
NO WAY.
WE'RE LETTING OUR SCHOOLGIRL IMAGINATIONS RUN WILD.
shhh!
THERE THEY ARE.
WHERE?
LOOK!
SO, KAWORU-KUN, ARE YOU GETTING A LITTLE USED TO THINGS AROUND HERE?
I AM, THANKS TO YOU, SHINJI-KUN.
THAT'S GREAT! IF YOU HAVE ANY QUESTIONS ABOUT ANYTHING, ELSE, JUST ASK!
...OH... THERE'S SOME RICE ON YOUR FACE--
HUH?
wetting finger with lips
reeling it in
SHOCK

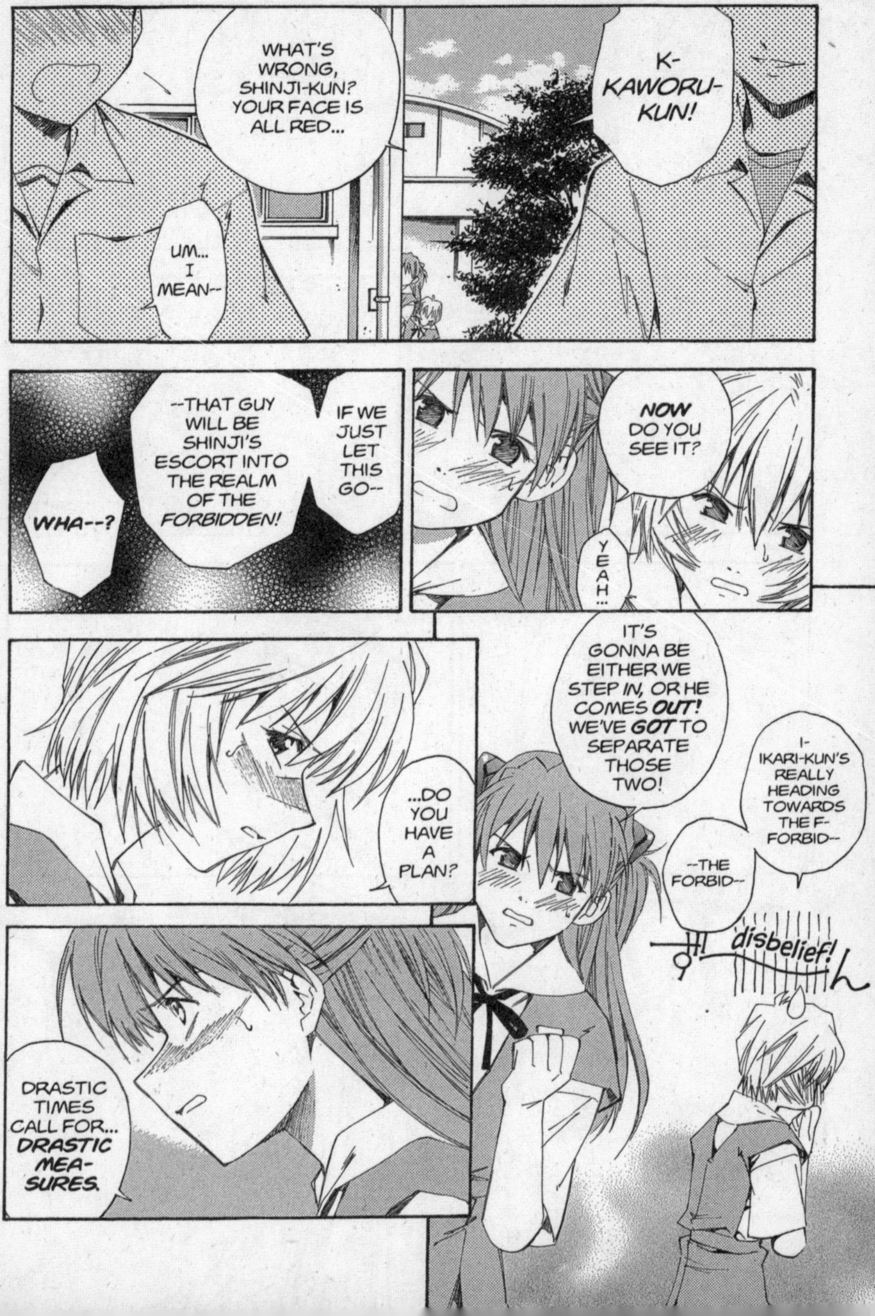
K-KAWORU-KUN!
WHAT'S WRONG, SHINJI-KUN? YOUR FACE IS ALL RED...
UM... I MEAN--
NOW DO YOU SEE IT?
YEAH...
IF WE JUST LET THIS GO--
--THAT GUY WILL BE SHINJI'S ESCORT INTO THE REALM OF THE FORBIDDEN!
WHA--?
IT'S GONNA BE EITHER WE STEP IN, OR HE COMES OUT! WE'VE GOT TO SEPARATE THOSE TWO!
I-IKARI-KUN'S REALLY HEADING TOWARDS THE F-FORBID--
--THE FORBID--
!!
disbelief!
...DO YOU HAVE A PLAN?
DRASTIC TIMES CALL FOR... DRASTIC MEA-SURES.

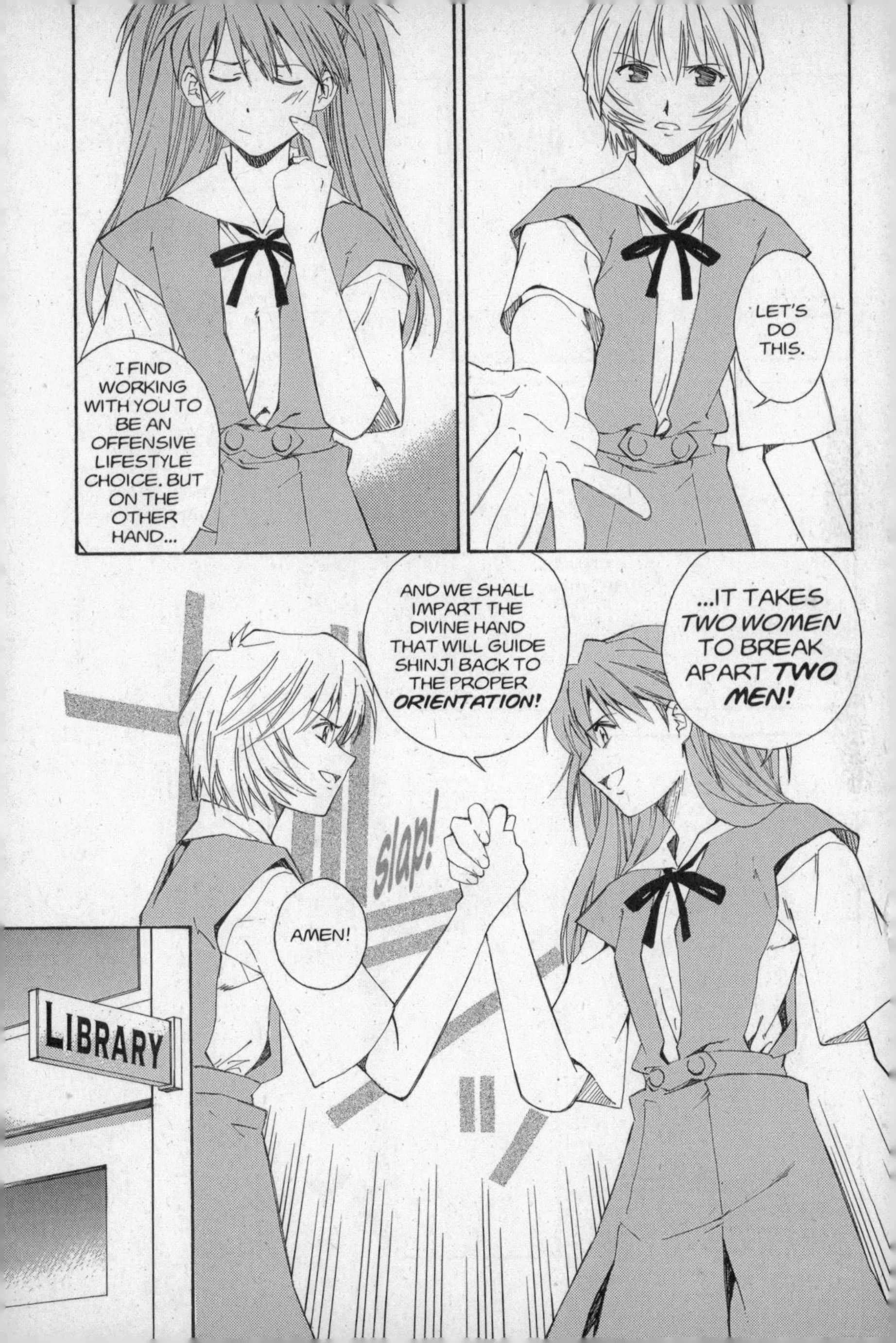
LET'S DO THIS.
I FIND WORKING WITH YOU TO BE AN OFFENSIVE LIFESTYLE CHOICE. BUT ON THE OTHER HAND...
...IT TAKES *TWO WOMEN* TO BREAK APART ***TWO MEN!***
AND WE SHALL IMPART THE DIVINE HAND THAT WILL GUIDE SHINJI BACK TO THE PROPER ***ORIENTATION!***
slap!
AMEN!
LIBRARY

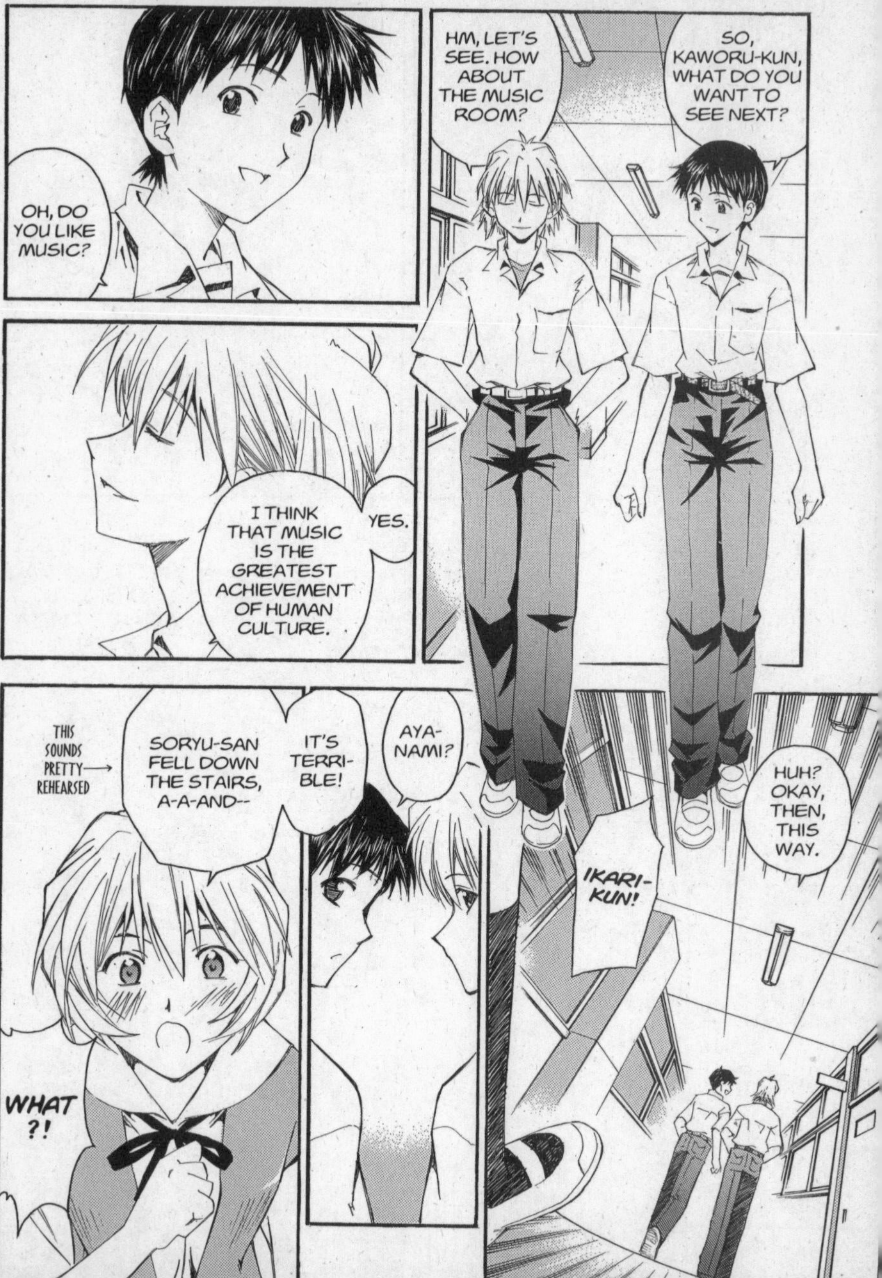
SO, KAWORU-KUN, WHAT DO YOU WANT TO SEE NEXT?
HM, LET'S SEE. HOW ABOUT THE MUSIC ROOM?
OH, DO YOU LIKE MUSIC?
YES.
I THINK THAT MUSIC IS THE GREATEST ACHIEVEMENT OF HUMAN CULTURE.
HUH? OKAY, THEN, THIS WAY.
IKARI-KUN!
AYA-NAMI?
IT'S TERRI-BLE!
SORYU-SAN FELL DOWN THE STAIRS, A-A-AND--
THIS SOUNDS PRETTY REHEARSED
WHAT ?!

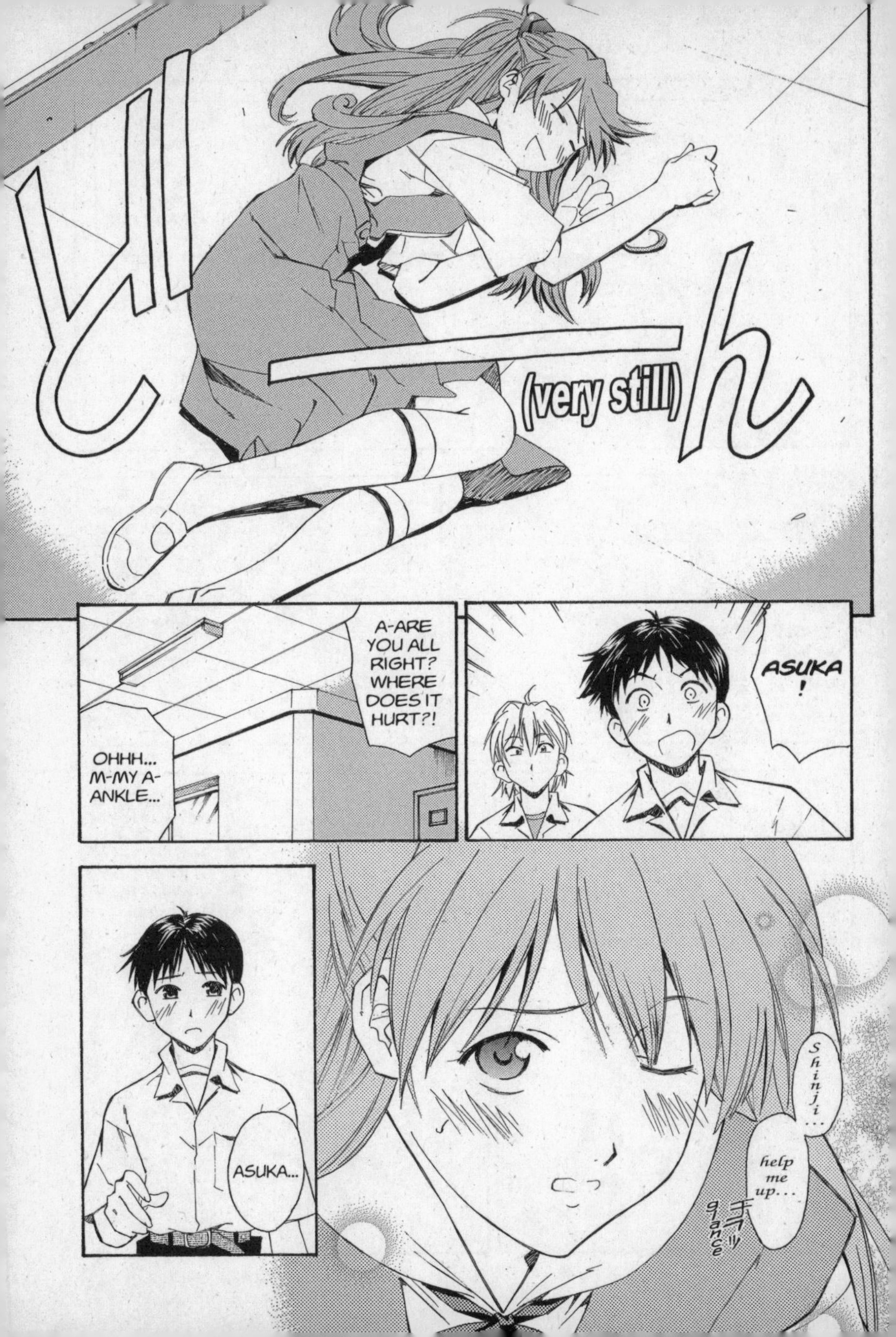
(very still)
ASUKA!
A-ARE YOU ALL RIGHT? WHERE DOES IT HURT?!
OHHH... M-MY A-ANKLE...
Shinji...
help me up...
glance
ASUKA...

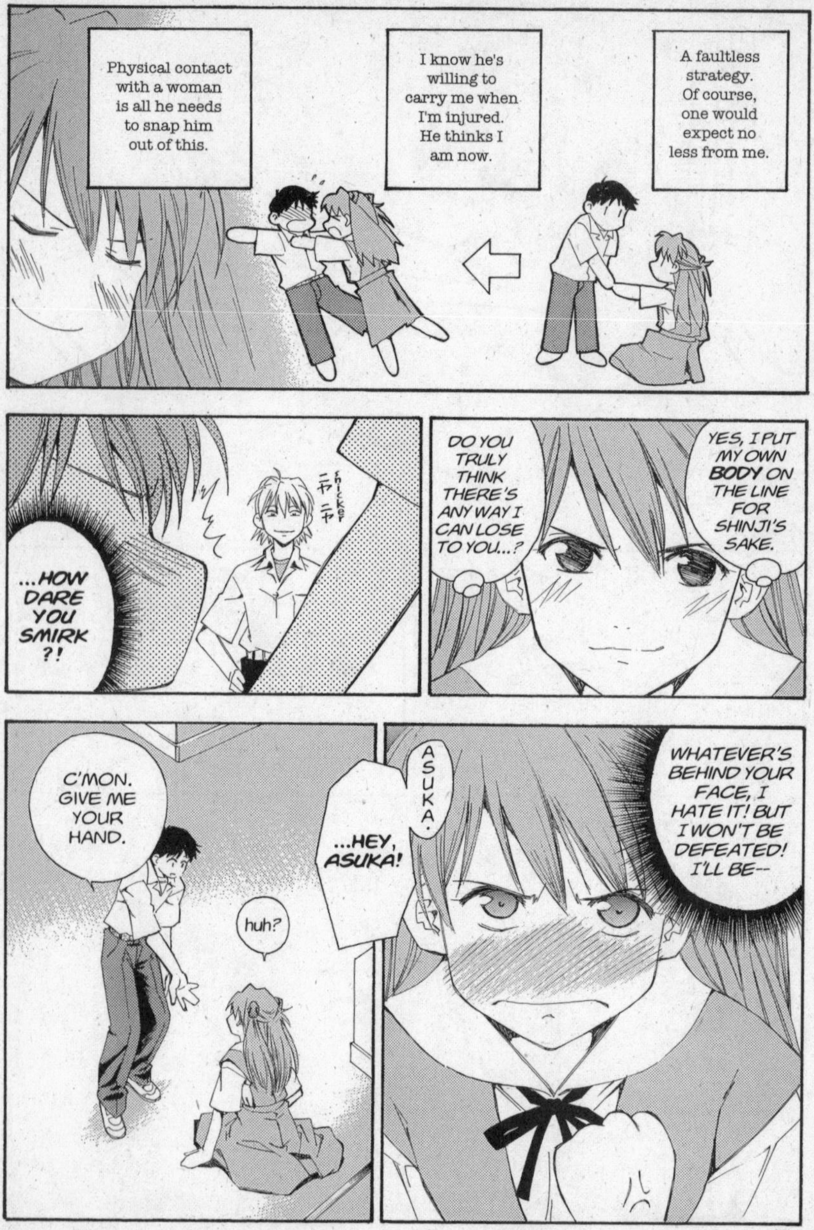
A faultless strategy. Of course, one would expect no less from me.
I know he's willing to carry me when I'm injured. He thinks I am now.
Physical contact with a woman is all he needs to snap him out of this.
YES, I PUT MY OWN **BODY** ON THE LINE FOR SHINJI'S SAKE.
DO YOU TRULY THINK THERE'S ANY WAY I CAN LOSE TO YOU...?
ニヤ ニヤ snicker
...HOW DARE YOU SMIRK?!
WHATEVER'S BEHIND YOUR FACE, I HATE IT! BUT I WON'T BE DEFEATED! I'LL BE--
ASUKA.
...HEY, ASUKA!
huh?
C'MON. GIVE ME YOUR HAND.

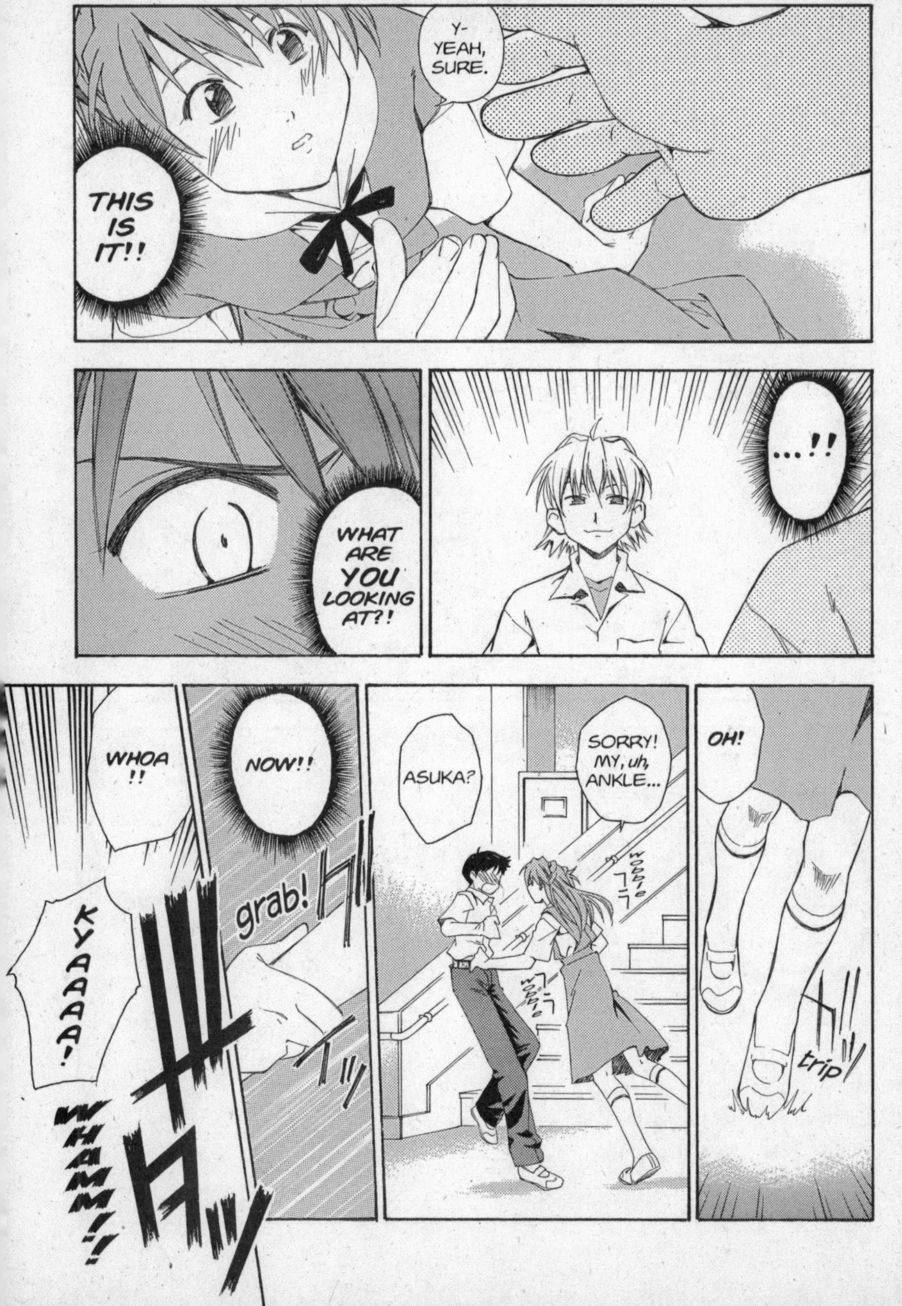
Y-
YEAH,
SURE.
THIS IS IT!!
...!!
WHAT ARE YOU LOOKING AT?!
OH!
trip
SORRY! MY, uh, ANKLE...
ASUKA?
wobble
wobble
NOW!!
grab!
WHOA!!
KYAAAAA!
WHAMM!!

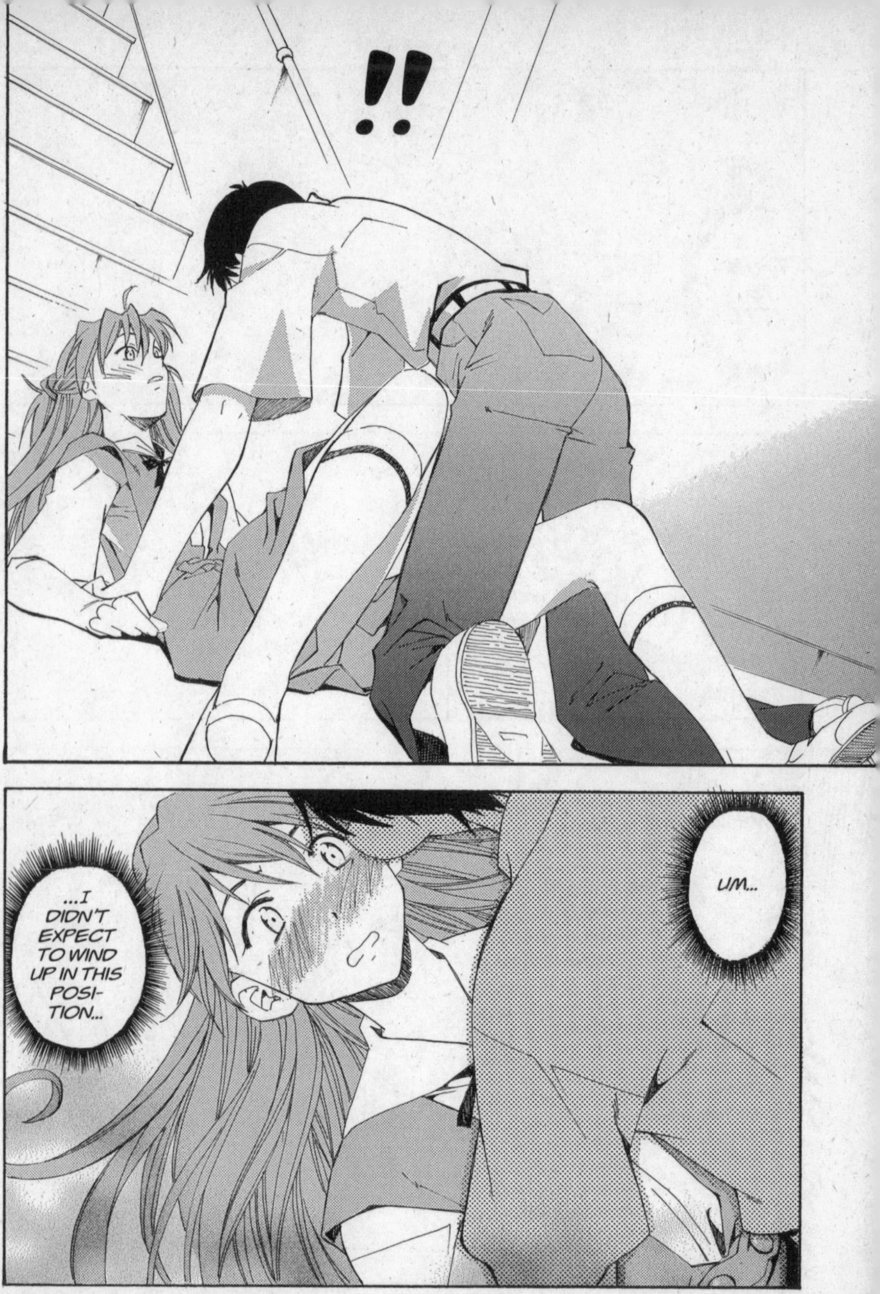
!!
UM...
...I DIDN'T EXPECT TO WIND UP IN THIS POSI-TION...

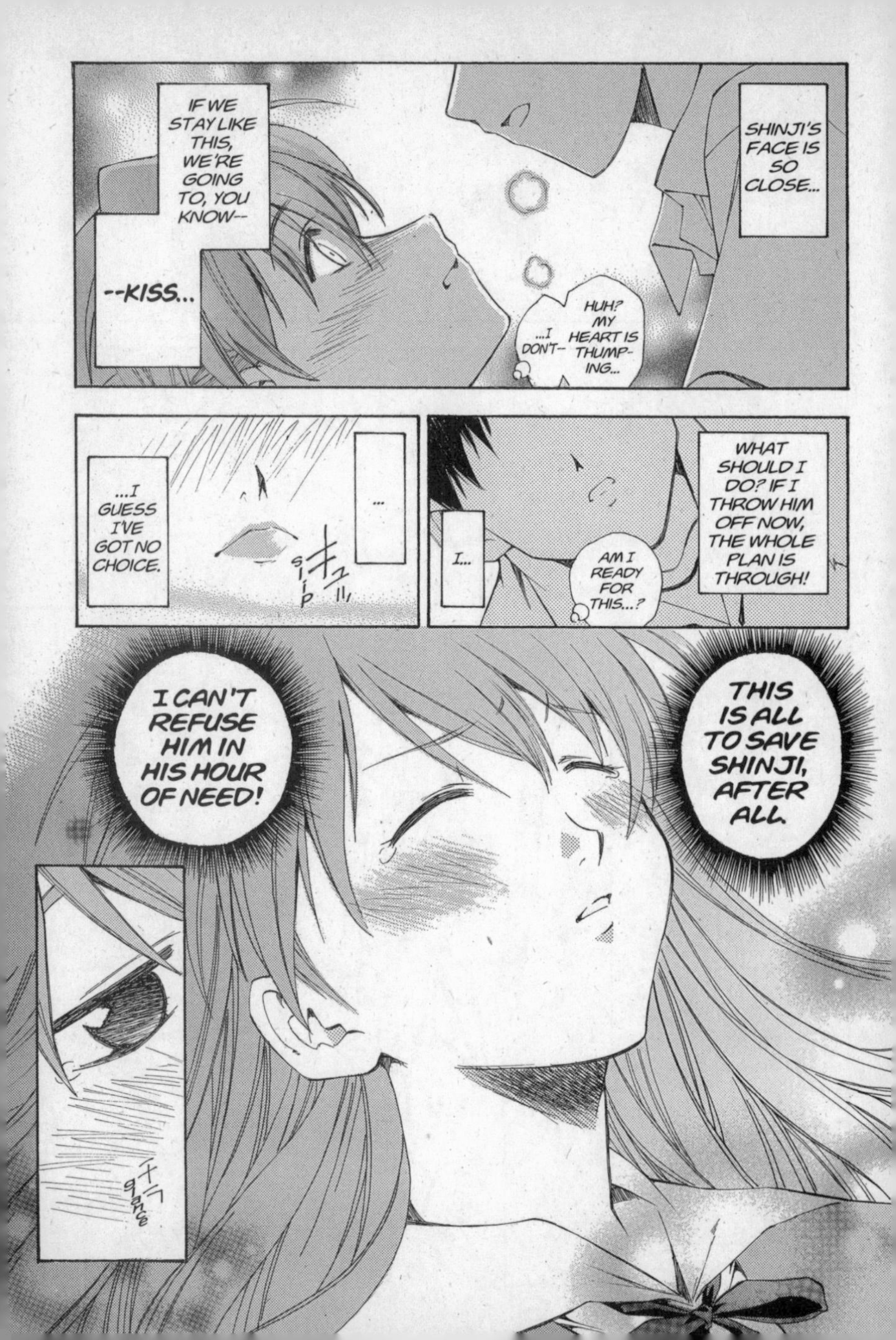
SHINJI'S FACE IS SO CLOSE...
IF WE STAY LIKE THIS, WE'RE GOING TO, YOU KNOW--
--KISS...
HUH? MY HEART IS THUMPING...
...I DON'T--
WHAT SHOULD I DO? IF I THROW HIM OFF NOW, THE WHOLE PLAN IS THROUGH!
AM I READY FOR THIS...?
I...
...
...I GUESS I'VE GOT NO CHOICE.
sip
THIS IS ALL TO SAVE SHINJI, AFTER ALL.
I CAN'T REFUSE HIM IN HIS HOUR OF NEED!
glance

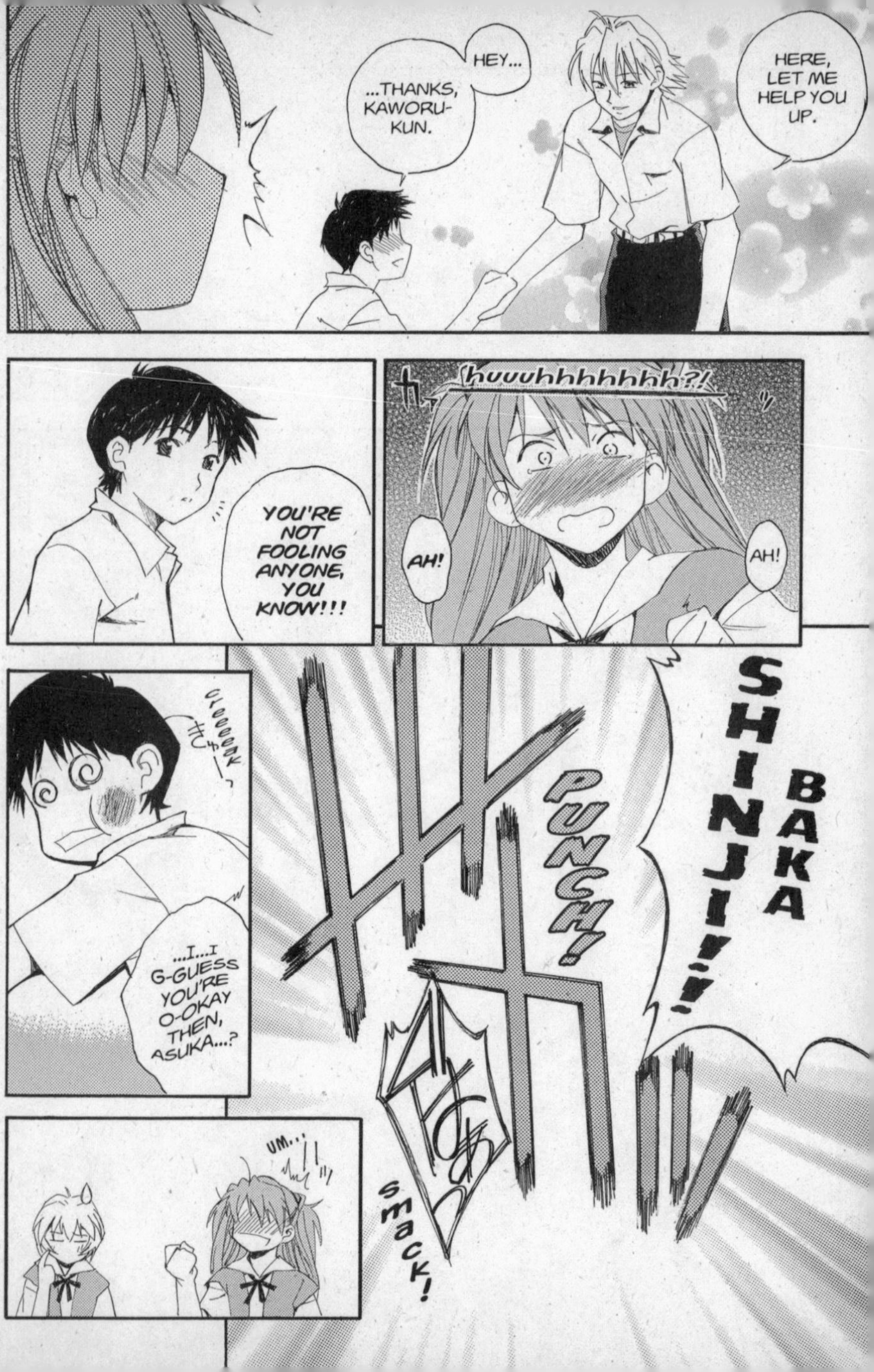
HERE, LET ME HELP YOU UP.
HEY...
...THANKS, KAWORU-KUN.
huuuhhhhhhh?!
AH!
AH!
YOU'RE NOT FOOLING ANYONE, YOU KNOW!!!
BAKA
SHINJI!!!
PUNCH!
smack!
creeeeak
...I...I G-GUESS YOU'RE O-OKAY THEN, ASUKA...?
UM...

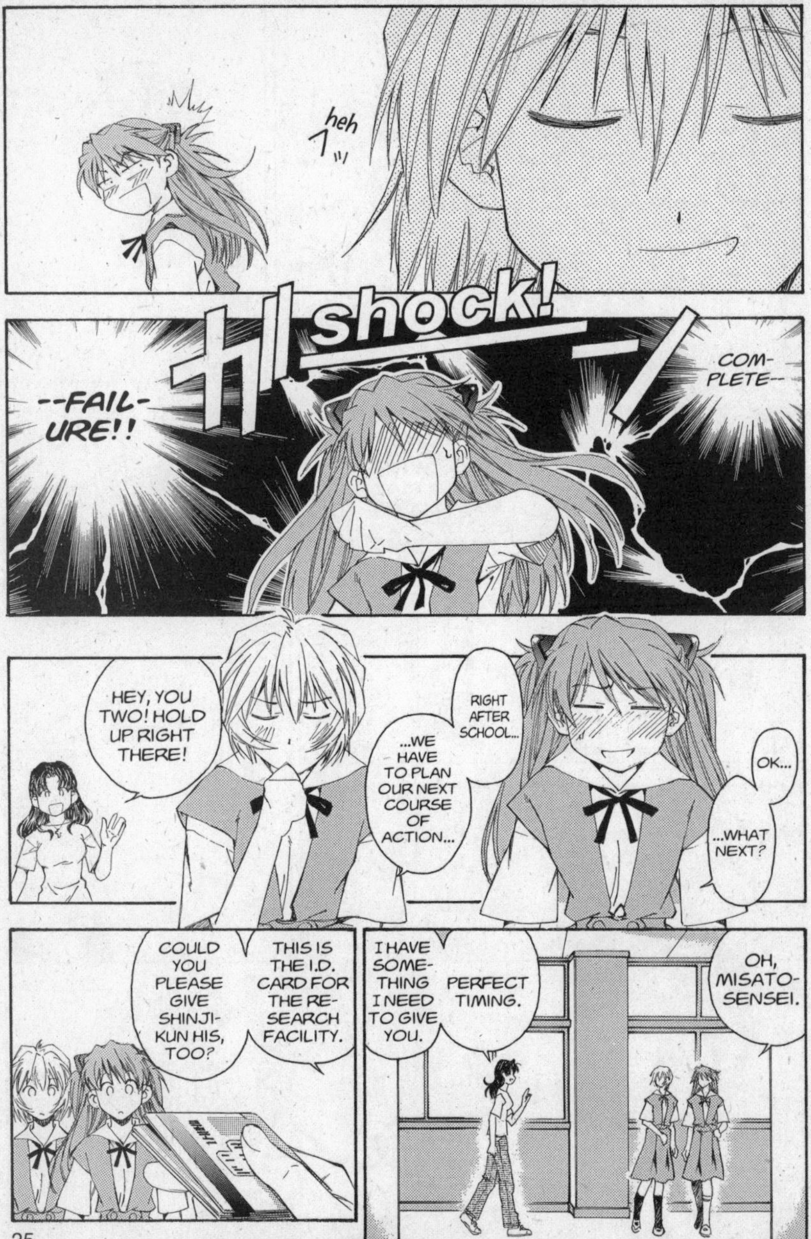
heh
COM-PLETE--
--FAIL-URE!!
shock!
OK...
...WHAT NEXT?
RIGHT AFTER SCHOOL...
...WE HAVE TO PLAN OUR NEXT COURSE OF ACTION...
HEY, YOU TWO! HOLD UP RIGHT THERE!
OH, MISATO-SENSEI.
PERFECT TIMING.
I HAVE SOME-THING I NEED TO GIVE YOU.
THIS IS THE I.D. CARD FOR THE RE-SEARCH FACILITY.
COULD YOU PLEASE GIVE SHINJI-KUN HIS, TOO?

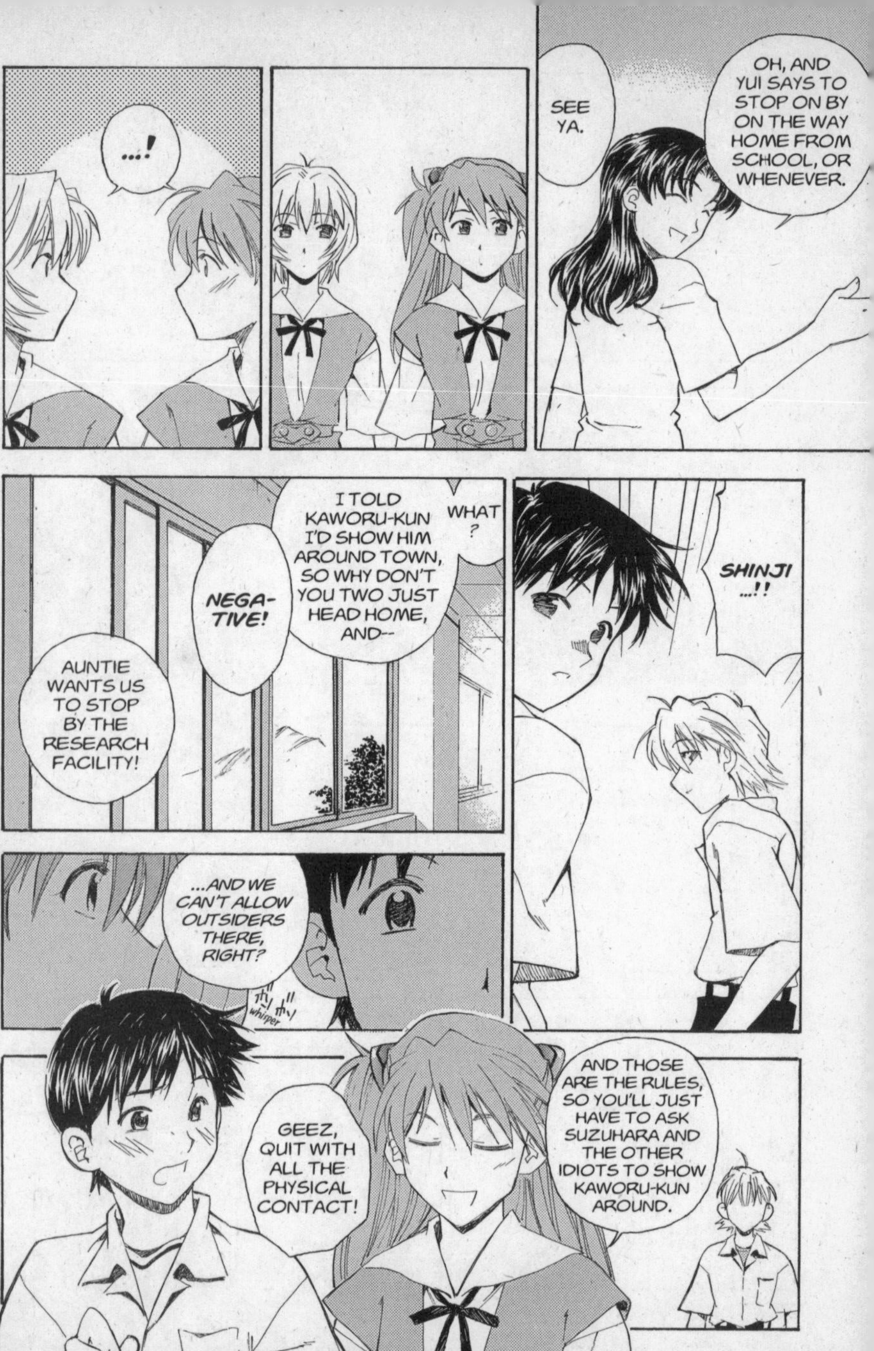
OH, AND YUI SAYS TO STOP ON BY ON THE WAY HOME FROM SCHOOL, OR WHENEVER.
SEE YA.
...!
SHINJI ...!!
WHAT?
I TOLD KAWORU-KUN I'D SHOW HIM AROUND TOWN, SO WHY DON'T YOU TWO JUST HEAD HOME, AND--
NEGA-TIVE!
AUNTIE WANTS US TO STOP BY THE RESEARCH FACILITY!
...AND WE CAN'T ALLOW OUTSIDERS THERE, RIGHT?
whisper
AND THOSE ARE THE RULES, SO YOU'LL JUST HAVE TO ASK SUZUHARA AND THE OTHER IDIOTS TO SHOW KAWORU-KUN AROUND.
GEEZ, QUIT WITH ALL THE PHYSICAL CONTACT!

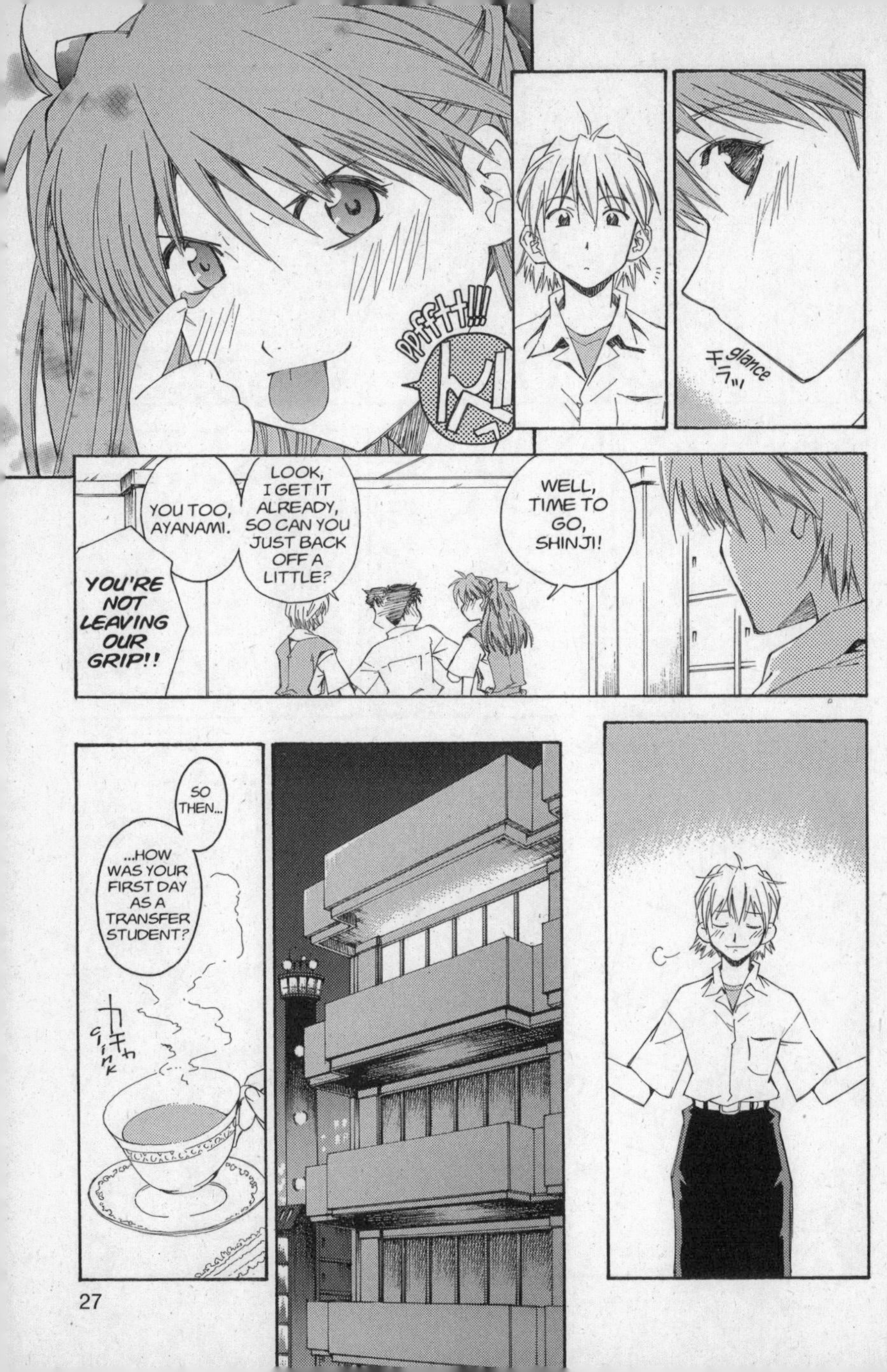

glance
チラッ
PPFFTT!!!
WELL, TIME TO GO, SHINJI!
LOOK, I GET IT ALREADY, SO CAN YOU JUST BACK OFF A LITTLE?
YOU TOO, AYANAMI.
YOU'RE NOT LEAVING OUR GRIP!!
SO THEN...
...HOW WAS YOUR FIRST DAY AS A TRANSFER STUDENT?
カチャ
clink

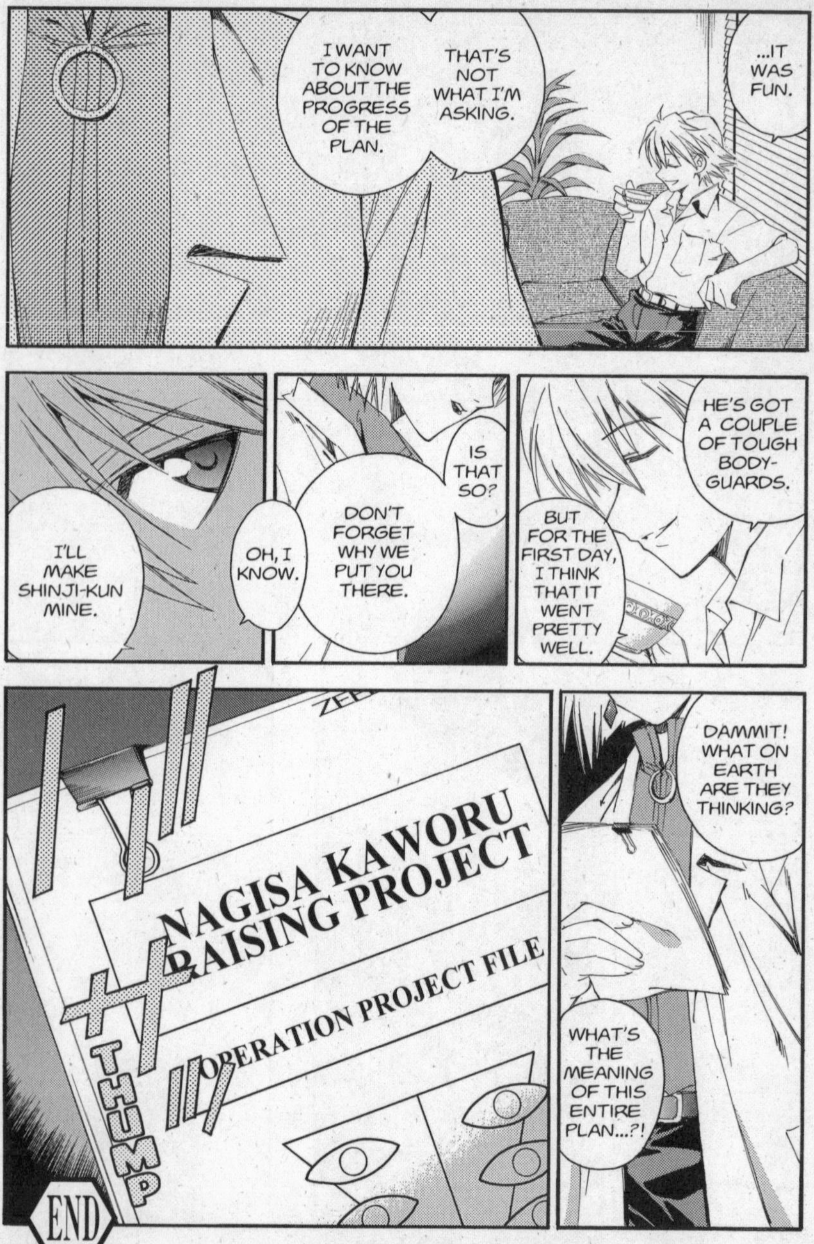
...IT WAS FUN.
THAT'S NOT WHAT I'M ASKING.
I WANT TO KNOW ABOUT THE PROGRESS OF THE PLAN.
HE'S GOT A COUPLE OF TOUGH BODY-GUARDS.
BUT FOR THE FIRST DAY, I THINK THAT IT WENT PRETTY WELL.
IS THAT SO?
DON'T FORGET WHY WE PUT YOU THERE.
OH, I KNOW.
I'LL MAKE SHINJI-KUN MINE.
DAMMIT! WHAT ON EARTH ARE THEY THINKING?
WHAT'S THE MEANING OF THIS ENTIRE PLAN...?!
NAGISA KAWORU RAISING PROJECT
OPERATION PROJECT FILE
THUMP
END

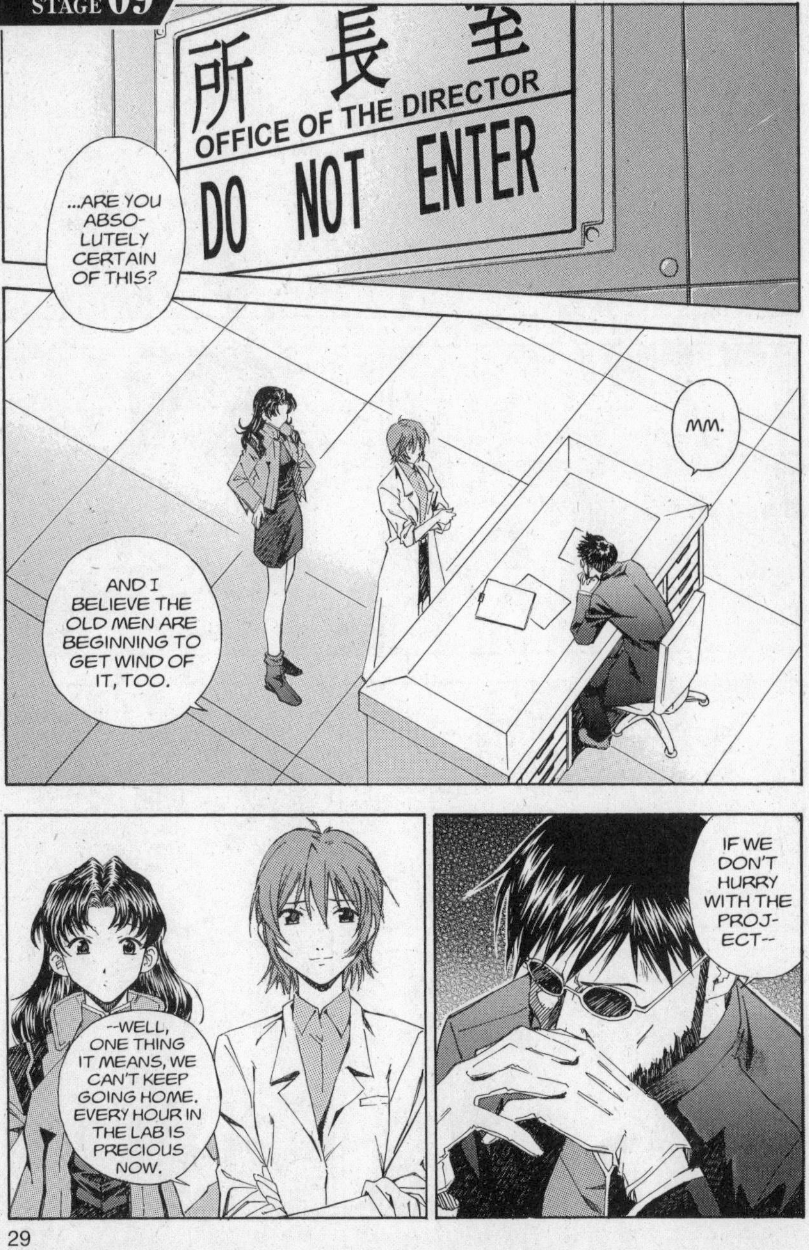
所長室
OFFICE OF THE DIRECTOR
DO NOT ENTER
...ARE YOU ABSO-LUTELY CERTAIN OF THIS?
MM.
AND I BELIEVE THE OLD MEN ARE BEGINNING TO GET WIND OF IT, TOO.
IF WE DON'T HURRY WITH THE PROJ-ECT--
--WELL, ONE THING IT MEANS, WE CAN'T KEEP GOING HOME. EVERY HOUR IN THE LAB IS PRECIOUS NOW.

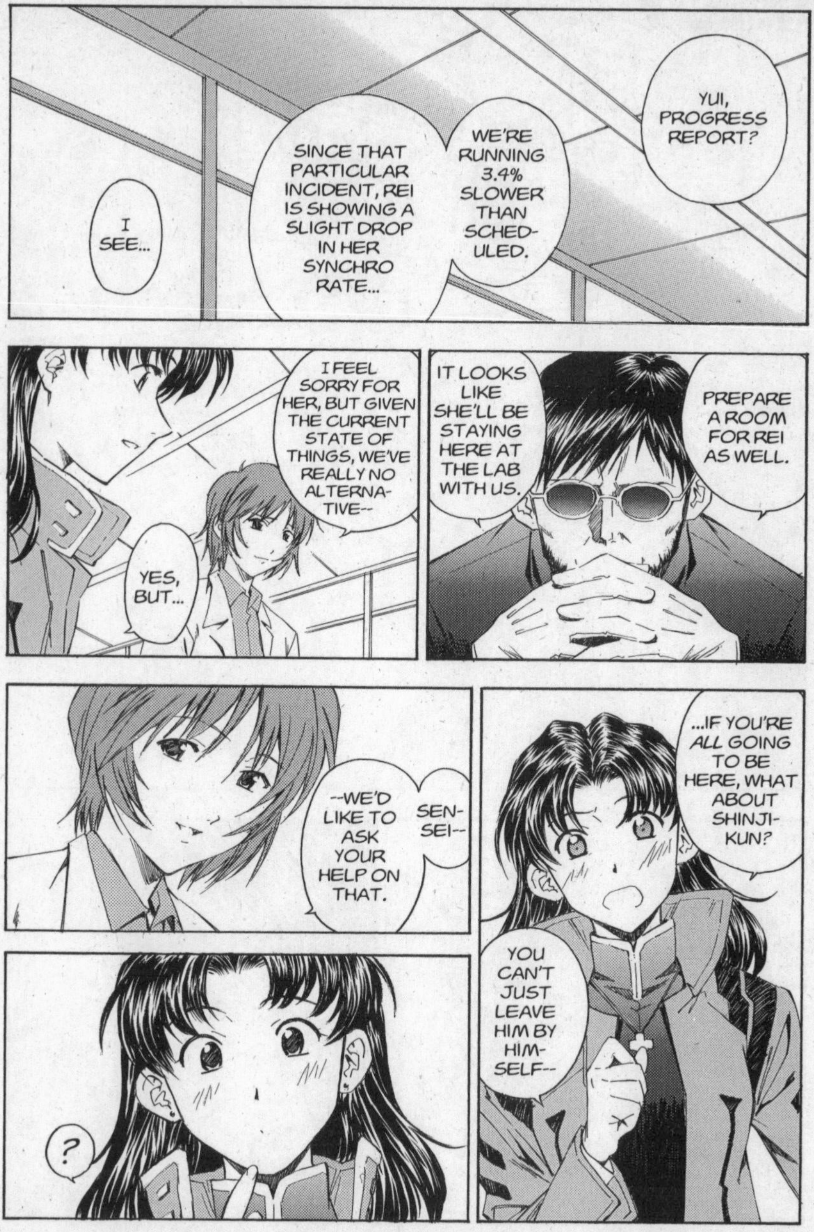

YUI, PROGRESS REPORT?
WE'RE RUNNING 3.4% SLOWER THAN SCHED-ULED.
SINCE THAT PARTICULAR INCIDENT, REI IS SHOWING A SLIGHT DROP IN HER SYNCHRO RATE...
I SEE...
PREPARE A ROOM FOR REI AS WELL.
IT LOOKS LIKE SHE'LL BE STAYING HERE AT THE LAB WITH US.
I FEEL SORRY FOR HER, BUT GIVEN THE CURRENT STATE OF THINGS, WE'VE REALLY NO ALTERNA-TIVE--
YES, BUT...
...IF YOU'RE ALL GOING TO BE HERE, WHAT ABOUT SHINJI-KUN?
YOU CAN'T JUST LEAVE HIM BY HIM-SELF--
SEN-SEI--
--WE'D LIKE TO ASK YOUR HELP ON THAT.
?

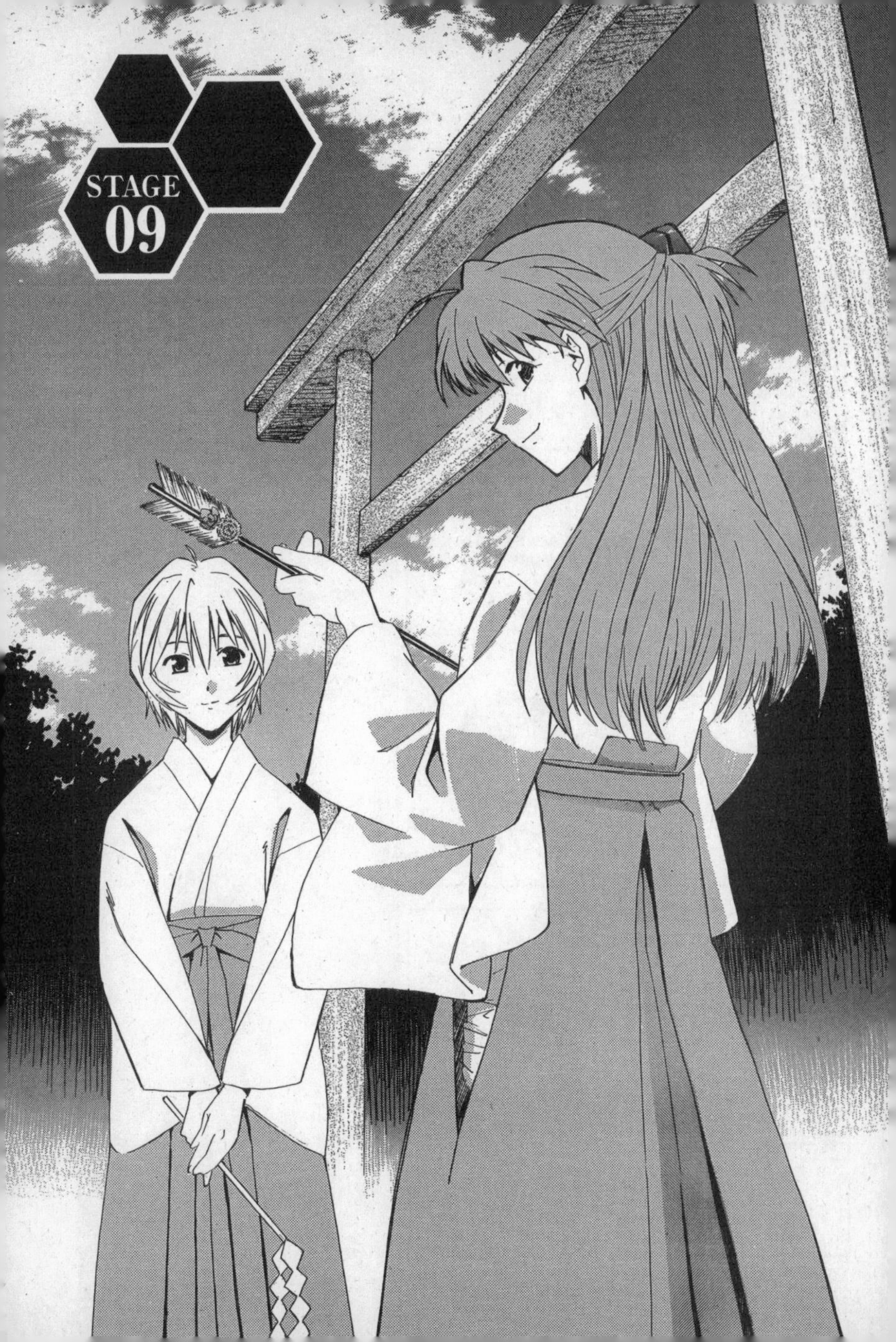
STAGE
09

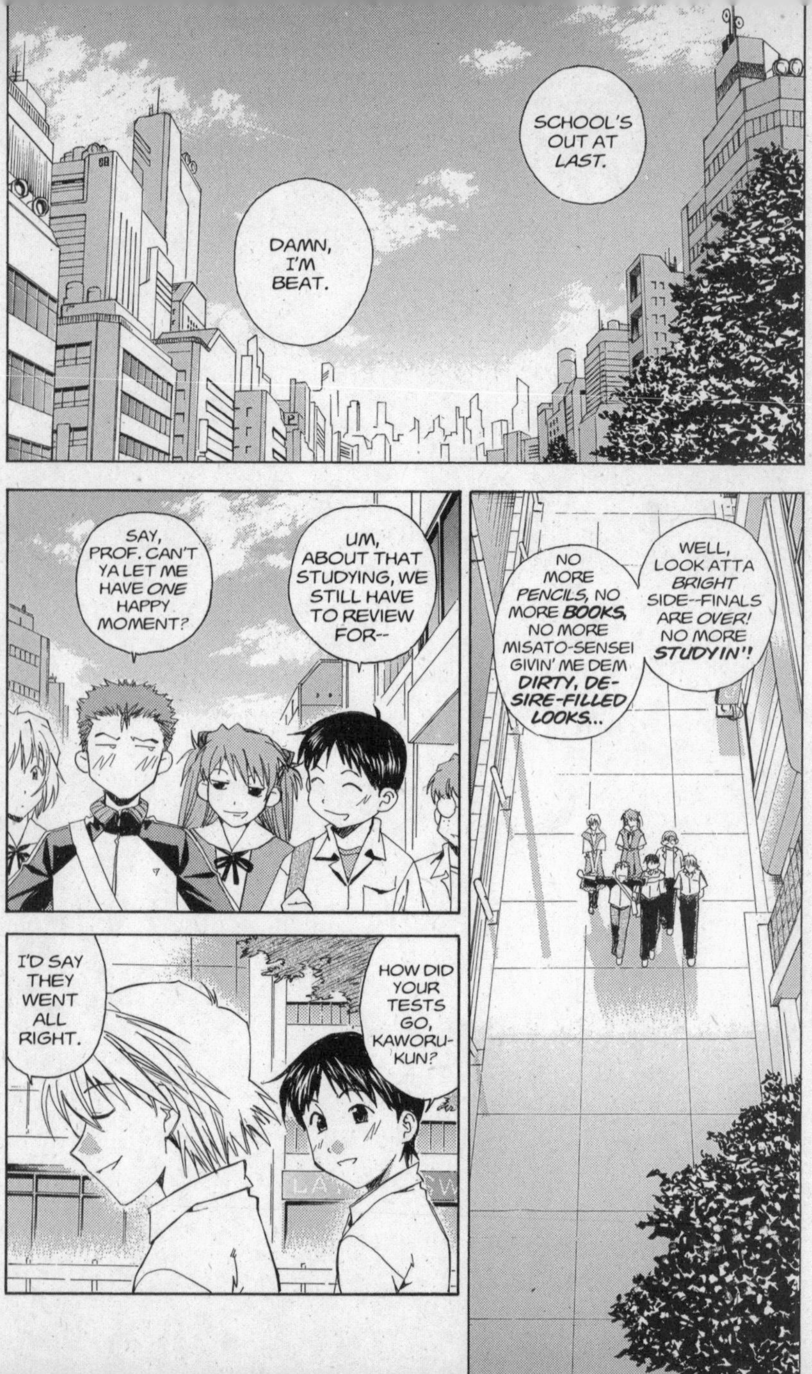
SCHOOL'S OUT AT LAST.
DAMN, I'M BEAT.
WELL, LOOK ATTA BRIGHT SIDE--FINALS ARE OVER! NO MORE STUDYIN'!
NO MORE PENCILS, NO MORE BOOKS, NO MORE MISATO-SENSEI GIVIN' ME DEM DIRTY, DESIRE-FILLED LOOKS...
UM, ABOUT THAT STUDYING, WE STILL HAVE TO REVIEW FOR--
SAY, PROF. CAN'T YA LET ME HAVE ONE HAPPY MOMENT?
HOW DID YOUR TESTS GO, KAWORU-KUN?
I'D SAY THEY WENT ALL RIGHT.

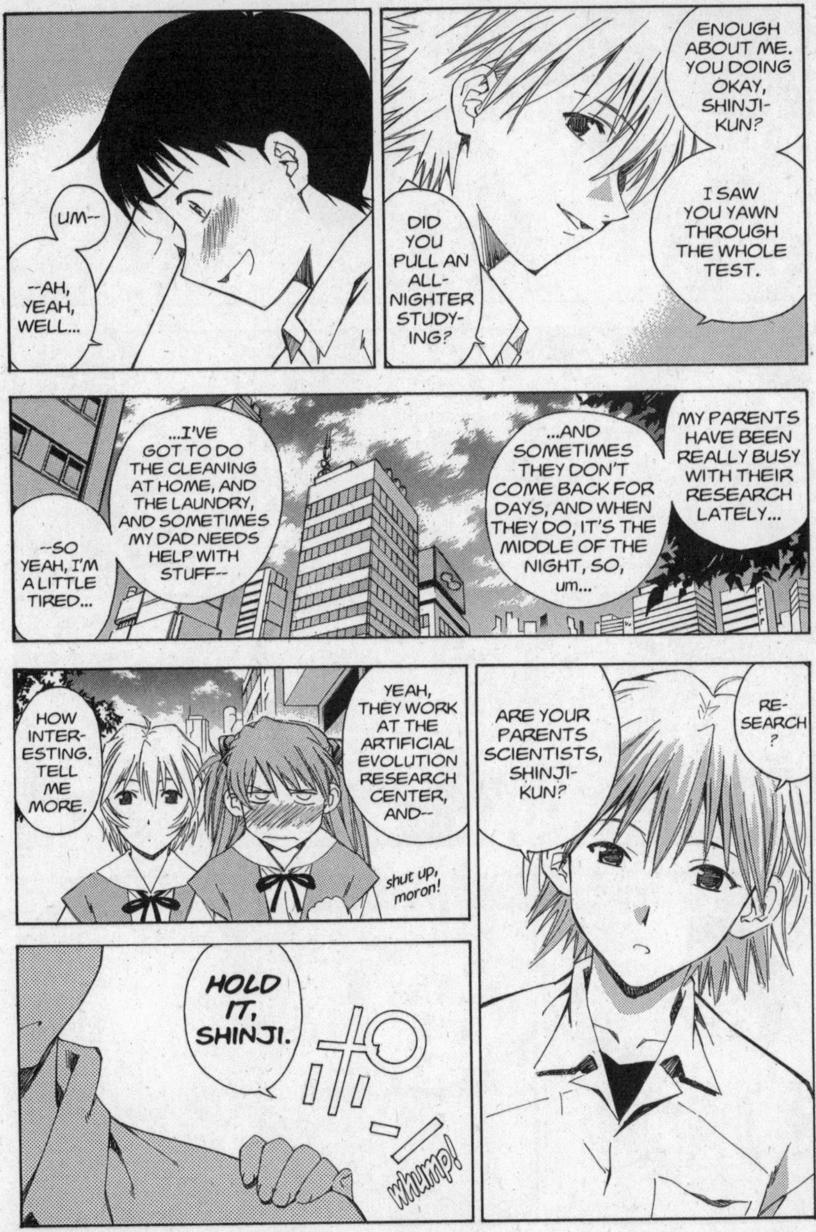
ENOUGH ABOUT ME. YOU DOING OKAY, SHINJI-KUN?
I SAW YOU YAWN THROUGH THE WHOLE TEST.
DID YOU PULL AN ALL-NIGHTER STUDYING?
UM--
--AH, YEAH, WELL...
MY PARENTS HAVE BEEN REALLY BUSY WITH THEIR RESEARCH LATELY...
...AND SOMETIMES THEY DON'T COME BACK FOR DAYS, AND WHEN THEY DO, IT'S THE MIDDLE OF THE NIGHT, SO, um...
...I'VE GOT TO DO THE CLEANING AT HOME, AND THE LAUNDRY, AND SOMETIMES MY DAD NEEDS HELP WITH STUFF--
--SO YEAH, I'M A LITTLE TIRED...
RE-SEARCH?
ARE YOUR PARENTS SCIENTISTS, SHINJI-KUN?
YEAH, THEY WORK AT THE ARTIFICIAL EVOLUTION RESEARCH CENTER, AND--
shut up, moron!
HOW INTERESTING. TELL ME MORE.
HOLD IT, SHINJI.
whump!

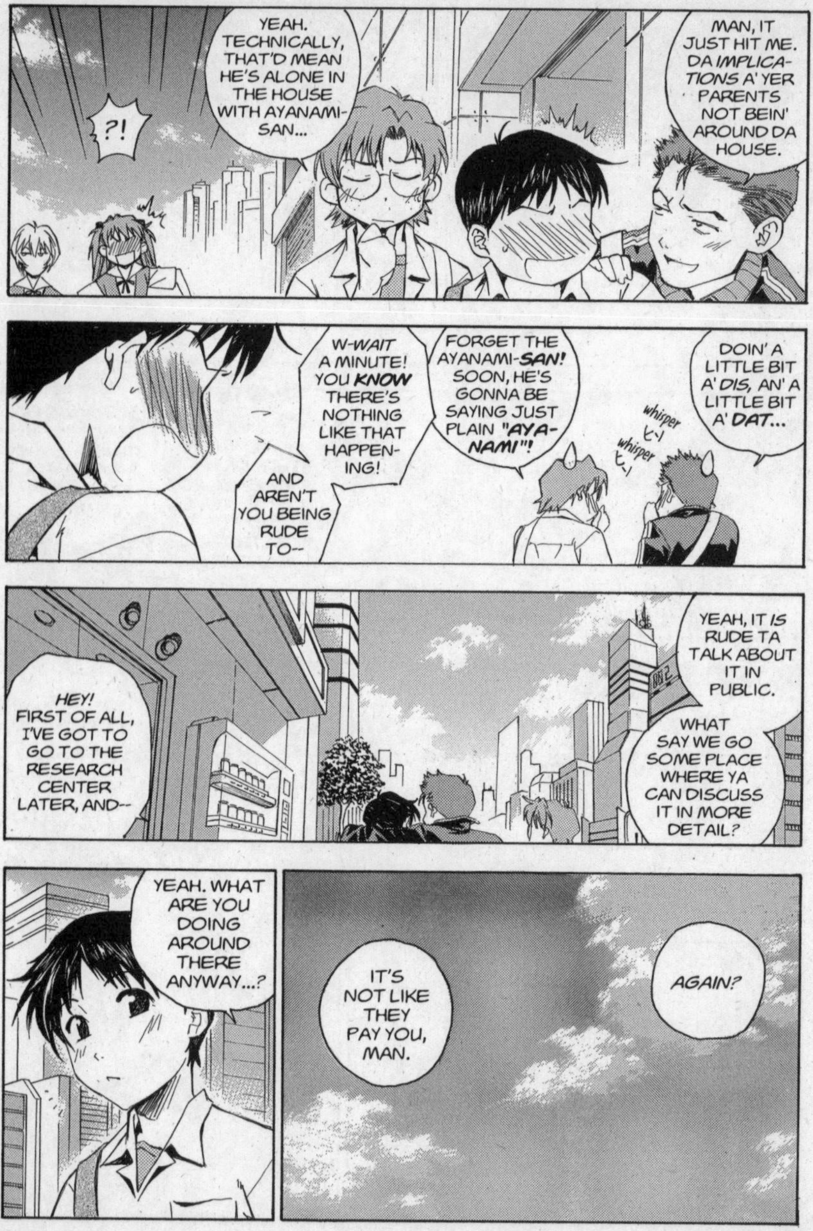

MAN, IT JUST HIT ME. DA IMPLICATIONS A' YER PARENTS NOT BEIN' AROUND DA HOUSE.
YEAH. TECHNICALLY, THAT'D MEAN HE'S ALONE IN THE HOUSE WITH AYANAMI-SAN...
?!
DOIN' A LITTLE BIT A' DIS, AN' A LITTLE BIT A' DAT...
whisper
whisper
FORGET THE AYANAMI-SAN! SOON, HE'S GONNA BE SAYING JUST PLAIN "AYA-NAMI"!
W-WAIT A MINUTE! YOU KNOW THERE'S NOTHING LIKE THAT HAPPEN-ING!
AND AREN'T YOU BEING RUDE TO--
YEAH, IT IS RUDE TA TALK ABOUT IT IN PUBLIC.
WHAT SAY WE GO SOME PLACE WHERE YA CAN DISCUSS IT IN MORE DETAIL?
HEY! FIRST OF ALL, I'VE GOT TO GO TO THE RESEARCH CENTER LATER, AND--
AGAIN?
IT'S NOT LIKE THEY PAY YOU, MAN.
YEAH. WHAT ARE YOU DOING AROUND THERE ANYWAY...?

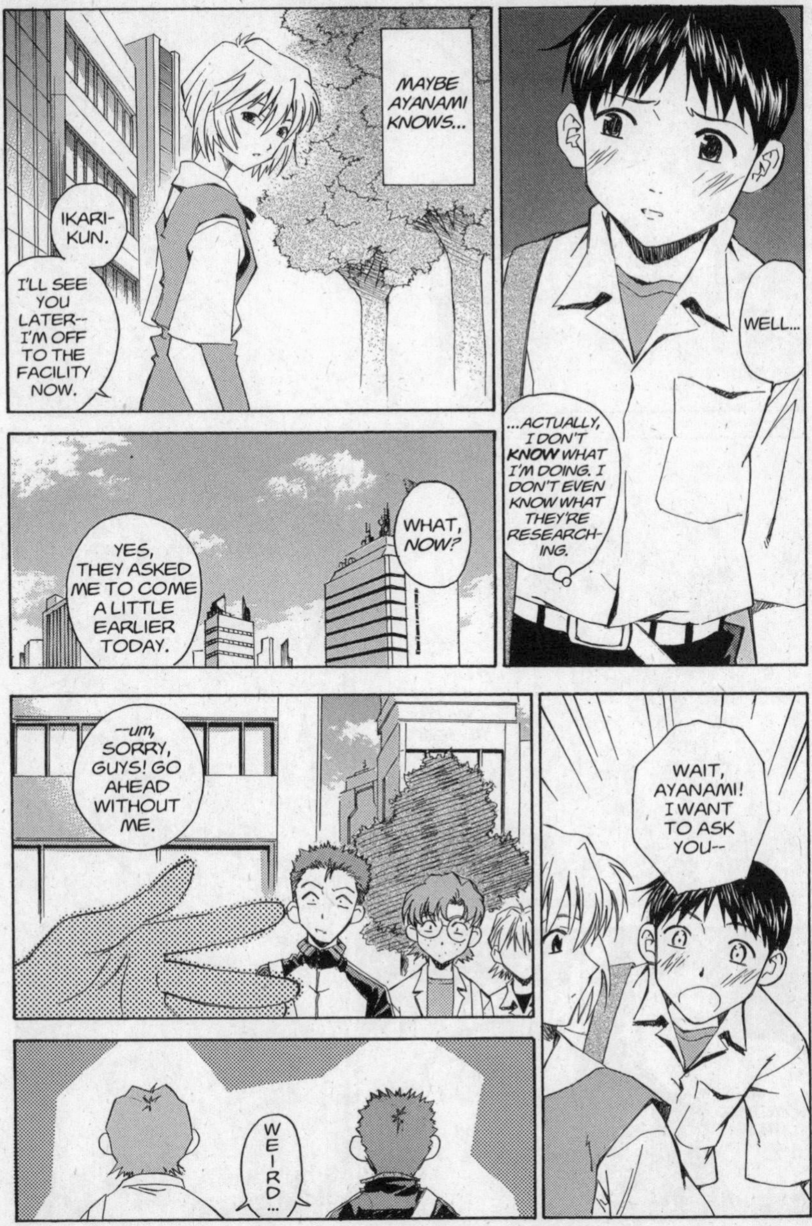
WELL...
...ACTUALLY, I DON'T KNOW WHAT I'M DOING. I DON'T EVEN KNOW WHAT THEY'RE RESEARCHING.
MAYBE AYANAMI KNOWS...
IKARI-KUN.
I'LL SEE YOU LATER-- I'M OFF TO THE FACILITY NOW.
WHAT, NOW?
YES, THEY ASKED ME TO COME A LITTLE EARLIER TODAY.
WAIT, AYANAMI! I WANT TO ASK YOU--
--um, SORRY, GUYS! GO AHEAD WITHOUT ME.
WEIRD...

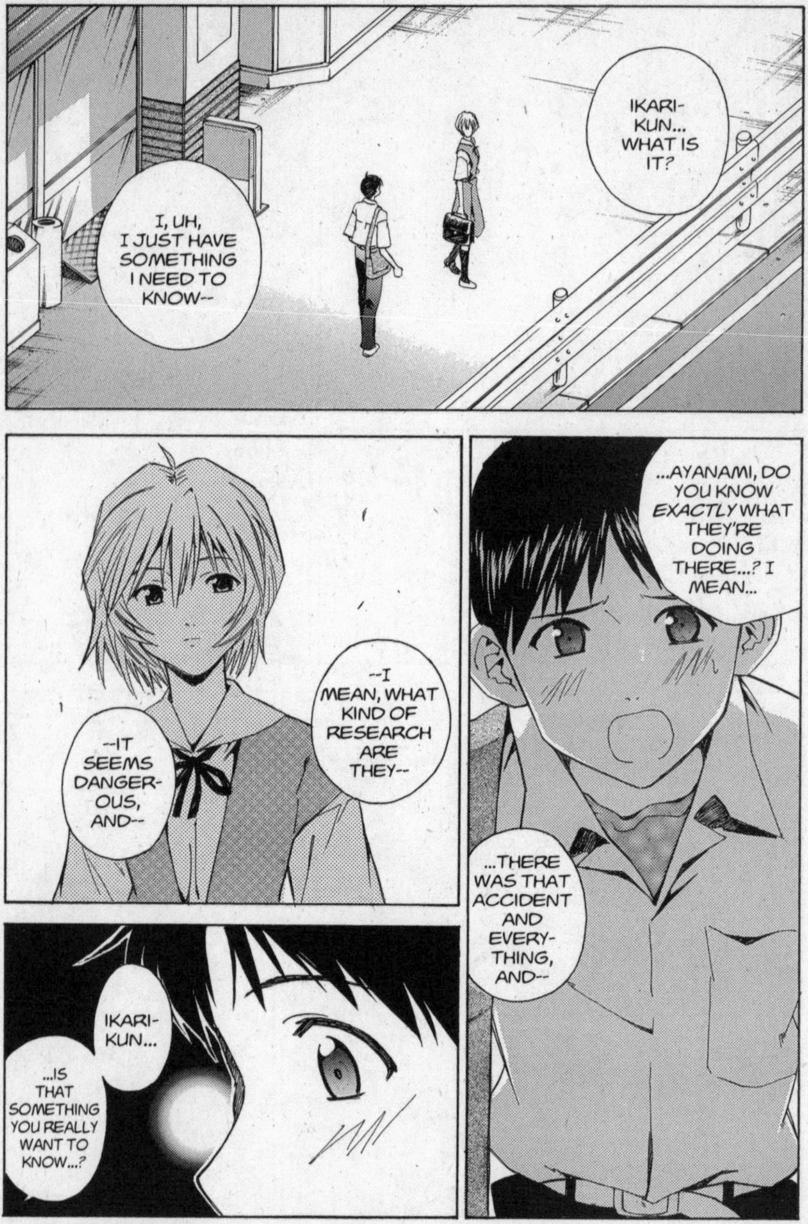
IKARI-KUN... WHAT IS IT?
I, UH, I JUST HAVE SOMETHING I NEED TO KNOW--
...AYANAMI, DO YOU KNOW *EXACTLY* WHAT THEY'RE DOING THERE...? I MEAN...
...THERE WAS THAT ACCIDENT AND EVERYTHING, AND--
--I MEAN, WHAT KIND OF RESEARCH ARE THEY--
--IT SEEMS DANGEROUS, AND--
IKARI-KUN...
...IS THAT SOMETHING YOU REALLY WANT TO KNOW...?

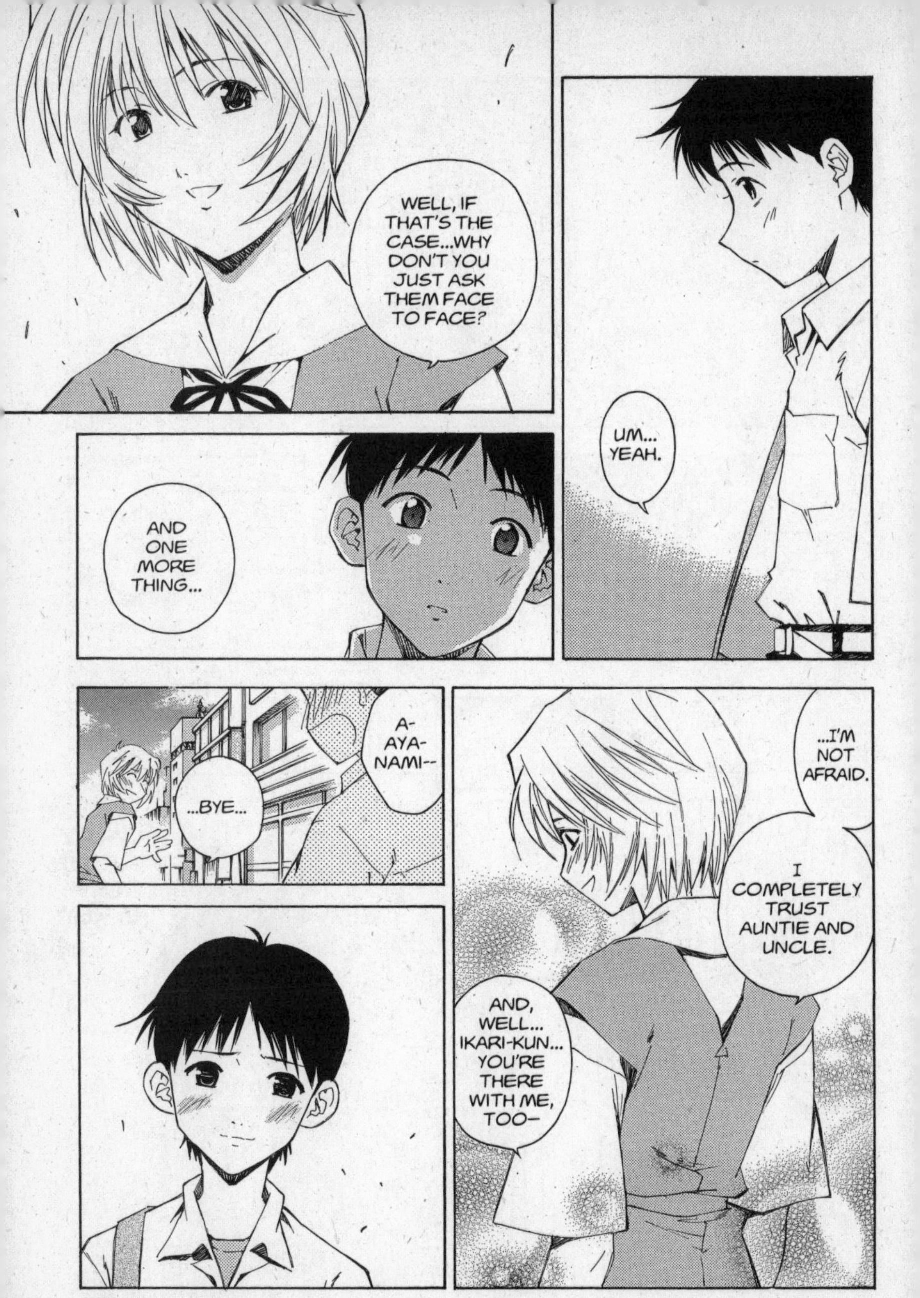
WELL, IF THAT'S THE CASE...WHY DON'T YOU JUST ASK THEM FACE TO FACE?
UM... YEAH.
AND ONE MORE THING...
...I'M NOT AFRAID.
I COMPLETELY TRUST AUNTIE AND UNCLE.
AND, WELL... IKARI-KUN... YOU'RE THERE WITH ME, TOO–
A-AYANAMI--
...BYE...

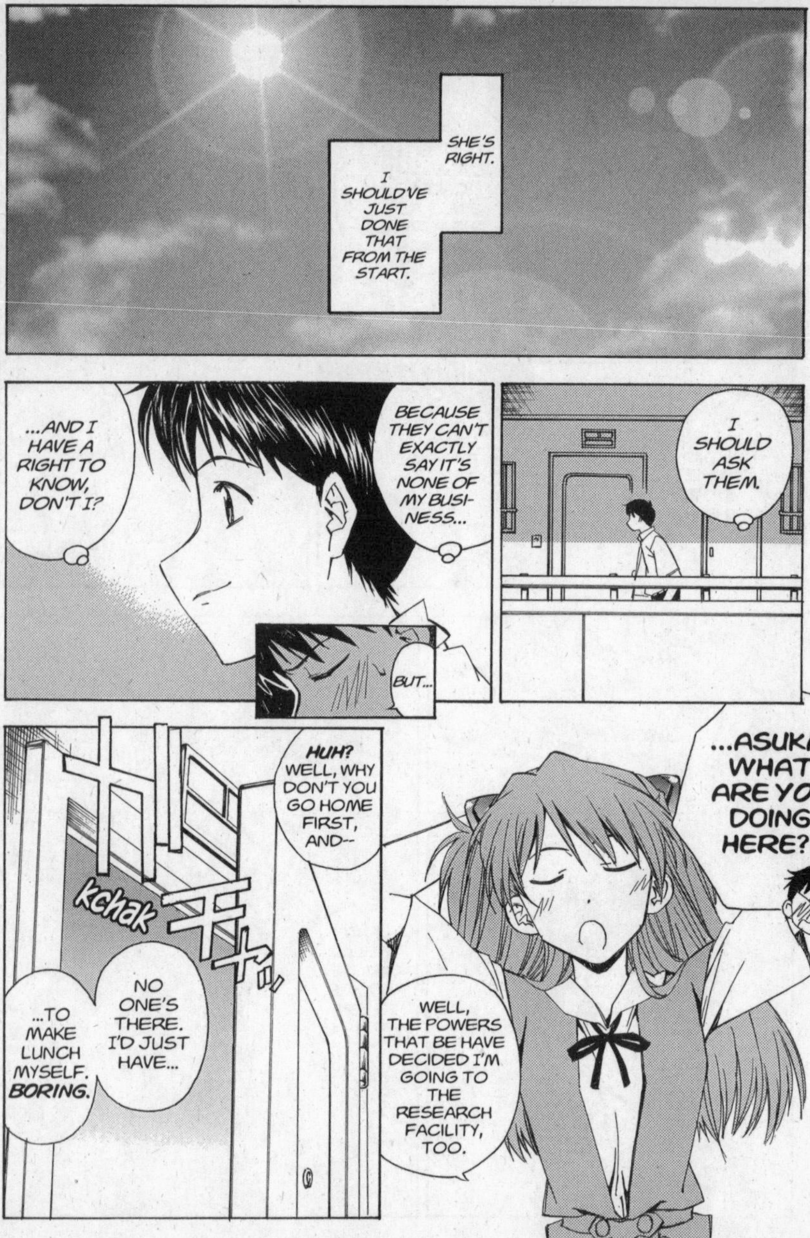
SHE'S RIGHT.
I SHOULD'VE JUST DONE THAT FROM THE START.
I SHOULD ASK THEM.
BECAUSE THEY CAN'T EXACTLY SAY IT'S NONE OF MY BUSINESS...
...AND I HAVE A RIGHT TO KNOW, DON'T I?
BUT...
...ASUKA, WHAT ARE YOU DOING HERE?!
WELL, THE POWERS THAT BE HAVE DECIDED I'M GOING TO THE RESEARCH FACILITY, TOO.
kchak
HUH? WELL, WHY DON'T YOU GO HOME FIRST, AND--
NO ONE'S THERE. I'D JUST HAVE...
...TO MAKE LUNCH MYSELF. **BORING.**

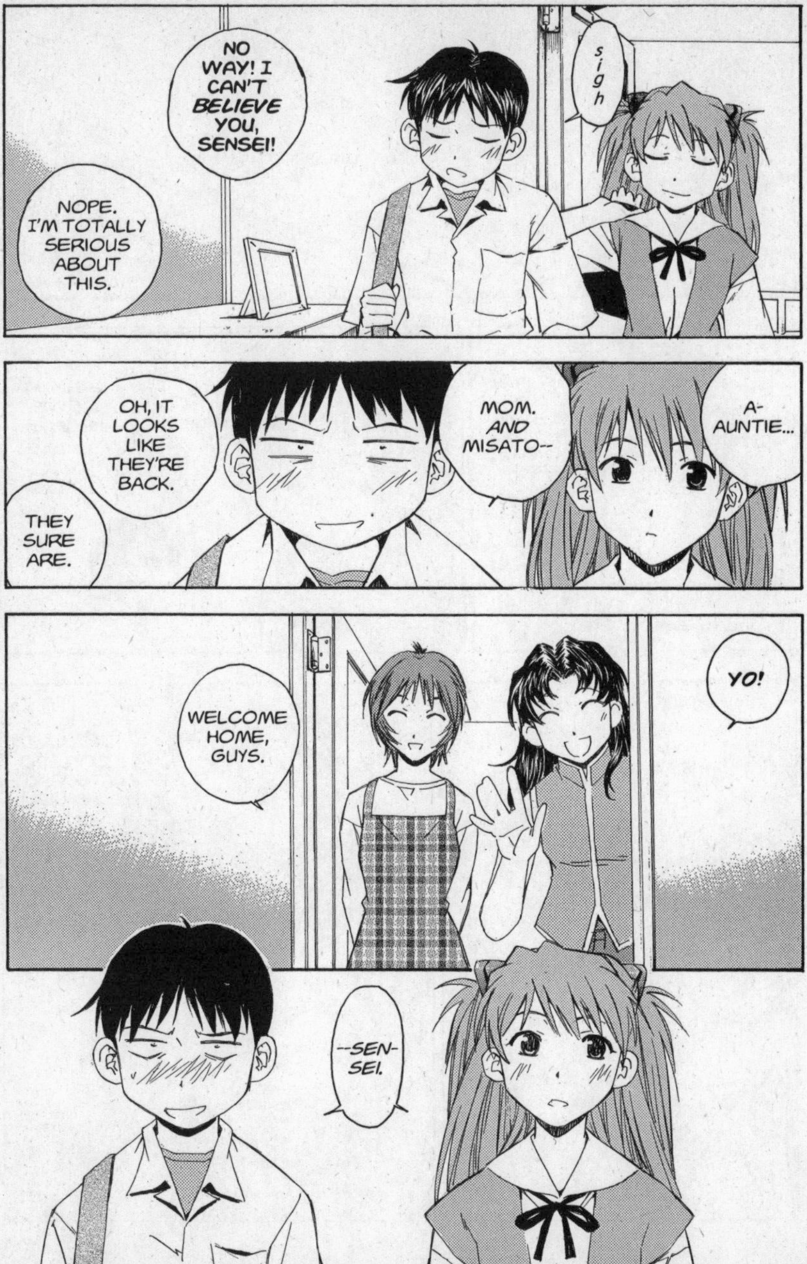
sigh
NO WAY! I CAN'T *BELIEVE* YOU, SENSEI!
NOPE. I'M TOTALLY SERIOUS ABOUT THIS.
A- AUNTIE...
MOM. AND MISATO--
OH, IT LOOKS LIKE THEY'RE BACK.
THEY SURE ARE.
YO!
WELCOME HOME, GUYS.
--SEN- SEI.

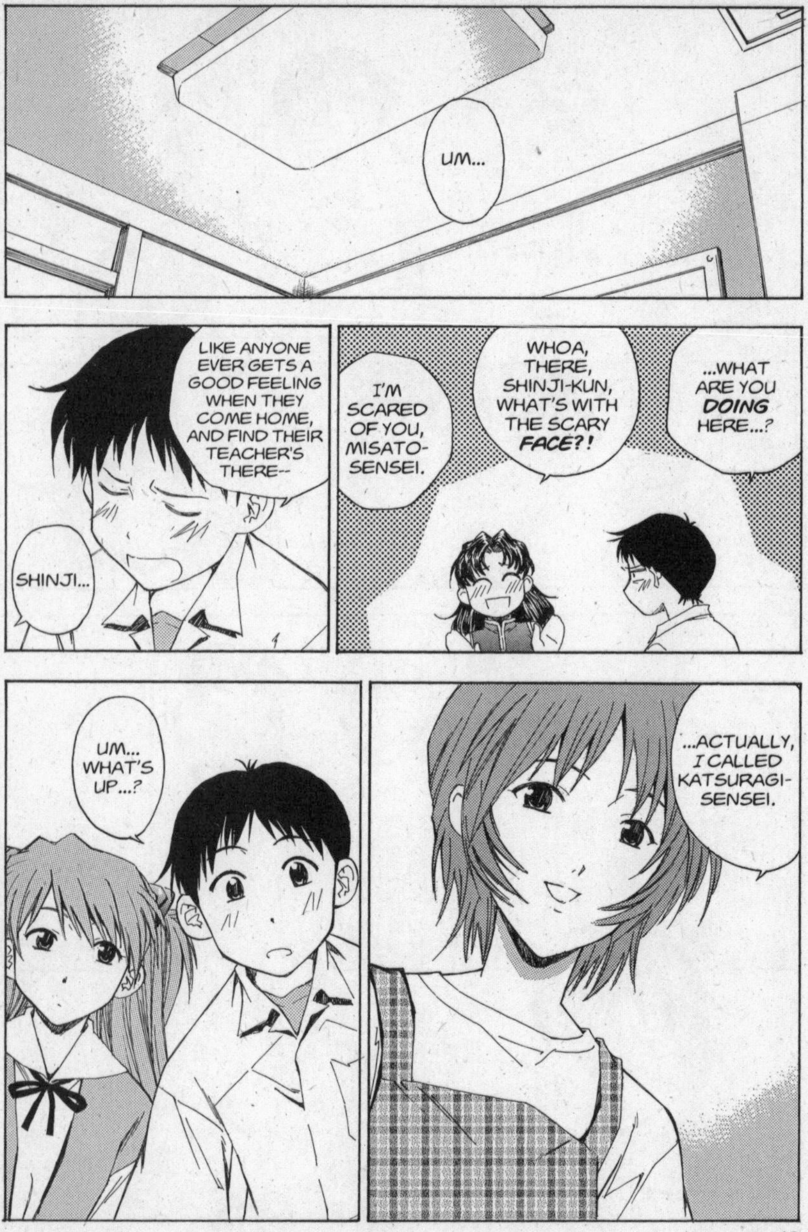
UM...
...WHAT ARE YOU DOING HERE...?
WHOA, THERE, SHINJI-KUN, WHAT'S WITH THE SCARY FACE?!
I'M SCARED OF YOU, MISATO-SENSEI.
LIKE ANYONE EVER GETS A GOOD FEELING WHEN THEY COME HOME, AND FIND THEIR TEACHER'S THERE--
SHINJI...
...ACTUALLY, I CALLED KATSURAGI-SENSEI.
UM... WHAT'S UP...?

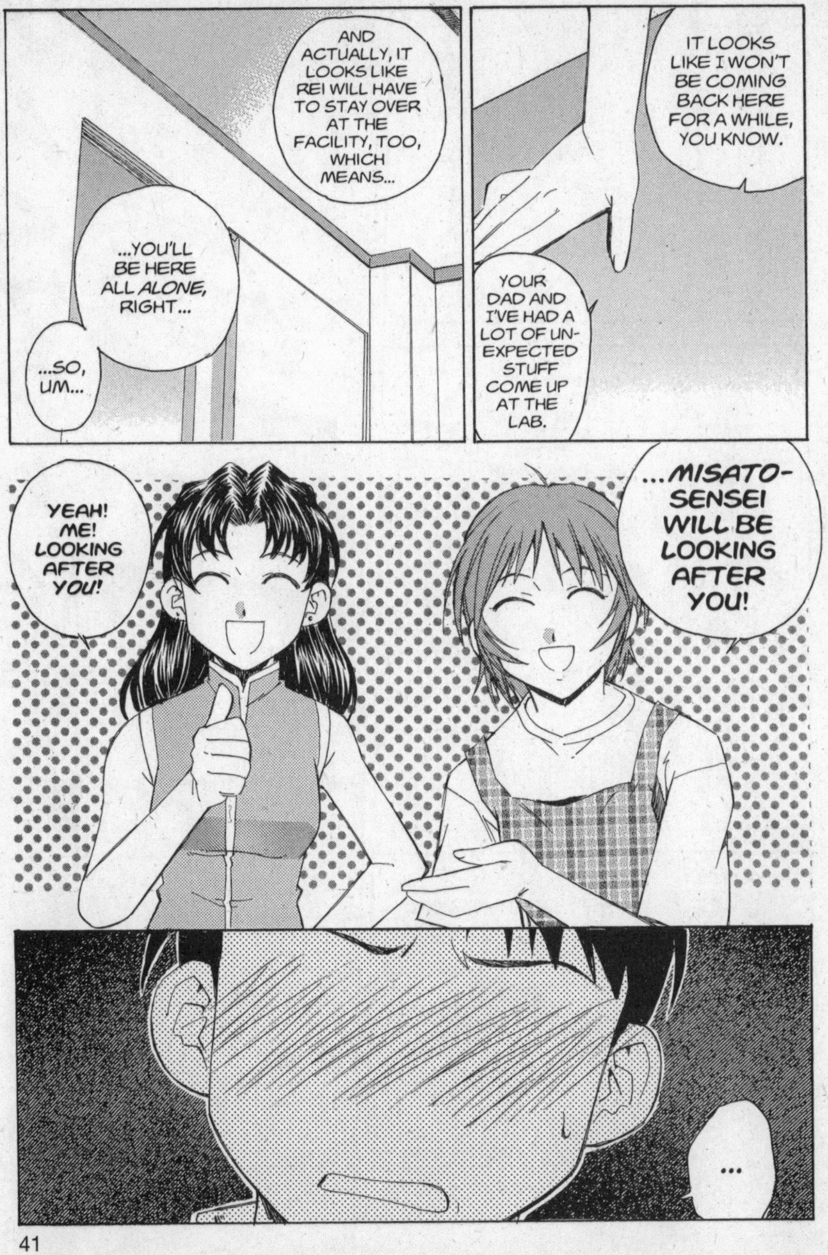
IT LOOKS LIKE I WON'T BE COMING BACK HERE FOR A WHILE, YOU KNOW.
YOUR DAD AND I'VE HAD A LOT OF UN-EXPECTED STUFF COME UP AT THE LAB.
AND ACTUALLY, IT LOOKS LIKE REI WILL HAVE TO STAY OVER AT THE FACILITY, TOO, WHICH MEANS...
...YOU'LL BE HERE ALL *ALONE*, RIGHT...
...SO, UM...
...**MISATO-SENSEI WILL BE LOOKING AFTER YOU!**
YEAH! ME! LOOKING AFTER *YOU!*
...

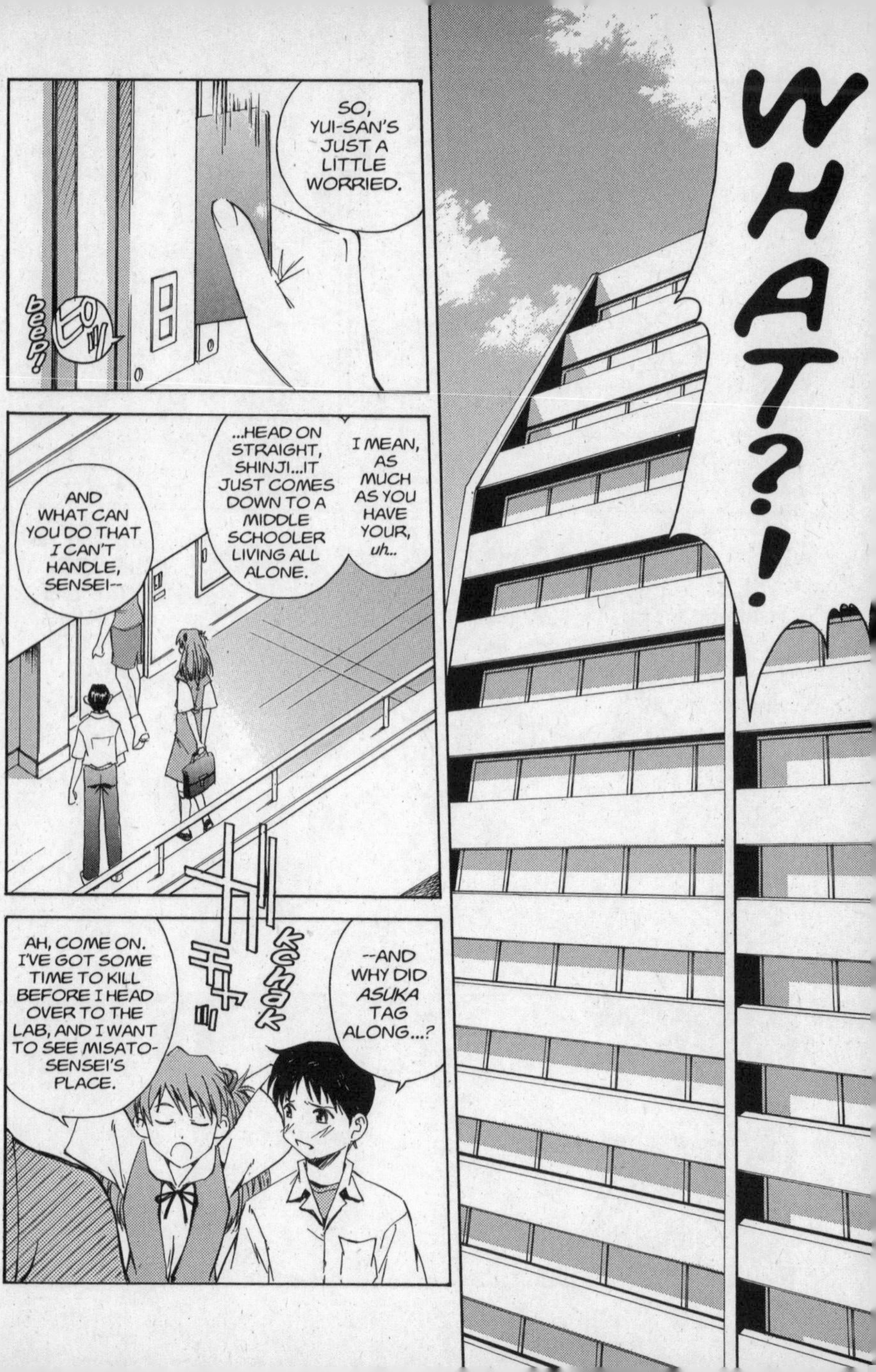
WHAT?!
SO, YUI-SAN'S JUST A LITTLE WORRIED.
beep!
I MEAN, AS MUCH AS YOU HAVE YOUR, uh..
...HEAD ON STRAIGHT, SHINJI...IT JUST COMES DOWN TO A MIDDLE SCHOOLER LIVING ALL ALONE.
AND WHAT CAN YOU DO THAT I CAN'T HANDLE, SENSEI--
--AND WHY DID ASUKA TAG ALONG...?
kchak
AH, COME ON. I'VE GOT SOME TIME TO KILL BEFORE I HEAD OVER TO THE LAB, AND I WANT TO SEE MISATO-SENSEI'S PLACE.

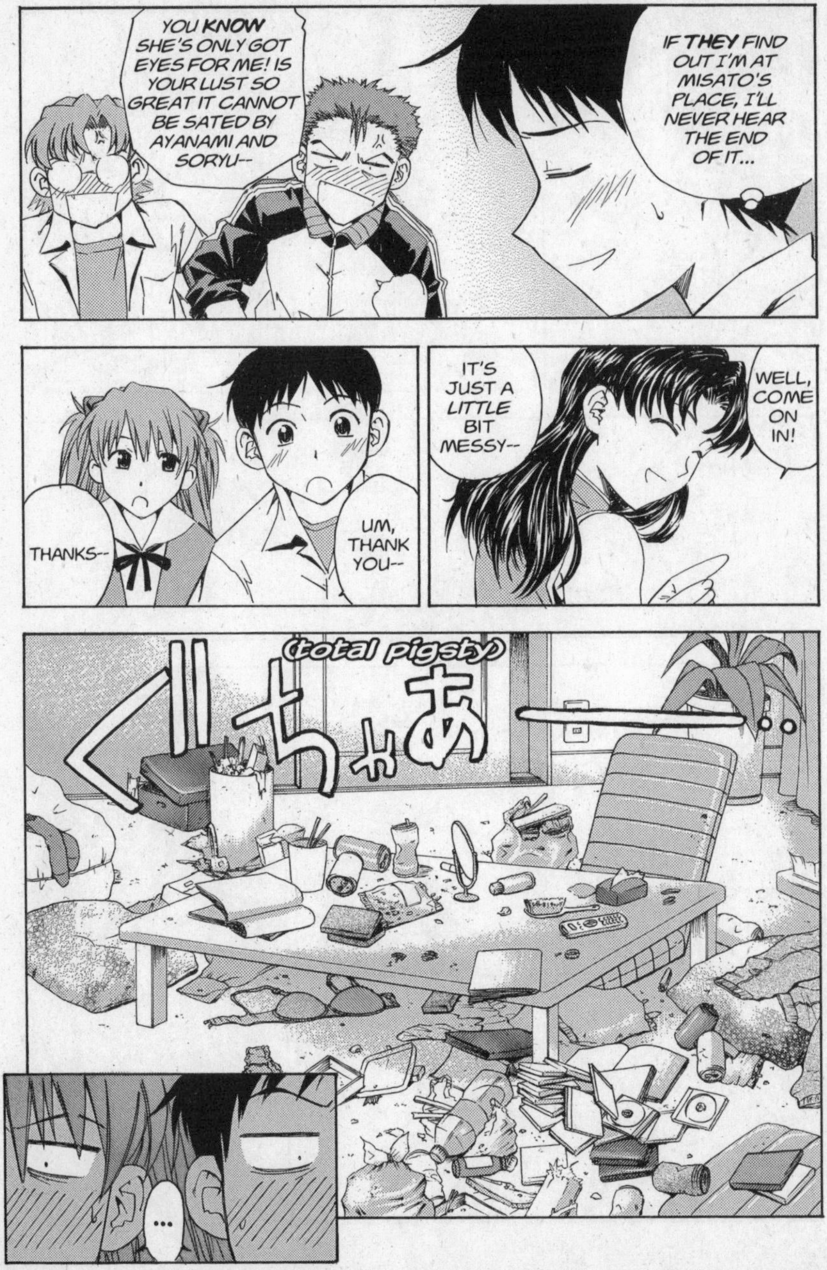
IF THEY FIND OUT I'M AT MISATO'S PLACE, I'LL NEVER HEAR THE END OF IT...
YOU KNOW SHE'S ONLY GOT EYES FOR ME! IS YOUR LUST SO GREAT IT CANNOT BE SATED BY AYANAMI AND SORYU--
WELL, COME ON IN!
IT'S JUST A LITTLE BIT MESSY--
UM, THANK YOU--
THANKS--
(total pigsty)
ぐちゃあー
...

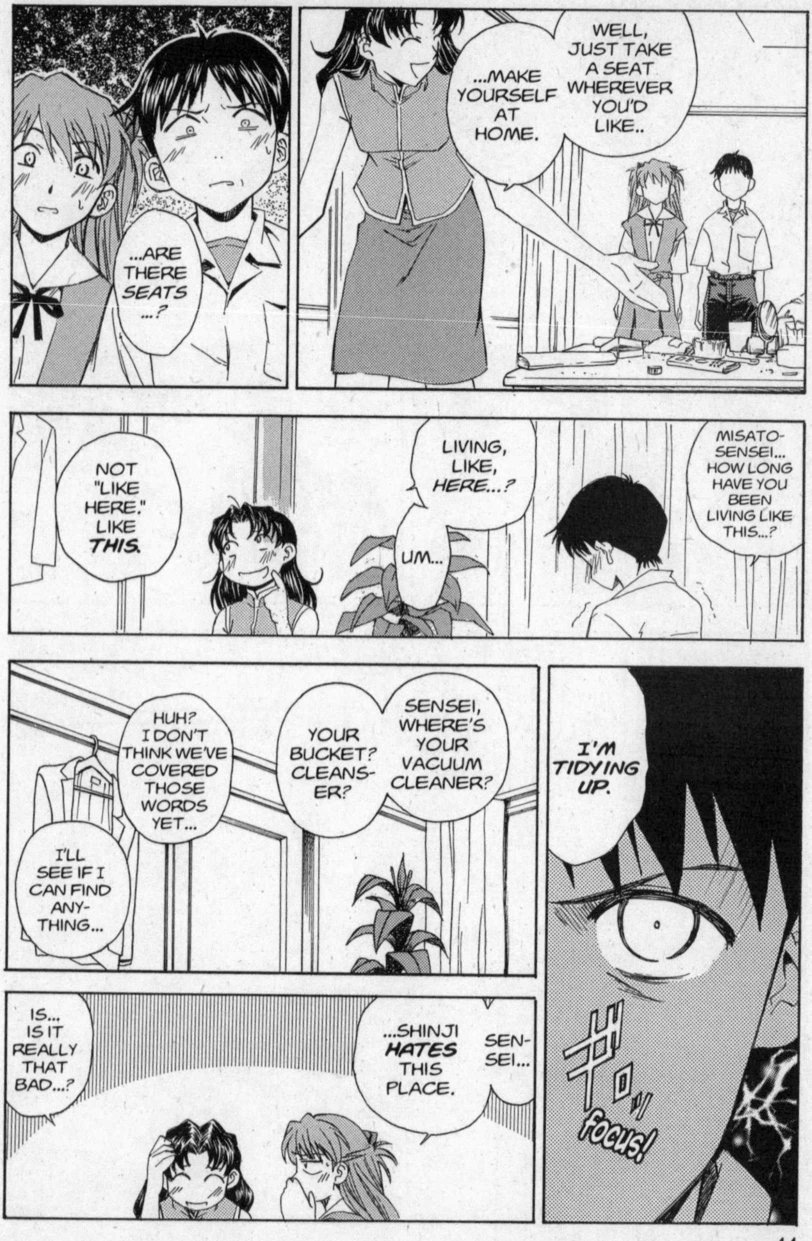
WELL, JUST TAKE A SEAT WHEREVER YOU'D LIKE..
...MAKE YOURSELF AT HOME.
...ARE THERE *SEATS* ...?
MISATO-SENSEI... HOW LONG HAVE YOU BEEN LIVING LIKE THIS...?
LIVING, LIKE, *HERE...?*
UM...
NOT "LIKE HERE." LIKE ***THIS.***
I'M TIDYING UP.
focus!
SENSEI, WHERE'S YOUR VACUUM CLEANER?
YOUR BUCKET? CLEANS-ER?
HUH? I DON'T THINK WE'VE COVERED THOSE WORDS YET...
I'LL SEE IF I CAN FIND ANY-THING...
SEN-SEI...
...SHINJI ***HATES*** THIS PLACE.
IS... IS IT REALLY THAT BAD...?

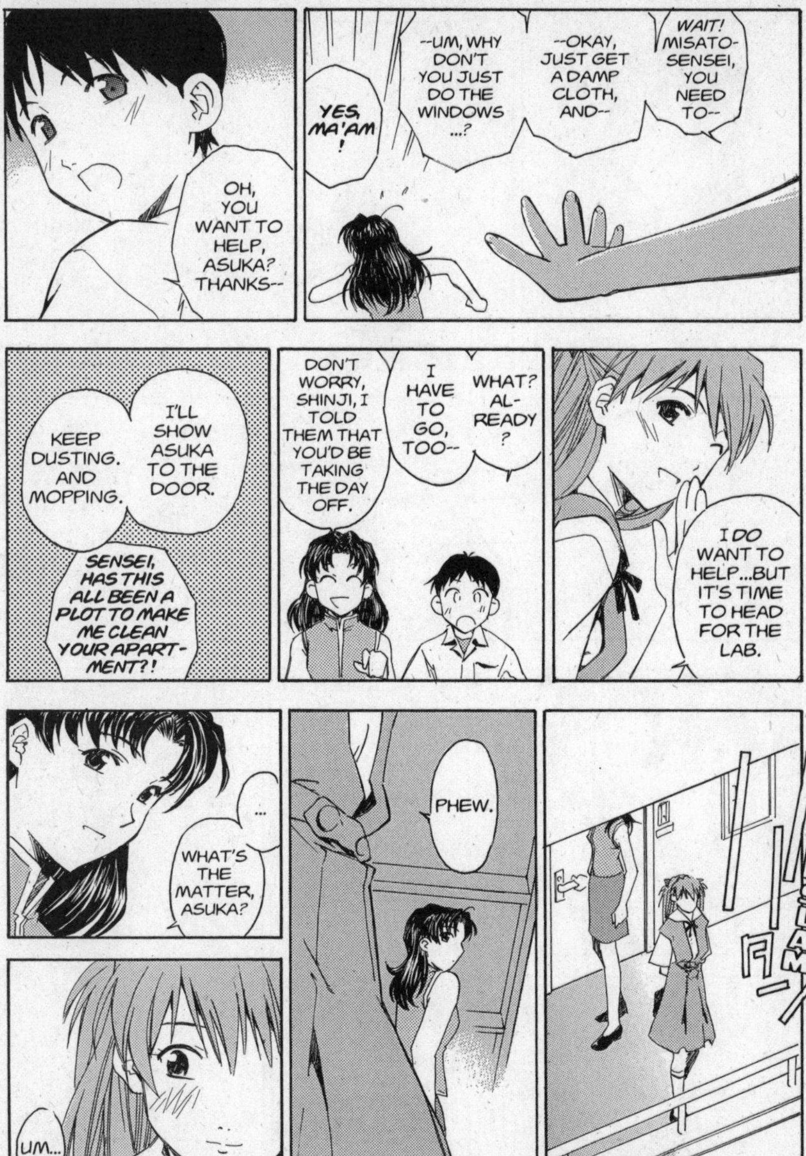
WAIT! MISATO-SENSEI, YOU NEED TO--
--OKAY, JUST GET A DAMP CLOTH, AND--
--UM, WHY DON'T YOU JUST DO THE WINDOWS ...?
YES, MA'AM!
OH, YOU WANT TO HELP, ASUKA? THANKS--
I DO WANT TO HELP...BUT IT'S TIME TO HEAD FOR THE LAB.
WHAT? AL-READY?
I HAVE TO GO, TOO--
DON'T WORRY, SHINJI, I TOLD THEM THAT YOU'D BE TAKING THE DAY OFF.
I'LL SHOW ASUKA TO THE DOOR.
KEEP DUSTING. AND MOPPING.
SENSEI, HAS THIS ALL BEEN A PLOT TO MAKE ME CLEAN YOUR APARTMENT?!
SLAM
PHEW.
...
WHAT'S THE MATTER, ASUKA?
UM...

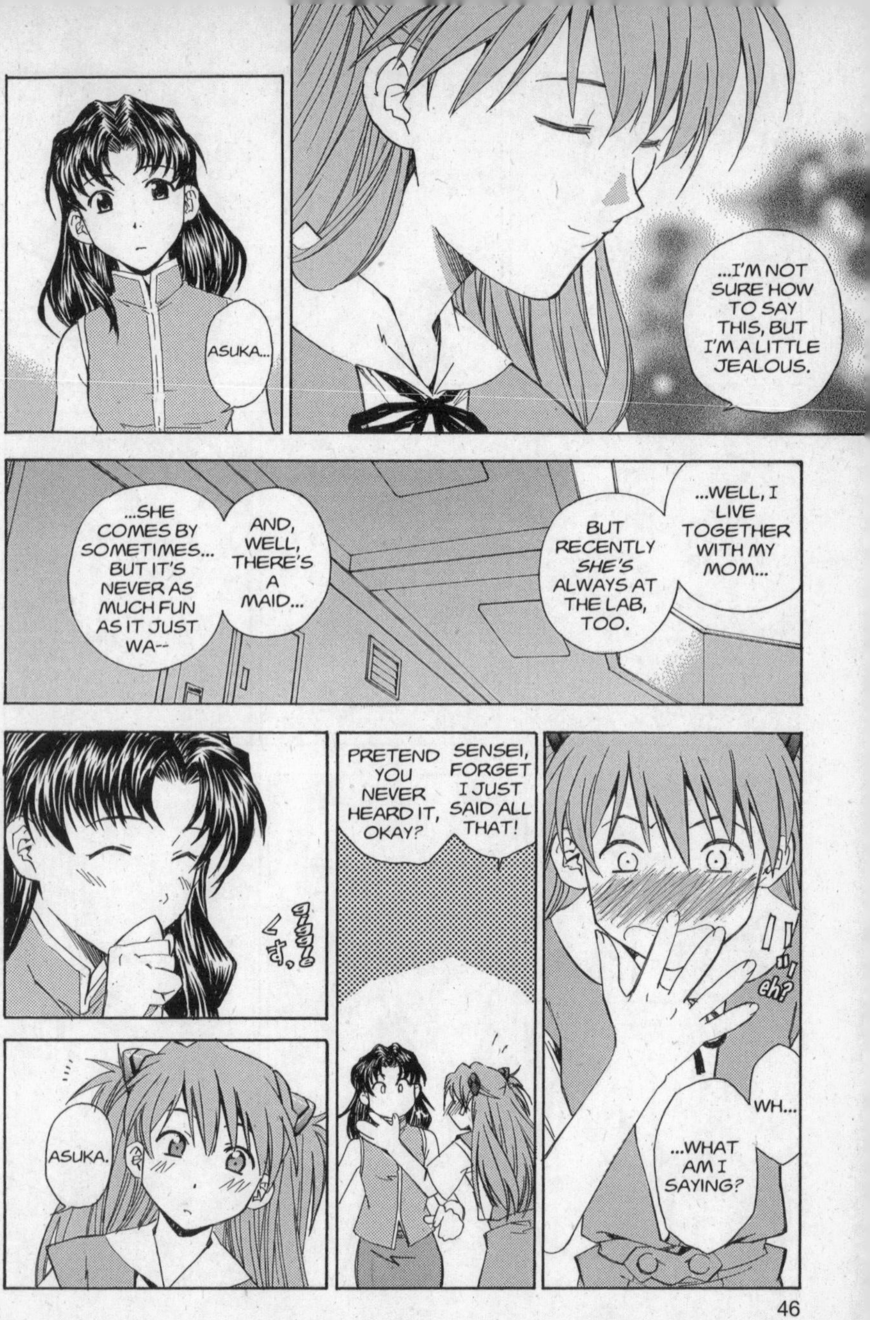
...I'M NOT SURE HOW TO SAY THIS, BUT I'M A LITTLE JEALOUS.
ASUKA...
...WELL, I LIVE TOGETHER WITH MY MOM...
BUT RECENTLY SHE'S ALWAYS AT THE LAB, TOO.
AND, WELL, THERE'S A MAID...
...SHE COMES BY SOMETIMES... BUT IT'S NEVER AS MUCH FUN AS IT JUST WA--
!!
eh?
WH...
...WHAT AM I SAYING?
SENSEI, FORGET I JUST SAID ALL THAT!
PRETEND YOU NEVER HEARD IT, OKAY?
くす。
giggle
ASUKA.

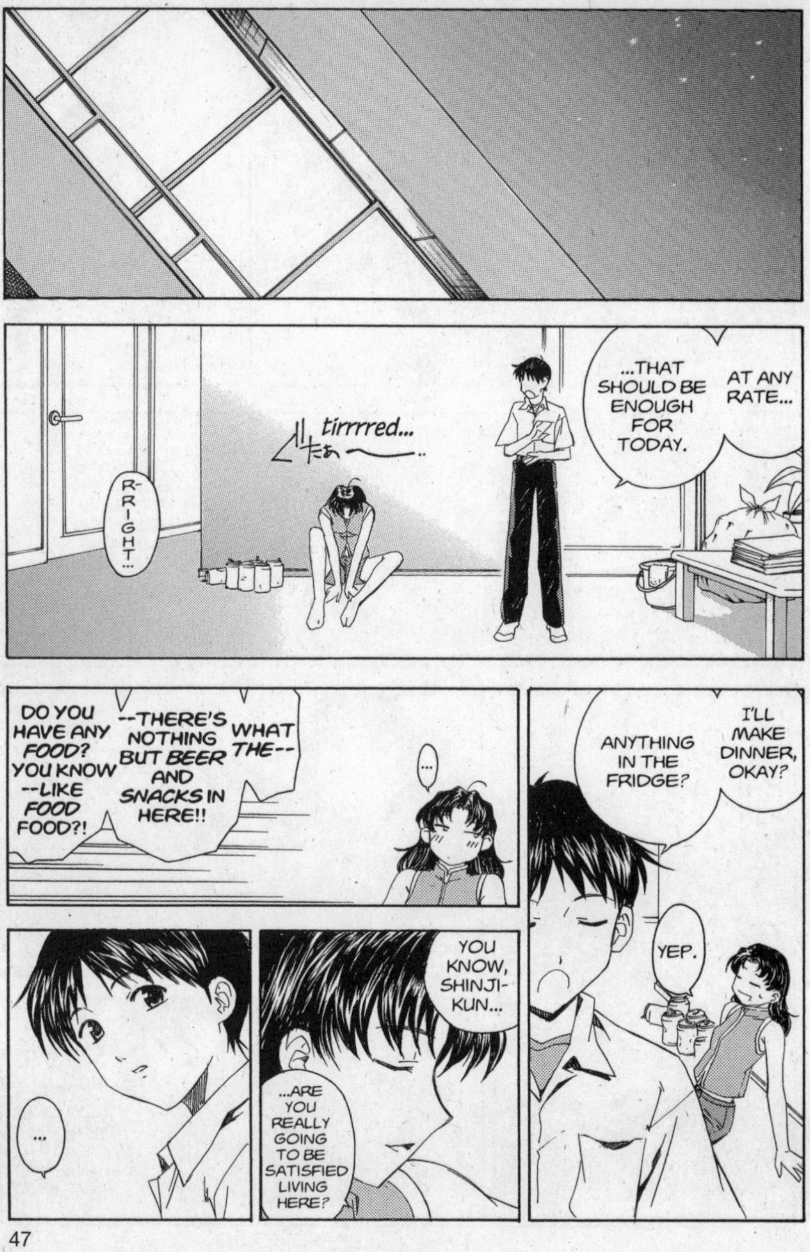
AT ANY RATE...
...THAT SHOULD BE ENOUGH FOR TODAY.
tirrrred...
R-RIGHT...
I'LL MAKE DINNER, OKAY?
ANYTHING IN THE FRIDGE?
YEP.
...
WHAT THE--
--THERE'S NOTHING BUT BEER AND SNACKS IN HERE!!
DO YOU HAVE ANY FOOD? YOU KNOW --LIKE FOOD FOOD?!
YOU KNOW, SHINJI-KUN...
...ARE YOU REALLY GOING TO BE SATISFIED LIVING HERE?
...

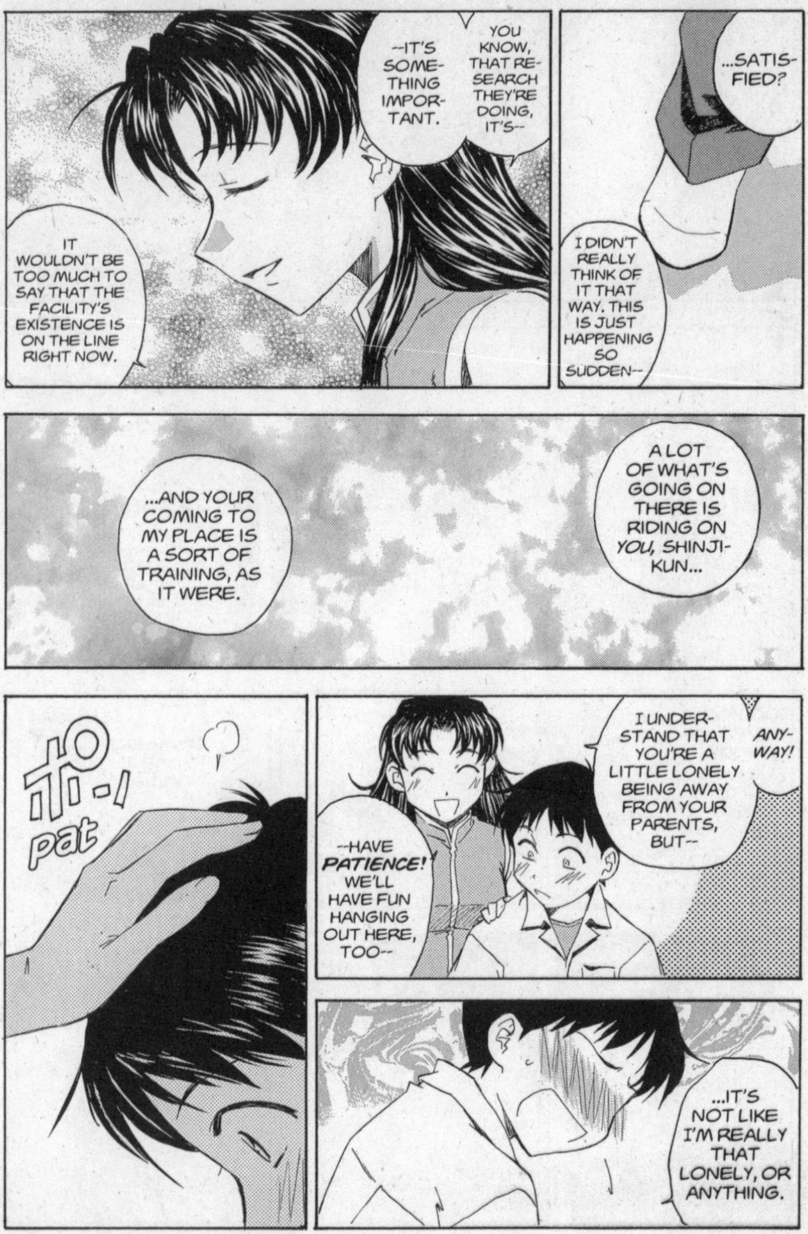
...SATISFIED?
I DIDN'T REALLY THINK OF IT THAT WAY. THIS IS JUST HAPPENING SO SUDDEN--
YOU KNOW, THAT RESEARCH THEY'RE DOING, IT'S--
--IT'S SOMETHING IMPORTANT.
IT WOULDN'T BE TOO MUCH TO SAY THAT THE FACILITY'S EXISTENCE IS ON THE LINE RIGHT NOW.
A LOT OF WHAT'S GOING ON THERE IS RIDING ON *YOU,* SHINJI-KUN...
...AND YOUR COMING TO MY PLACE IS A SORT OF TRAINING, AS IT WERE.
ANYWAY!
I UNDERSTAND THAT YOU'RE A LITTLE LONELY BEING AWAY FROM YOUR PARENTS, BUT--
--HAVE **PATIENCE!** WE'LL HAVE FUN HANGING OUT HERE, TOO--
...IT'S NOT LIKE I'M REALLY THAT LONELY, OR ANYTHING.
pat

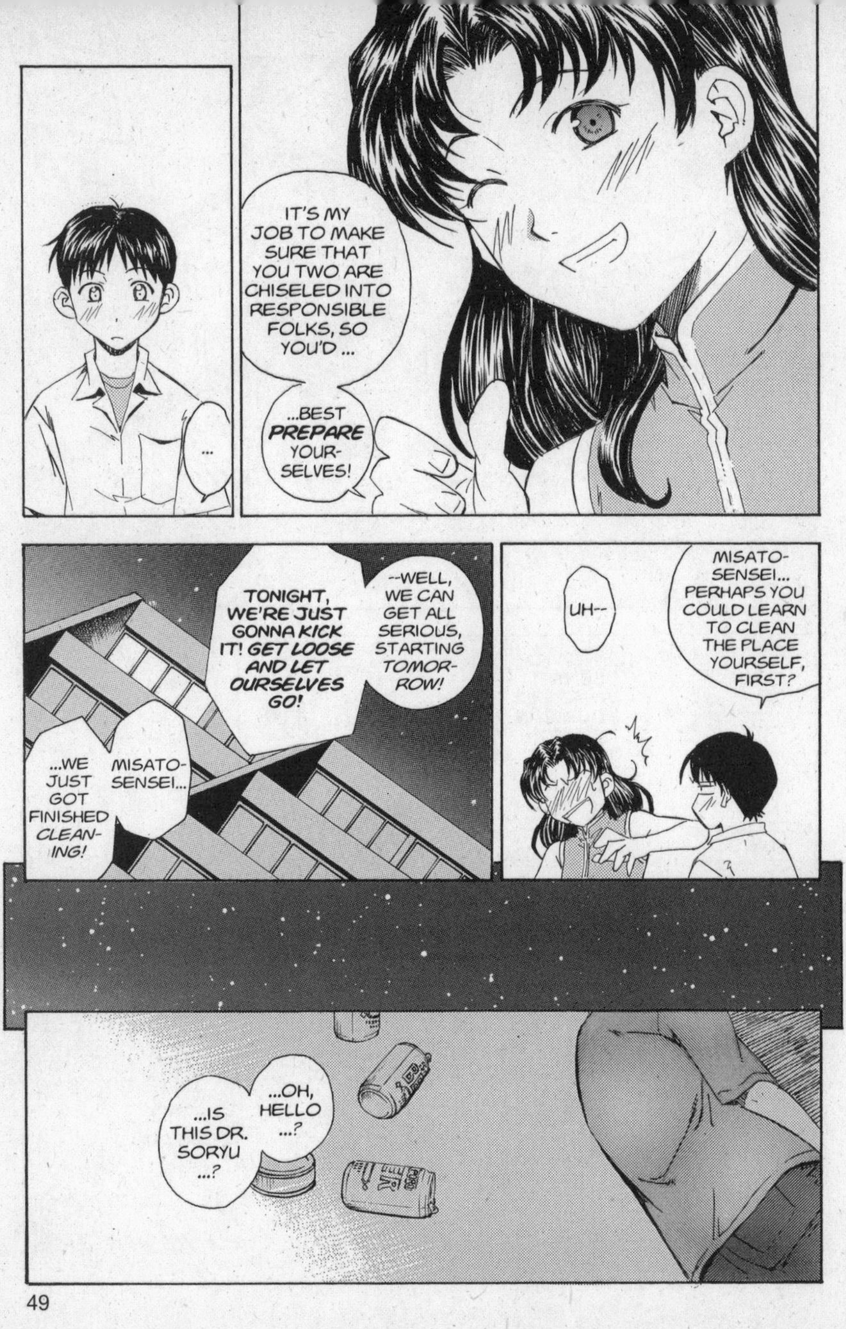
IT'S MY JOB TO MAKE SURE THAT YOU TWO ARE CHISELED INTO RESPONSIBLE FOLKS, SO YOU'D ...
...BEST PREPARE YOURSELVES!
...
MISATO-SENSEI... PERHAPS YOU COULD LEARN TO CLEAN THE PLACE YOURSELF, FIRST?
UH--
--WELL, WE CAN GET ALL SERIOUS, STARTING TOMORROW!
TONIGHT, WE'RE JUST GONNA KICK IT! GET LOOSE AND LET OURSELVES GO!
MISATO-SENSEI...
...WE JUST GOT FINISHED CLEANING!
...OH, HELLO ...?
...IS THIS DR. SORYU ...?

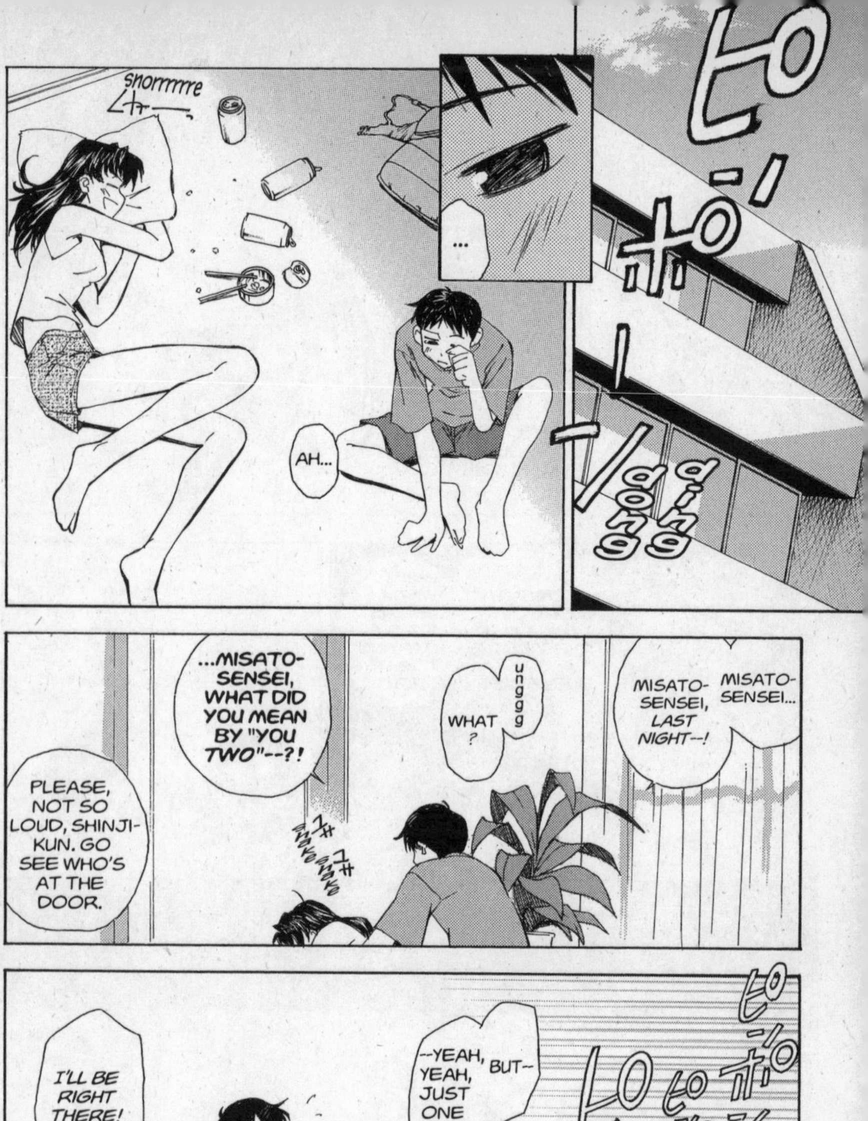
ピンポーン
ding
dong
...
snorrrrrre
AH...
MISATO-SENSEI...
MISATO-SENSEI, LAST NIGHT--!
unggg
WHAT?
...MISATO-SENSEI, WHAT DID YOU MEAN BY "YOU TWO"--?!
PLEASE, NOT SO LOUD, SHINJI-KUN. GO SEE WHO'S AT THE DOOR.
smoke smoke
ding-dong
ding-dong
ding-dong
BUT--
--YEAH, YEAH, JUST ONE SEC!
I'LL BE RIGHT THERE!

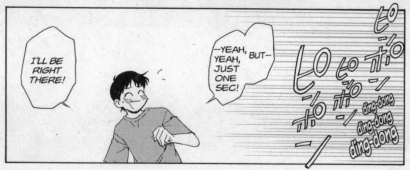

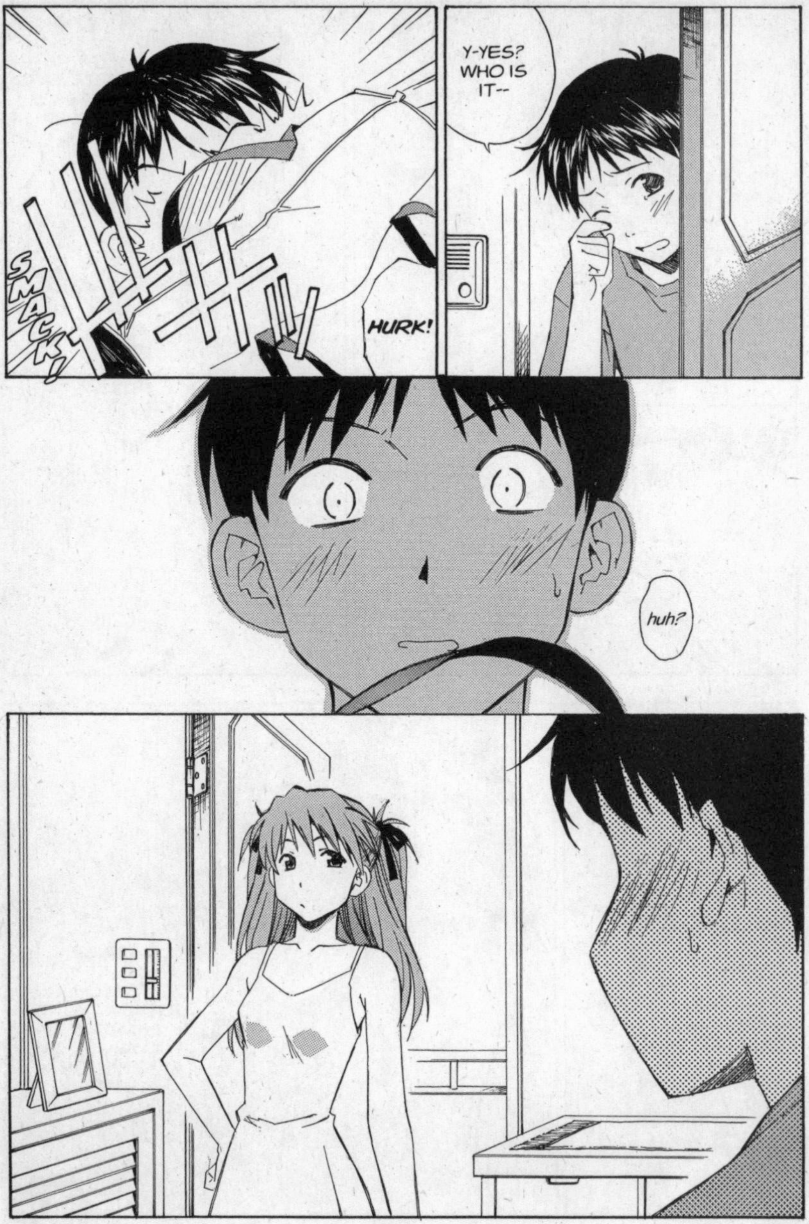
Y-YES? WHO IS IT--
SMACK!
HURK!
huh?

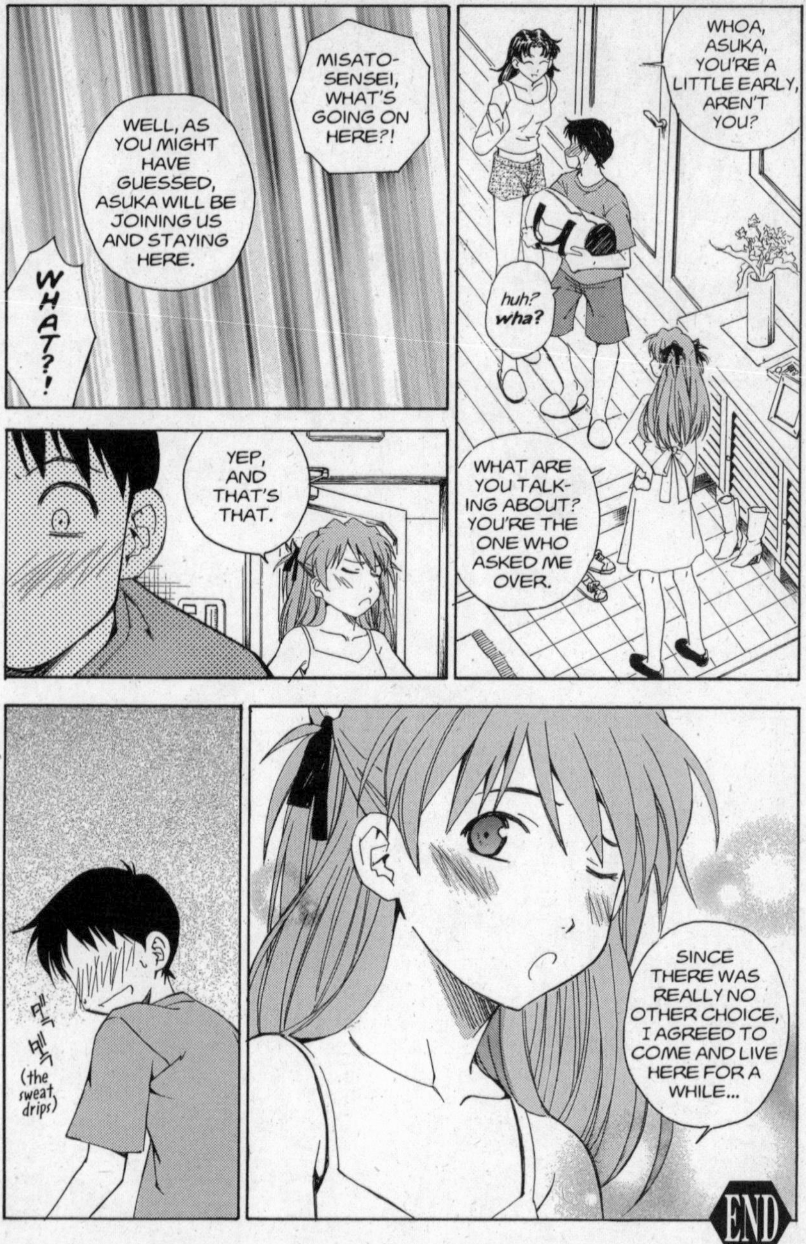
WHOA, ASUKA, YOU'RE A LITTLE EARLY, AREN'T YOU?
huh? wha?
WHAT ARE YOU TALKING ABOUT? YOU'RE THE ONE WHO ASKED ME OVER.
MISATO-SENSEI, WHAT'S GOING ON HERE?!
WELL, AS YOU MIGHT HAVE GUESSED, ASUKA WILL BE JOINING US AND STAYING HERE.
WHAT?!
YEP, AND THAT'S THAT.
SINCE THERE WAS REALLY NO OTHER CHOICE, I AGREED TO COME AND LIVE HERE FOR A WHILE...
END
(the sweat drips)

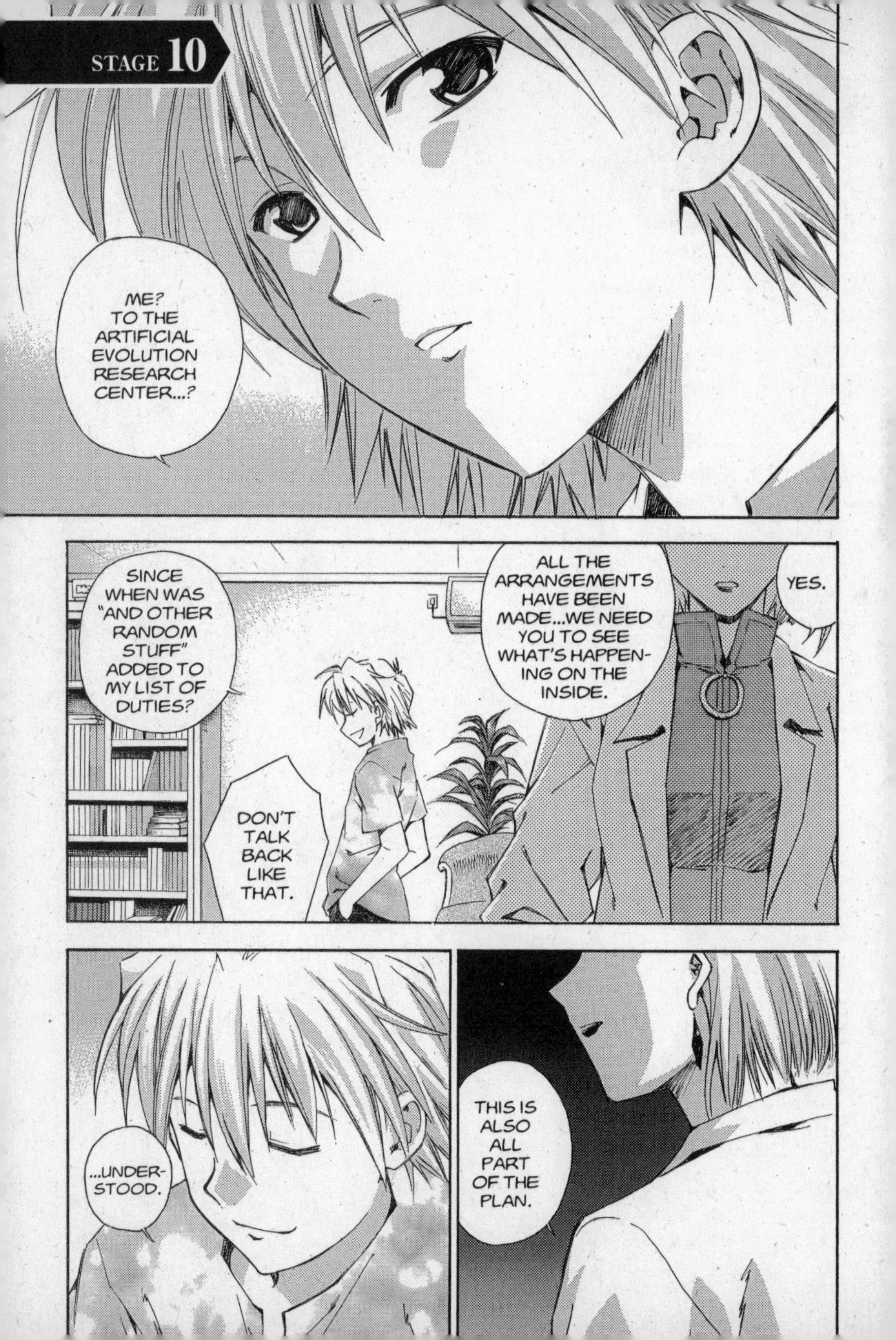
STAGE 10
ME? TO THE ARTIFICIAL EVOLUTION RESEARCH CENTER...?
YES.
ALL THE ARRANGEMENTS HAVE BEEN MADE...WE NEED YOU TO SEE WHAT'S HAPPENING ON THE INSIDE.
SINCE WHEN WAS "AND OTHER RANDOM STUFF" ADDED TO MY LIST OF DUTIES?
DON'T TALK BACK LIKE THAT.
THIS IS ALSO ALL PART OF THE PLAN.
...UNDERSTOOD.

STAGE 10

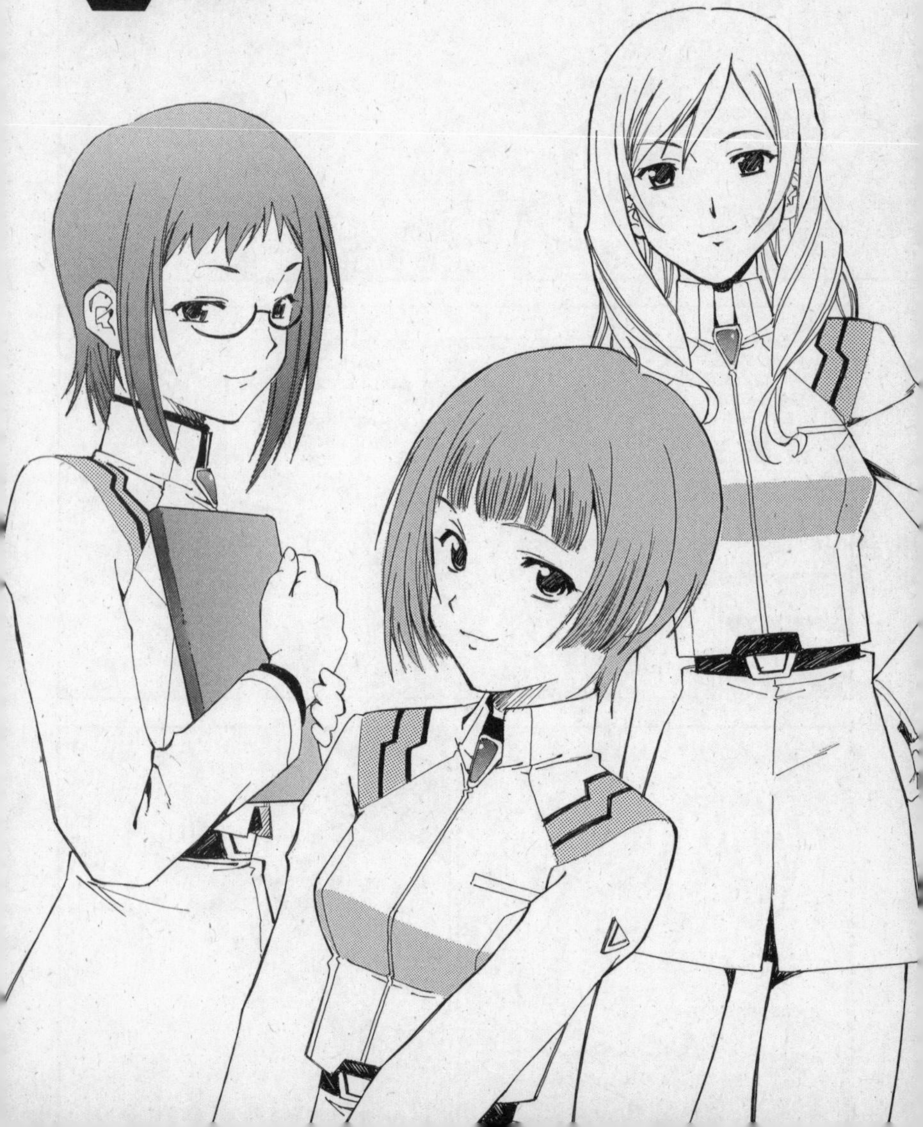

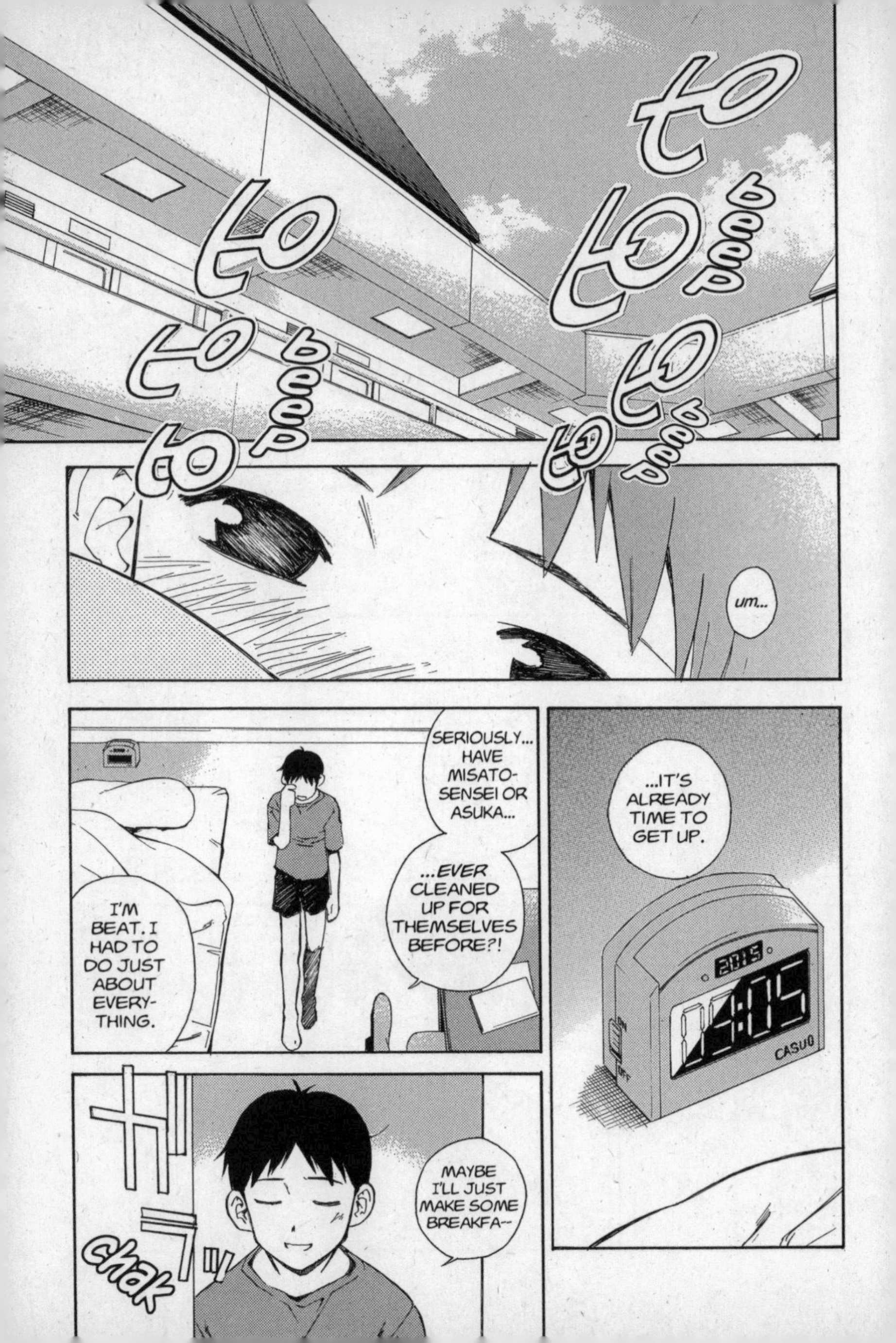
beep
beep
beep
um...
...IT'S ALREADY TIME TO GET UP.
CASUO
SERIOUSLY... HAVE MISATO-SENSEI OR ASUKA...
...EVER CLEANED UP FOR THEMSELVES BEFORE?!
I'M BEAT. I HAD TO DO JUST ABOUT EVERY-THING.
MAYBE I'LL JUST MAKE SOME BREAKFA--
chak

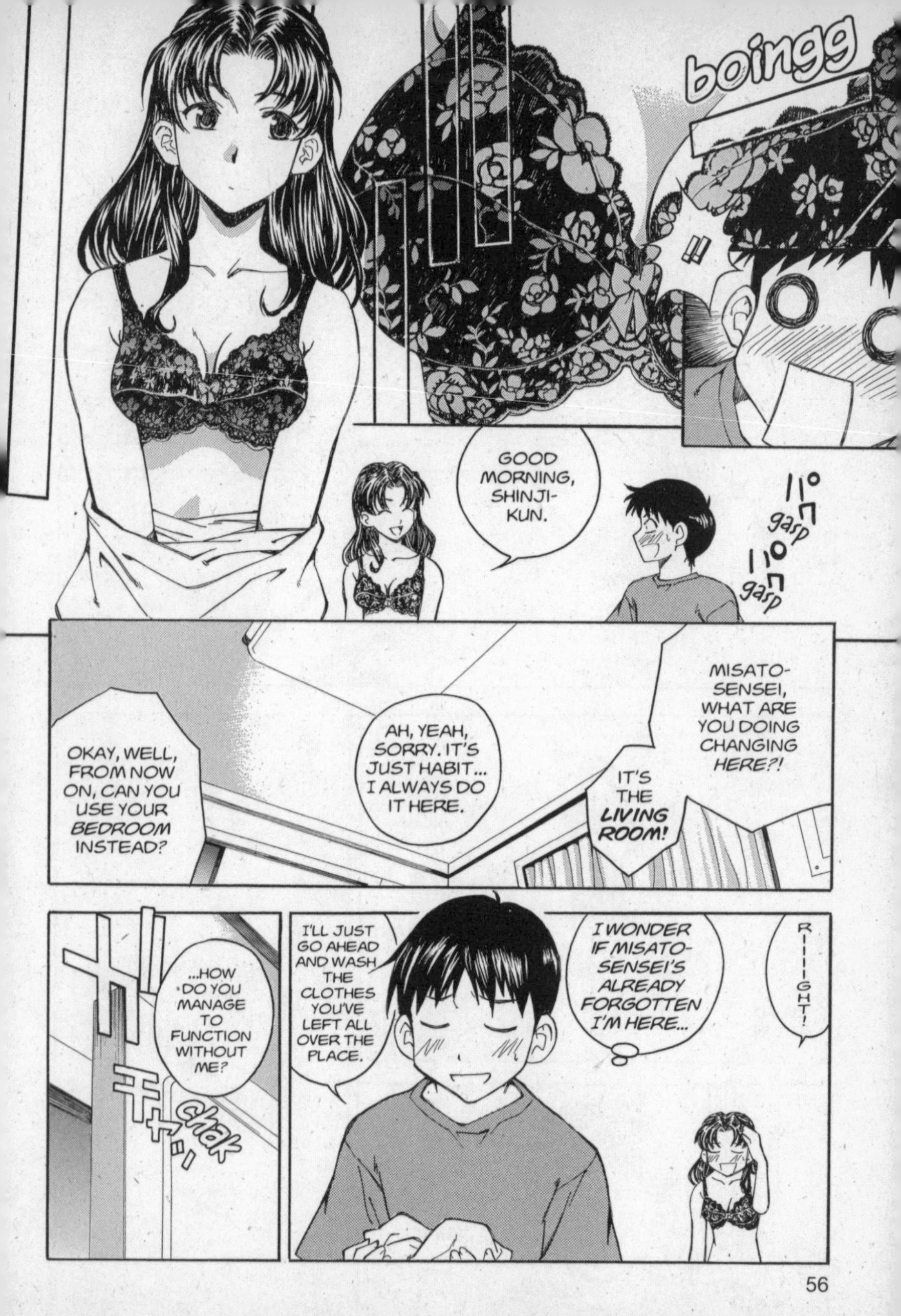
boingg
!!
gasp
gasp
GOOD MORNING, SHINJI-KUN.
MISATO-SENSEI, WHAT ARE YOU DOING CHANGING HERE?!
IT'S THE LIVING ROOM!
AH, YEAH, SORRY. IT'S JUST HABIT... I ALWAYS DO IT HERE.
OKAY, WELL, FROM NOW ON, CAN YOU USE YOUR BEDROOM INSTEAD?
R-I-I-I-GHT!
I WONDER IF MISATO-SENSEI'S ALREADY FORGOTTEN I'M HERE...
I'LL JUST GO AHEAD AND WASH THE CLOTHES YOU'VE LEFT ALL OVER THE PLACE.
...HOW DO YOU MANAGE TO FUNCTION WITHOUT ME?
chak

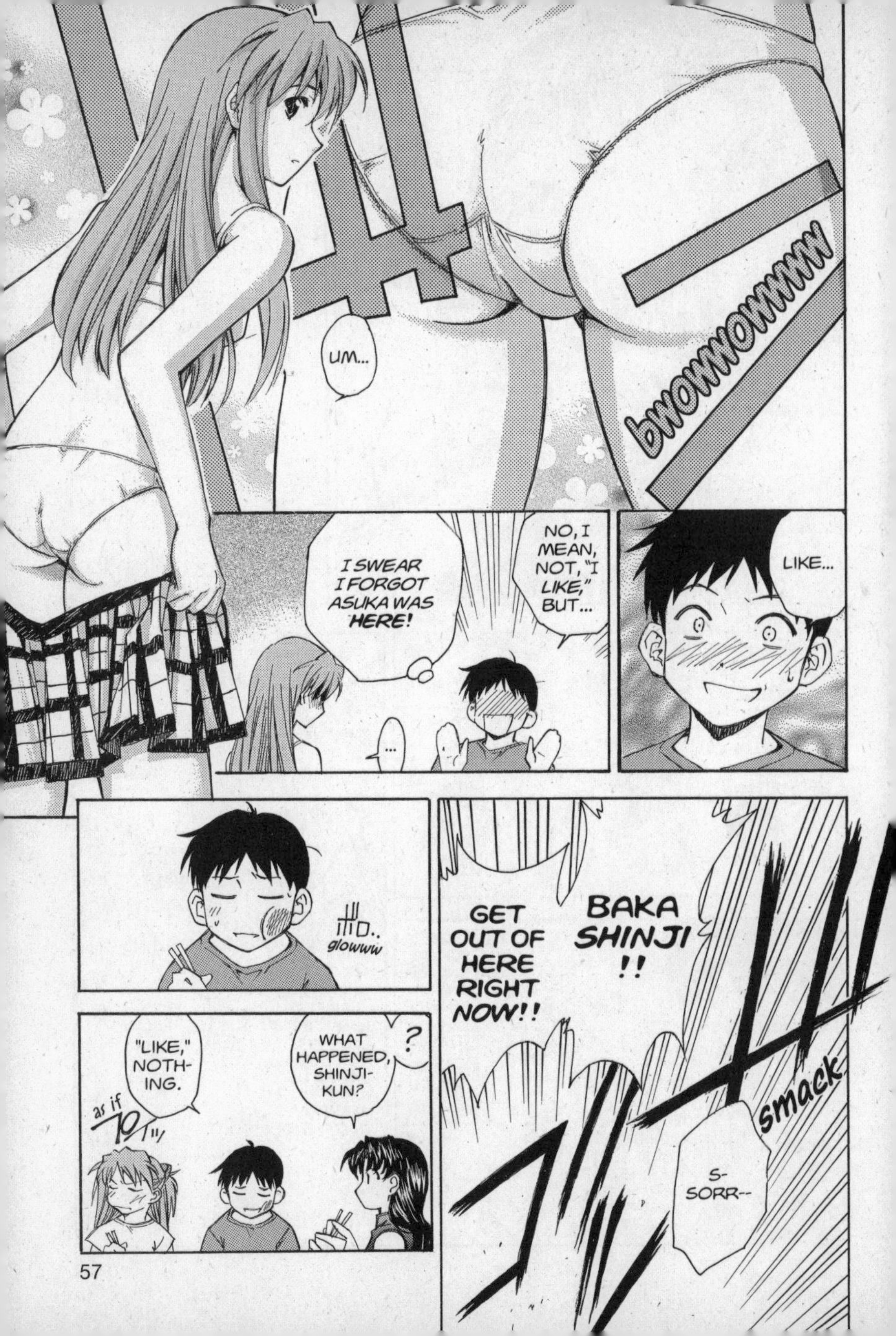
bwowowwww
UM...
LIKE...
NO, I MEAN, NOT, "I LIKE," BUT...
I SWEAR I FORGOT ASUKA WAS HERE!
...
BAKA SHINJI!!
GET OUT OF HERE RIGHT NOW!!
smack
S-SORR--
glowww
WHAT HAPPENED, SHINJI-KUN?
?
"LIKE," NOTHING.
as if

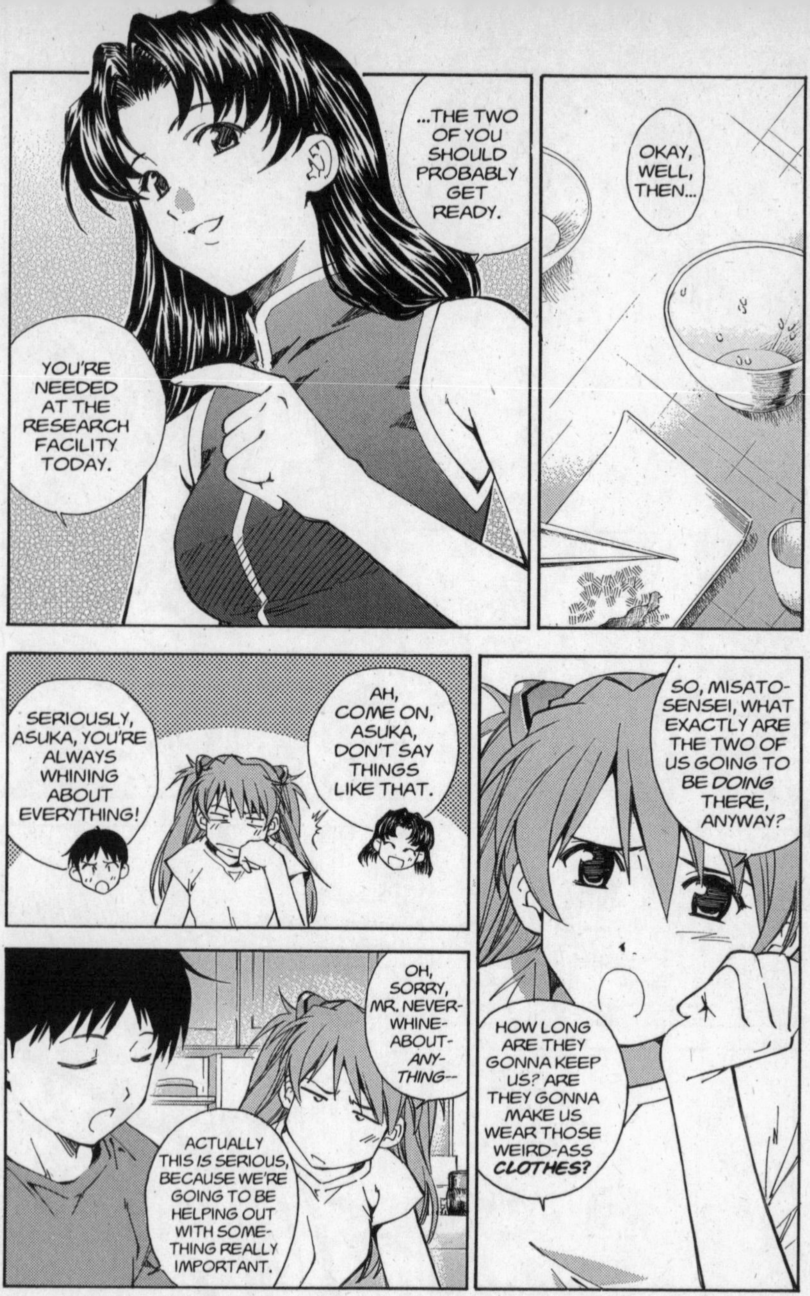
OKAY, WELL, THEN...
...THE TWO OF YOU SHOULD PROBABLY GET READY.
YOU'RE NEEDED AT THE RESEARCH FACILITY TODAY.
SO, MISATO-SENSEI, WHAT EXACTLY ARE THE TWO OF US GOING TO BE *DOING* THERE, ANYWAY?
HOW LONG ARE THEY GONNA KEEP US? ARE THEY GONNA MAKE US WEAR THOSE WEIRD-ASS ***CLOTHES?***
AH, COME ON, ASUKA, DON'T SAY THINGS LIKE THAT.
SERIOUSLY, ASUKA, YOU'RE ALWAYS WHINING ABOUT EVERYTHING!
OH, SORRY, MR. NEVER-WHINE-ABOUT-*ANY-THING--*
ACTUALLY THIS *IS* SERIOUS, BECAUSE WE'RE GOING TO BE HELPING OUT WITH SOME-THING REALLY IMPORTANT.

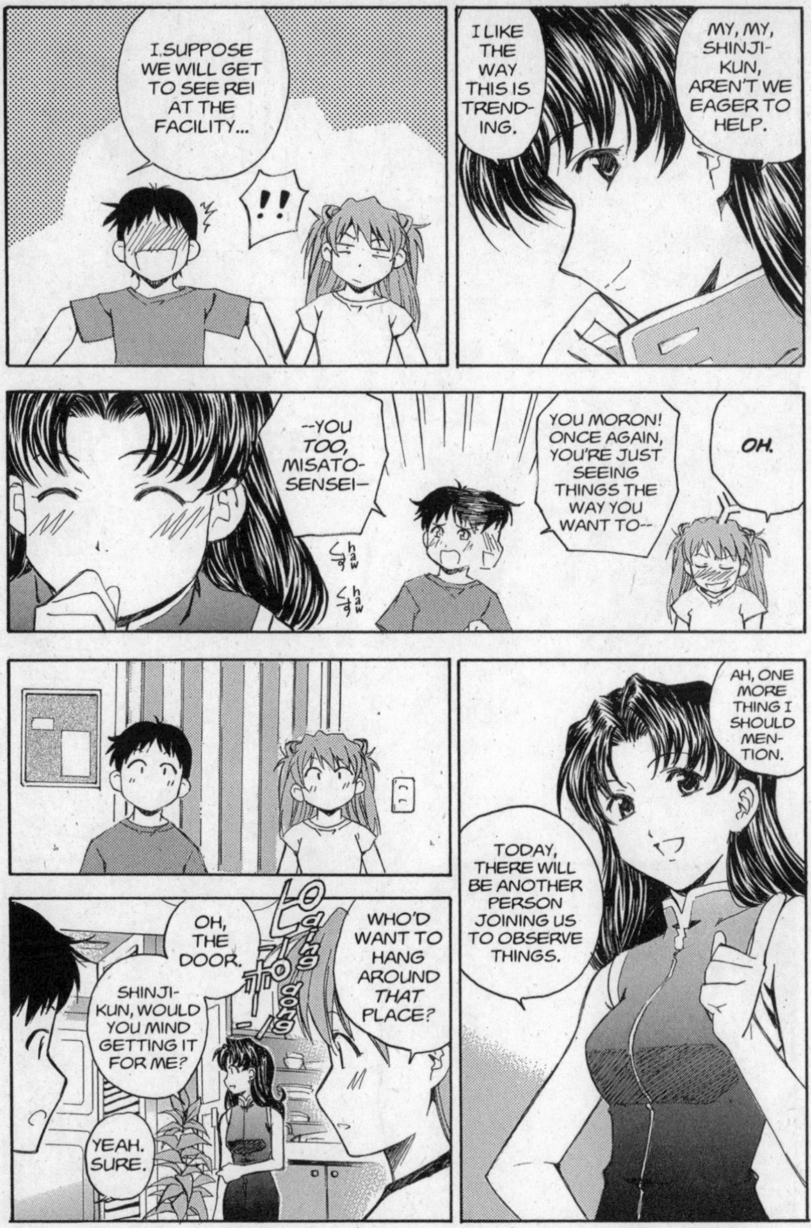
MY, MY, SHINJI-KUN, AREN'T WE EAGER TO HELP.
I LIKE THE WAY THIS IS TRENDING.
I.SUPPOSE WE WILL GET TO SEE REI AT THE FACILITY...
!!
OH.
YOU MORON! ONCE AGAIN, YOU'RE JUST SEEING THINGS THE WAY YOU WANT TO--
--YOU *TOO*, MISATO-SENSEI-
haw
haw
AH, ONE MORE THING I SHOULD MEN-TION.
TODAY, THERE WILL BE ANOTHER PERSON JOINING US TO OBSERVE THINGS.
WHO'D WANT TO HANG AROUND *THAT* PLACE?
ding dong
OH, THE DOOR.
SHINJI-KUN, WOULD YOU MIND GETTING IT FOR ME?
YEAH. SURE.

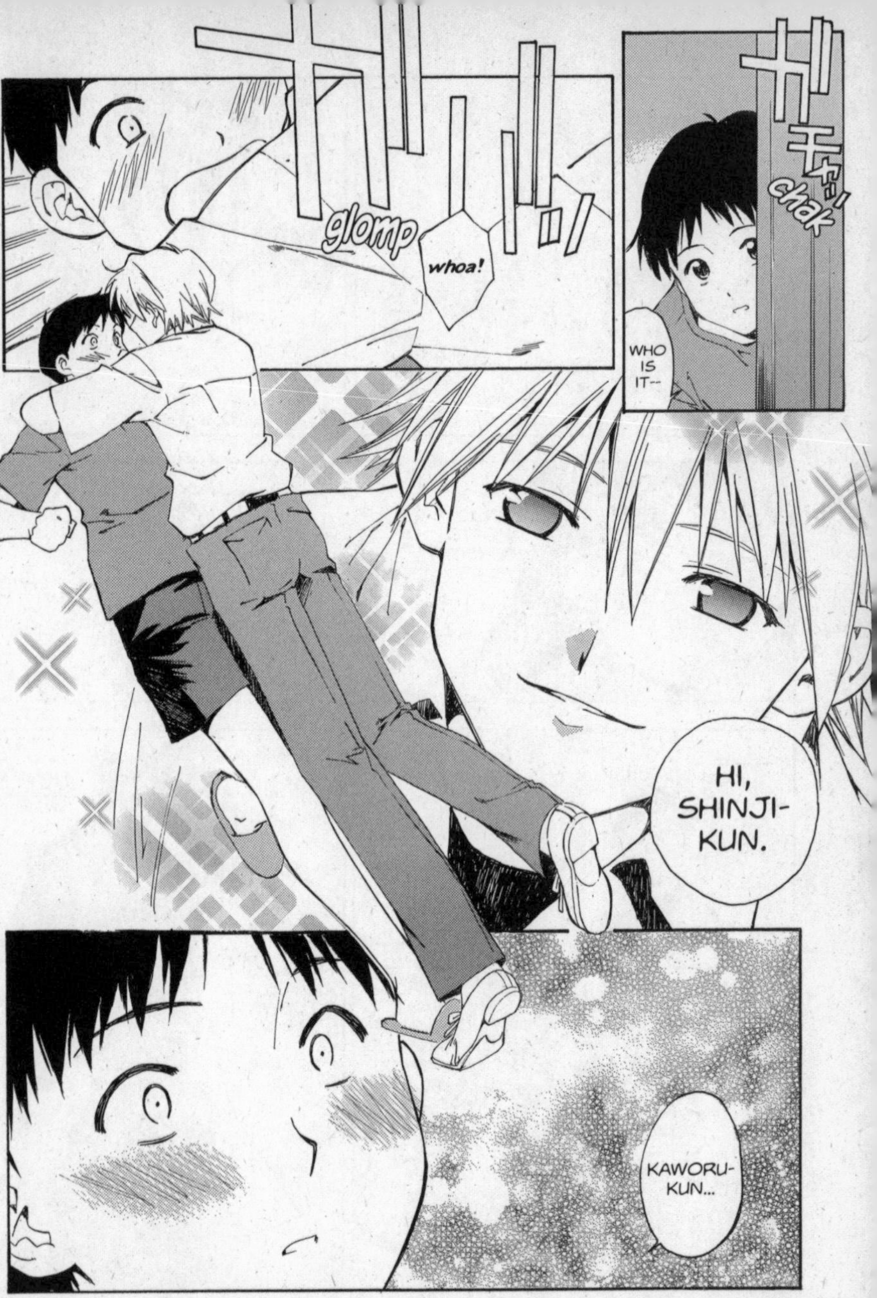
chak
WHO IS IT--
glomp
whoa!
HI, SHINJI-KUN.
KAWORU-KUN...

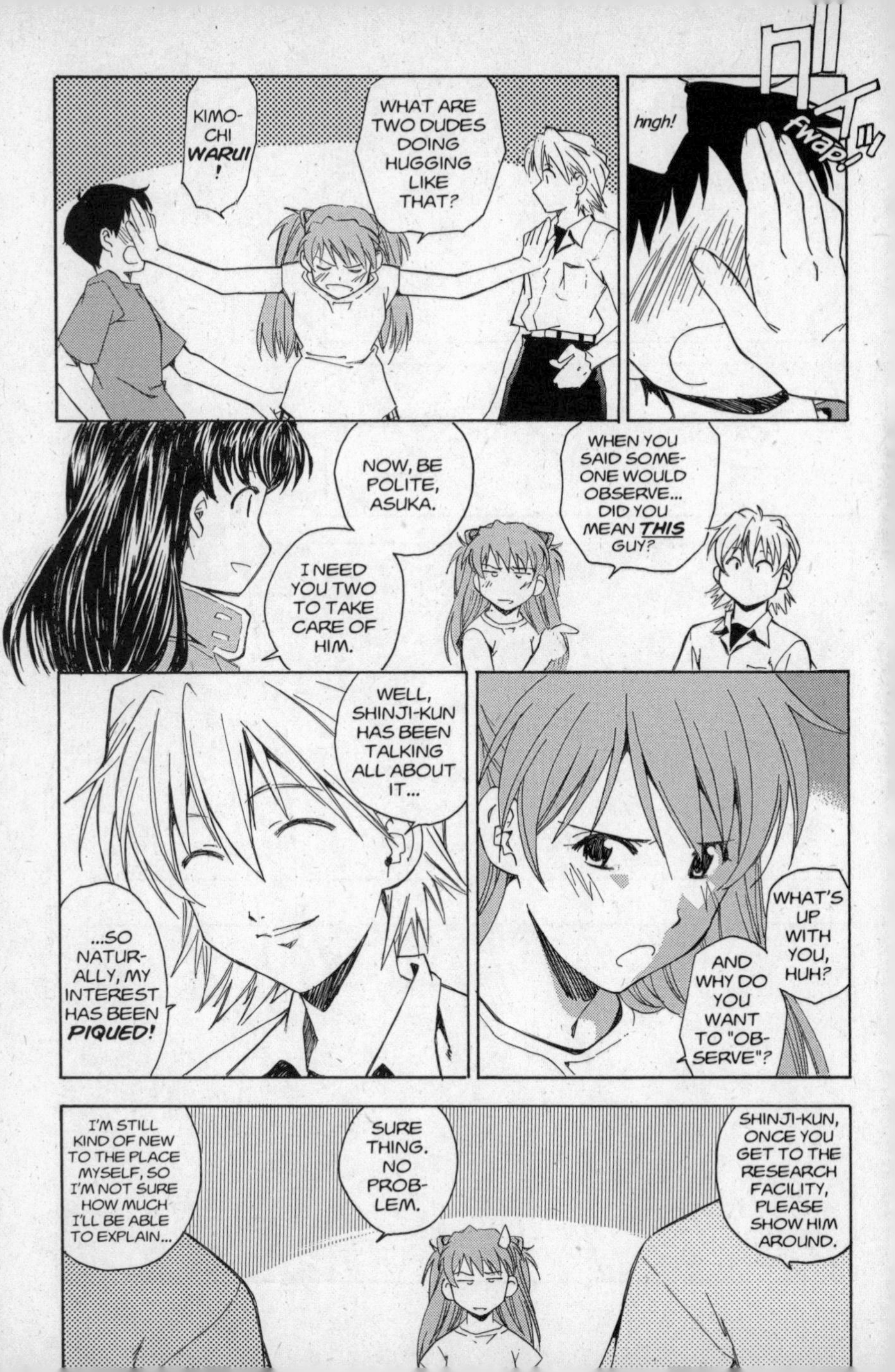
hngh!
fwap!!
WHAT ARE TWO DUDES DOING HUGGING LIKE THAT?
KIMO-CHI **WARUI**!
WHEN YOU SAID SOME-ONE WOULD OBSERVE... DID YOU MEAN ***THIS*** GUY?
NOW, BE POLITE, ASUKA.
I NEED YOU TWO TO TAKE CARE OF HIM.
WHAT'S UP WITH YOU, HUH?
AND WHY DO YOU WANT TO "OB-SERVE"?
WELL, SHINJI-KUN HAS BEEN TALKING ALL ABOUT IT...
...SO NATUR-ALLY, MY INTEREST HAS BEEN ***PIQUED!***
SHINJI-KUN, ONCE YOU GET TO THE RESEARCH FACILITY, PLEASE SHOW HIM AROUND.
SURE THING. NO PROB-LEM.
I'M STILL KIND OF NEW TO THE PLACE MYSELF, SO I'M NOT SURE HOW MUCH I'LL BE ABLE TO EXPLAIN...

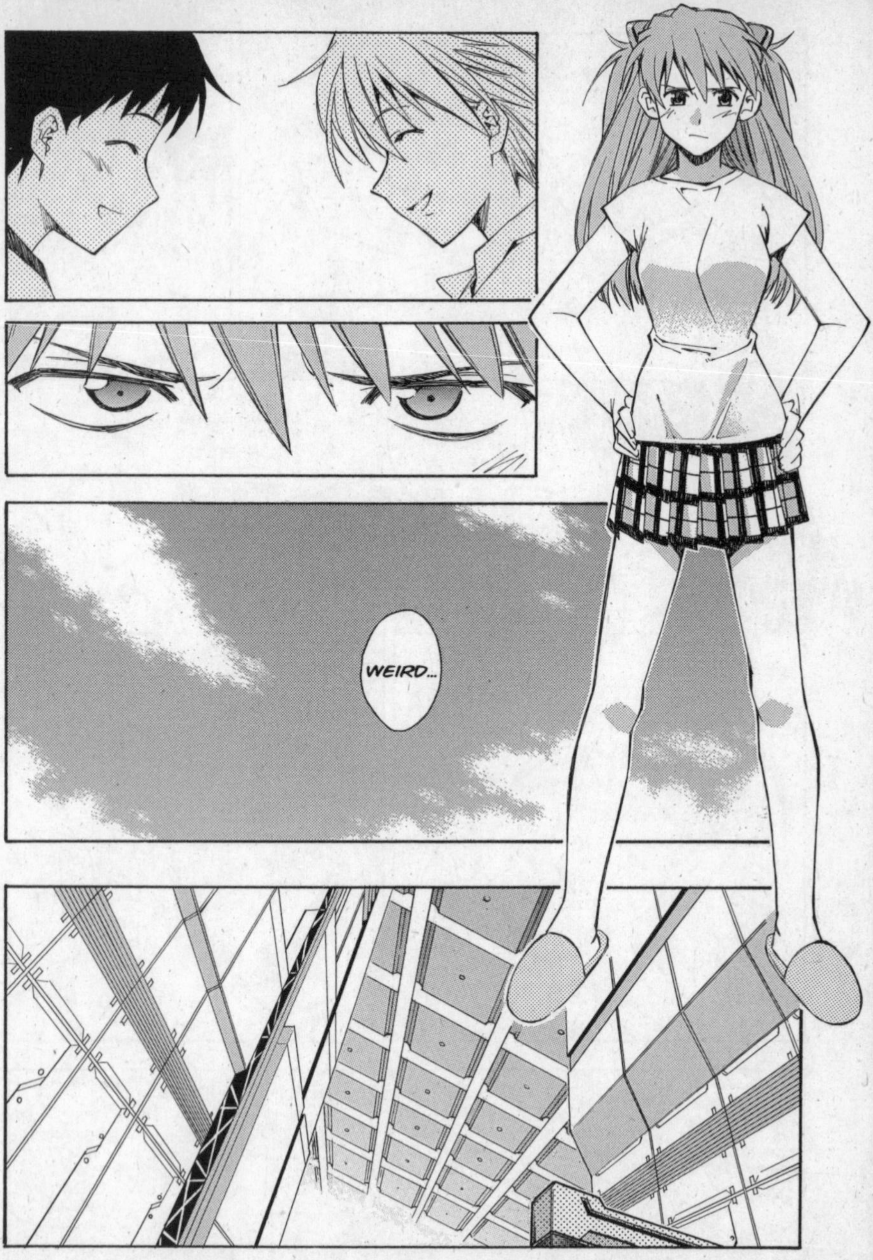
WEIRD...

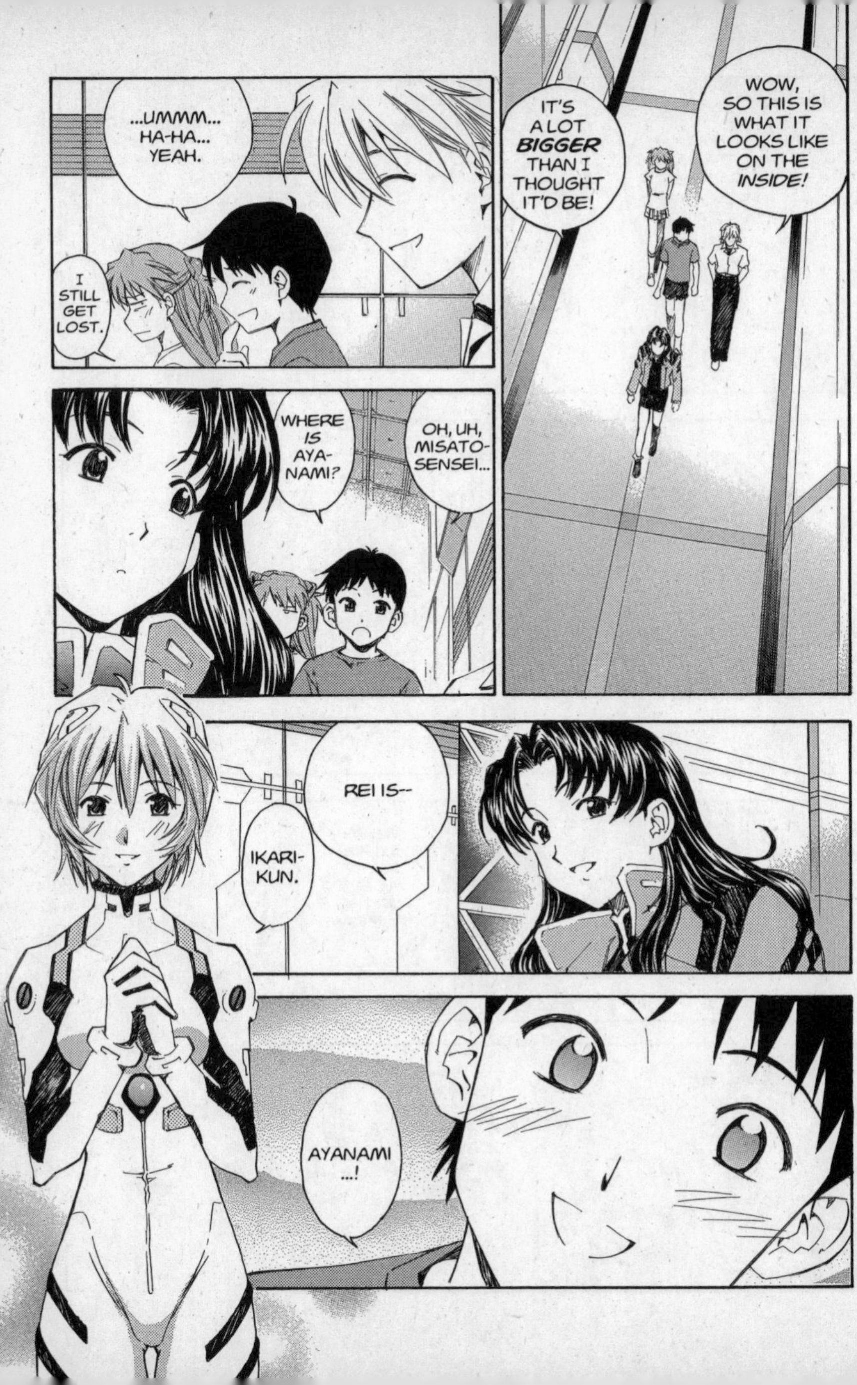
WOW, SO THIS IS WHAT IT LOOKS LIKE ON THE INSIDE!
IT'S A LOT BIGGER THAN I THOUGHT IT'D BE!
...UMMM... HA-HA... YEAH.
I STILL GET LOST.
OH, UH, MISATO-SENSEI...
WHERE IS AYANAMI?
REI IS--
IKARI-KUN.
AYANAMI ...!

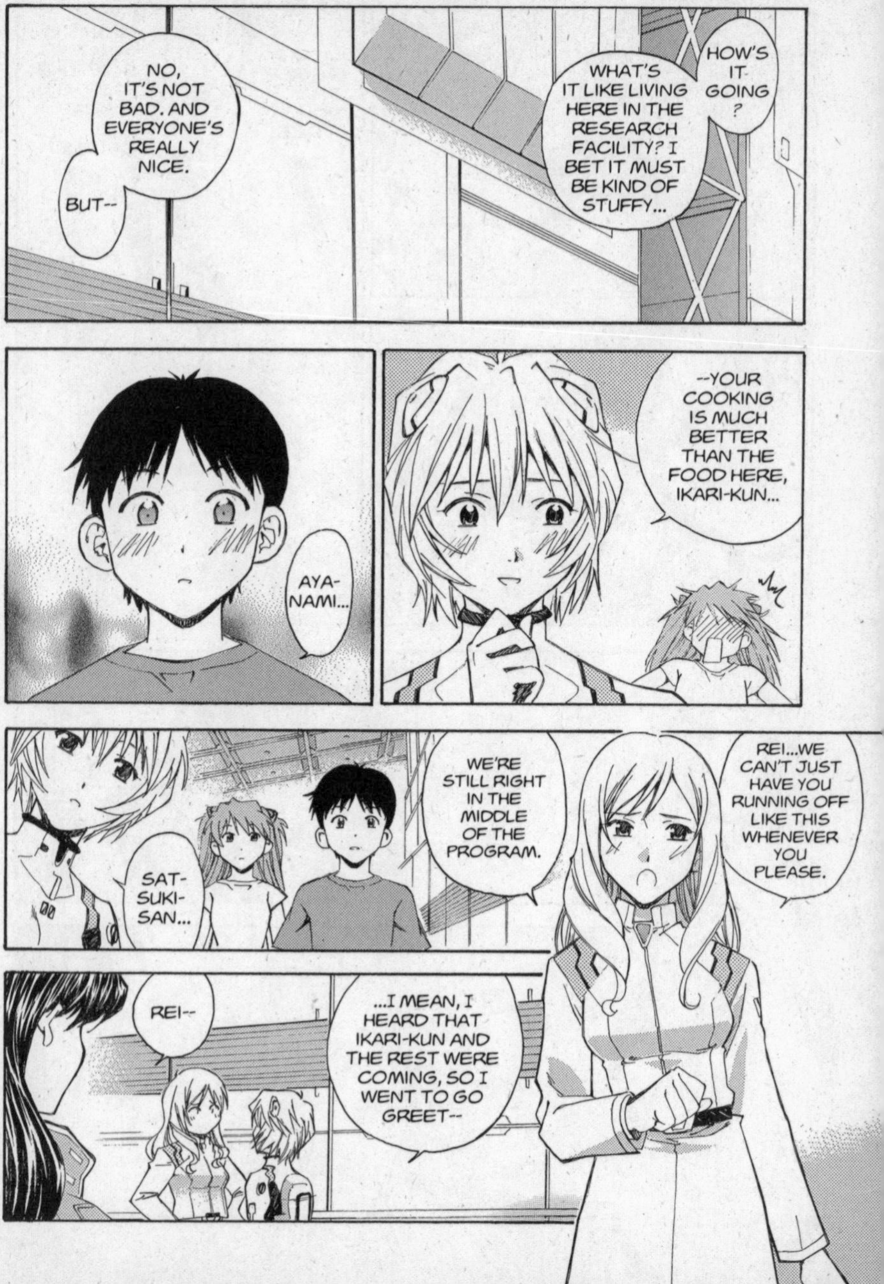
HOW'S IT GOING?
WHAT'S IT LIKE LIVING HERE IN THE RESEARCH FACILITY? I BET IT MUST BE KIND OF STUFFY...
NO, IT'S NOT BAD. AND EVERYONE'S REALLY NICE.
BUT--
--YOUR COOKING IS MUCH BETTER THAN THE FOOD HERE, IKARI-KUN...
AYA-NAMI...
REI...WE CAN'T JUST HAVE YOU RUNNING OFF LIKE THIS WHENEVER YOU PLEASE.
WE'RE STILL RIGHT IN THE MIDDLE OF THE PROGRAM.
SAT-SUKI-SAN...
...I MEAN, I HEARD THAT IKARI-KUN AND THE REST WERE COMING, SO I WENT TO GO GREET--
REI--

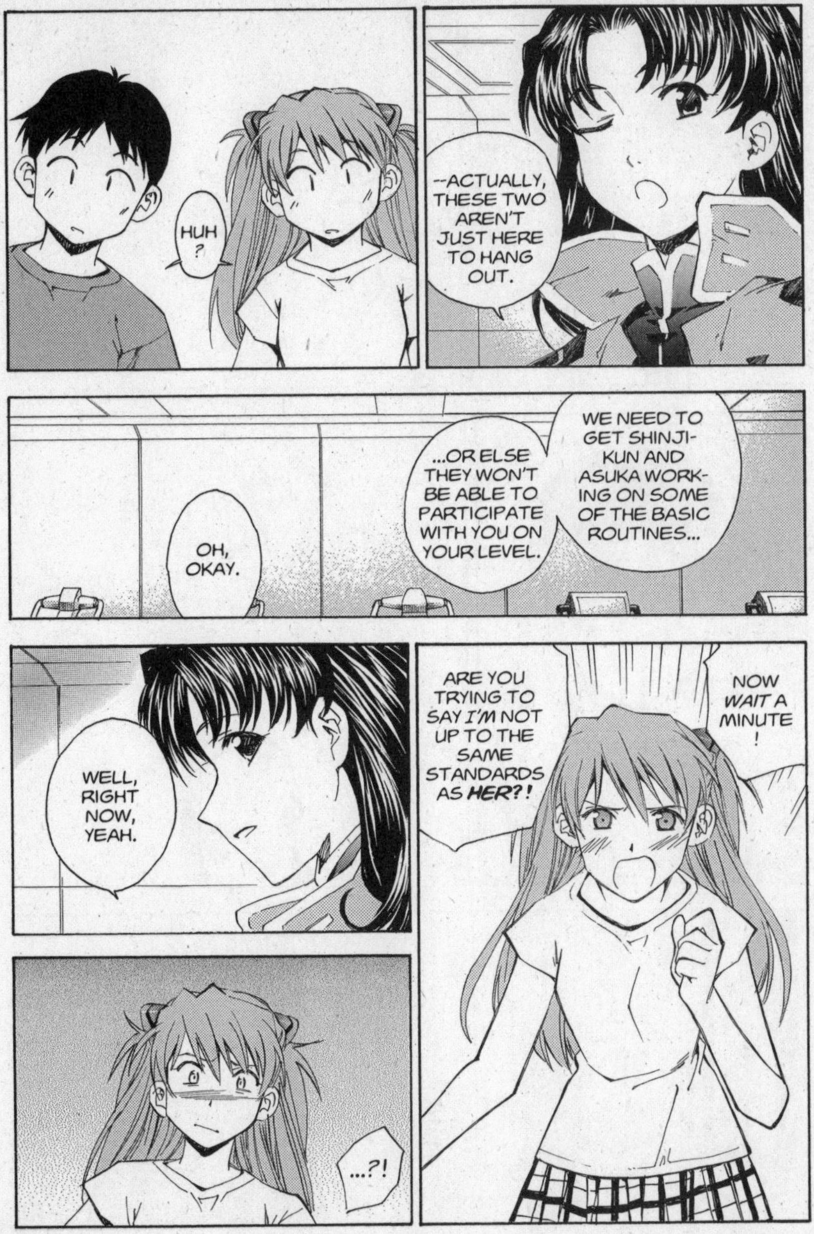

--ACTUALLY, THESE TWO AREN'T JUST HERE TO HANG OUT.
HUH?
WE NEED TO GET SHINJI-KUN AND ASUKA WORKING ON SOME OF THE BASIC ROUTINES...
...OR ELSE THEY WON'T BE ABLE TO PARTICIPATE WITH YOU ON YOUR LEVEL.
OH, OKAY.
NOW *WAIT* A MINUTE!
ARE YOU TRYING TO SAY *I'M* NOT UP TO THE SAME STANDARDS AS ***HER***?!
WELL, RIGHT NOW, YEAH.
...?!

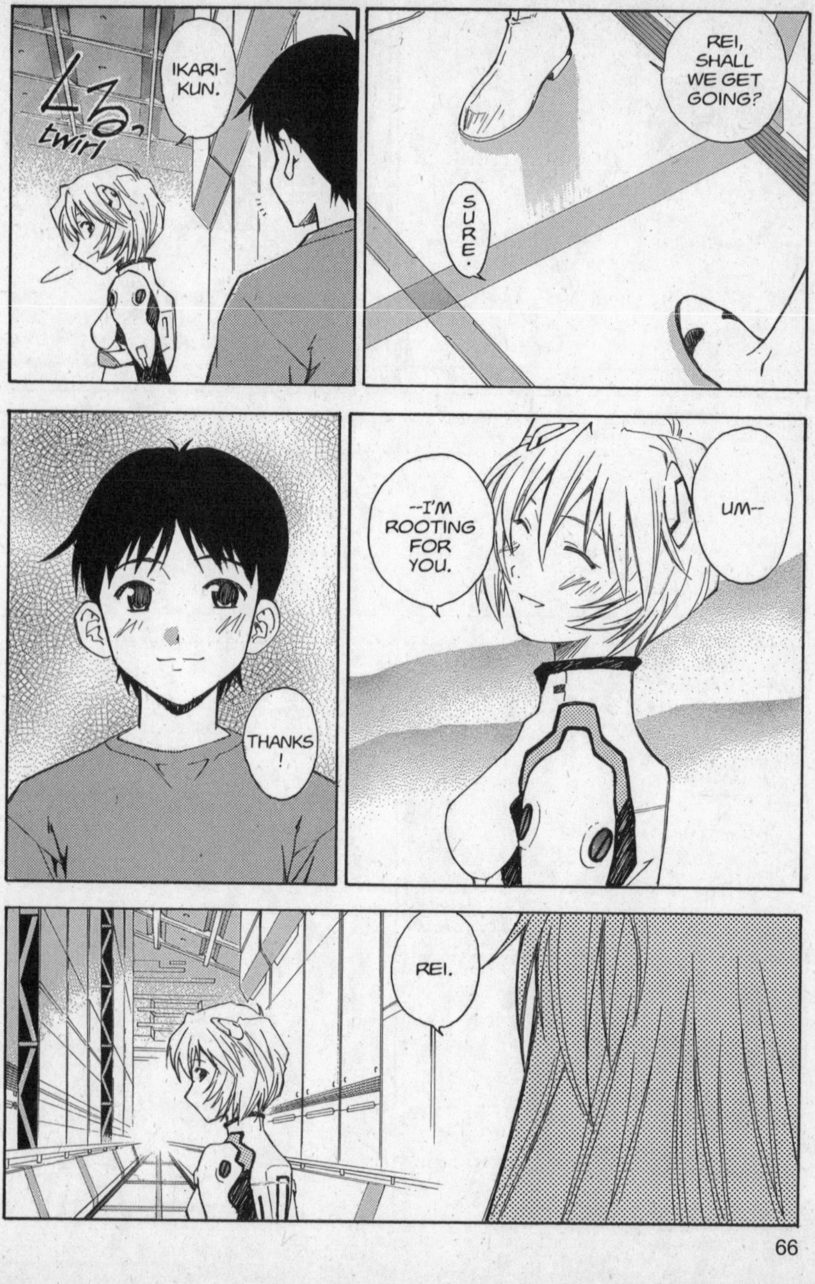
REI, SHALL WE GET GOING?
SURE.
IKARI-KUN.
twirl
UM--
--I'M ROOTING FOR YOU.
THANKS!
REI.

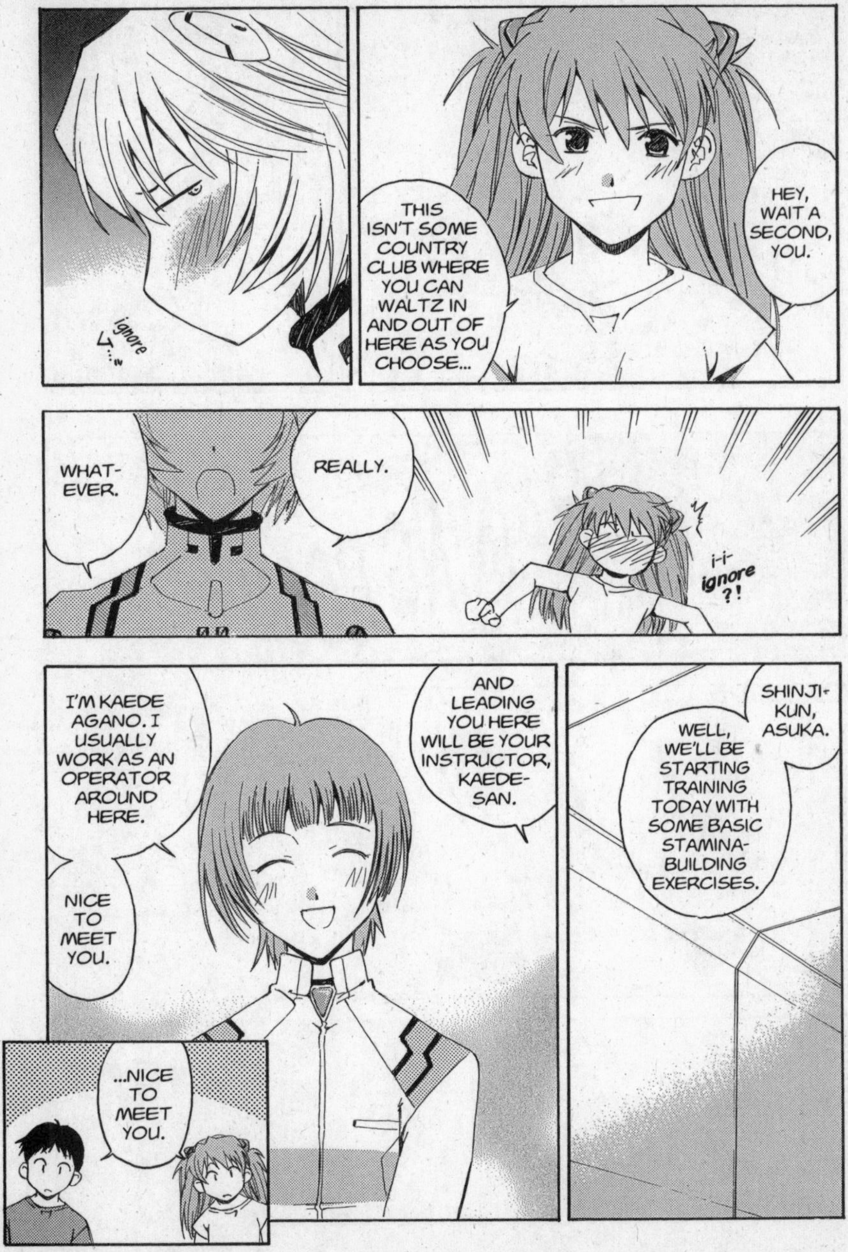
HEY, WAIT A SECOND, YOU.
THIS ISN'T SOME COUNTRY CLUB WHERE YOU CAN WALTZ IN AND OUT OF HERE AS YOU CHOOSE...
ignore
i-i-ignore ?!
REALLY.
WHAT-EVER.
SHINJI-KUN, ASUKA.
WELL, WE'LL BE STARTING TRAINING TODAY WITH SOME BASIC STAMINA-BUILDING EXERCISES.
AND LEADING YOU HERE WILL BE YOUR INSTRUCTOR, KAEDE-SAN.
I'M KAEDE AGANO. I USUALLY WORK AS AN OPERATOR AROUND HERE.
NICE TO MEET YOU.
...NICE TO MEET YOU.

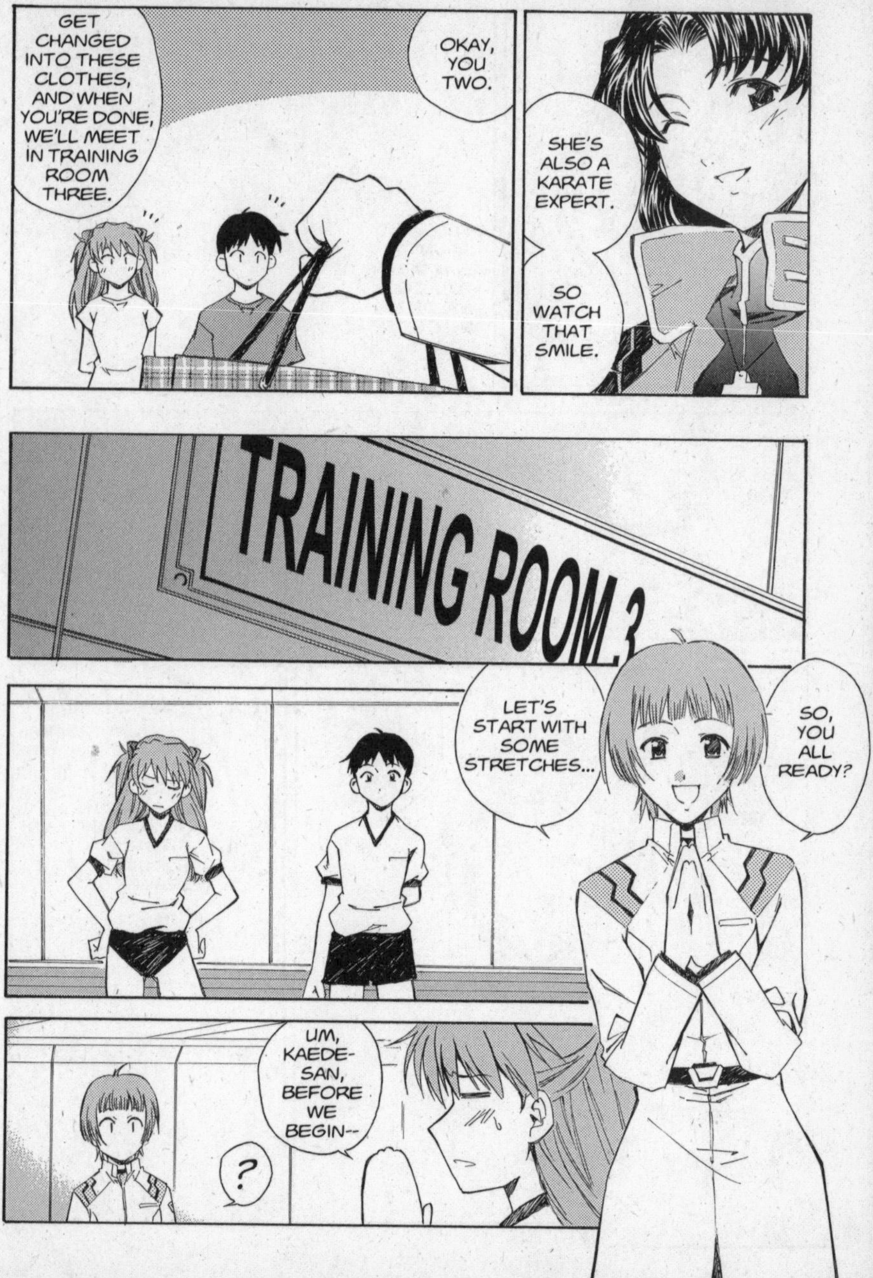
SHE'S ALSO A KARATE EXPERT.
SO WATCH THAT SMILE.
OKAY, YOU TWO.
GET CHANGED INTO THESE CLOTHES, AND WHEN YOU'RE DONE, WE'LL MEET IN TRAINING ROOM THREE.
TRAINING ROOM 3
SO, YOU ALL READY?
LET'S START WITH SOME STRETCHES...
UM, KAEDE-SAN, BEFORE WE BEGIN--
?

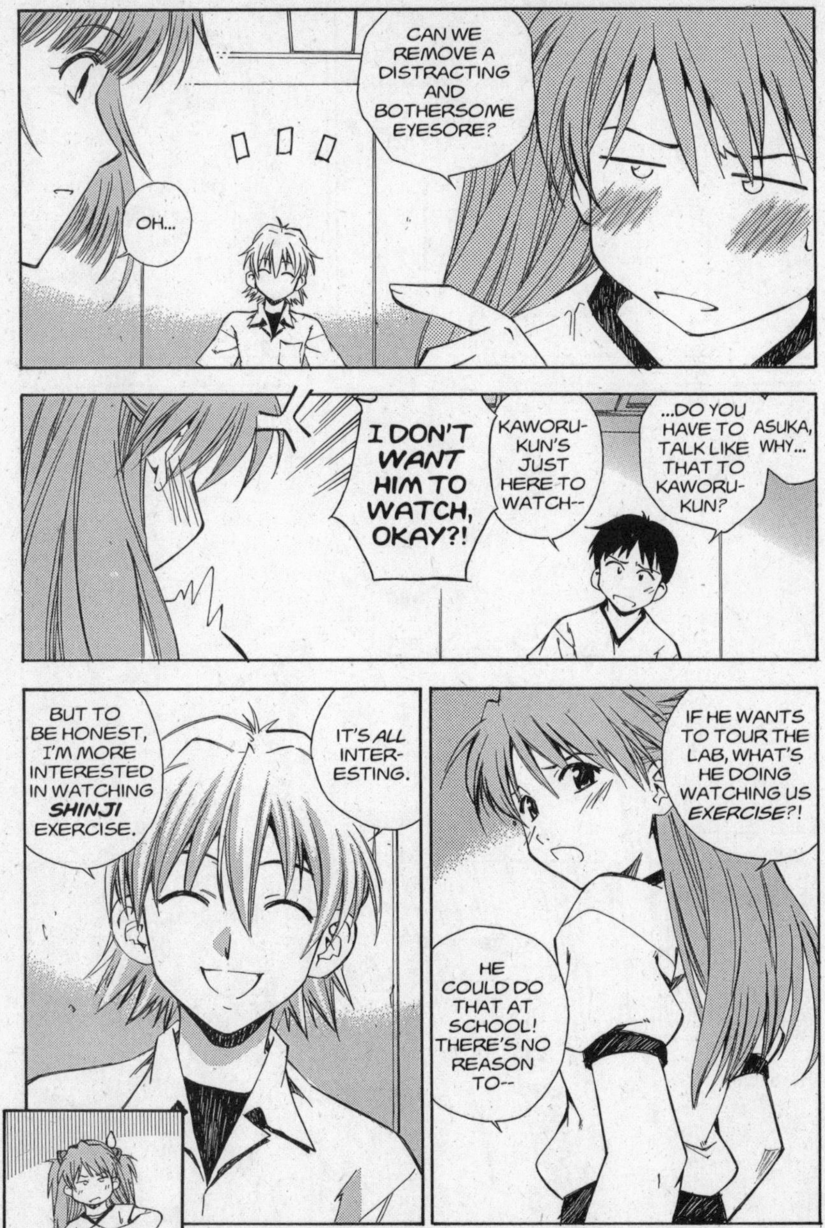
CAN WE REMOVE A DISTRACTING AND BOTHERSOME EYESORE?
OH...
ASUKA, WHY...
...DO YOU HAVE TO TALK LIKE THAT TO KAWORU-KUN?
KAWORU-KUN'S JUST HERE TO WATCH--
I DON'T *WANT* HIM TO WATCH, OKAY?!
IF HE WANTS TO TOUR THE LAB, WHAT'S HE DOING WATCHING US *EXERCISE*?!
HE COULD DO THAT AT SCHOOL! THERE'S NO REASON TO--
IT'S *ALL* INTERESTING.
BUT TO BE HONEST, I'M MORE INTERESTED IN WATCHING ***SHINJI*** EXERCISE.

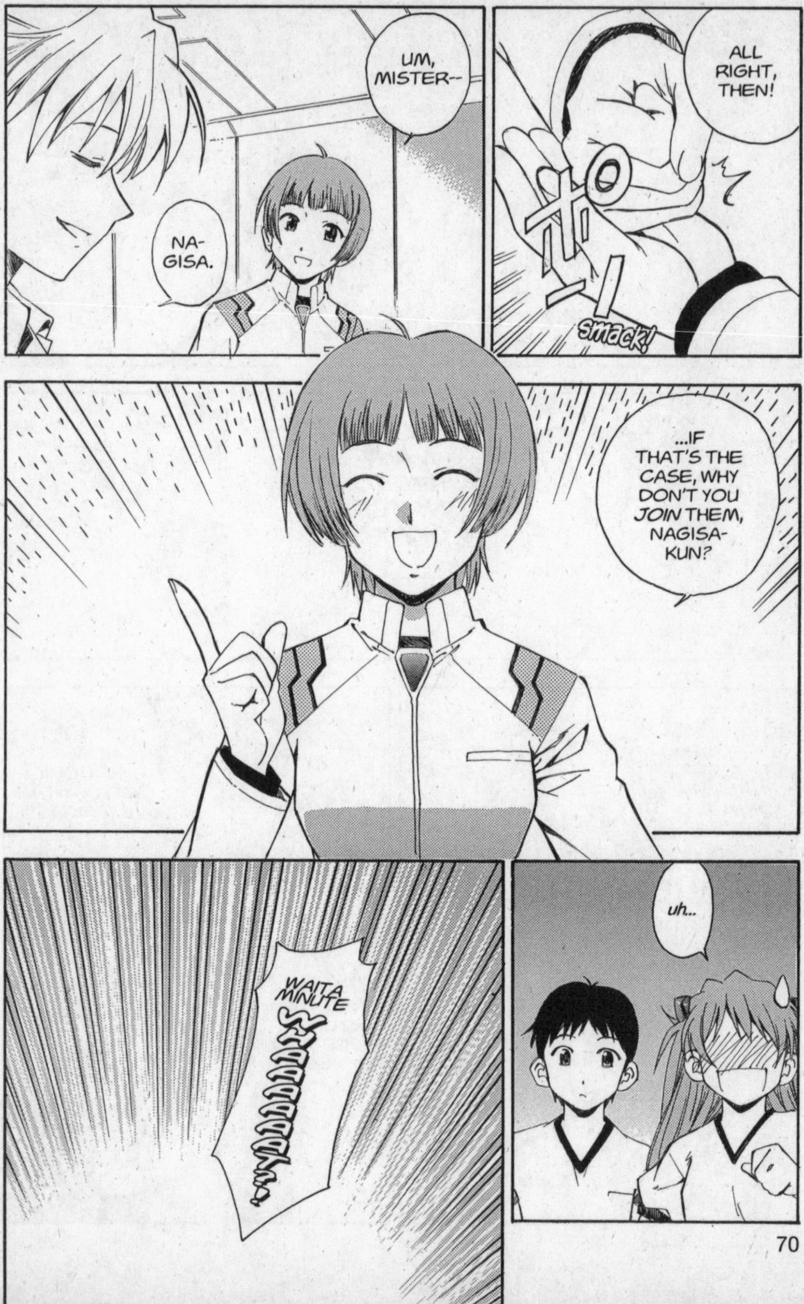
ALL RIGHT, THEN!
smack!
UM, MISTER--
NA-GISA.
...IF THAT'S THE CASE, WHY DON'T YOU JOIN THEM, NAGISA-KUN?
uh..
WAIT A MINUTE

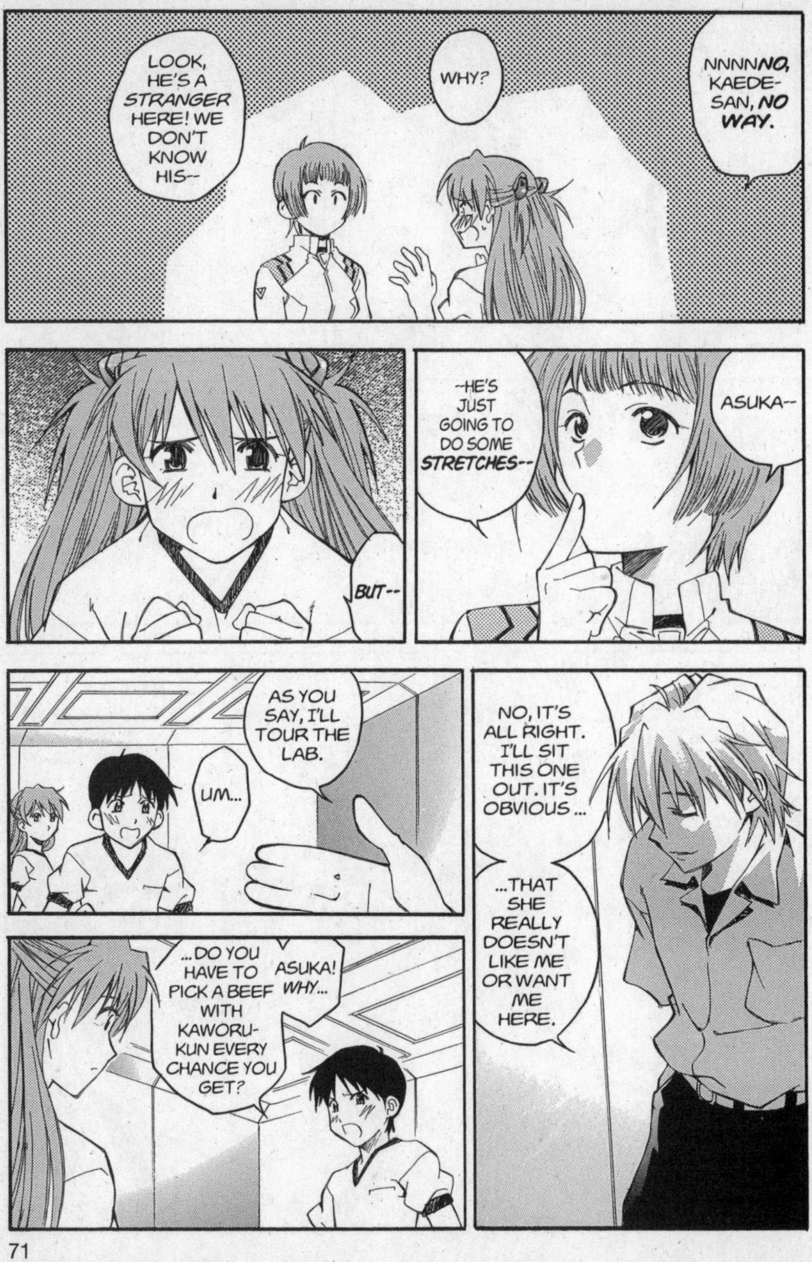
NNNNNO, KAEDE-SAN, NO WAY.
WHY?
LOOK, HE'S A STRANGER HERE! WE DON'T KNOW HIS--
ASUKA--
--HE'S JUST GOING TO DO SOME STRETCHES--
BUT--
NO, IT'S ALL RIGHT. I'LL SIT THIS ONE OUT. IT'S OBVIOUS ...
...THAT SHE REALLY DOESN'T LIKE ME OR WANT ME HERE.
AS YOU SAY, I'LL TOUR THE LAB.
UM...
ASUKA! WHY...
...DO YOU HAVE TO PICK A BEEF WITH KAWORU-KUN EVERY CHANCE YOU GET?

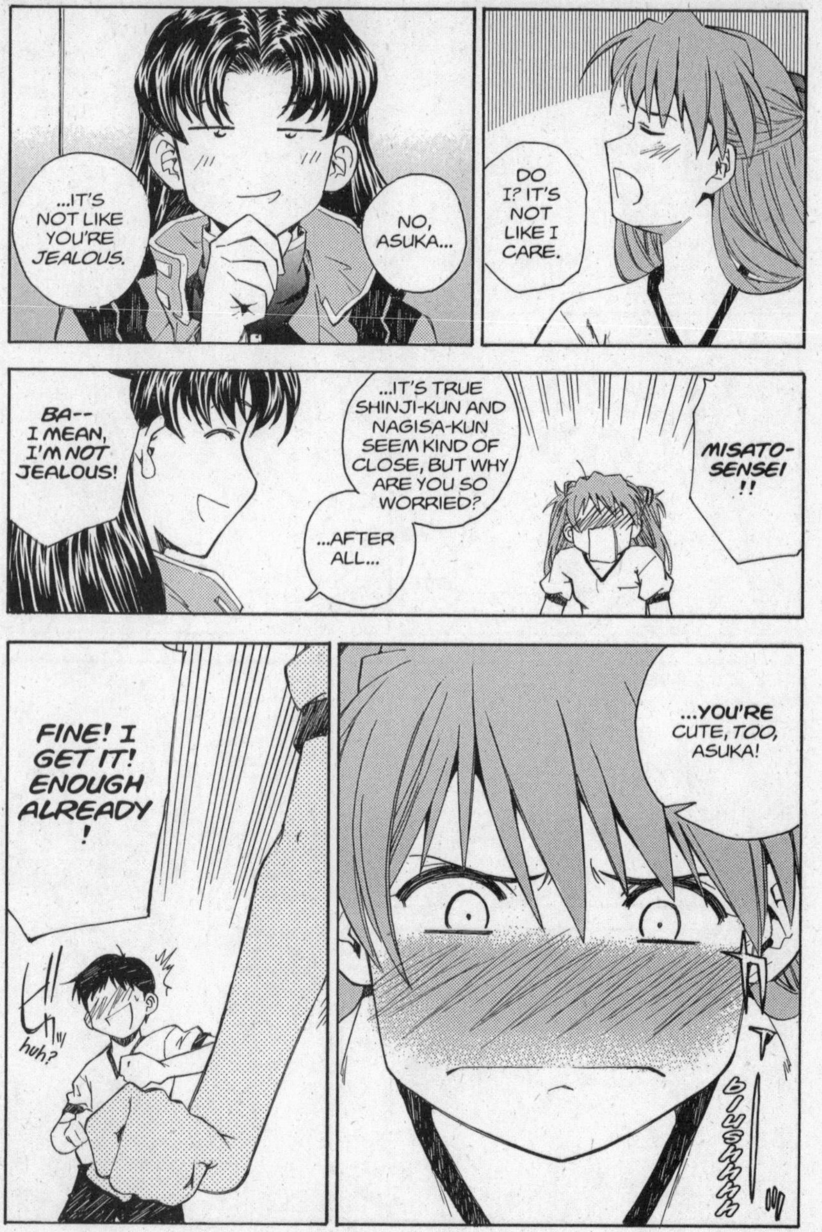
DO I? IT'S NOT LIKE I CARE.
NO, ASUKA...
...IT'S NOT LIKE YOU'RE JEALOUS.
MISATO-SENSEI !!
...IT'S TRUE SHINJI-KUN AND NAGISA-KUN SEEM KIND OF CLOSE, BUT WHY ARE YOU SO WORRIED?
...AFTER ALL...
BA-- I MEAN, I'M NOT JEALOUS!
...YOU'RE CUTE, TOO, ASUKA!
BLUSHHHH
FINE! I GET IT! ENOUGH ALREADY !
Uh
huh?

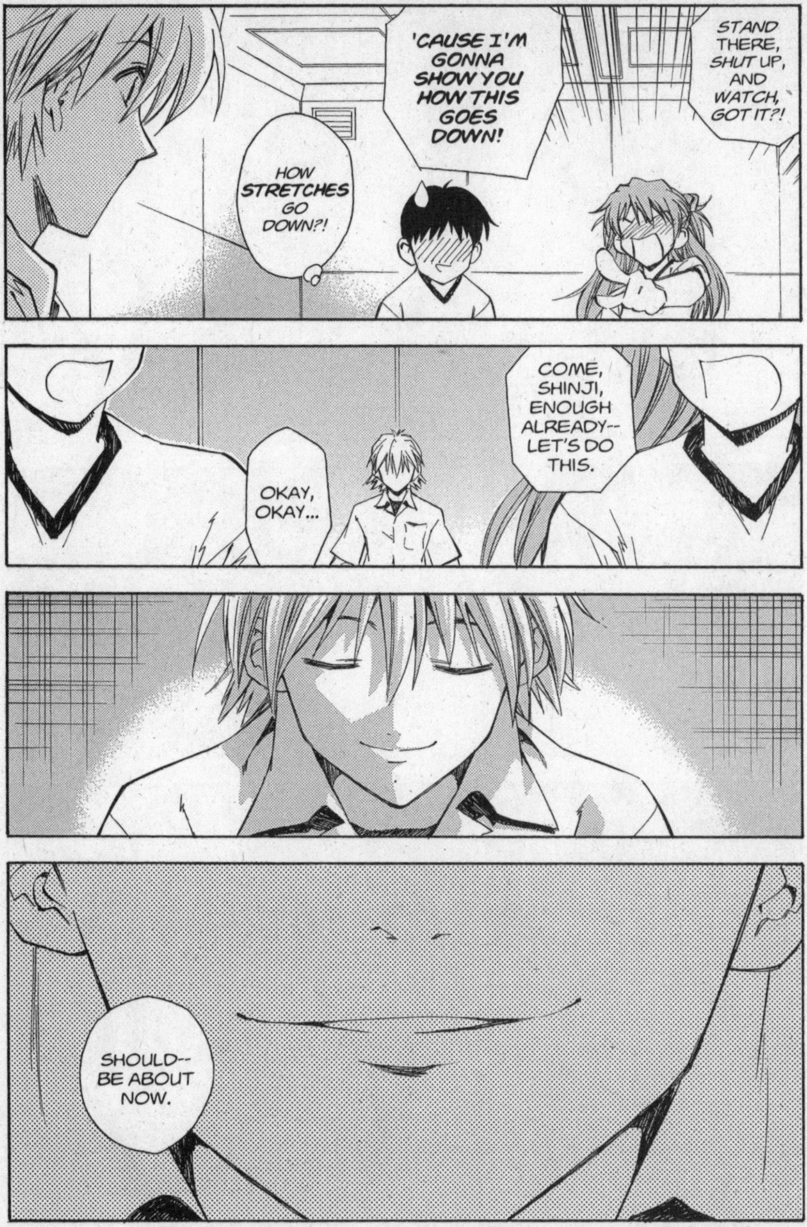
STAND THERE, SHUT UP, AND WATCH, GOT IT?!
'CAUSE I'M GONNA SHOW YOU HOW THIS GOES DOWN!
HOW STRETCHES GO DOWN?!
COME, SHINJI, ENOUGH ALREADY-- LET'S DO THIS.
OKAY, OKAY...
SHOULD-- BE ABOUT NOW.

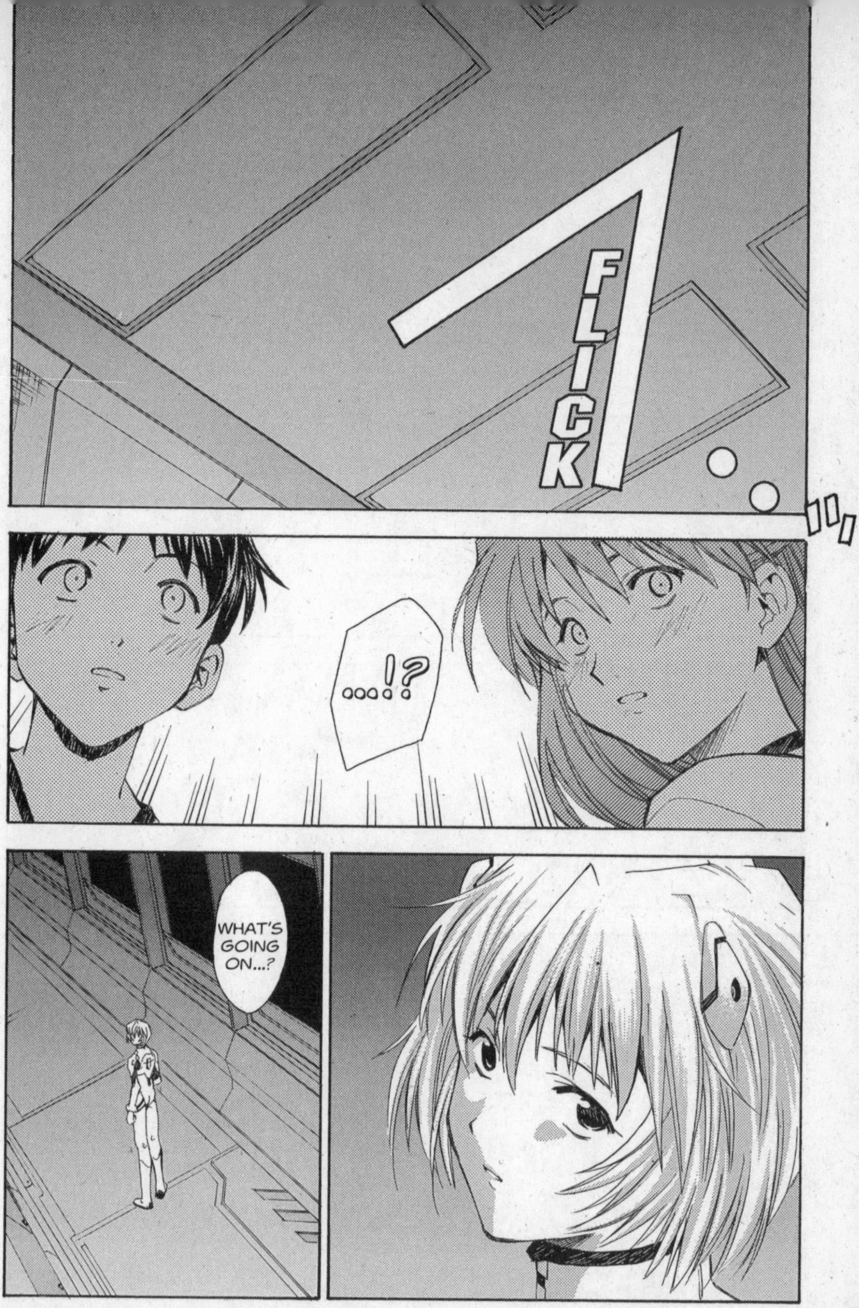
FLICK
...!?
WHAT'S GOING ON...?

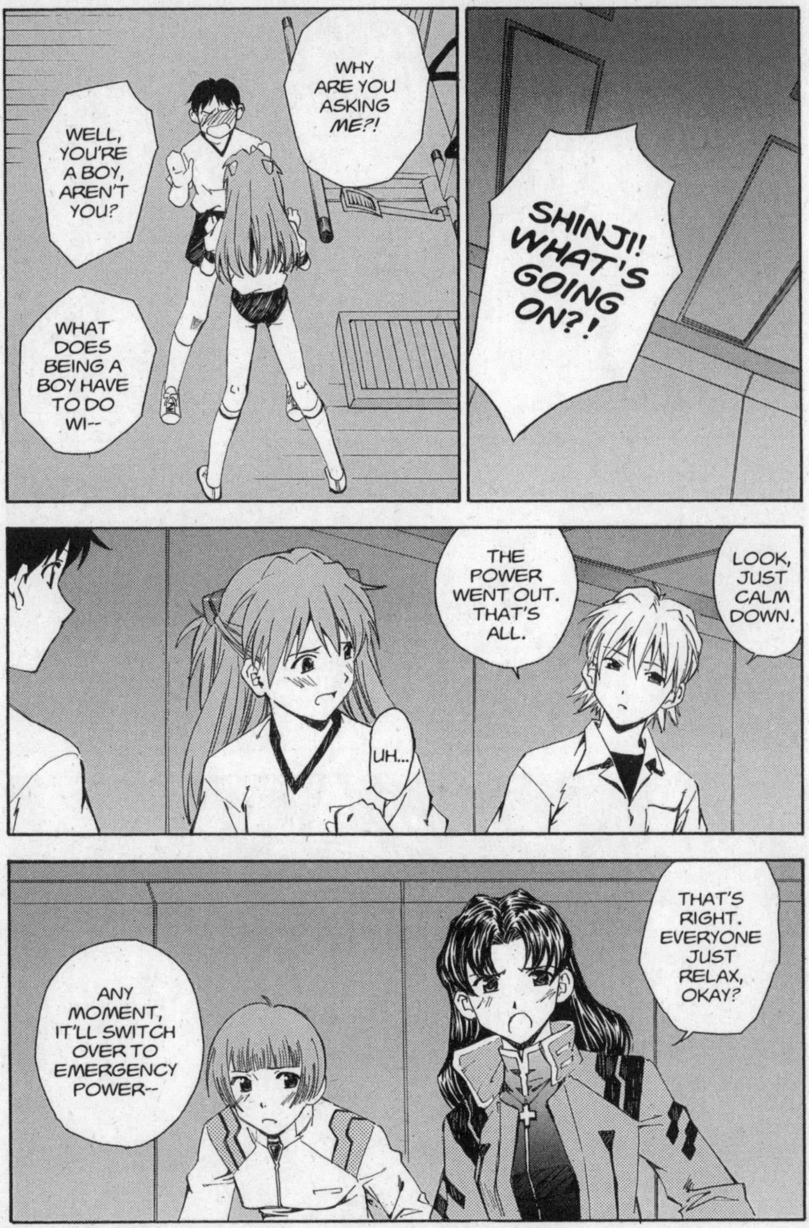
SHINJI!! WHAT'S GOING ON?!
WHY ARE YOU ASKING *ME*?!
WELL, YOU'RE A BOY, AREN'T YOU?
WHAT DOES BEING A BOY HAVE TO DO WI--
LOOK, JUST CALM DOWN.
THE POWER WENT OUT. THAT'S ALL.
UH...
THAT'S RIGHT. EVERYONE JUST RELAX, OKAY?
ANY MOMENT, IT'LL SWITCH OVER TO EMERGENCY POWER--

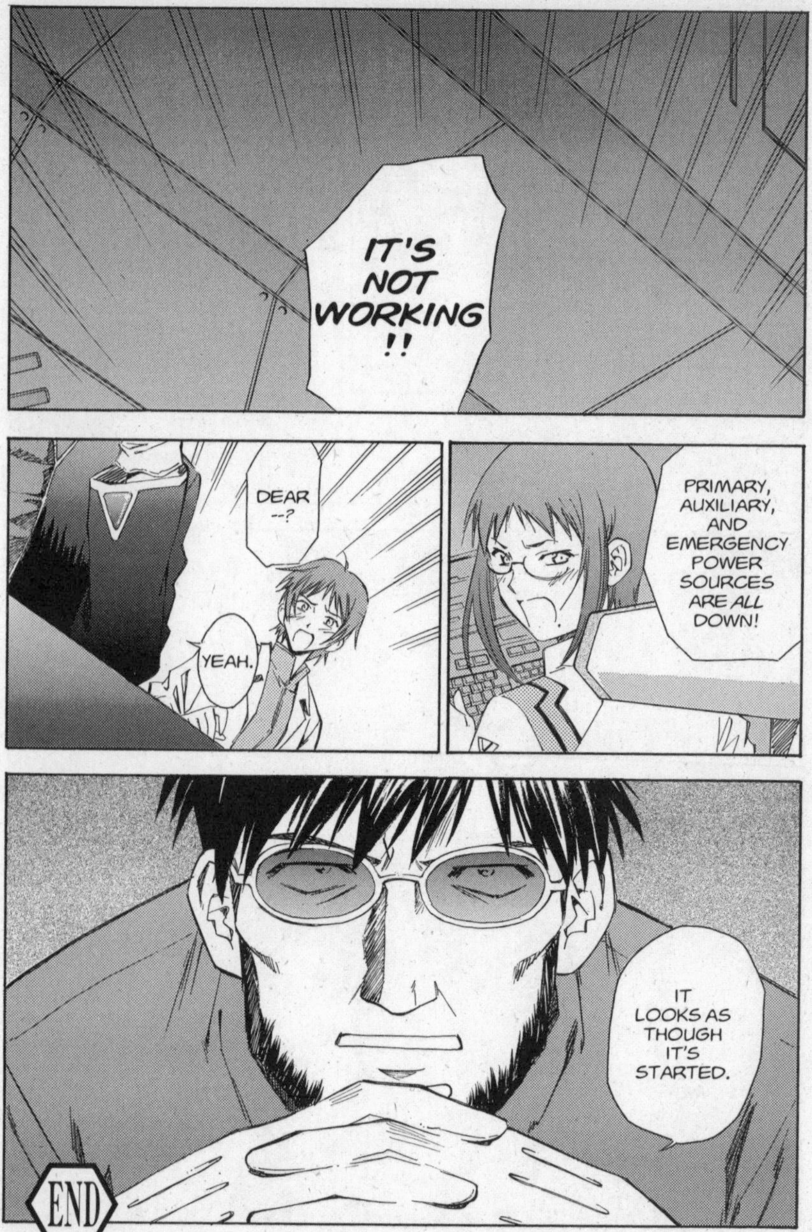
IT'S NOT WORKING !!
PRIMARY, AUXILIARY, AND EMERGENCY POWER SOURCES ARE ALL DOWN!
DEAR --?
YEAH.
IT LOOKS AS THOUGH IT'S STARTED.
END

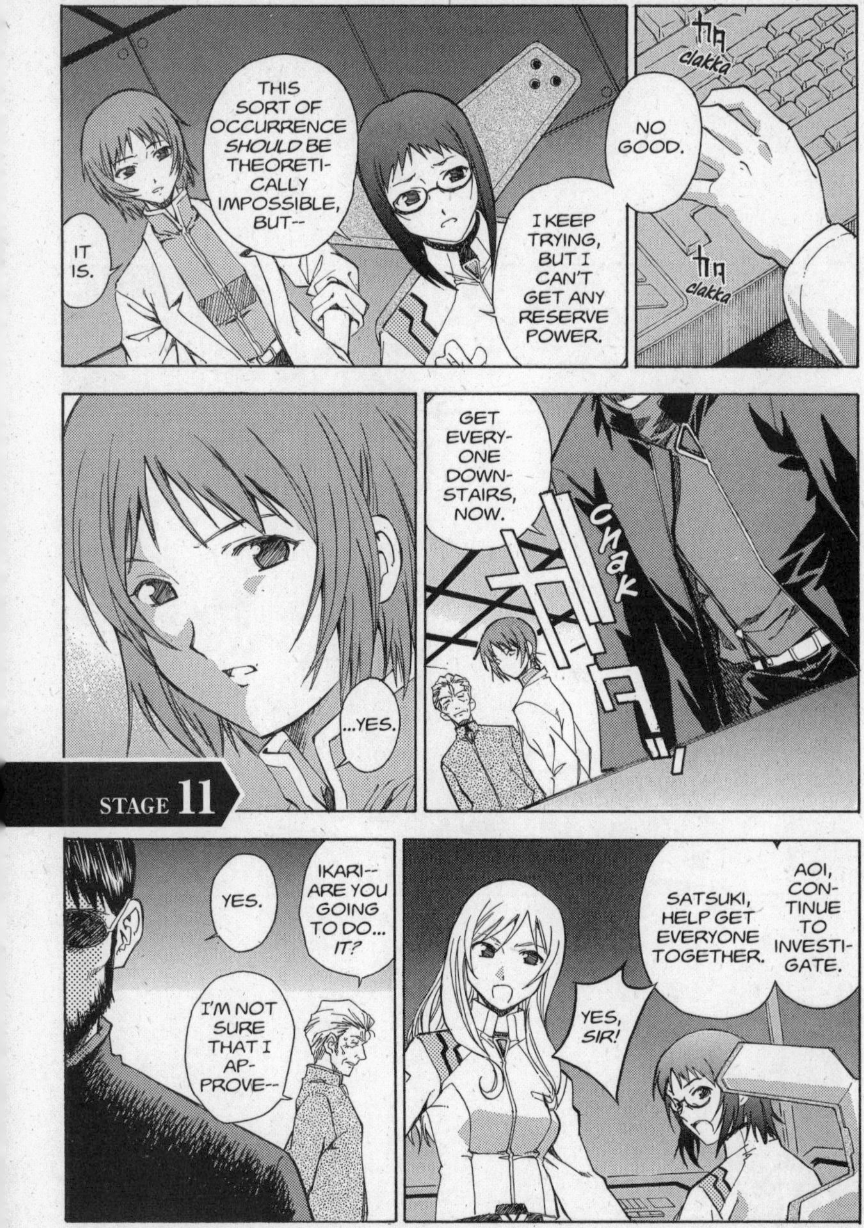
clakka
NO GOOD.
clakka
I KEEP TRYING, BUT I CAN'T GET ANY RESERVE POWER.
THIS SORT OF OCCURRENCE *SHOULD* BE THEORETICALLY IMPOSSIBLE, BUT--
IT IS.
GET EVERYONE DOWNSTAIRS, NOW.
chak
...YES.
STAGE 11
AOI, CONTINUE TO INVESTIGATE.
SATSUKI, HELP GET EVERYONE TOGETHER.
YES, SIR!
IKARI--ARE YOU GOING TO DO... IT?
YES.
I'M NOT SURE THAT I APPROVE--

STAGE
11

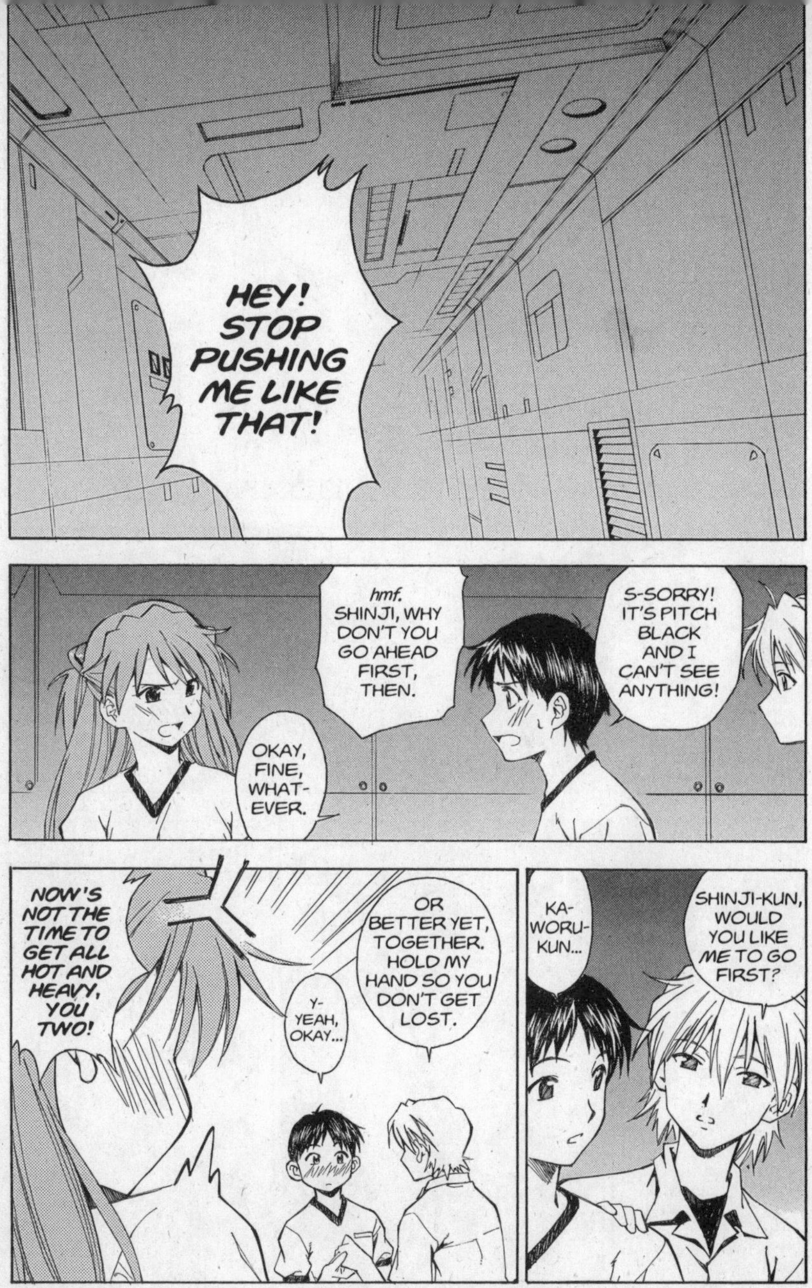
HEY! STOP PUSHING ME LIKE THAT!
S-SORRY! IT'S PITCH BLACK AND I CAN'T SEE ANYTHING!
hmf. SHINJI, WHY DON'T YOU GO AHEAD FIRST, THEN.
OKAY, FINE, WHATEVER.
SHINJI-KUN, WOULD YOU LIKE ME TO GO FIRST?
KAWORU-KUN...
OR BETTER YET, TOGETHER. HOLD MY HAND SO YOU DON'T GET LOST.
Y-YEAH, OKAY...
NOW'S NOT THE TIME TO GET ALL HOT AND HEAVY, YOU TWO!

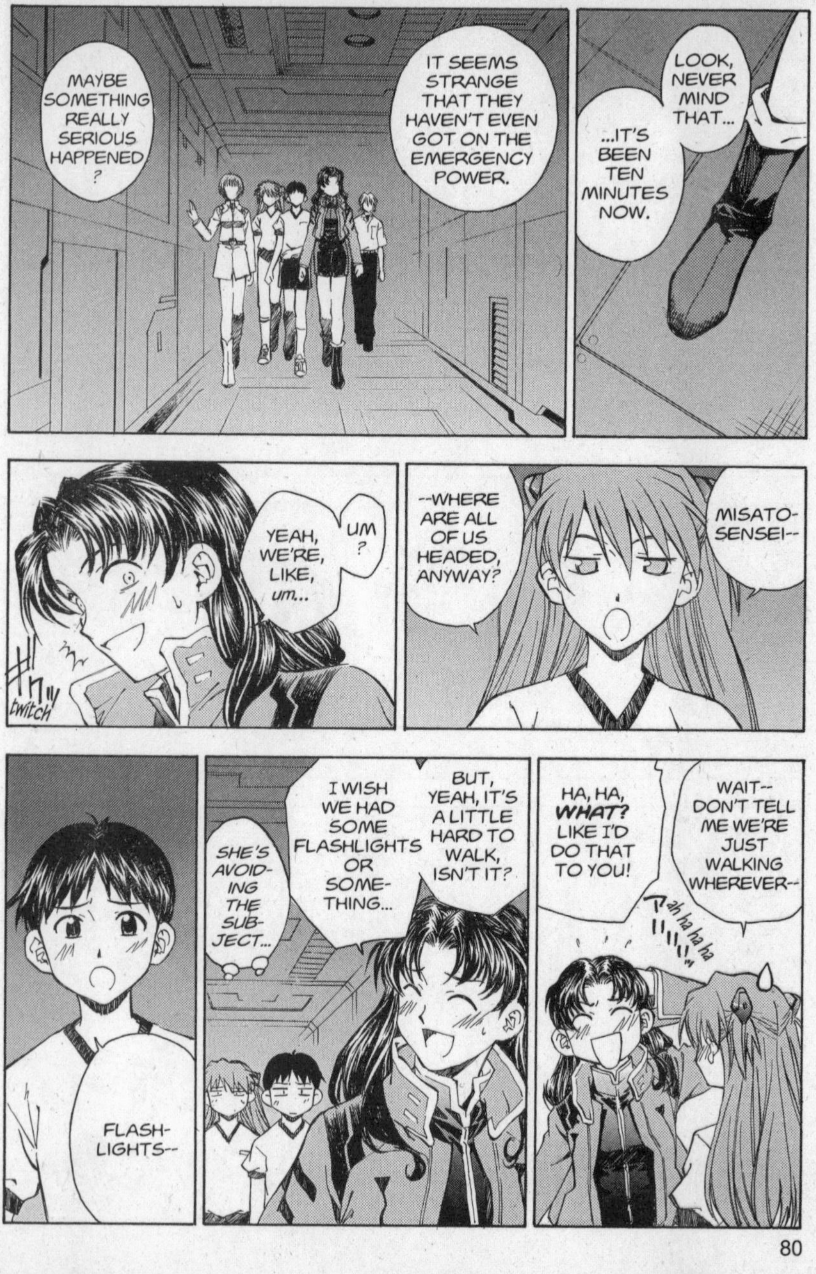
LOOK, NEVER MIND THAT...
...IT'S BEEN TEN MINUTES NOW.
IT SEEMS STRANGE THAT THEY HAVEN'T EVEN GOT ON THE EMERGENCY POWER.
MAYBE SOMETHING REALLY SERIOUS HAPPENED?
MISATO-SENSEI--
--WHERE ARE ALL OF US HEADED, ANYWAY?
UM?
YEAH, WE'RE, LIKE, *um...*
twitch
WAIT-- DON'T TELL ME WE'RE JUST WALKING WHEREVER--
HA, HA, ***WHAT?*** LIKE I'D DO THAT TO YOU!
ah ha ha ha
BUT, YEAH, IT'S A LITTLE HARD TO WALK, ISN'T IT?
I WISH WE HAD SOME FLASHLIGHTS OR SOMETHING...
SHE'S AVOIDING THE SUBJECT...
FLASHLIGHTS--

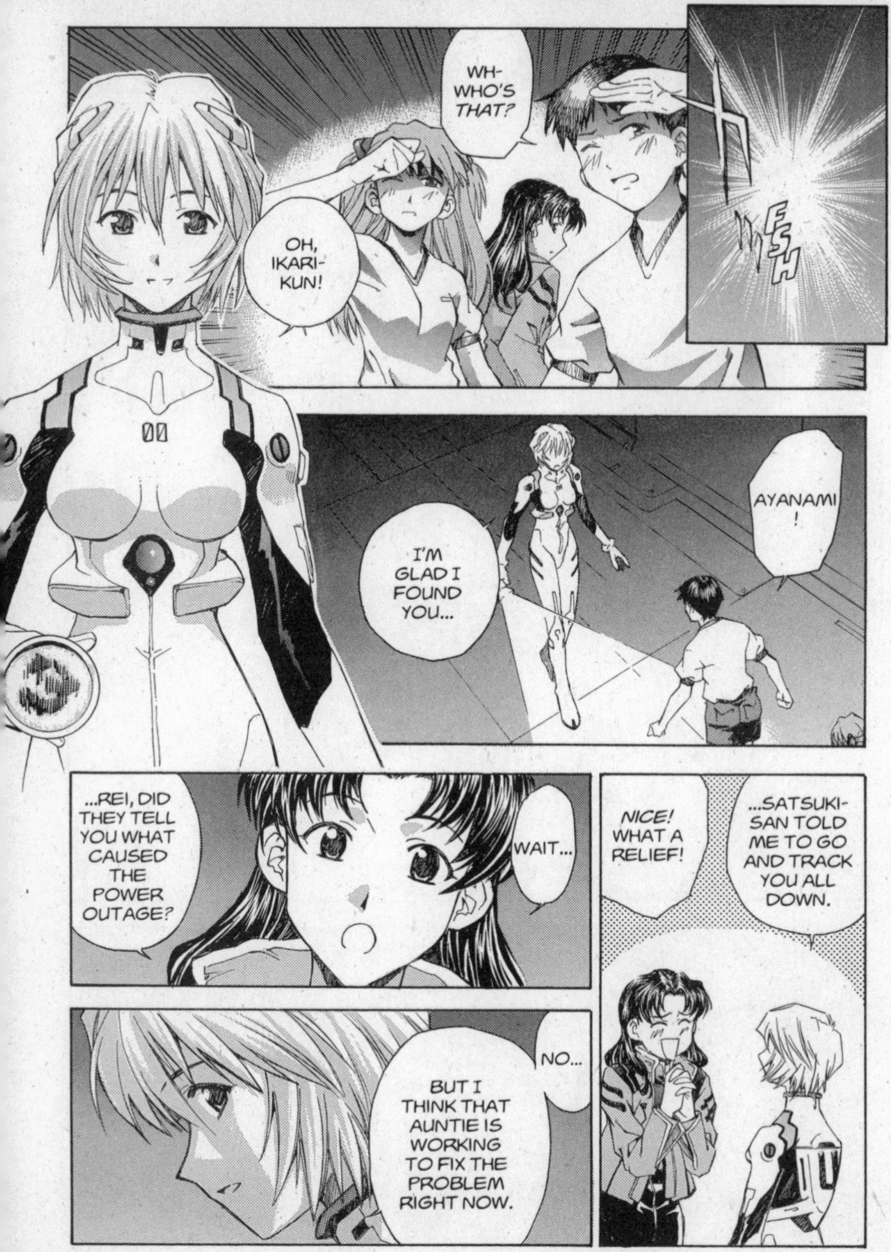
FSH
WH-WHO'S THAT?
OH, IKARI-KUN!
AYANAMI!
I'M GLAD I FOUND YOU...
...SATSUKI-SAN TOLD ME TO GO AND TRACK YOU ALL DOWN.
NICE! WHAT A RELIEF!
WAIT...
...REI, DID THEY TELL YOU WHAT CAUSED THE POWER OUTAGE?
NO...
BUT I THINK THAT AUNTIE IS WORKING TO FIX THE PROBLEM RIGHT NOW.

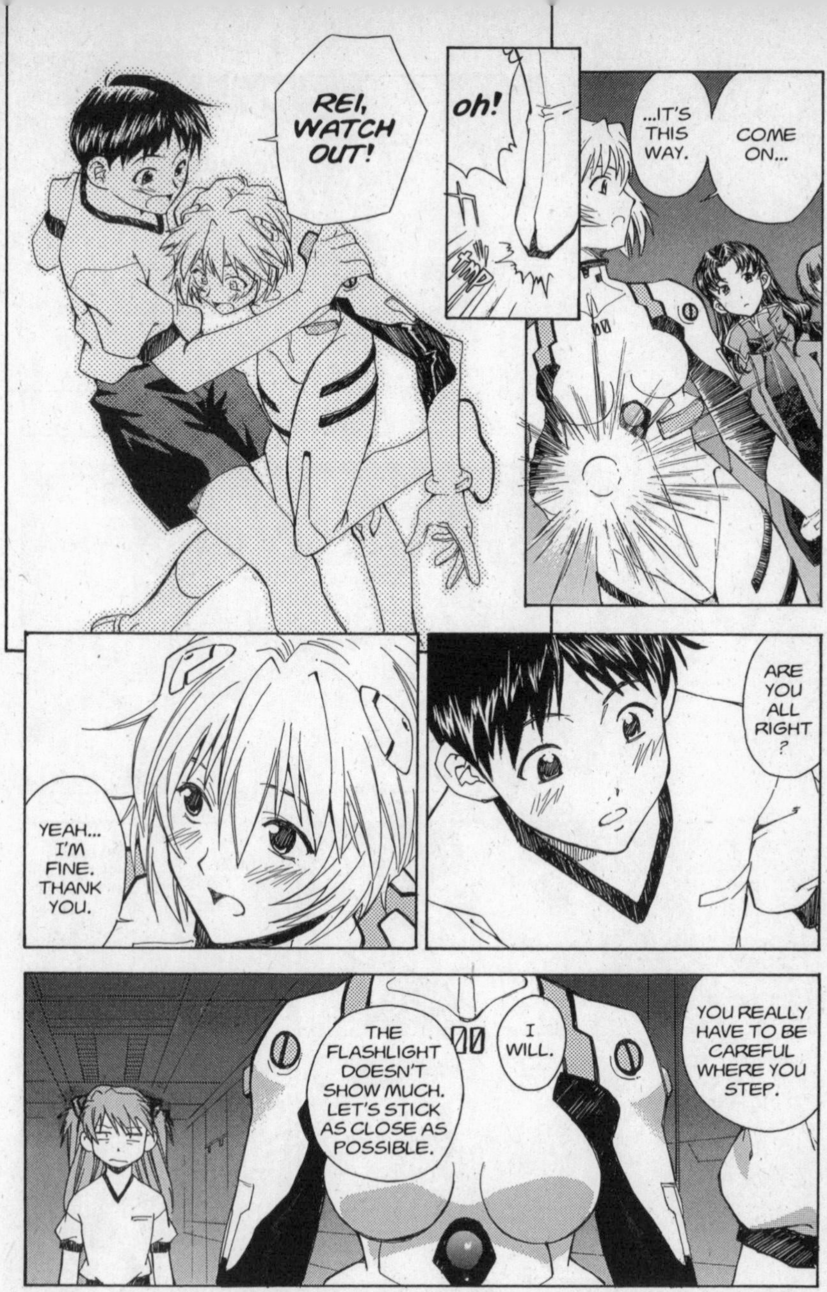
COME ON...
...IT'S THIS WAY.
oh!
tmp
REI, WATCH OUT!
ARE YOU ALL RIGHT?
YEAH... I'M FINE. THANK YOU.
YOU REALLY HAVE TO BE CAREFUL WHERE YOU STEP.
I WILL.
THE FLASHLIGHT DOESN'T SHOW MUCH. LET'S STICK AS CLOSE AS POSSIBLE.

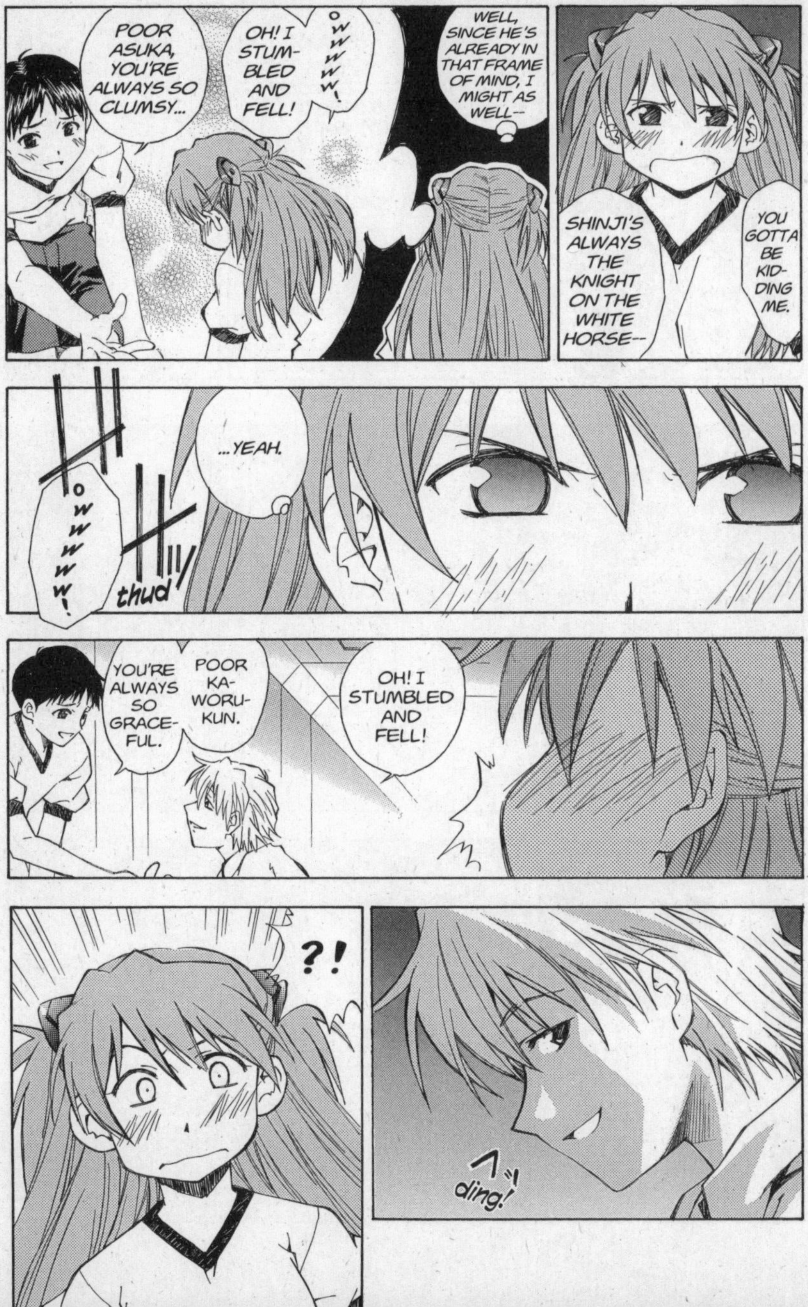
YOU GOTTA BE KIDDING ME.
SHINJI'S ALWAYS THE KNIGHT ON THE WHITE HORSE--
WELL, SINCE HE'S ALREADY IN THAT FRAME OF MIND, I MIGHT AS WELL--
OWWWWWW!
OH! I STUMBLED AND FELL!
POOR ASUKA, YOU'RE ALWAYS SO CLUMSY...
...YEAH.
OWWWWWW!
thud
OH! I STUMBLED AND FELL!
POOR KAWORU-KUN.
YOU'RE ALWAYS SO GRACEFUL.
ding!
?!

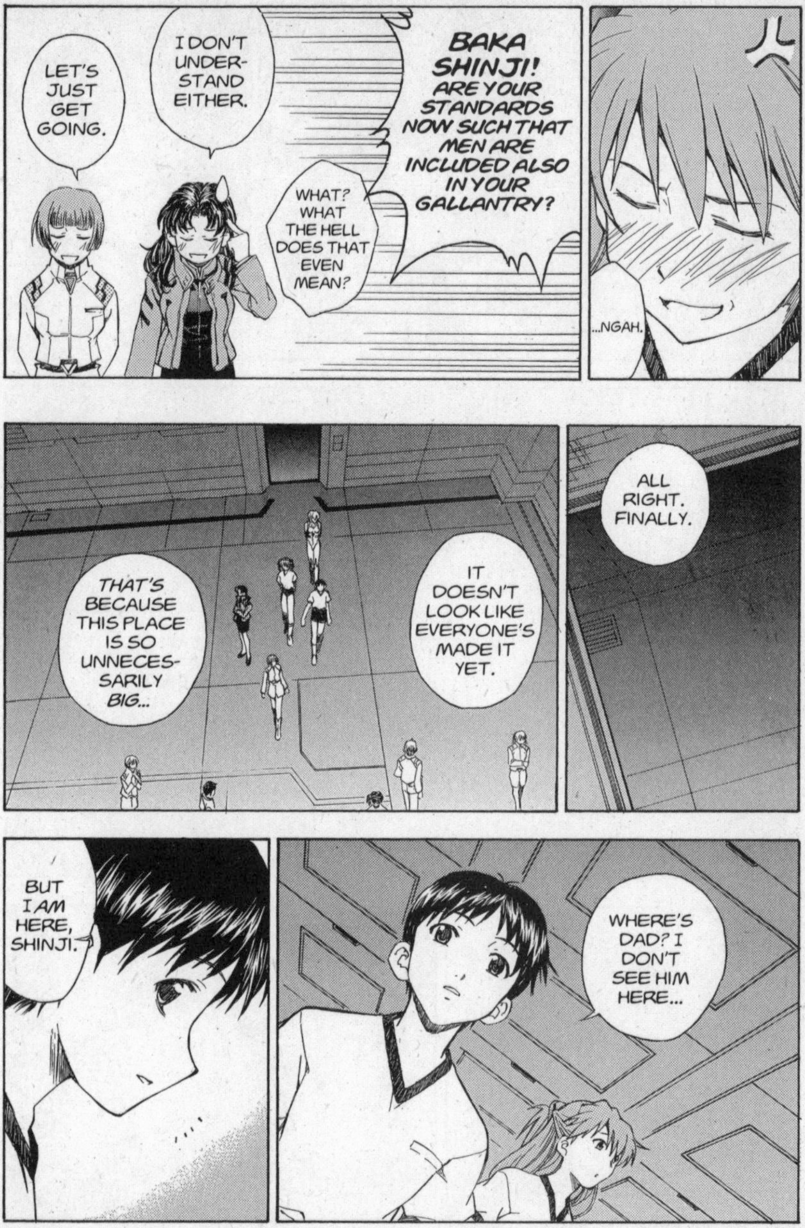
...NGAH.
BAKA SHINJI! ARE YOUR STANDARDS NOW SUCH THAT MEN ARE INCLUDED ALSO IN YOUR GALLANTRY?
WHAT? WHAT THE HELL DOES THAT EVEN MEAN?
I DON'T UNDER-STAND EITHER.
LET'S JUST GET GOING.
ALL RIGHT. FINALLY.
IT DOESN'T LOOK LIKE EVERYONE'S MADE IT YET.
THAT'S BECAUSE THIS PLACE IS SO UNNECES-SARILY BIG...
WHERE'S DAD? I DON'T SEE HIM HERE...
BUT I AM HERE, SHINJI.
...

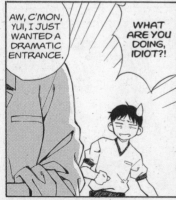

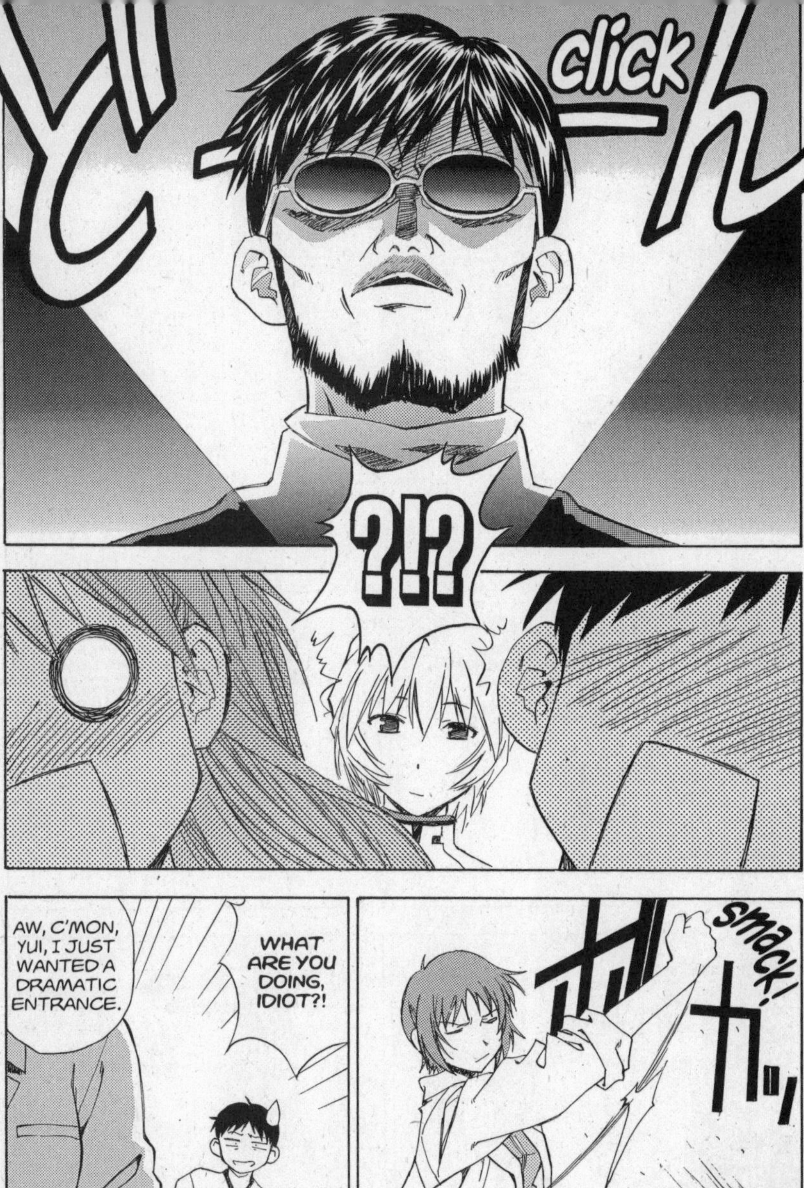
どーん
click
?!?
smack!
ガッ
WHAT ARE YOU DOING, IDIOT?!
AW, C'MON, YUI, I JUST WANTED A DRAMATIC ENTRANCE.

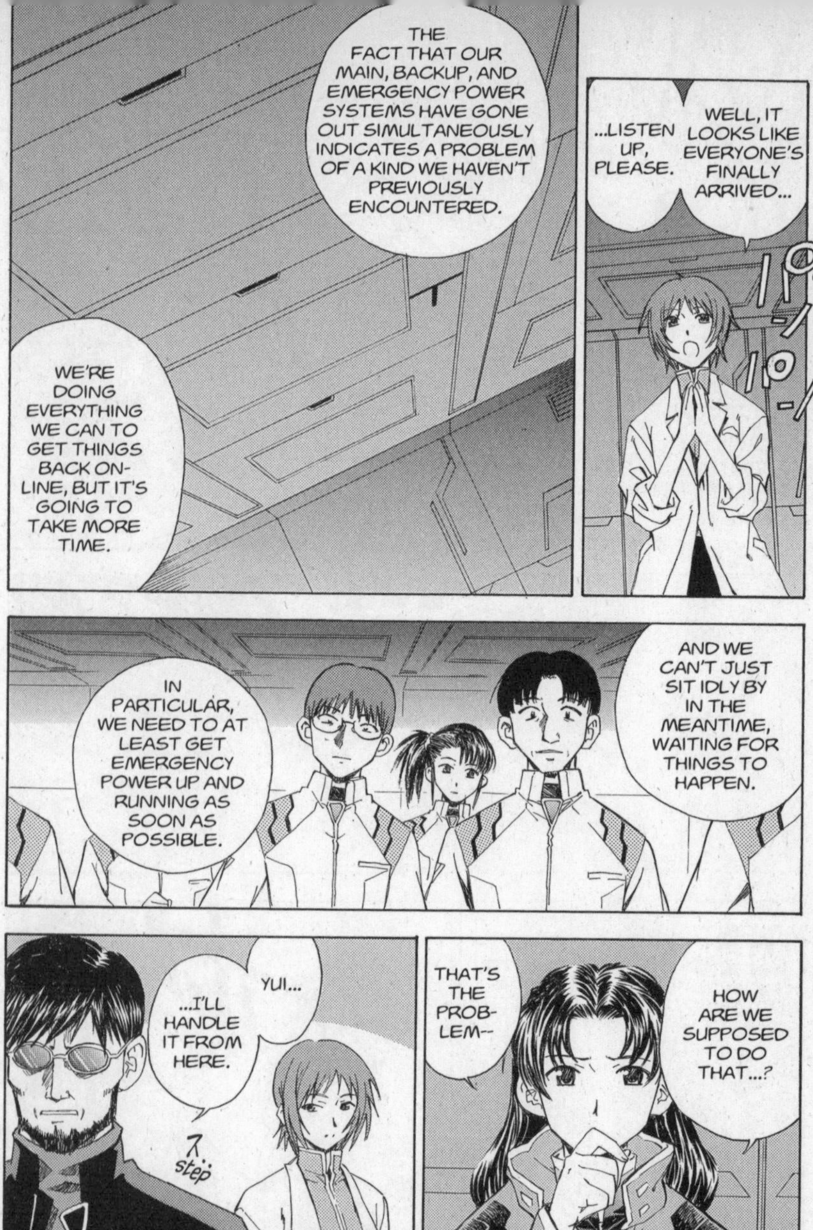
WELL, IT LOOKS LIKE EVERYONE'S FINALLY ARRIVED...
...LISTEN UP, PLEASE.
clap clap
THE FACT THAT OUR MAIN, BACKUP, AND EMERGENCY POWER SYSTEMS HAVE GONE OUT SIMULTANEOUSLY INDICATES A PROBLEM OF A KIND WE HAVEN'T PREVIOUSLY ENCOUNTERED.
WE'RE DOING EVERYTHING WE CAN TO GET THINGS BACK ON-LINE, BUT IT'S GOING TO TAKE MORE TIME.
AND WE CAN'T JUST SIT IDLY BY IN THE MEANTIME, WAITING FOR THINGS TO HAPPEN.
IN PARTICULAR, WE NEED TO AT LEAST GET EMERGENCY POWER UP AND RUNNING AS SOON AS POSSIBLE.
HOW ARE WE SUPPOSED TO DO THAT...?
THAT'S THE PROB-LEM--
YUI...
...I'LL HANDLE IT FROM HERE.
step

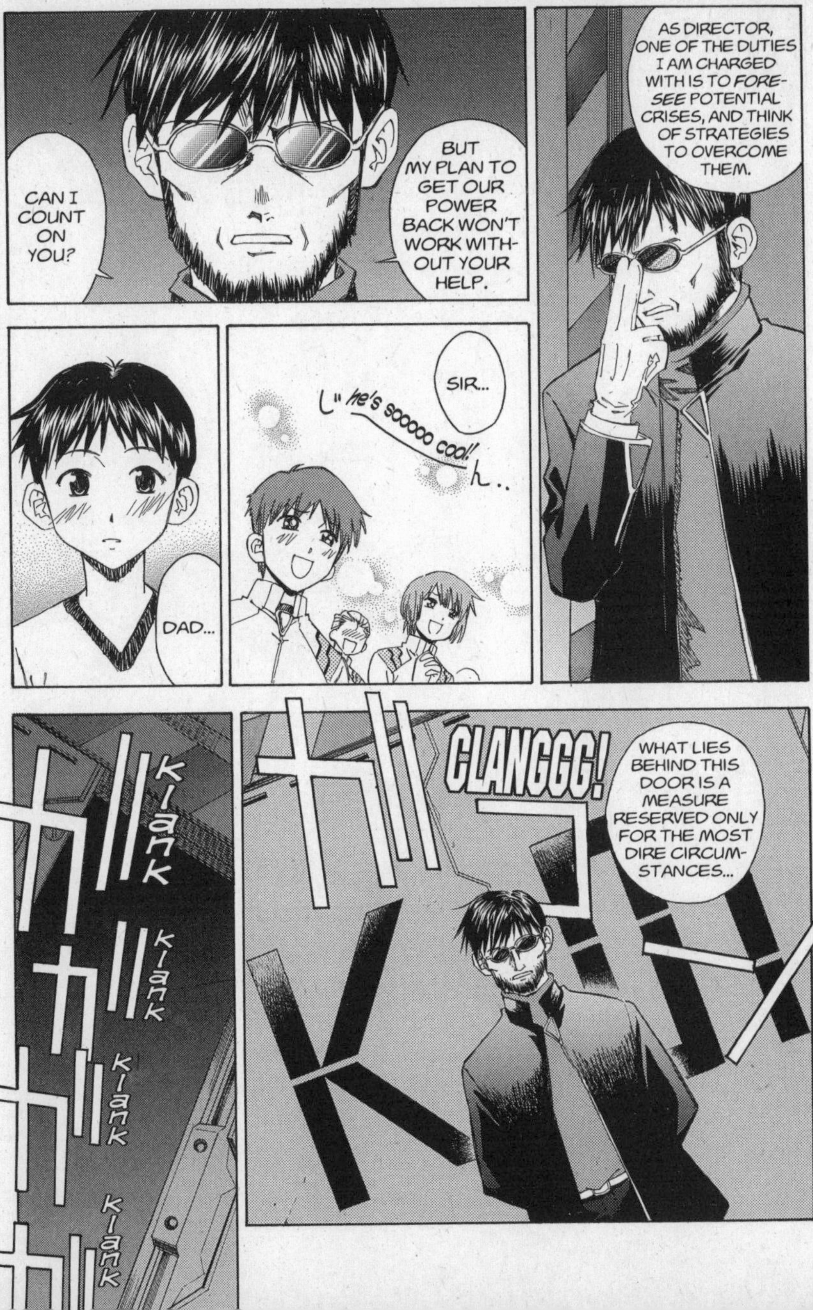
AS DIRECTOR, ONE OF THE DUTIES I AM CHARGED WITH IS TO *FORESEE* POTENTIAL CRISES, AND THINK OF STRATEGIES TO OVERCOME THEM.
BUT MY PLAN TO GET OUR POWER BACK WON'T WORK WITHOUT YOUR HELP.
CAN I COUNT ON YOU?
SIR...
he's sooooo cool!
DAD...
CLANGGG!
WHAT LIES BEHIND THIS DOOR IS A MEASURE RESERVED ONLY FOR THE MOST DIRE CIRCUMSTANCES...
klank
klank
klank
klank

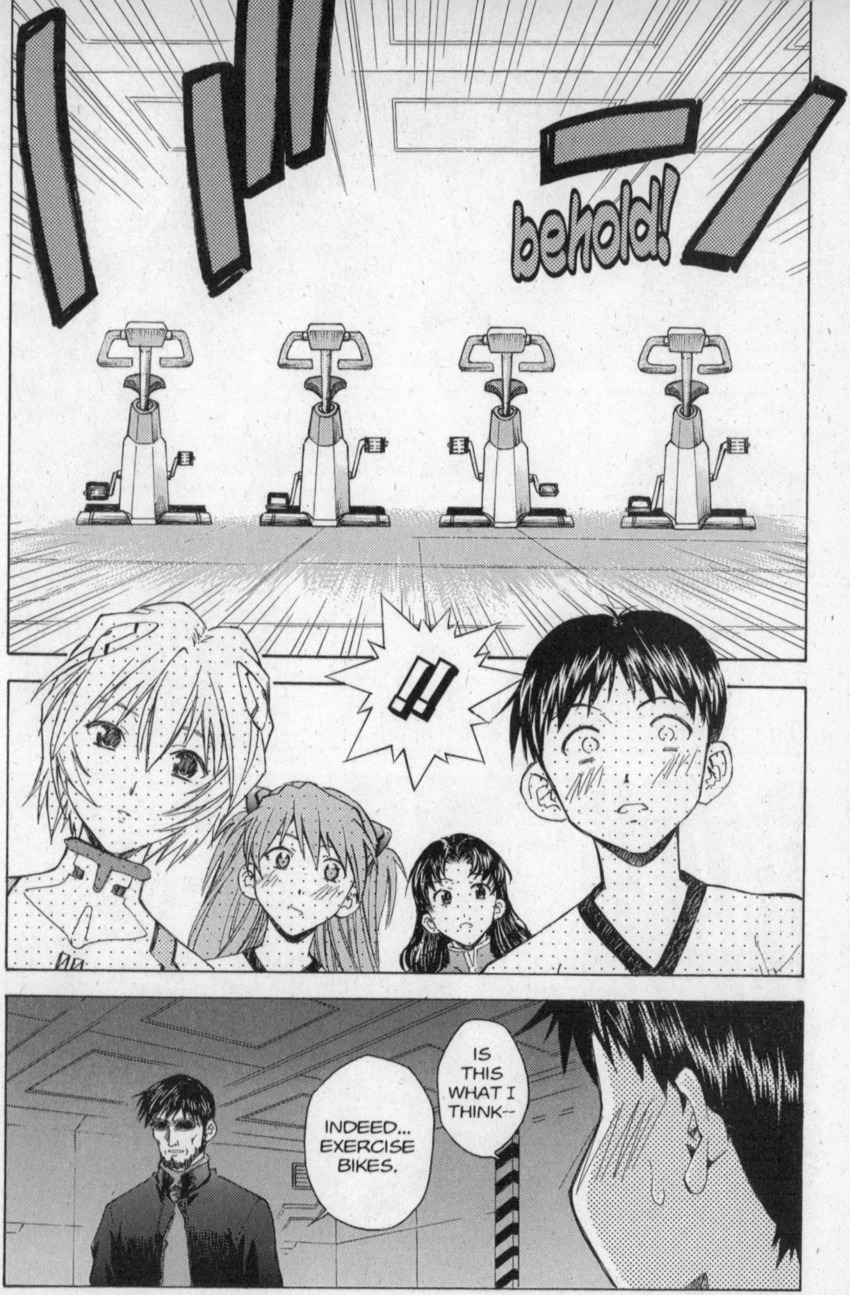
behold!
!!
IS THIS WHAT I THINK--
INDEED... EXERCISE BIKES.

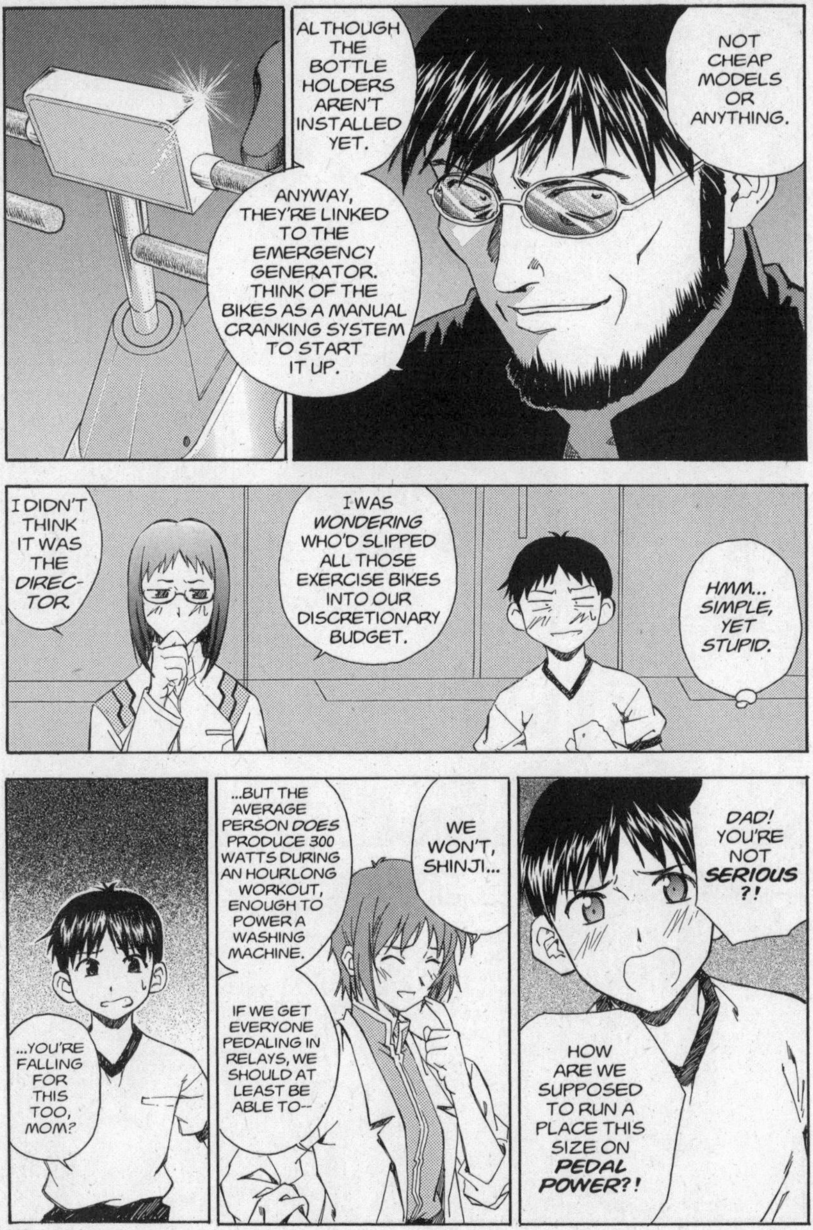
NOT CHEAP MODELS OR ANYTHING.
ALTHOUGH THE BOTTLE HOLDERS AREN'T INSTALLED YET.
ANYWAY, THEY'RE LINKED TO THE EMERGENCY GENERATOR. THINK OF THE BIKES AS A MANUAL CRANKING SYSTEM TO START IT UP.
HMM... SIMPLE, YET STUPID.
I WAS WONDERING WHO'D SLIPPED ALL THOSE EXERCISE BIKES INTO OUR DISCRETIONARY BUDGET.
I DIDN'T THINK IT WAS THE DIRECTOR.
DAD! YOU'RE NOT SERIOUS?!
HOW ARE WE SUPPOSED TO RUN A PLACE THIS SIZE ON PEDAL POWER?!
WE WON'T, SHINJI...
...BUT THE AVERAGE PERSON DOES PRODUCE 300 WATTS DURING AN HOURLONG WORKOUT, ENOUGH TO POWER A WASHING MACHINE.
IF WE GET EVERYONE PEDALING IN RELAYS, WE SHOULD AT LEAST BE ABLE TO--
...YOU'RE FALLING FOR THIS TOO, MOM?

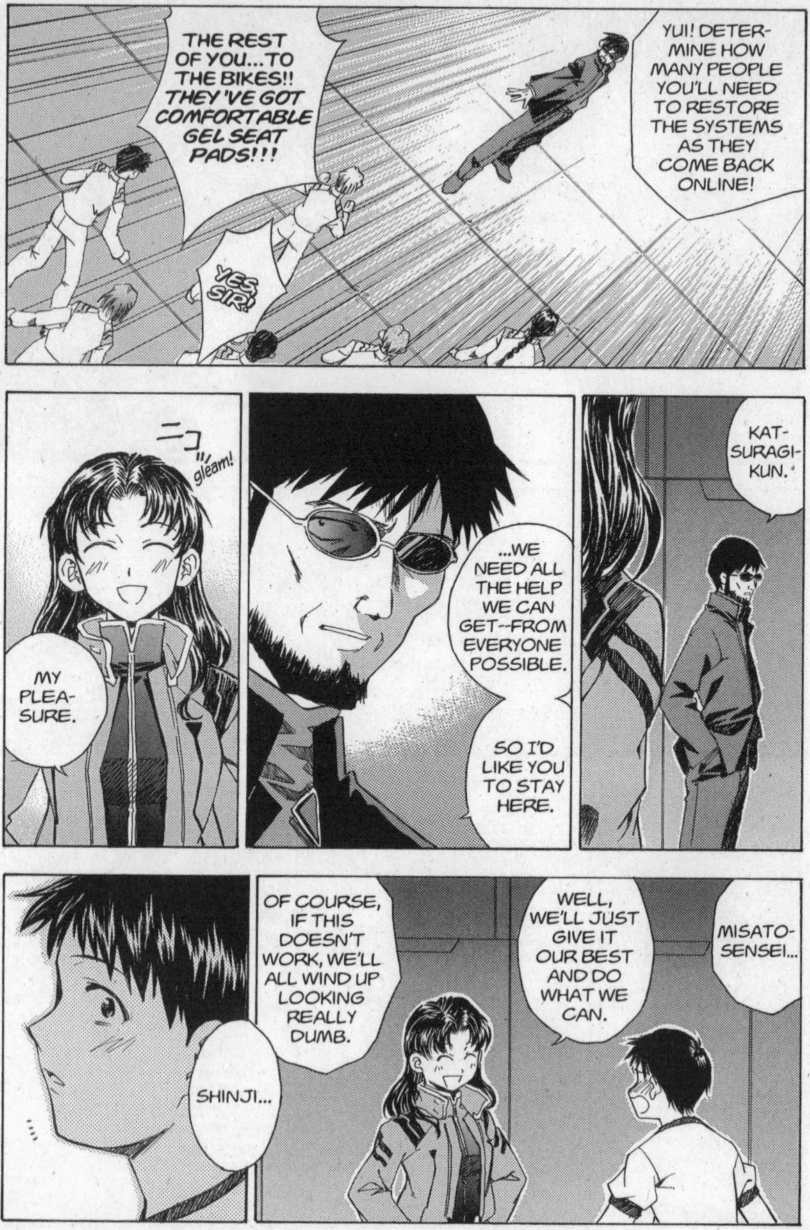
YUI! DETER-MINE HOW MANY PEOPLE YOU'LL NEED TO RESTORE THE SYSTEMS AS THEY COME BACK ONLINE!
THE REST OF YOU...TO THE BIKES!! THEY'VE GOT COMFORTABLE GEL SEAT PADS!!!
YES, SIR!
KAT-SURAGI-KUN.
...WE NEED ALL THE HELP WE CAN GET--FROM EVERYONE POSSIBLE.
SO I'D LIKE YOU TO STAY HERE.
ニコ
gleam!
MY PLEA-SURE.
MISATO-SENSEI...
WELL, WE'LL JUST GIVE IT OUR BEST AND DO WHAT WE CAN.
OF COURSE, IF THIS DOESN'T WORK, WE'LL ALL WIND UP LOOKING REALLY DUMB.
SHINJI...
...

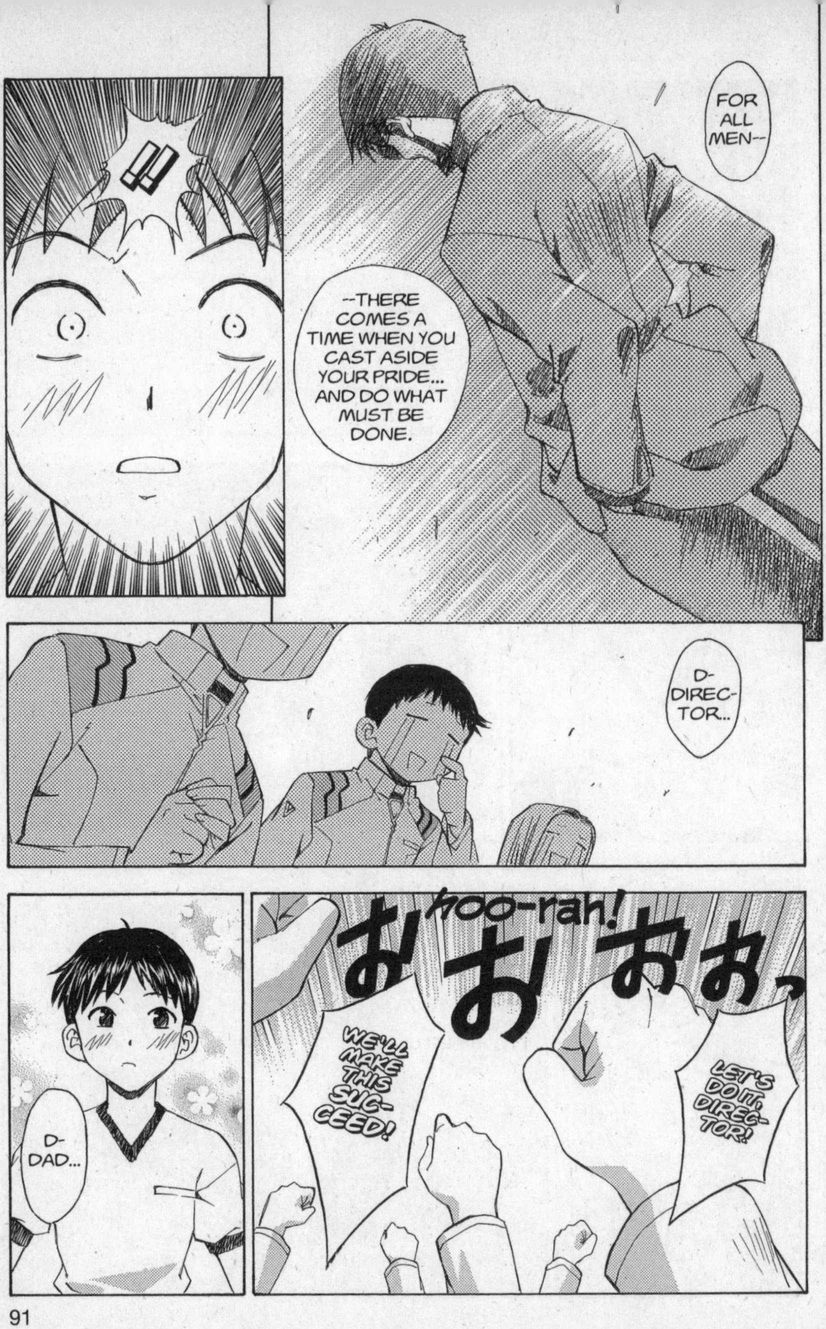
FOR ALL MEN--
--THERE COMES A TIME WHEN YOU CAST ASIDE YOUR PRIDE... AND DO WHAT MUST BE DONE.
!!
D-DIRECTOR...
hoo-rah!
おおおおっ
LET'S DO IT, DIRECTOR!
WE'LL MAKE THIS SUCCEED!
D-DAD...

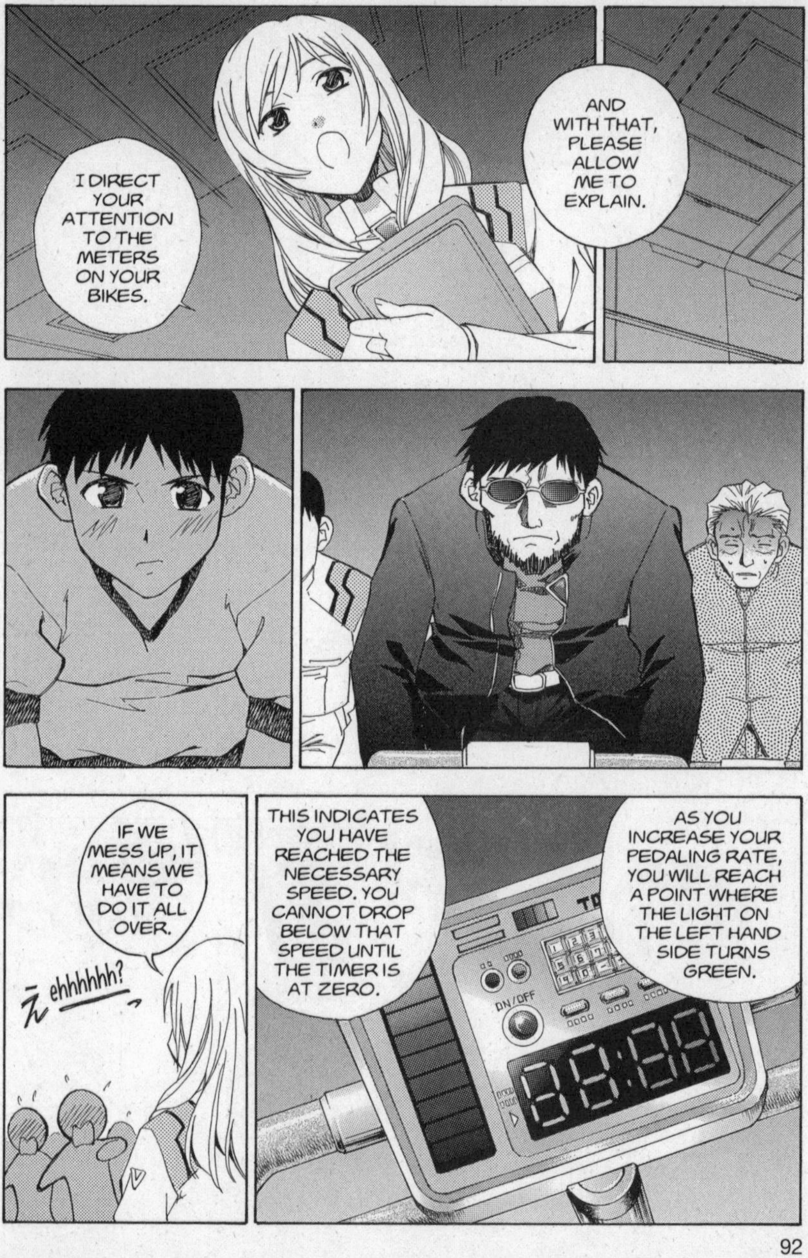

AND WITH THAT, PLEASE ALLOW ME TO EXPLAIN.
I DIRECT YOUR ATTENTION TO THE METERS ON YOUR BIKES.
AS YOU INCREASE YOUR PEDALING RATE, YOU WILL REACH A POINT WHERE THE LIGHT ON THE LEFT HAND SIDE TURNS GREEN.
THIS INDICATES YOU HAVE REACHED THE NECESSARY SPEED. YOU CANNOT DROP BELOW THAT SPEED UNTIL THE TIMER IS AT ZERO.
ON/OFF
IF WE MESS UP, IT MEANS WE HAVE TO DO IT ALL OVER.
ehhhhhh?

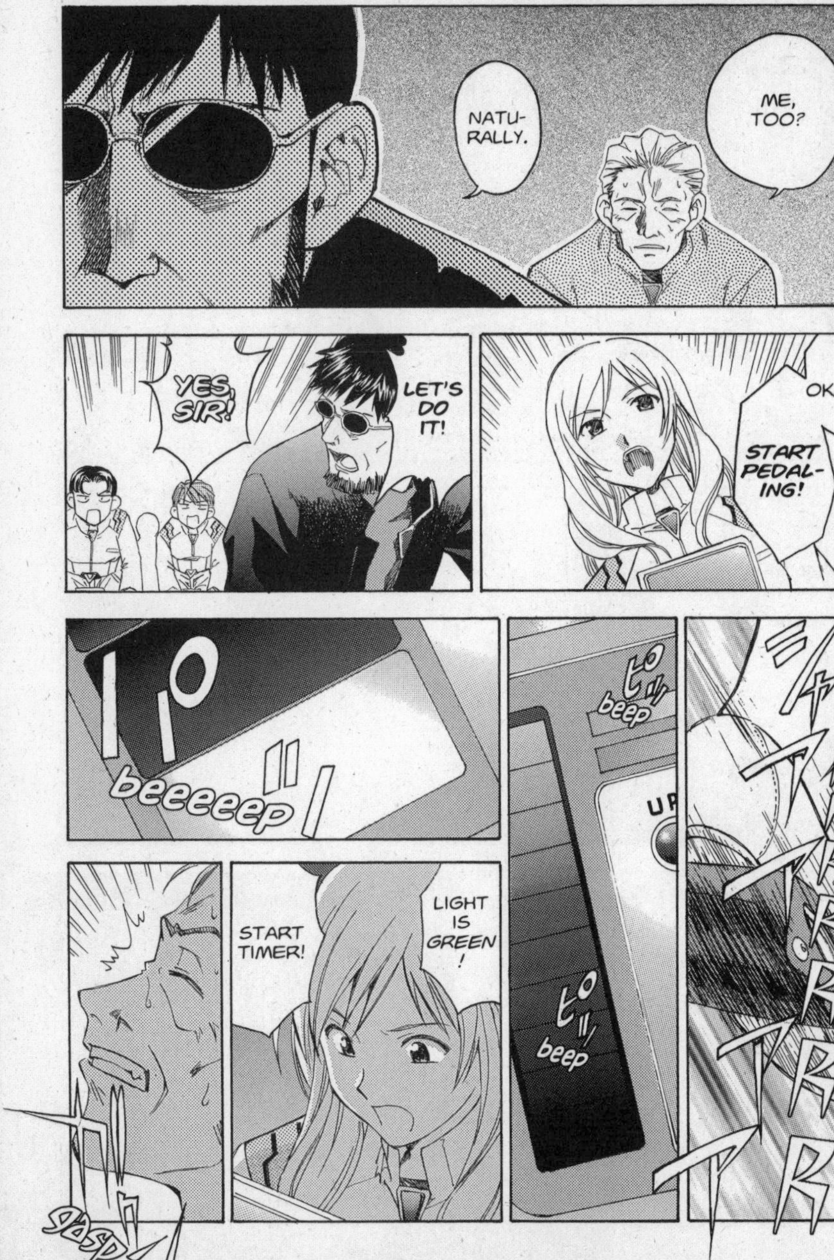
ME, TOO?
NATU-RALLY.
OKAY.
START PEDAL-ING!
LET'S DO IT!
YES, SIR!
WHHHIRRRRRRRR
beep
UP
beep
beeeeeep
LIGHT IS GREEN!
START TIMER!
gasp

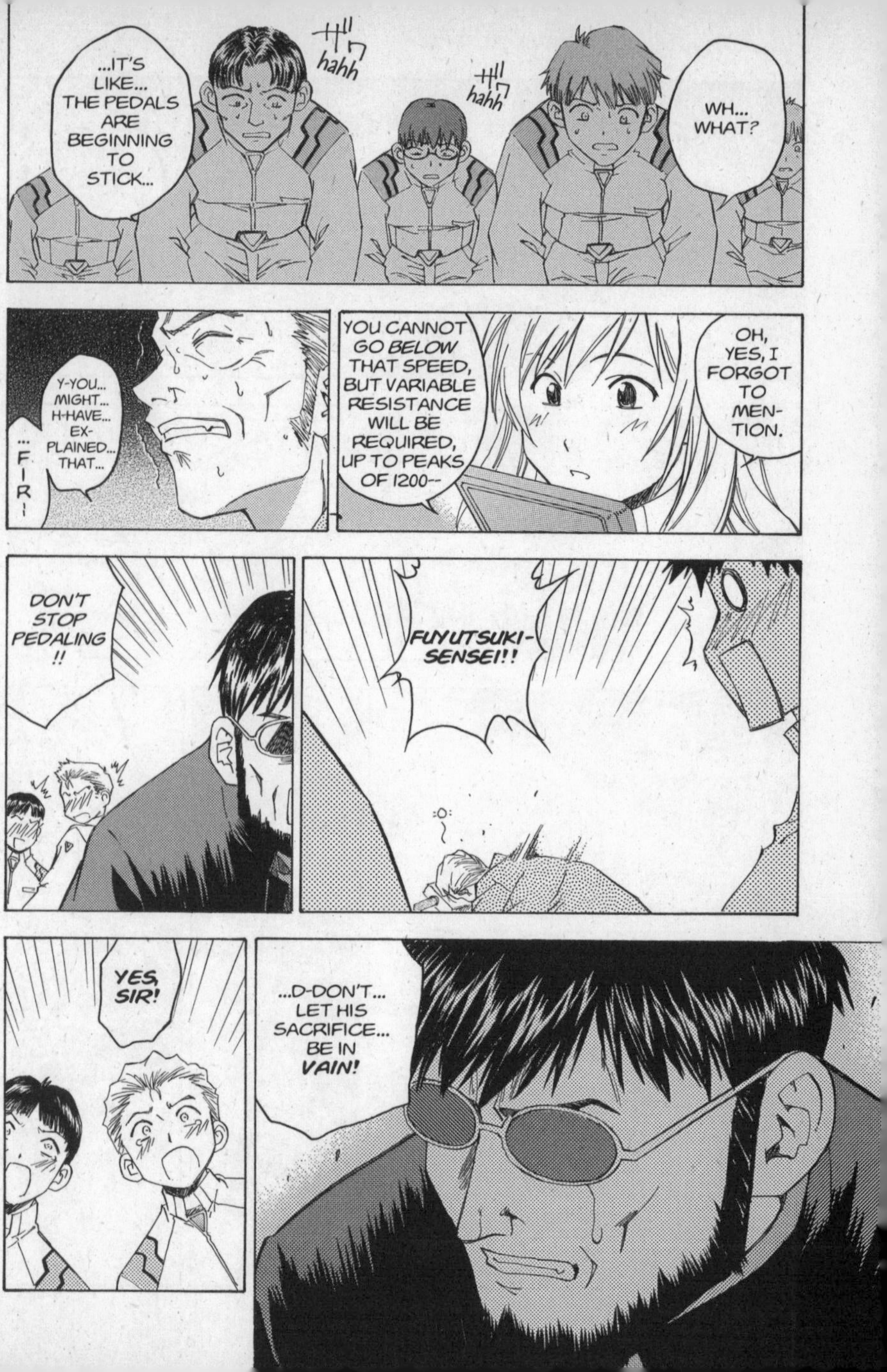
WH... WHAT?
hahh
hahh
...IT'S LIKE... THE PEDALS ARE BEGINNING TO STICK...
OH, YES, I FORGOT TO MEN-TION.
YOU CANNOT GO *BELOW* THAT SPEED, BUT VARIABLE RESISTANCE WILL BE REQUIRED, UP TO PEAKS OF 1200--
Y-YOU... MIGHT... H-HAVE... EX-PLAINED... THAT...
...FIRI
FUYUTSUKI-SENSEI!!
DON'T STOP PEDALING!!
...D-DON'T... LET HIS SACRIFICE... BE IN ***VAIN!***
YES, SIR!

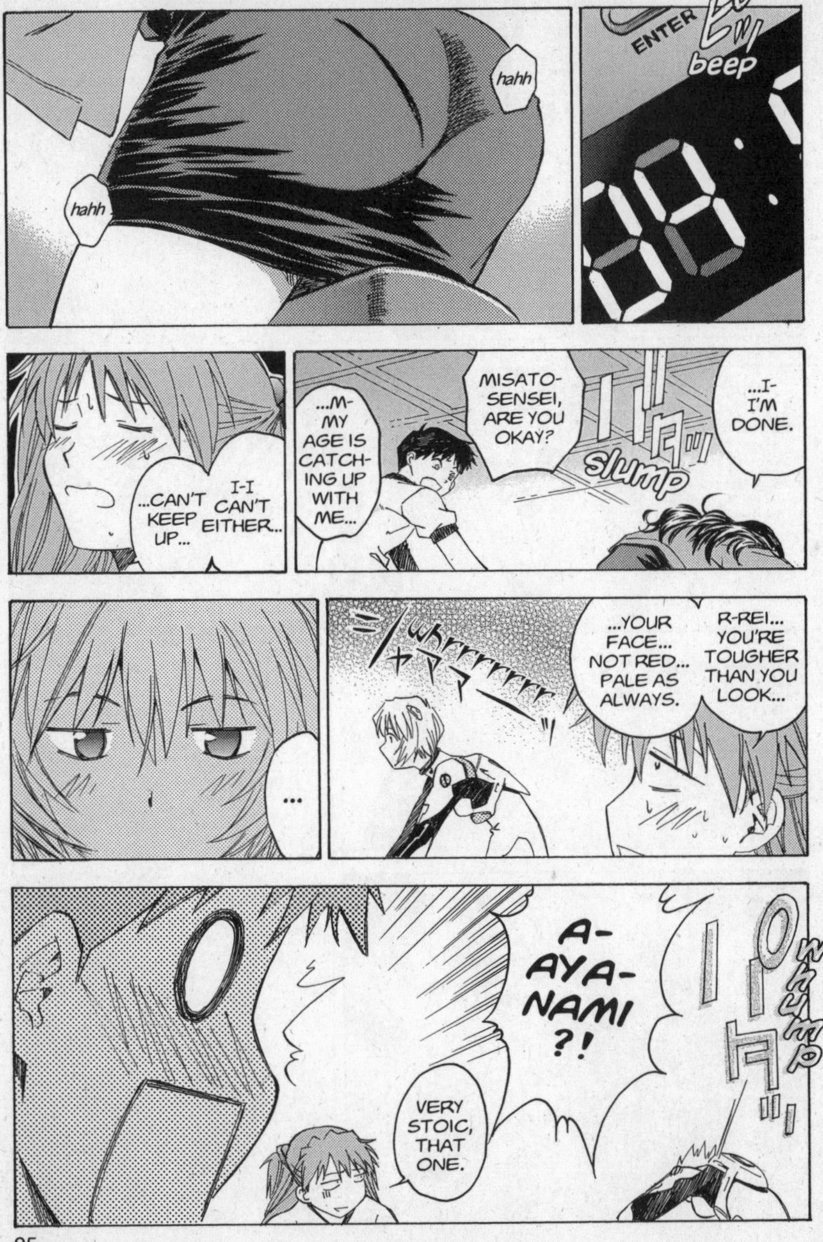
ENTER
beep
hahh
hahh
...I- I'M DONE.
slump
MISATO-SENSEI, ARE YOU OKAY?
...M-MY AGE IS CATCHING UP WITH ME...
I-I CAN'T EITHER...
...CAN'T KEEP UP...
R-REI... YOU'RE TOUGHER THAN YOU LOOK...
...YOUR FACE... NOT RED... PALE AS ALWAYS.
whrrrrrrrr
...
whump
A-AYA-NAMI?!
VERY STOIC, THAT ONE.

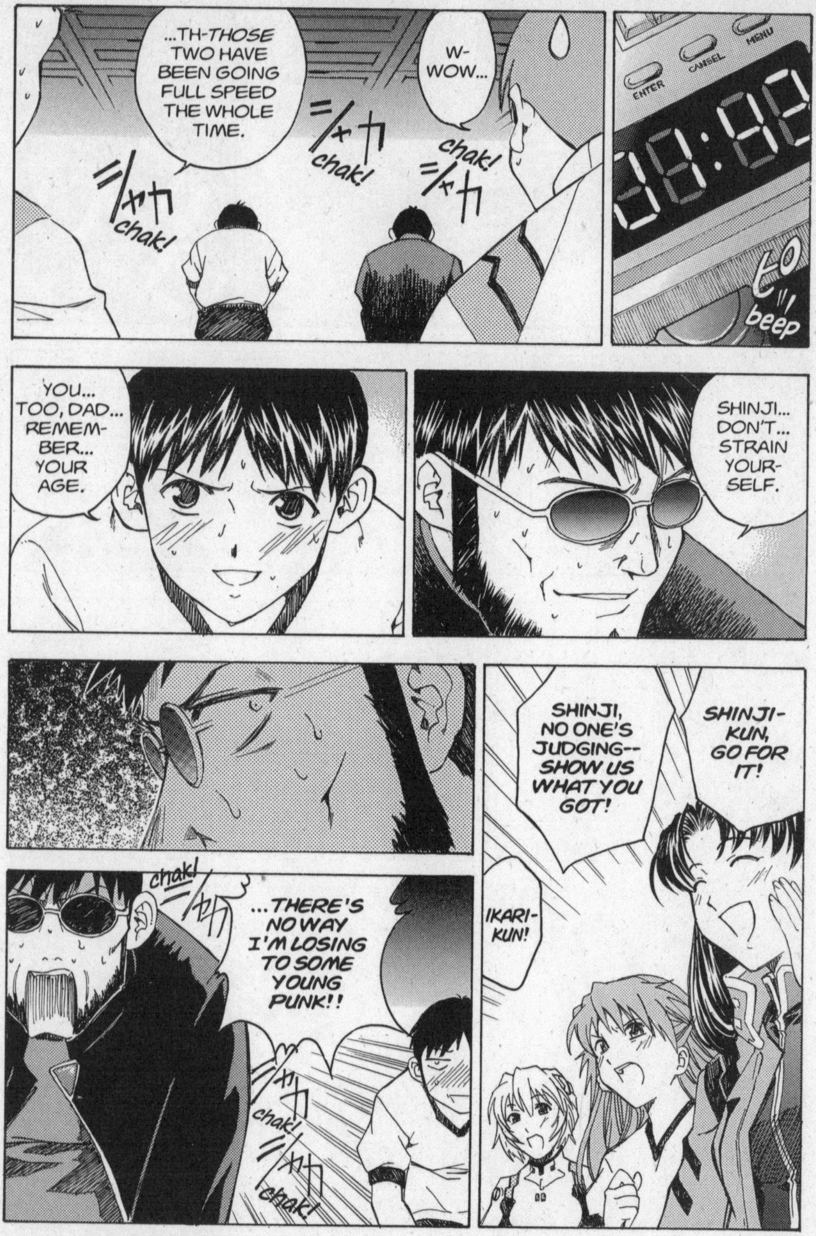
ENTER
CANSEL
MENU
beep
W-WOW...
chak!
chak!
...TH-THOSE TWO HAVE BEEN GOING FULL SPEED THE WHOLE TIME.
chak!
SHINJI... DON'T... STRAIN YOUR-SELF.
YOU... TOO, DAD... REMEM-BER... YOUR AGE.
SHINJI-KUN, GO FOR IT!
SHINJI, NO ONE'S JUDGING-- SHOW US WHAT YOU GOT!
IKARI-KUN!
chak!
...THERE'S NO WAY I'M LOSING TO SOME YOUNG PUNK!!
chak!
chak!

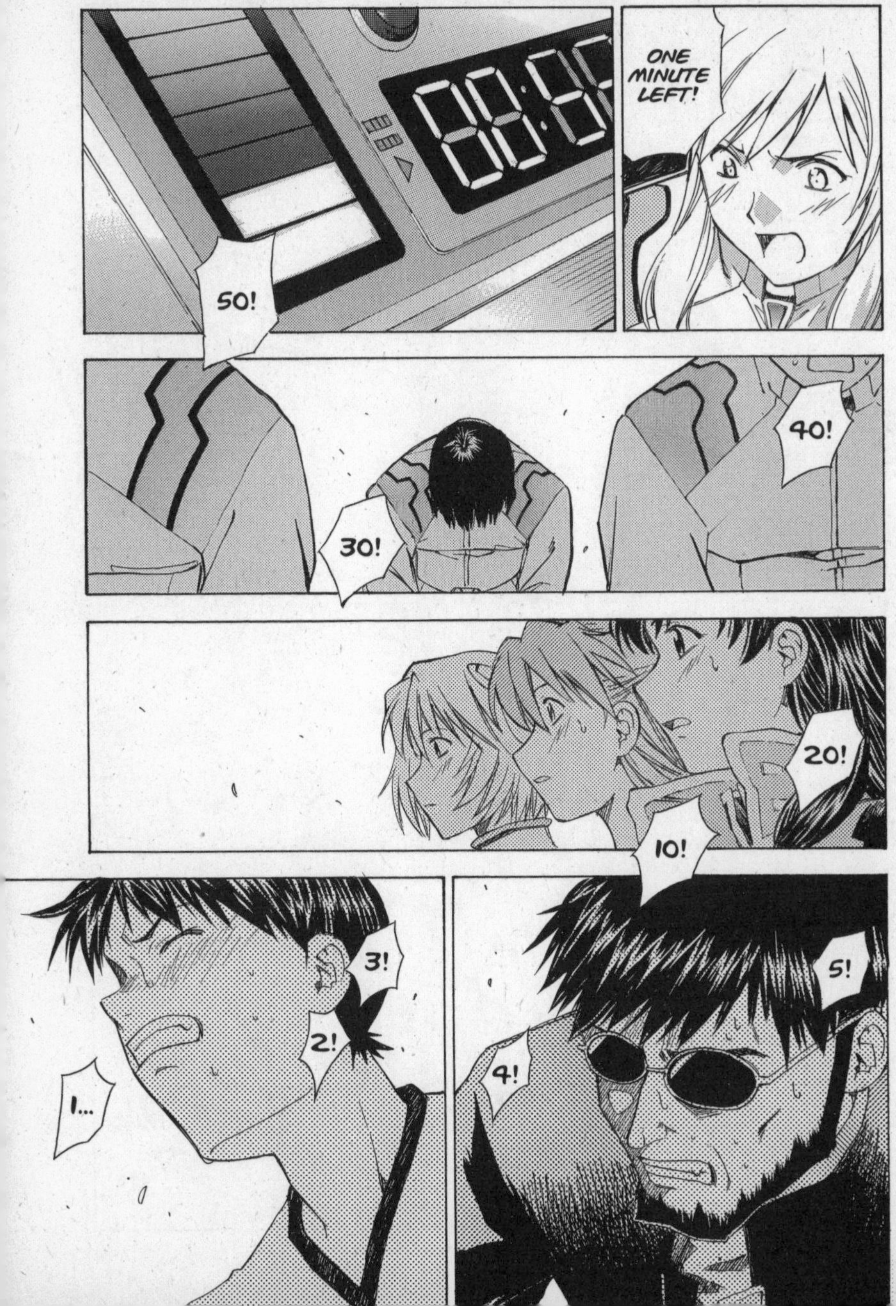
ONE MINUTE LEFT!
50!
40!
30!
20!
10!
5!
4!
3!
2!
1...

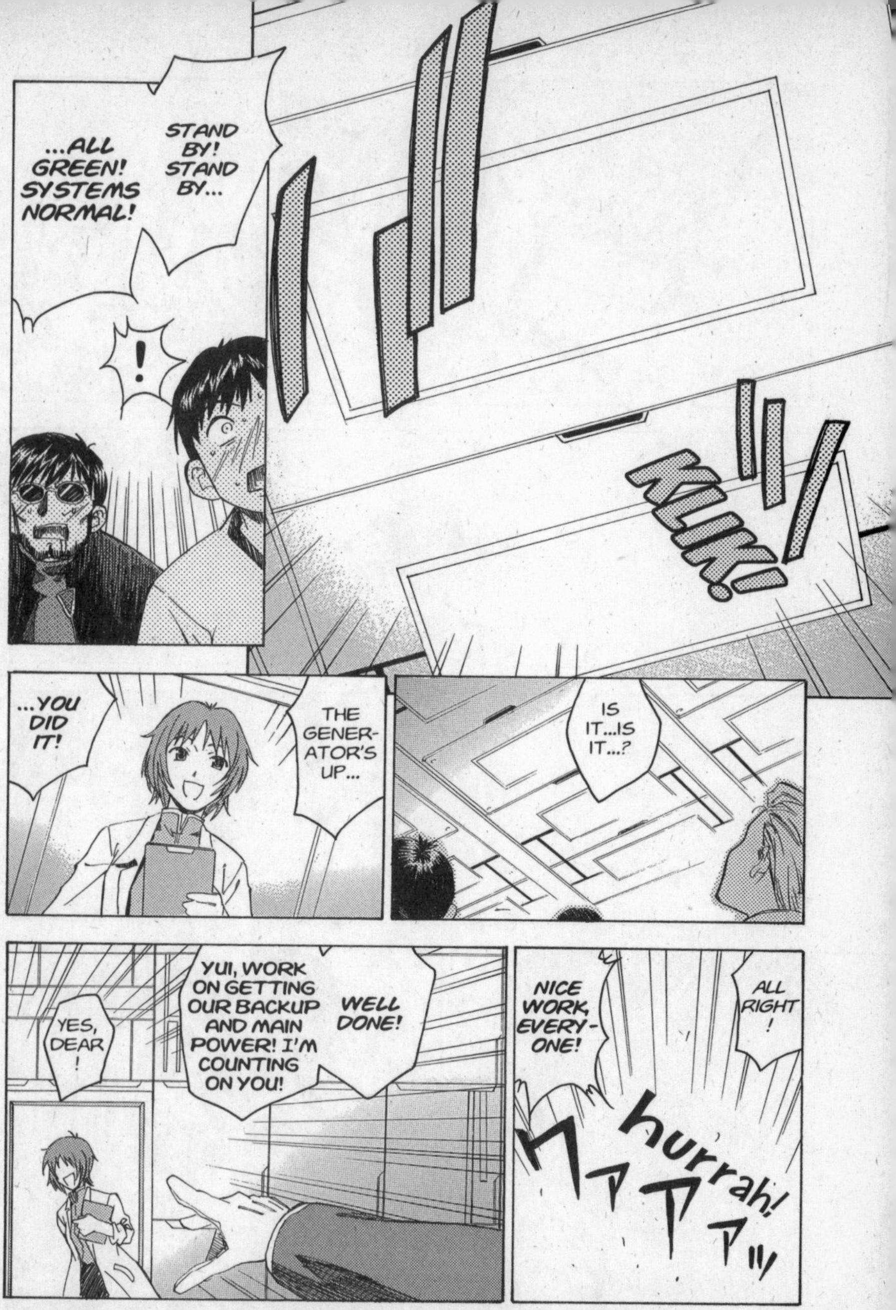
KLIK!
STAND BY! STAND BY...
...ALL GREEN! SYSTEMS NORMAL!
!
IS IT...IS IT...?
THE GENER-ATOR'S UP...
...YOU DID IT!
ALL RIGHT!
NICE WORK, EVERY-ONE!
hurrah!
ワァアァッ
WELL DONE!
YUI, WORK ON GETTING OUR BACKUP AND MAIN POWER! I'M COUNTING ON YOU!
YES, DEAR!

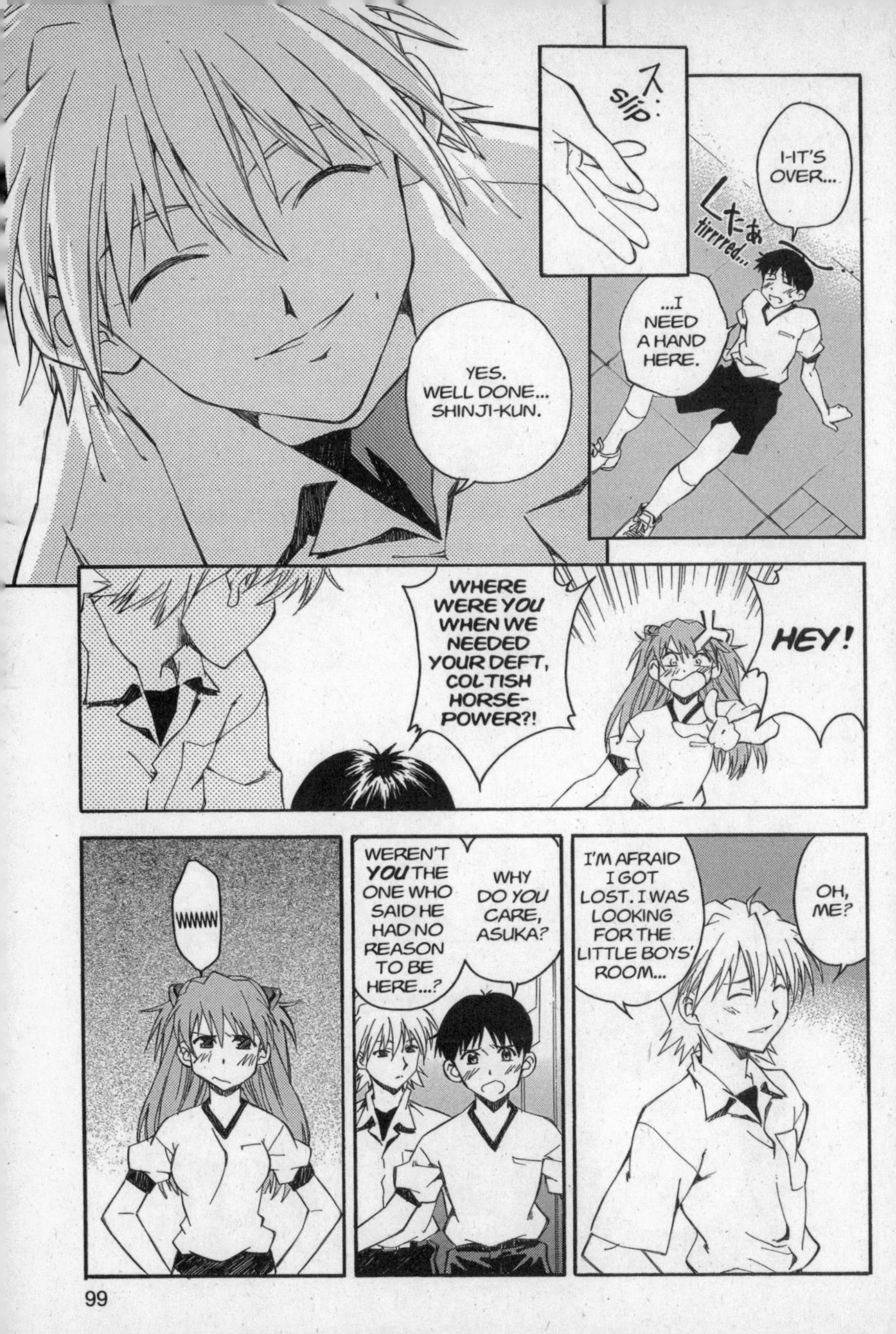
I-IT'S OVER...
くたぁ tirrrred...
...I NEED A HAND HERE.
ス slip
YES. WELL DONE... SHINJI-KUN.
HEY!
WHERE WERE *YOU* WHEN WE NEEDED YOUR DEFT, COLTISH HORSE-POWER?!
OH, ME?
I'M AFRAID I GOT LOST. I WAS LOOKING FOR THE LITTLE BOYS' ROOM...
WHY DO *YOU* CARE, ASUKA?
WEREN'T ***YOU*** THE ONE WHO SAID HE HAD NO REASON TO BE HERE...?
WWWWW

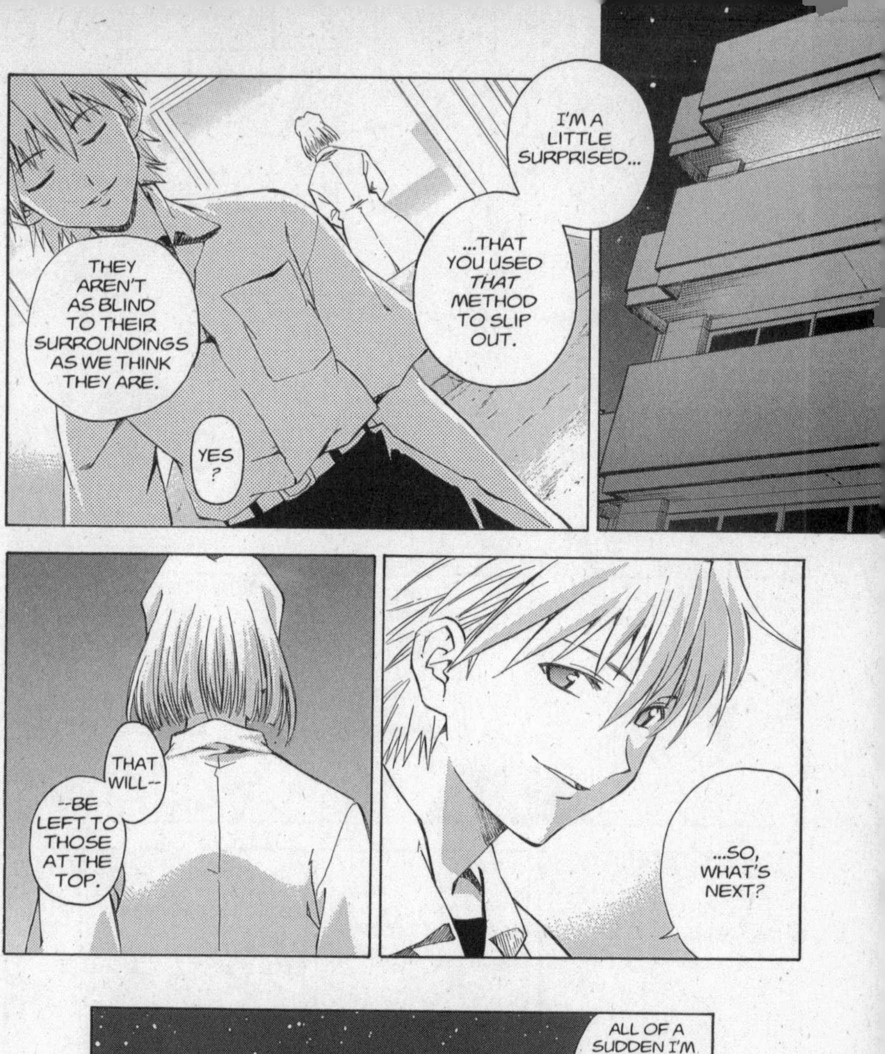
I'M A LITTLE SURPRISED...
...THAT YOU USED *THAT* METHOD TO SLIP OUT.
THEY AREN'T AS BLIND TO THEIR SURROUNDINGS AS WE THINK THEY ARE.
YES?
...SO, WHAT'S NEXT?
THAT WILL--
--BE LEFT TO THOSE AT THE TOP.
ALL OF A SUDDEN I'M GETTING MORE INTER-ESTED IN HOW THIS WHOLE MISSION WILL PLAY OUT.
MAYBE I SHOULD ACTUALLY START TO PLAY FOR KEEPS.
END

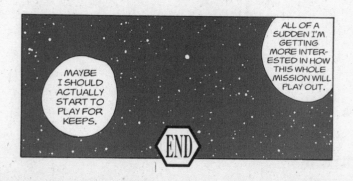

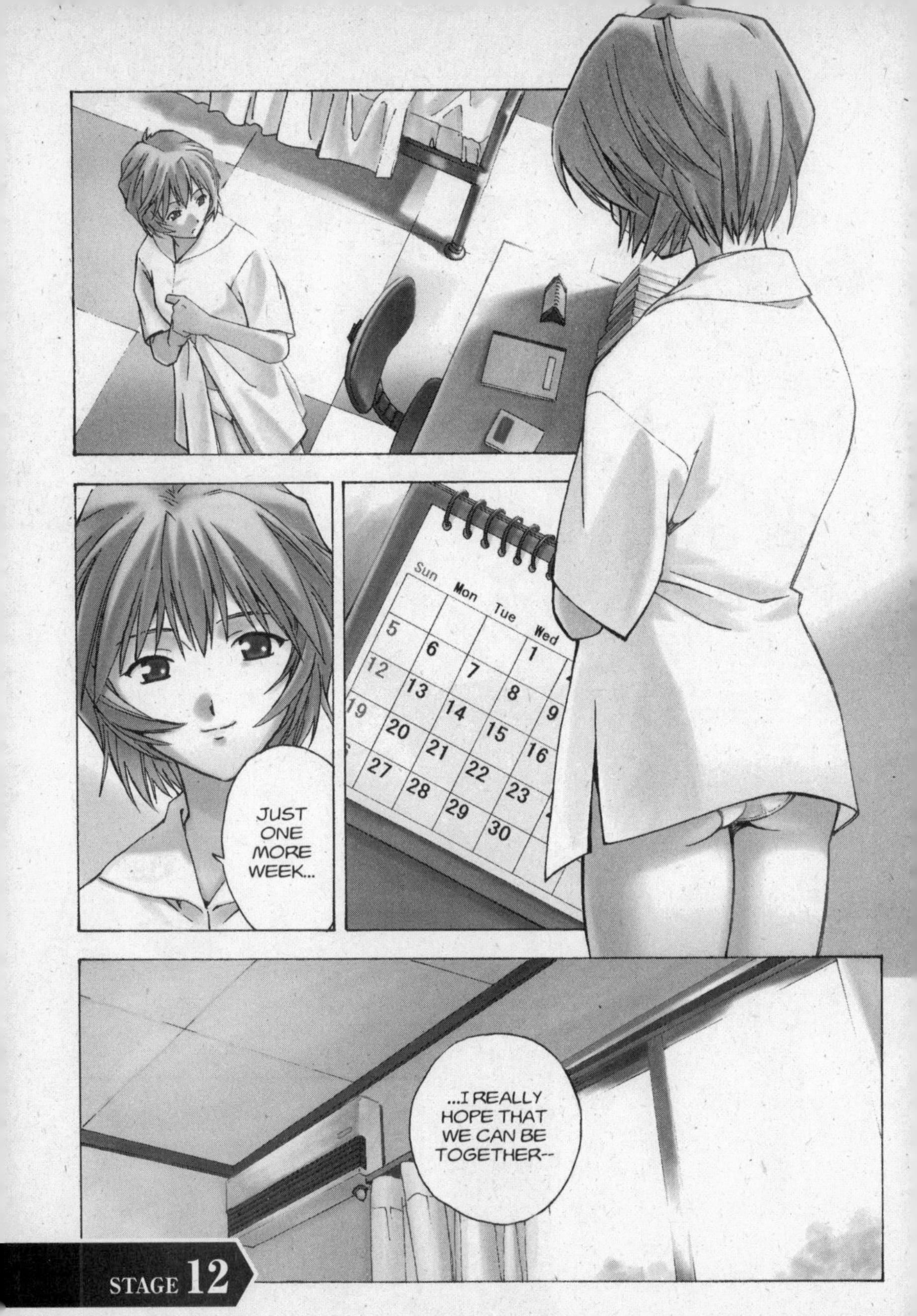
JUST ONE MORE WEEK...
...I REALLY HOPE THAT WE CAN BE TOGETHER--
STAGE 12

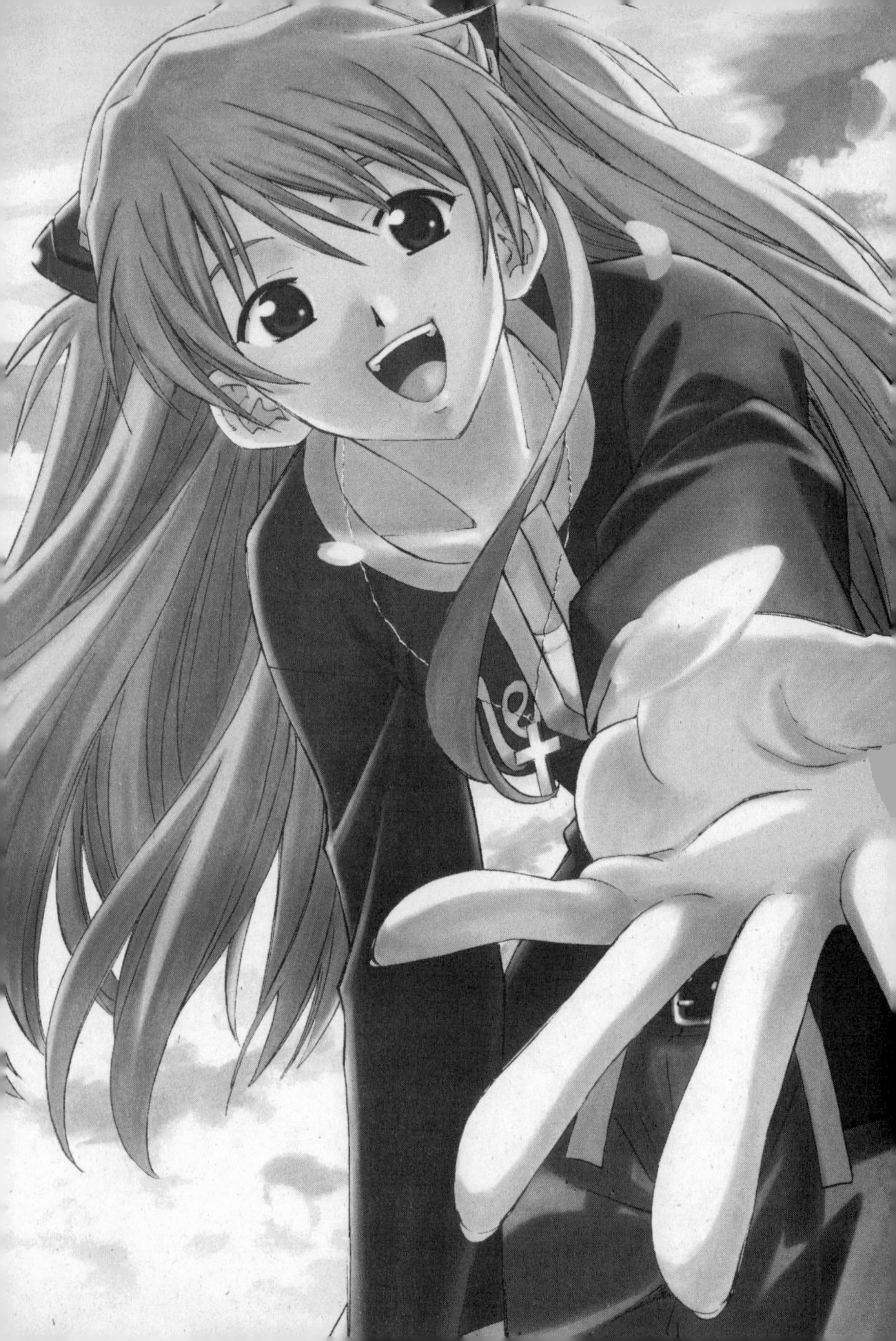

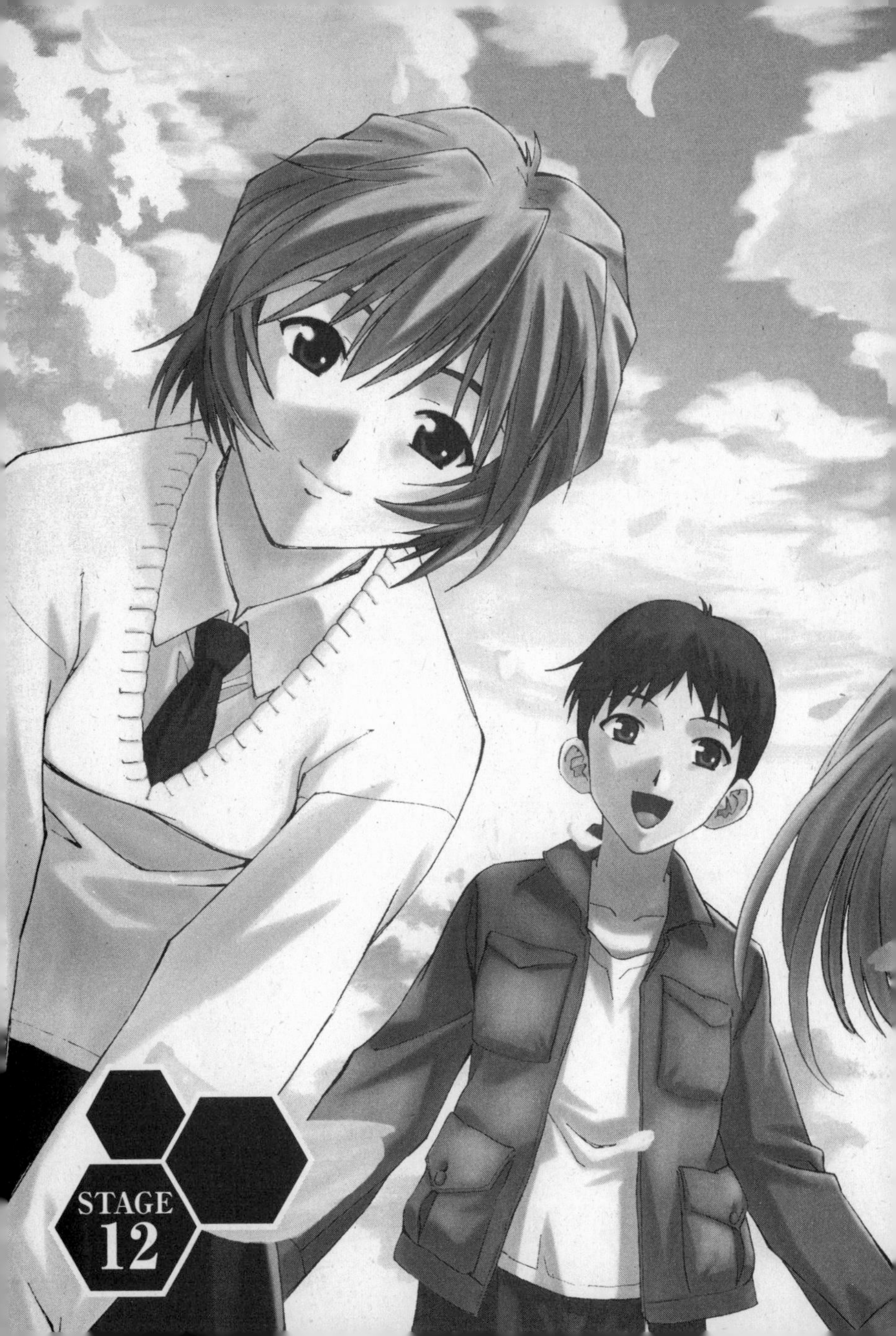
STAGE
12

NEON GENESIS EVANGELION
THE SHINJI IKARI RAISING PROJECT

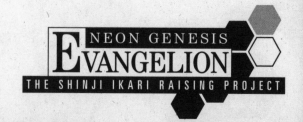

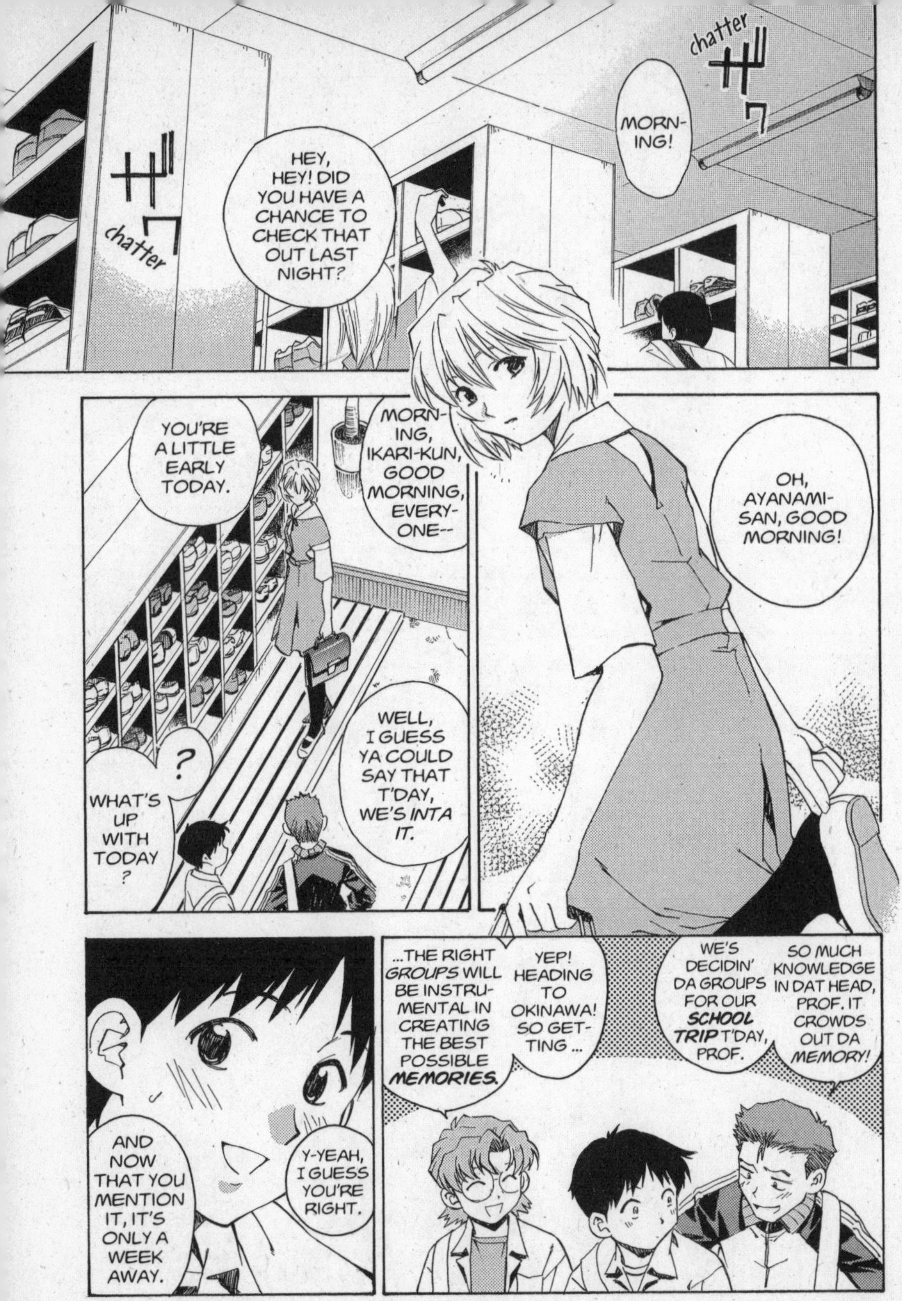
chatter
MORNING!
HEY, HEY! DID YOU HAVE A CHANCE TO CHECK THAT OUT LAST NIGHT?
chatter
OH, AYANAMI-SAN, GOOD MORNING!
MORNING, IKARI-KUN, GOOD MORNING, EVERYONE--
YOU'RE A LITTLE EARLY TODAY.
WELL, I GUESS YA COULD SAY THAT T'DAY, WE'S *INTA* IT.
?
WHAT'S UP WITH TODAY?
SO MUCH KNOWLEDGE IN DAT HEAD, PROF. IT CROWDS OUT DA *MEMORY*!
WE'S DECIDIN' DA GROUPS FOR OUR ***SCHOOL TRIP*** T'DAY, PROF.
YEP! HEADING TO OKINAWA! SO GETTING ...
...THE RIGHT *GROUPS* WILL BE INSTRUMENTAL IN CREATING THE BEST POSSIBLE ***MEMORIES.***
Y-YEAH, I GUESS YOU'RE RIGHT.
AND NOW THAT YOU MENTION IT, IT'S ONLY A WEEK AWAY.

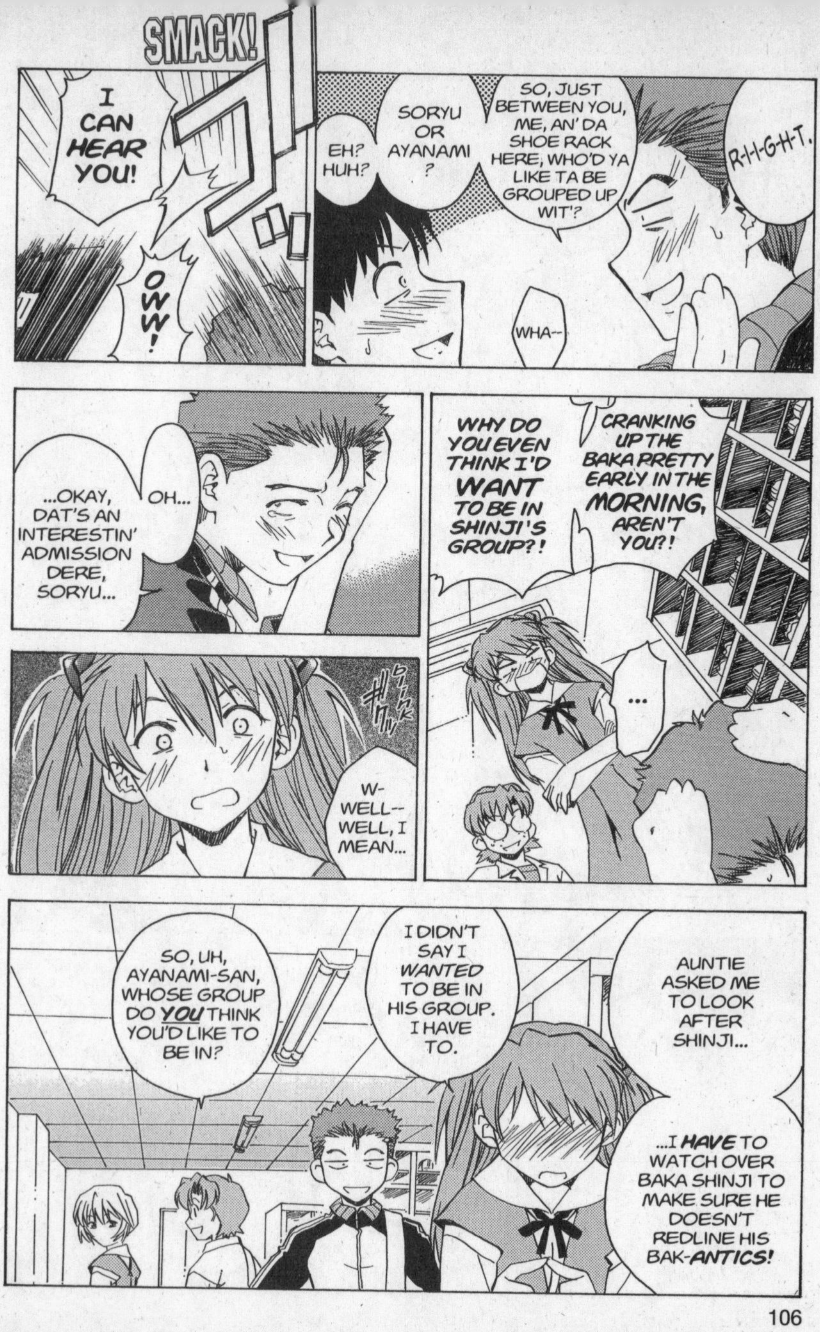
R-I-I-G-H-T.
SO, JUST BETWEEN YOU, ME, AN' DA SHOE RACK HERE, WHO'D YA LIKE TA BE GROUPED UP WIT'?
SORYU OR AYANAMI?
EH? HUH?
WHA--
SMACK!
I CAN HEAR YOU!
OWW!
CRANKING UP THE BAKA PRETTY EARLY IN THE MORNING, AREN'T YOU?!
WHY DO YOU EVEN THINK I'D WANT TO BE IN SHINJI'S GROUP?!
...
OH...
...OKAY, DAT'S AN INTERESTIN' ADMISSION DERE, SORYU...
W-WELL-- WELL, I MEAN...
I DIDN'T SAY I WANTED TO BE IN HIS GROUP. I HAVE TO.
AUNTIE ASKED ME TO LOOK AFTER SHINJI...
...I HAVE TO WATCH OVER BAKA SHINJI TO MAKE SURE HE DOESN'T REDLINE HIS BAK-ANTICS!
SO, UH, AYANAMI-SAN, WHOSE GROUP DO YOU THINK YOU'D LIKE TO BE IN?

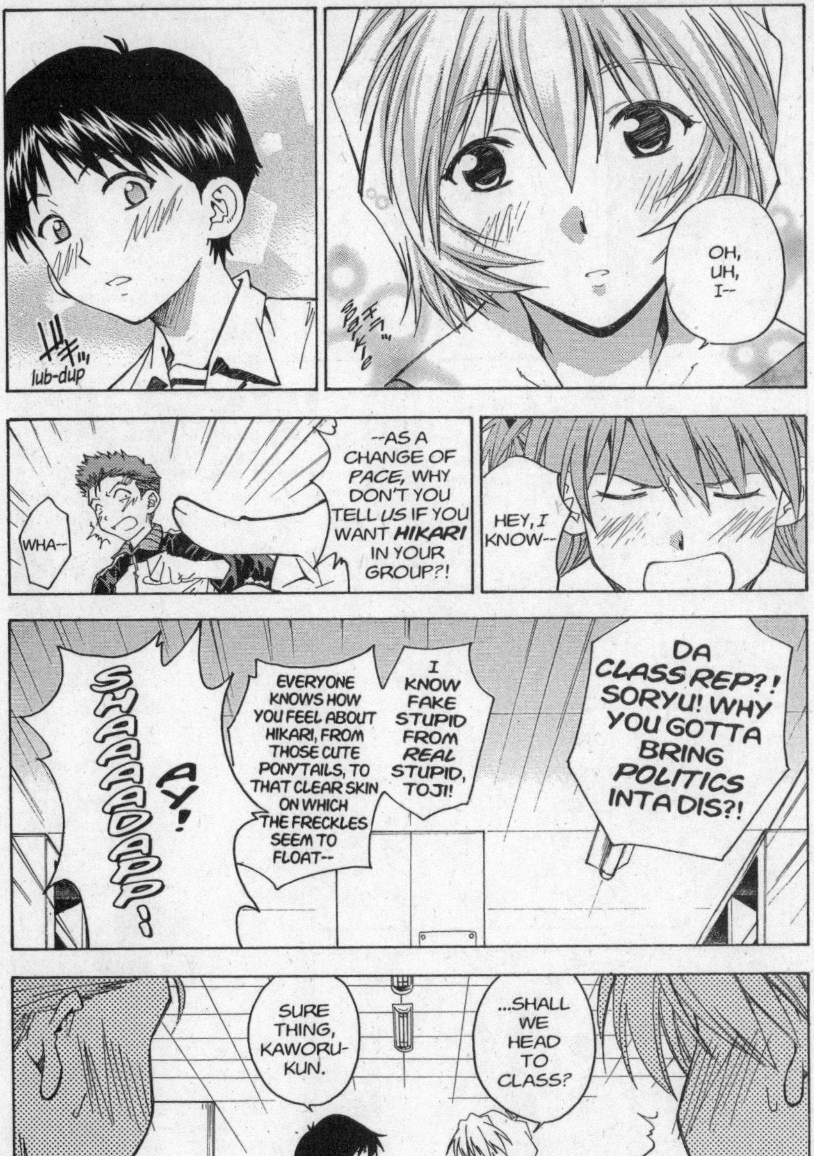
OH, UH, I--
lub-dup
HEY, I KNOW--
--AS A CHANGE OF PACE, WHY DON'T YOU TELL US IF YOU WANT HIKARI IN YOUR GROUP?!
WHA--
DA CLASS REP?! SORYU! WHY YOU GOTTA BRING POLITICS INTA DIS?!
I KNOW FAKE STUPID FROM REAL STUPID, TOJI!
EVERYONE KNOWS HOW YOU FEEL ABOUT HIKARI, FROM THOSE CUTE PONYTAILS, TO THAT CLEAR SKIN ON WHICH THE FRECKLES SEEM TO FLOAT--
AY!
SHAAAADAPP!
...SHALL WE HEAD TO CLASS?
SURE THING, KAWORU-KUN.

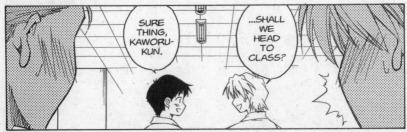

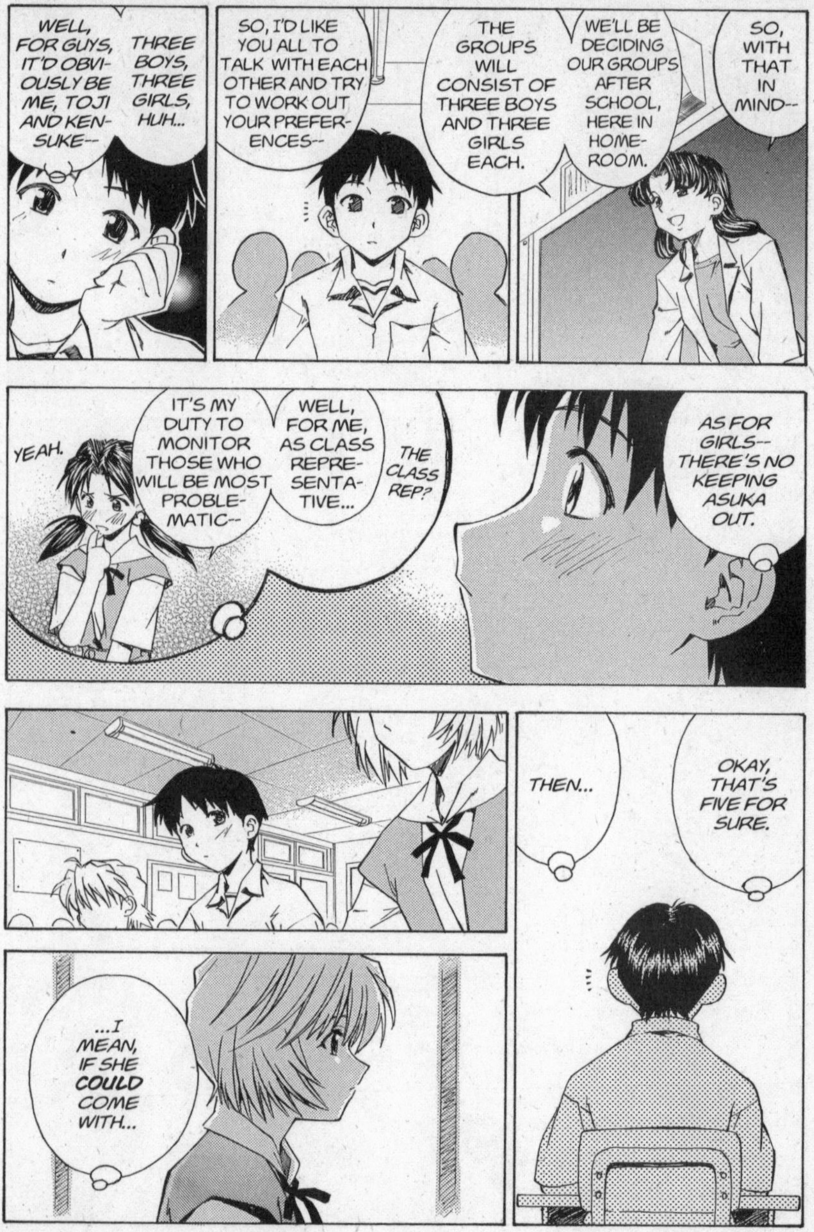
SO, WITH THAT IN MIND--
WE'LL BE DECIDING OUR GROUPS AFTER SCHOOL, HERE IN HOME-ROOM.
THE GROUPS WILL CONSIST OF THREE BOYS AND THREE GIRLS EACH.
SO, I'D LIKE YOU ALL TO TALK WITH EACH OTHER AND TRY TO WORK OUT YOUR PREFER-ENCES--
THREE BOYS, THREE GIRLS, HUH...
WELL, FOR GUYS, IT'D OBVI-OUSLY BE ME, TOJI AND KEN-SUKE--
AS FOR GIRLS-- THERE'S NO KEEPING ASUKA OUT.
THE CLASS REP?
WELL, FOR ME, AS CLASS REPRE-SENTA-TIVE...
IT'S MY DUTY TO MONITOR THOSE WHO WILL BE MOST PROBLE-MATIC--
YEAH.
OKAY, THAT'S FIVE FOR SURE.
THEN...
...I MEAN, IF SHE **COULD** COME WITH...

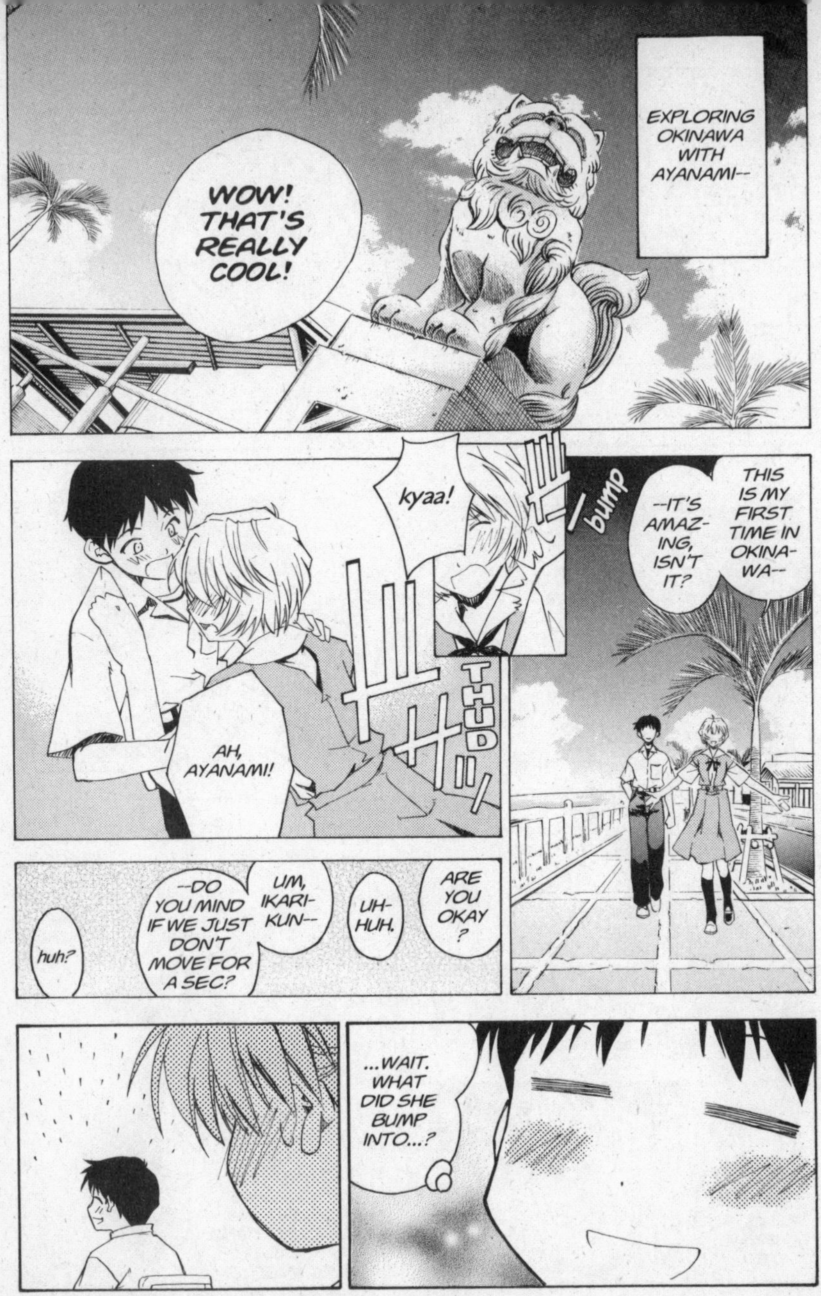
EXPLORING OKINAWA WITH AYANAMI--
WOW! THAT'S REALLY COOL!
THIS IS MY FIRST TIME IN OKINAWA--
--IT'S AMAZING, ISN'T IT?
bump
kyaa!
THUD
AH, AYANAMI!
ARE YOU OKAY?
UH-HUH.
UM, IKARI-KUN--
--DO YOU MIND IF WE JUST DON'T MOVE FOR A SEC?
huh?
...WAIT. WHAT DID SHE BUMP INTO...?

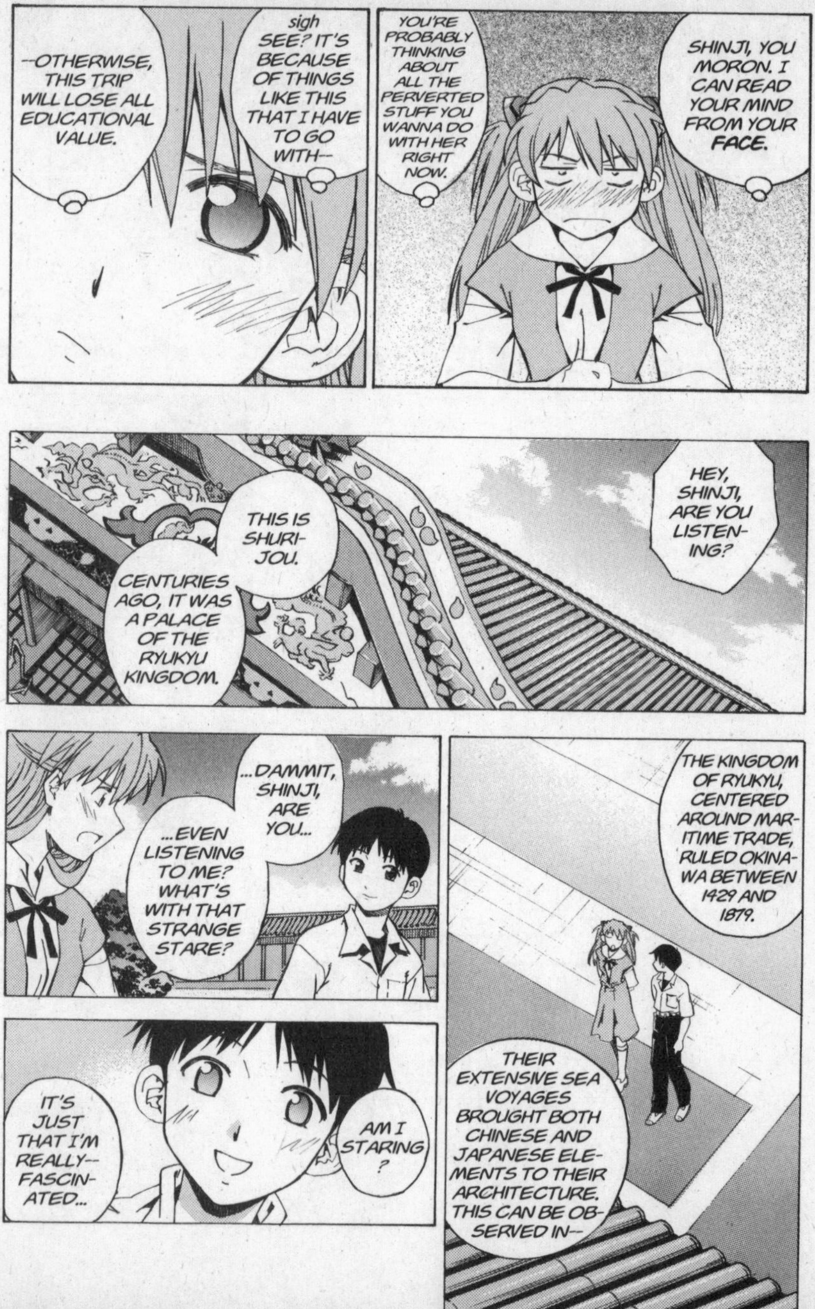
SHINJI, YOU MORON. I CAN READ YOUR MIND FROM YOUR **FACE.**
YOU'RE PROBABLY THINKING ABOUT ALL THE PERVERTED STUFF YOU WANNA DO WITH HER RIGHT NOW.
sigh SEE? IT'S BECAUSE OF THINGS LIKE THIS THAT I HAVE TO GO WITH--
--OTHERWISE, THIS TRIP WILL LOSE ALL EDUCATIONAL VALUE.
HEY, SHINJI, ARE YOU LISTENING?
THIS IS SHURI-JOU.
CENTURIES AGO, IT WAS A PALACE OF THE RYUKYU KINGDOM.
THE KINGDOM OF RYUKYU, CENTERED AROUND MARITIME TRADE, RULED OKINAWA BETWEEN 1429 AND 1879.
THEIR EXTENSIVE SEA VOYAGES BROUGHT BOTH CHINESE AND JAPANESE ELEMENTS TO THEIR ARCHITECTURE. THIS CAN BE OBSERVED IN--
...DAMMIT, SHINJI, ARE YOU...
...EVEN LISTENING TO ME? WHAT'S WITH THAT STRANGE STARE?
AM I STARING?
IT'S JUST THAT I'M REALLY--FASCINATED...

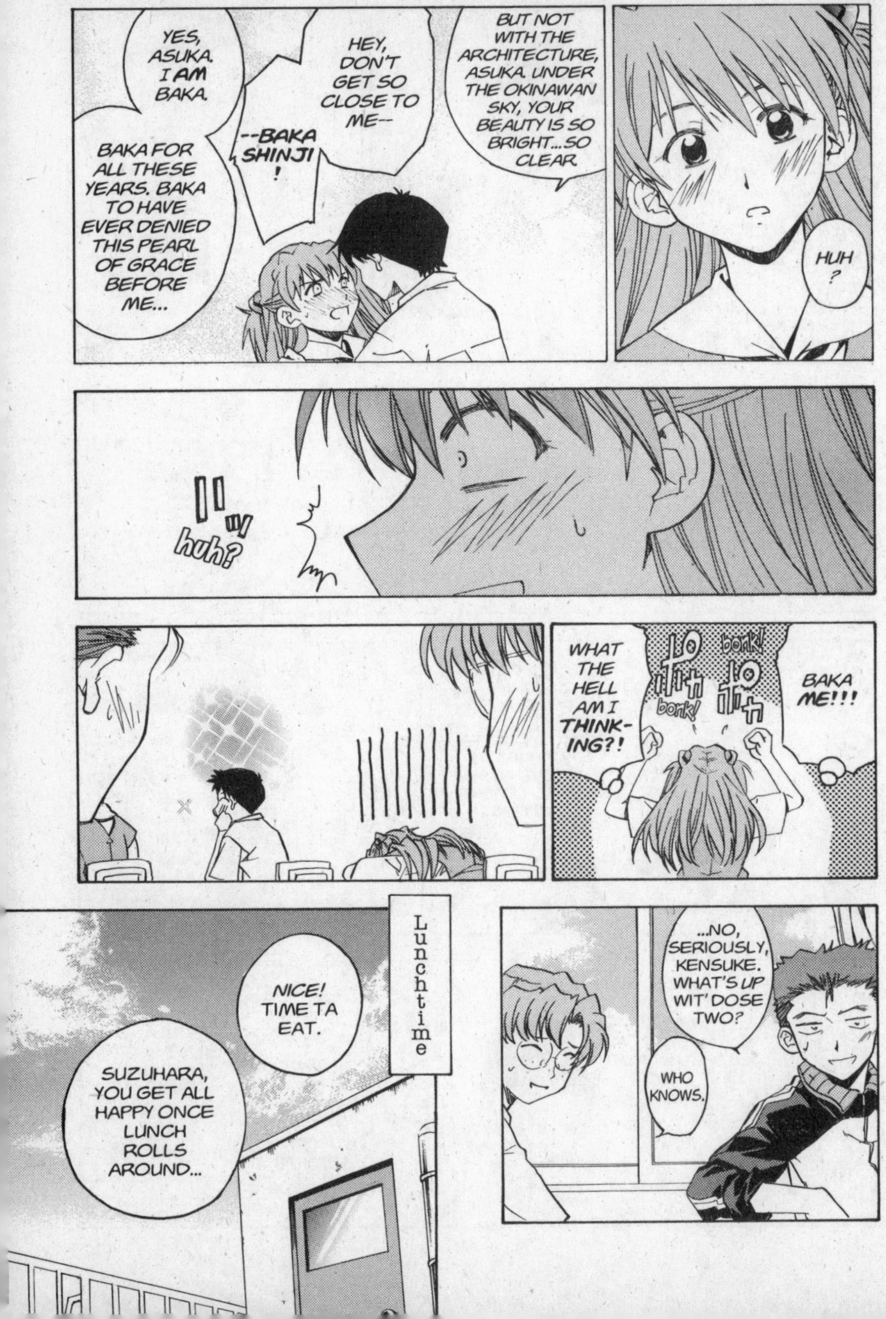
HUH ?
BUT NOT WITH THE ARCHITECTURE, ASUKA. UNDER THE OKINAWAN SKY, YOUR BEAUTY IS SO BRIGHT...SO CLEAR.
HEY, DON'T GET SO CLOSE TO ME--
--BAKA SHINJI !
YES, ASUKA. I **AM** BAKA.
BAKA FOR ALL THESE YEARS. BAKA TO HAVE EVER DENIED THIS PEARL OF GRACE BEFORE ME...
huh?
BAKA **ME!!!**
bonk!
bonk!
WHAT THE HELL AM I **THINKING?!**
...NO, SERIOUSLY, KENSUKE. WHAT'S UP WIT' DOSE TWO?
WHO KNOWS.
Lunchtime
NICE! TIME TA EAT.
SUZUHARA, YOU GET ALL HAPPY ONCE LUNCH ROLLS AROUND...

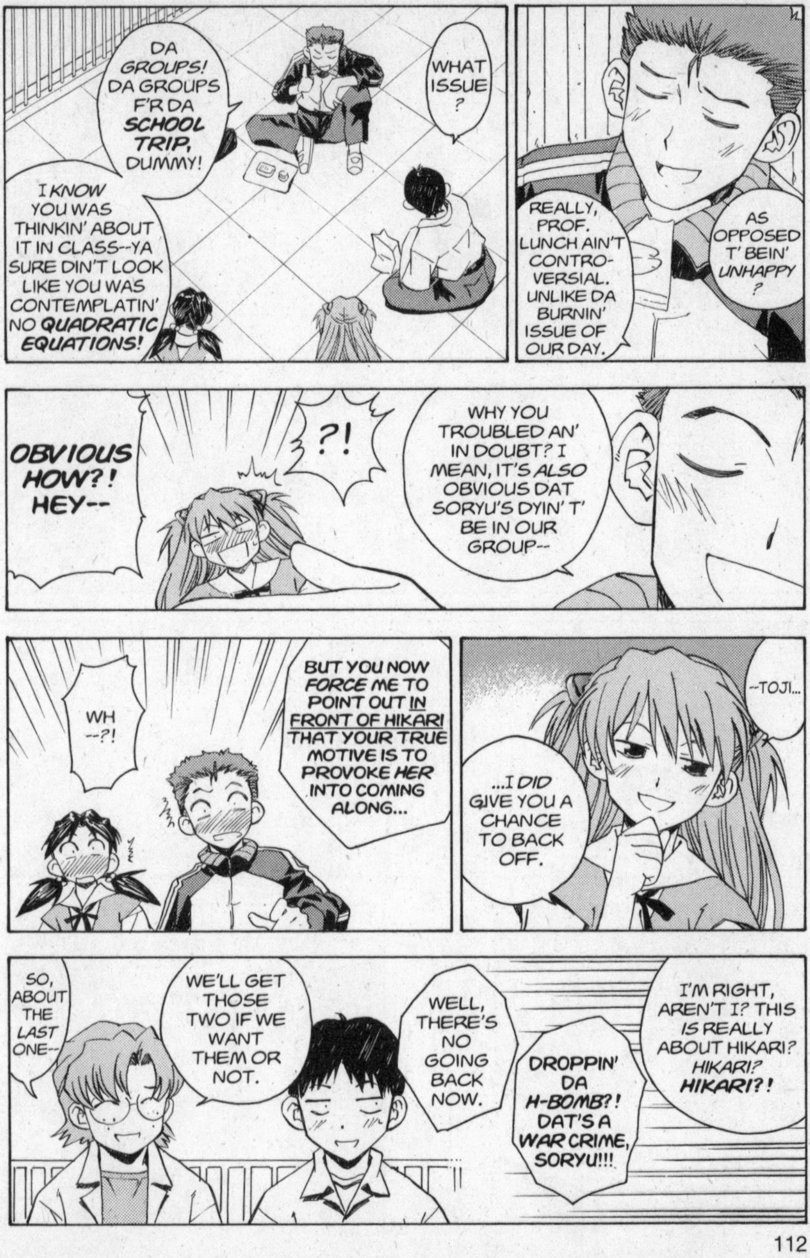
REALLY, PROF. LUNCH AIN'T CONTROVERSIAL. UNLIKE DA BURNIN' ISSUE OF OUR DAY.
AS OPPOSED T' BEIN' *UNHAPPY*?
WHAT ISSUE?
DA GROUPS! DA GROUPS F'R DA **SCHOOL TRIP,** DUMMY!
I KNOW YOU WAS THINKIN' ABOUT IT IN CLASS--YA SURE DIN'T LOOK LIKE YOU WAS CONTEMPLATIN' NO **QUADRATIC EQUATIONS!**
WHY YOU TROUBLED AN' IN DOUBT? I MEAN, IT'S *ALSO* OBVIOUS DAT SORYU'S DYIN' T' BE IN OUR GROUP--
?!
OBVIOUS HOW?! HEY--
--TOJI...
...I *DID* GIVE YOU A CHANCE TO BACK OFF.
BUT YOU NOW *FORCE* ME TO POINT OUT IN FRONT OF HIKARI THAT YOUR TRUE MOTIVE IS TO PROVOKE *HER* INTO COMING ALONG...
WH--?!
I'M RIGHT, AREN'T I? THIS *IS* REALLY ABOUT HIKARI? HIKARI? **HIKARI?!**
DROPPIN' DA *H-BOMB*?! DAT'S A *WAR* CRIME, SORYU!!!
WELL, THERE'S NO GOING BACK NOW.
WE'LL GET THOSE TWO IF WE WANT THEM OR NOT.
SO, ABOUT THE *LAST* ONE--

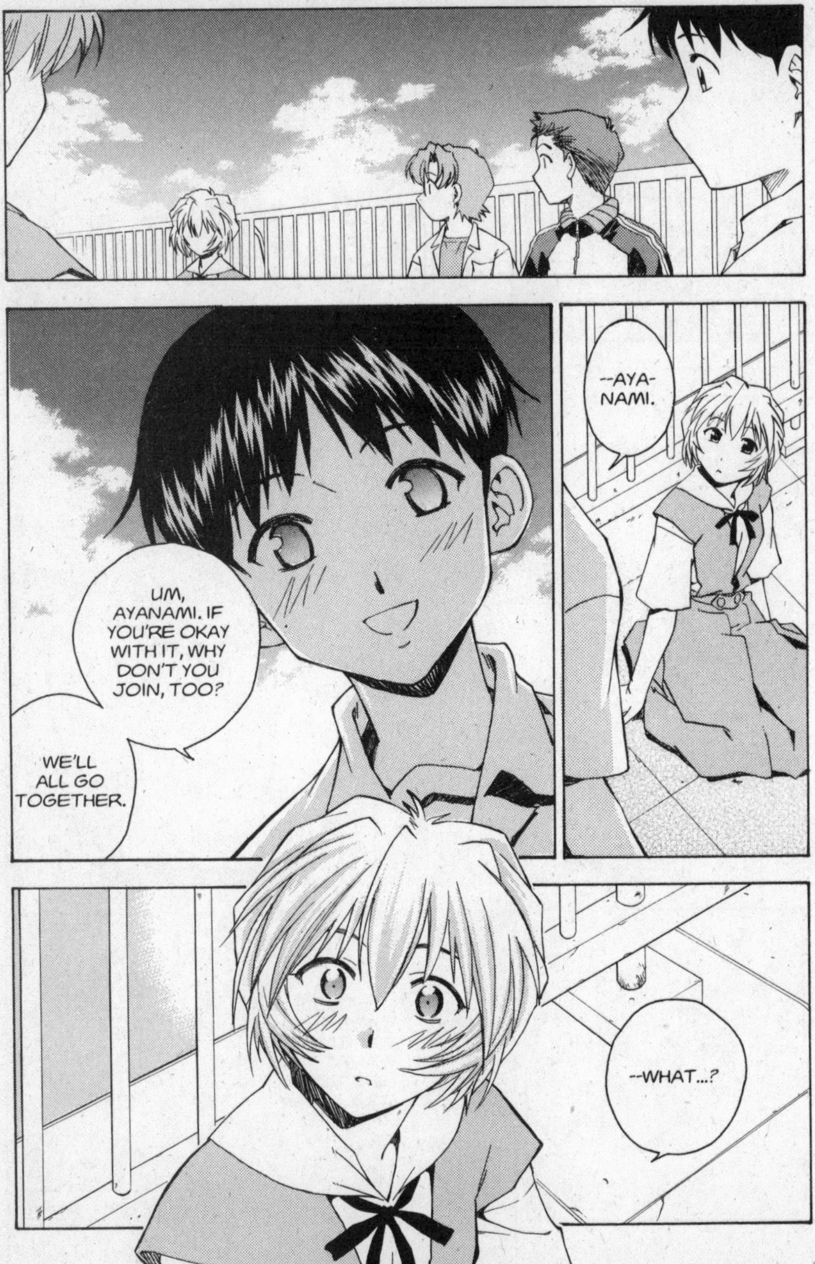
--AYA-NAMI.
UM, AYANAMI. IF YOU'RE OKAY WITH IT, WHY DON'T YOU JOIN, TOO?
WE'LL ALL GO TOGETHER.
--WHAT...?

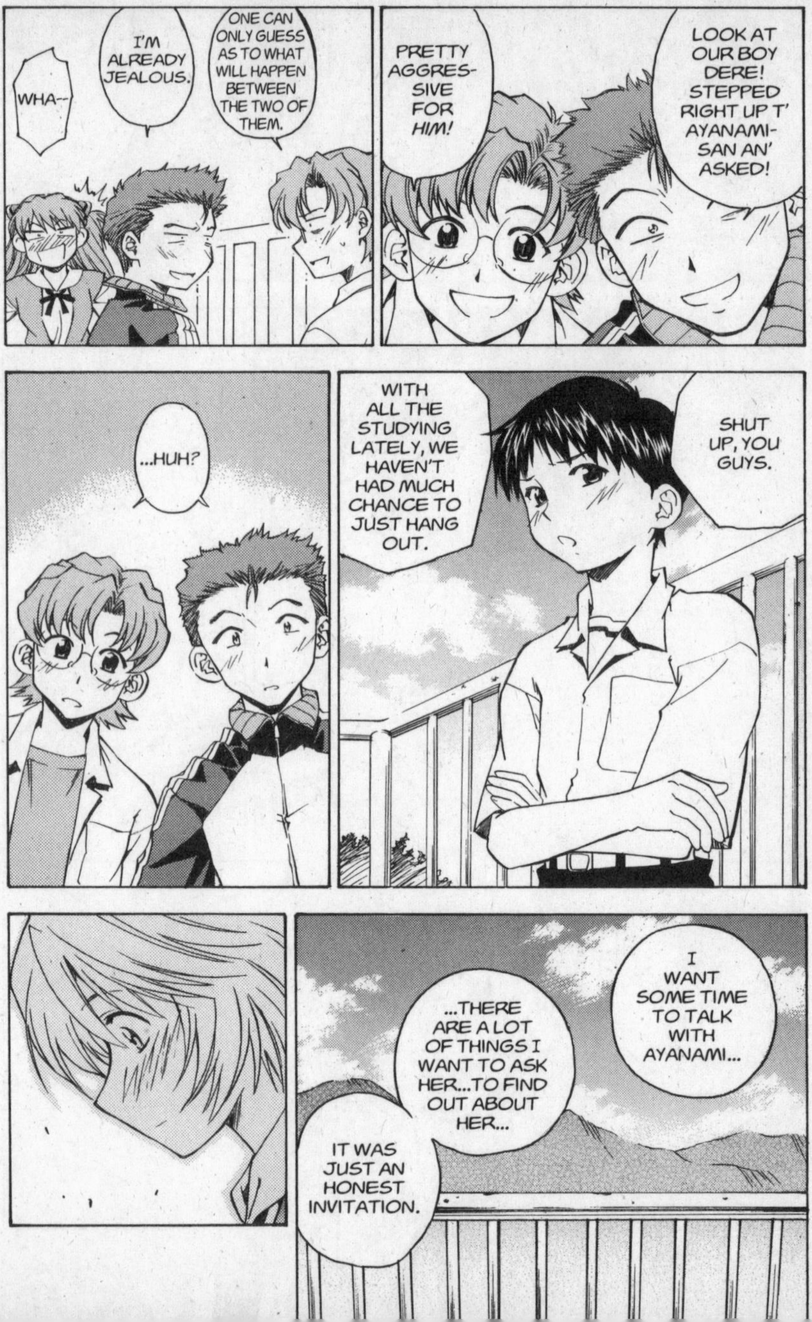

LOOK AT OUR BOY DERE! STEPPED RIGHT UP T' AYANAMI-SAN AN' ASKED!
PRETTY AGGRES-SIVE FOR HIM!
ONE CAN ONLY GUESS AS TO WHAT WILL HAPPEN BETWEEN THE TWO OF THEM.
I'M ALREADY JEALOUS.
WHA--
SHUT UP, YOU GUYS.
WITH ALL THE STUDYING LATELY, WE HAVEN'T HAD MUCH CHANCE TO JUST HANG OUT.
...HUH?
I WANT SOME TIME TO TALK WITH AYANAMI...
...THERE ARE A LOT OF THINGS I WANT TO ASK HER...TO FIND OUT ABOUT HER...
IT WAS JUST AN HONEST INVITATION.

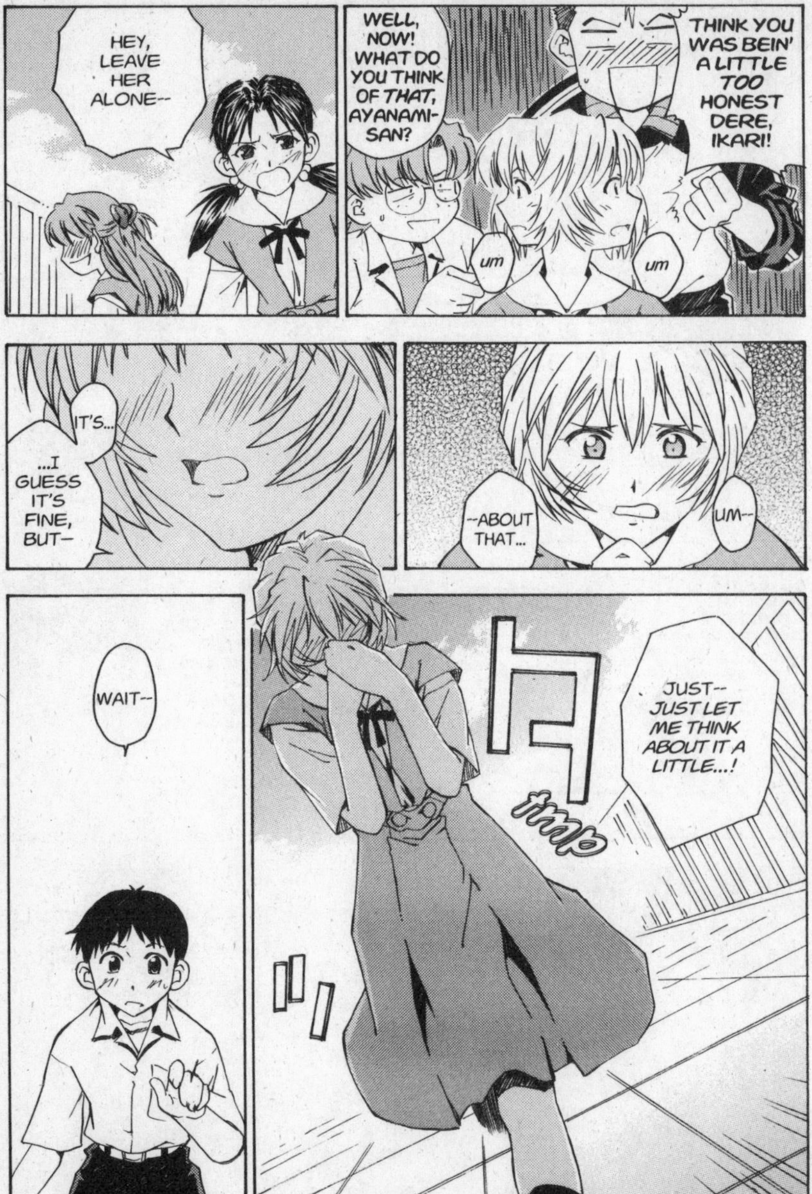
THINK YOU WAS BEIN' A LITTLE *TOO* HONEST DERE, IKARI!
WELL, NOW! WHAT DO YOU THINK OF *THAT*, AYANAMI-SAN?
um
um
HEY, LEAVE HER ALONE--
UM--
--ABOUT THAT...
IT'S...
...I GUESS IT'S FINE, BUT--
JUST-- JUST LET ME THINK ABOUT IT A LITTLE...!
tmp
WAIT--

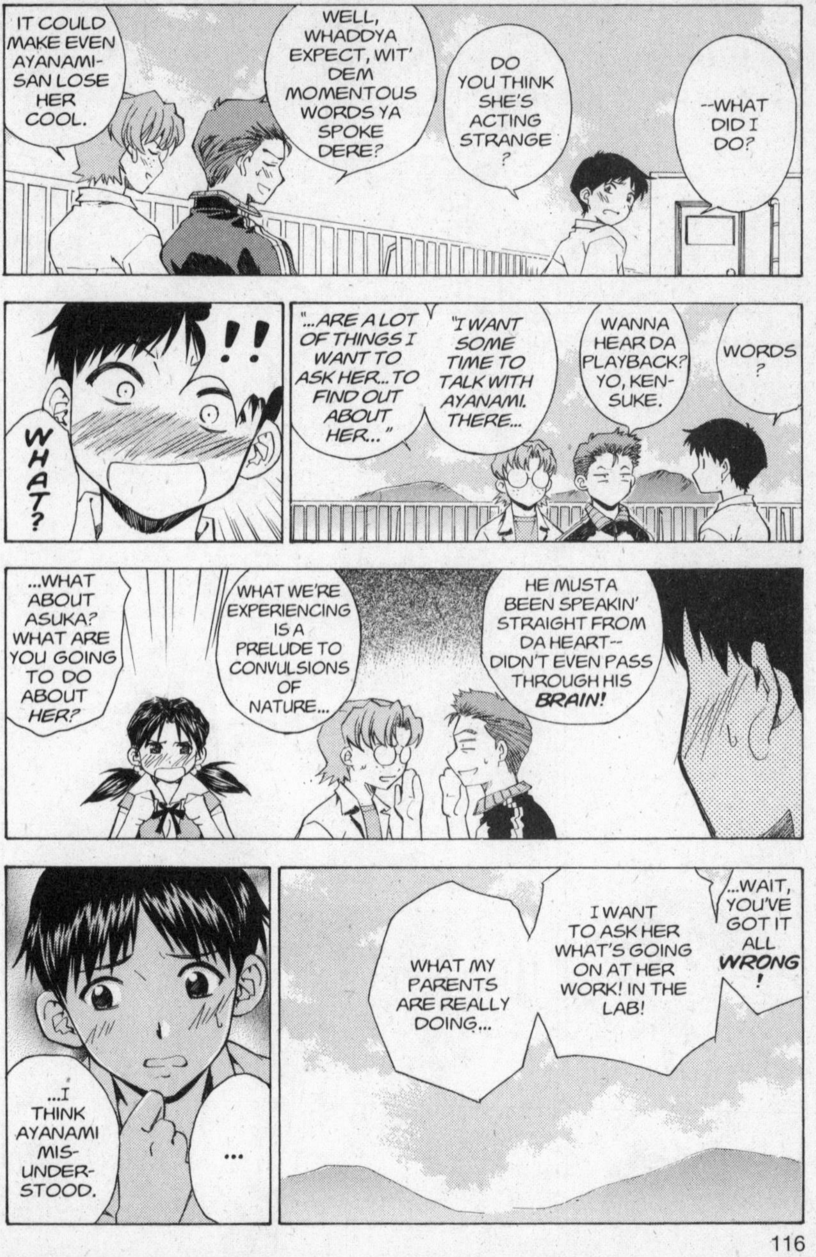
--WHAT DID I DO?
DO YOU THINK SHE'S ACTING STRANGE?
WELL, WHADDYA EXPECT, WIT' DEM MOMENTOUS WORDS YA SPOKE DERE?
IT COULD MAKE EVEN AYANAMI-SAN LOSE HER COOL.
WORDS?
WANNA HEAR DA PLAYBACK? YO, KEN-SUKE.
"I WANT SOME TIME TO TALK WITH AYANAMI. THERE...
"...ARE A LOT OF THINGS I WANT TO ASK HER...TO FIND OUT ABOUT HER..."
!!
WHAT?
HE MUSTA BEEN SPEAKIN' STRAIGHT FROM DA HEART--DIDN'T EVEN PASS THROUGH HIS **BRAIN!**
WHAT WE'RE EXPERIENCING IS A PRELUDE TO CONVULSIONS OF NATURE...
...WHAT ABOUT ASUKA? WHAT ARE YOU GOING TO DO ABOUT HER?
...WAIT, YOU'VE GOT IT ALL **WRONG!**
I WANT TO ASK HER WHAT'S GOING ON AT HER WORK! IN THE LAB!
WHAT MY PARENTS ARE REALLY DOING...
...
...I THINK AYANAMI MIS-UNDER-STOOD.

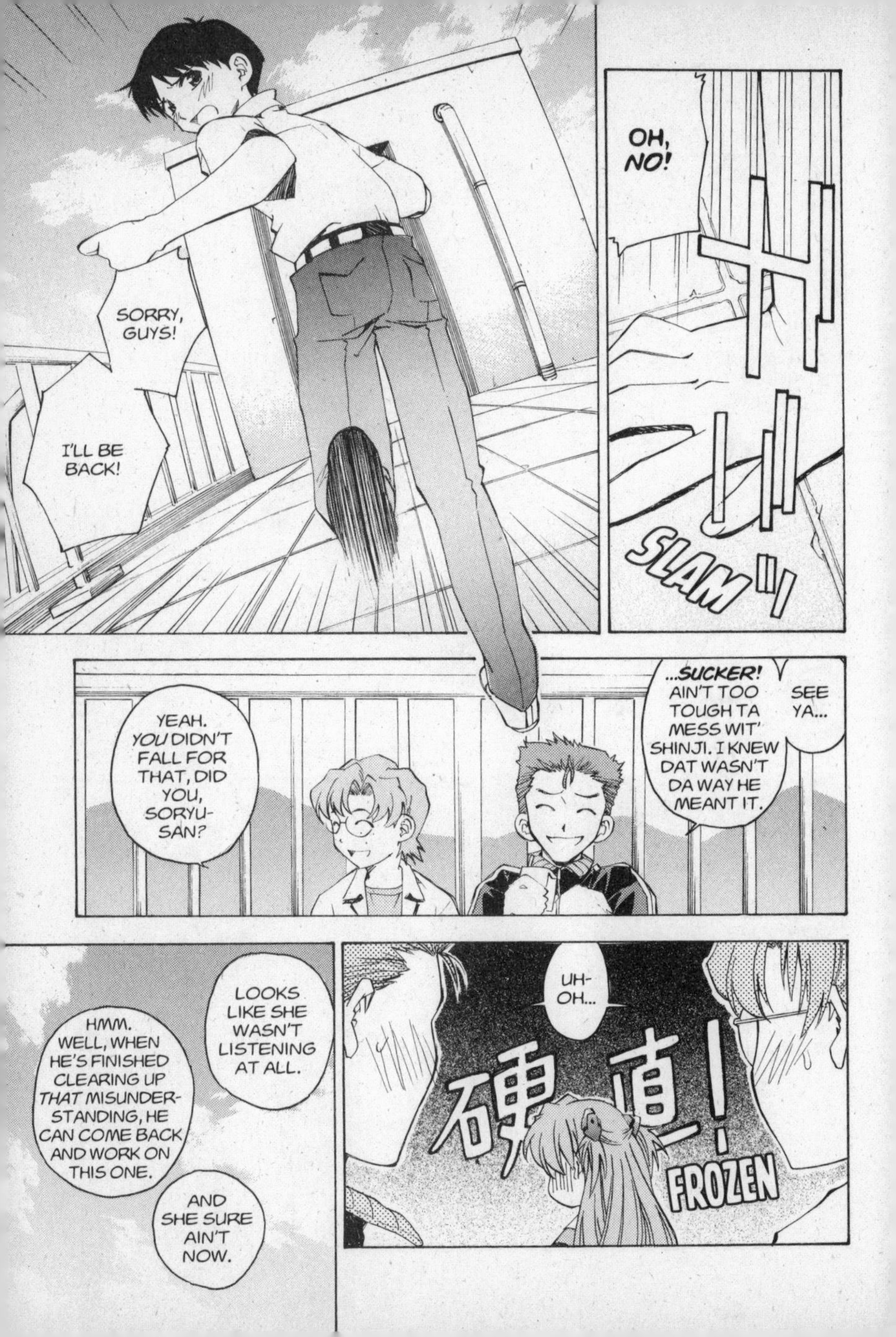
OH, NO!
SLAM
SORRY, GUYS!
I'LL BE BACK!
SEE YA...
...SUCKER! AIN'T TOO TOUGH TA MESS WIT' SHINJI. I KNEW DAT WASN'T DA WAY HE MEANT IT.
YEAH. YOU DIDN'T FALL FOR THAT, DID YOU, SORYU-SAN?
UH-OH...
硬直!
FROZEN
LOOKS LIKE SHE WASN'T LISTENING AT ALL.
HMM. WELL, WHEN HE'S FINISHED CLEARING UP THAT MISUNDER-STANDING, HE CAN COME BACK AND WORK ON THIS ONE.
AND SHE SURE AIN'T NOW.

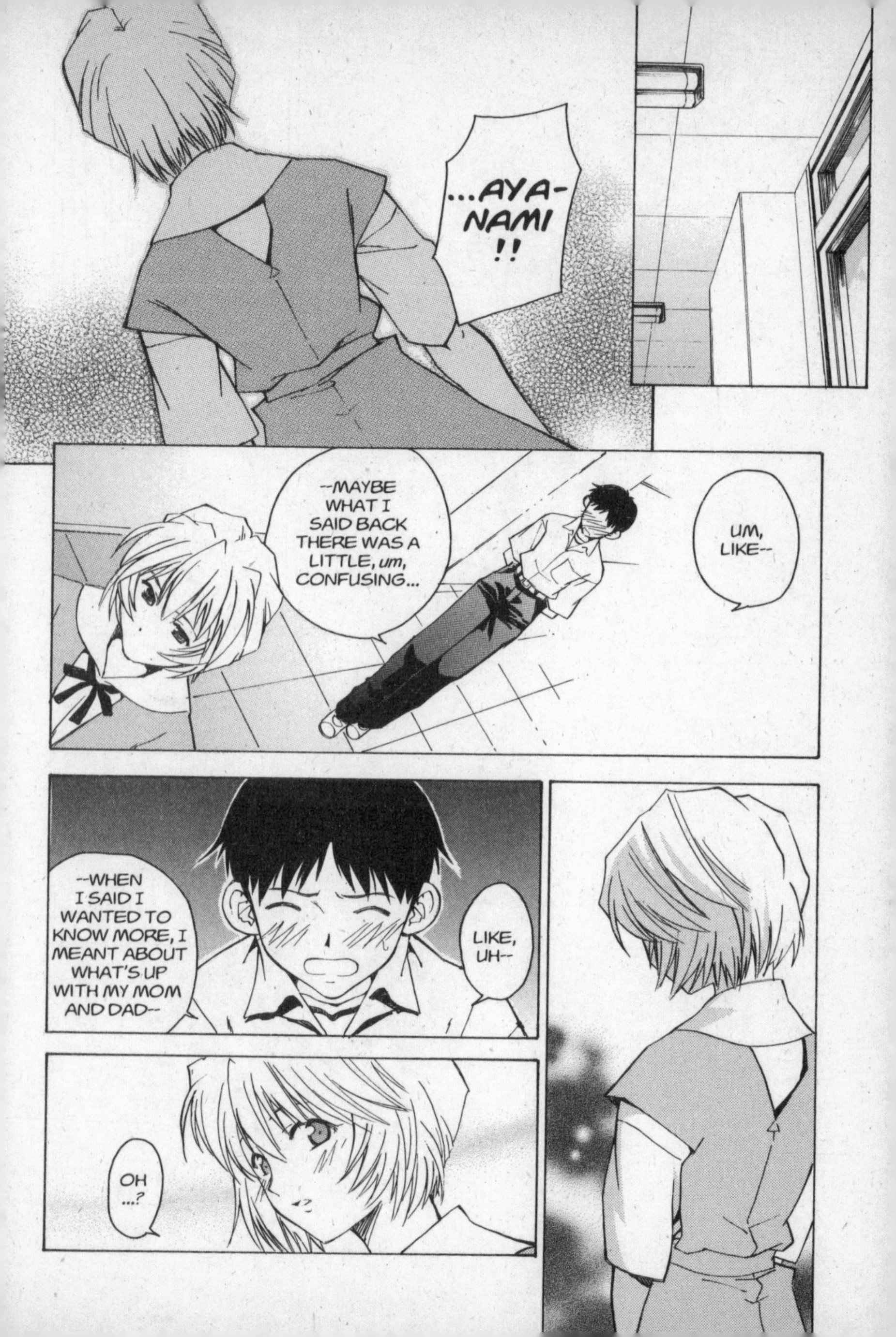
...AYA-NAMI !!
UM, LIKE--
--MAYBE WHAT I SAID BACK THERE WAS A LITTLE, *um*, CONFUSING...
LIKE, UH--
--WHEN I SAID I WANTED TO KNOW MORE, I MEANT ABOUT WHAT'S UP WITH MY MOM AND DAD--
OH ...?

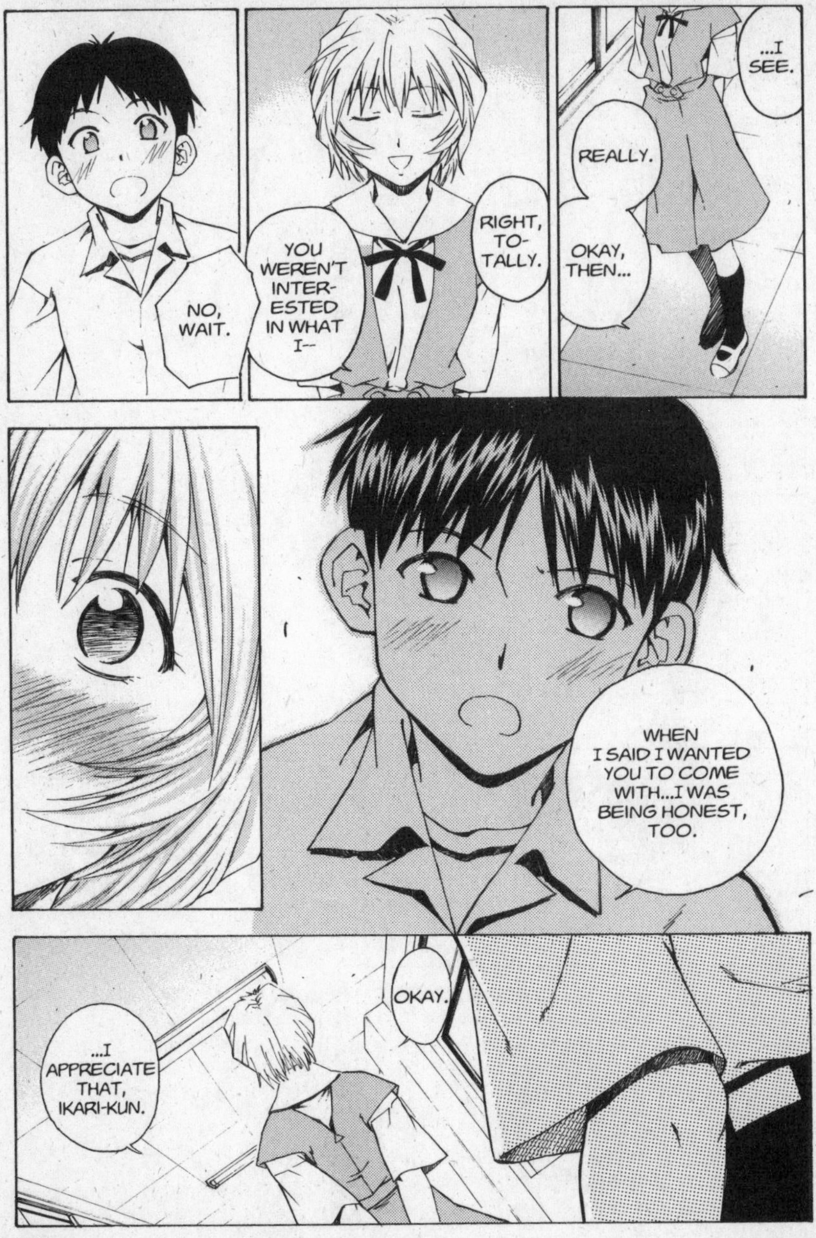
...I SEE.
REALLY.
OKAY, THEN...
RIGHT, TO-TALLY.
YOU WEREN'T INTER-ESTED IN WHAT I--
NO, WAIT.
WHEN I SAID I WANTED YOU TO COME WITH...I WAS BEING HONEST, TOO.
OKAY.
...I APPRECIATE THAT, IKARI-KUN.

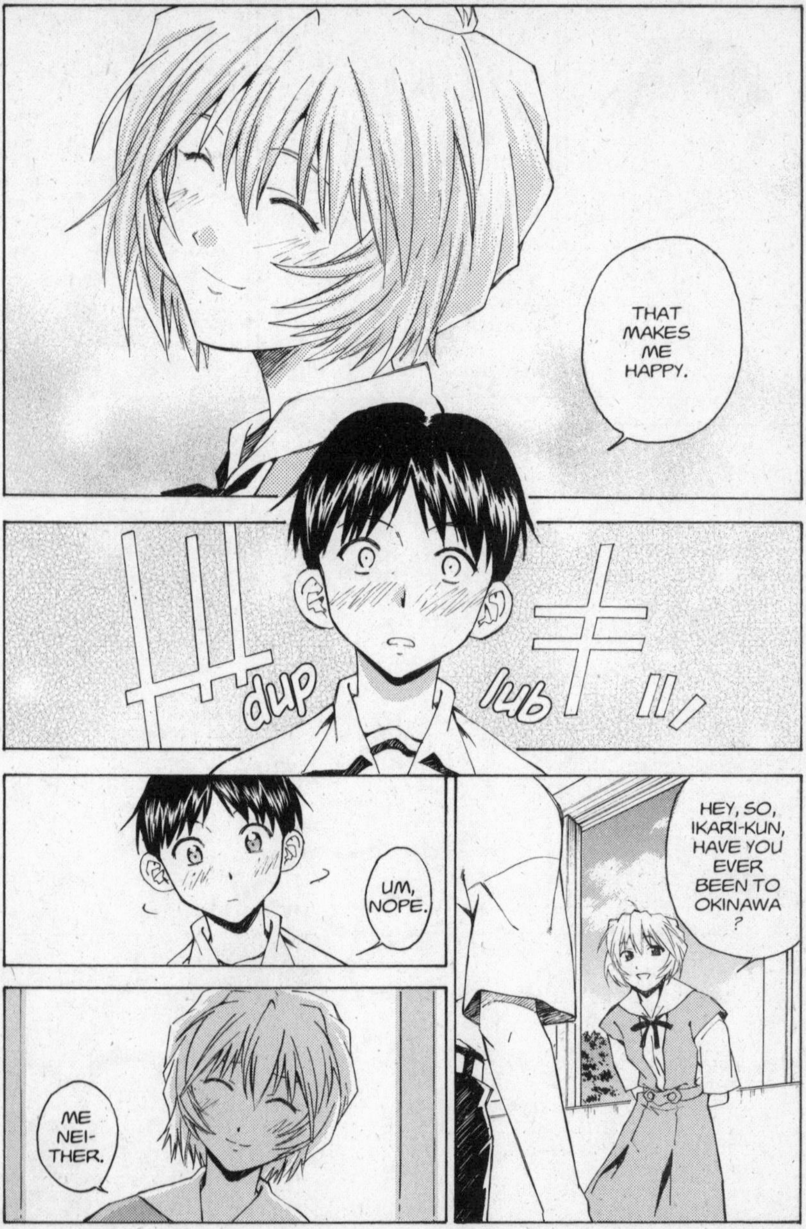
THAT MAKES ME HAPPY.
lub
dup
HEY, SO, IKARI-KUN, HAVE YOU EVER BEEN TO OKINAWA?
UM, NOPE.
ME NEI-THER.

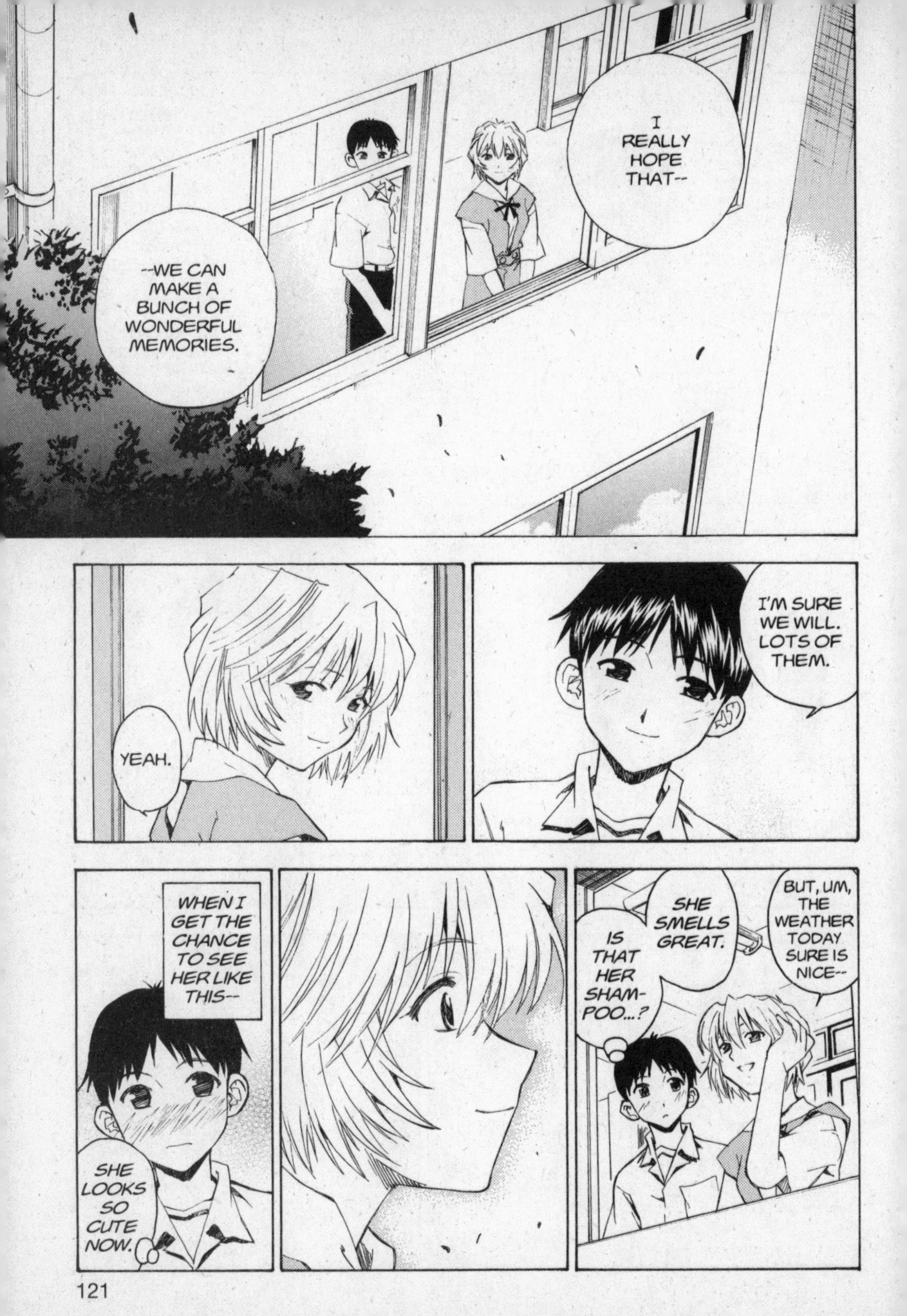
I REALLY HOPE THAT--
--WE CAN MAKE A BUNCH OF WONDERFUL MEMORIES.
I'M SURE WE WILL. LOTS OF THEM.
YEAH.
BUT, UM, THE WEATHER TODAY SURE IS NICE--
SHE SMELLS GREAT.
IS THAT HER SHAM-POO...?
WHEN I GET THE CHANCE TO SEE HER LIKE THIS--
SHE LOOKS SO CUTE NOW.

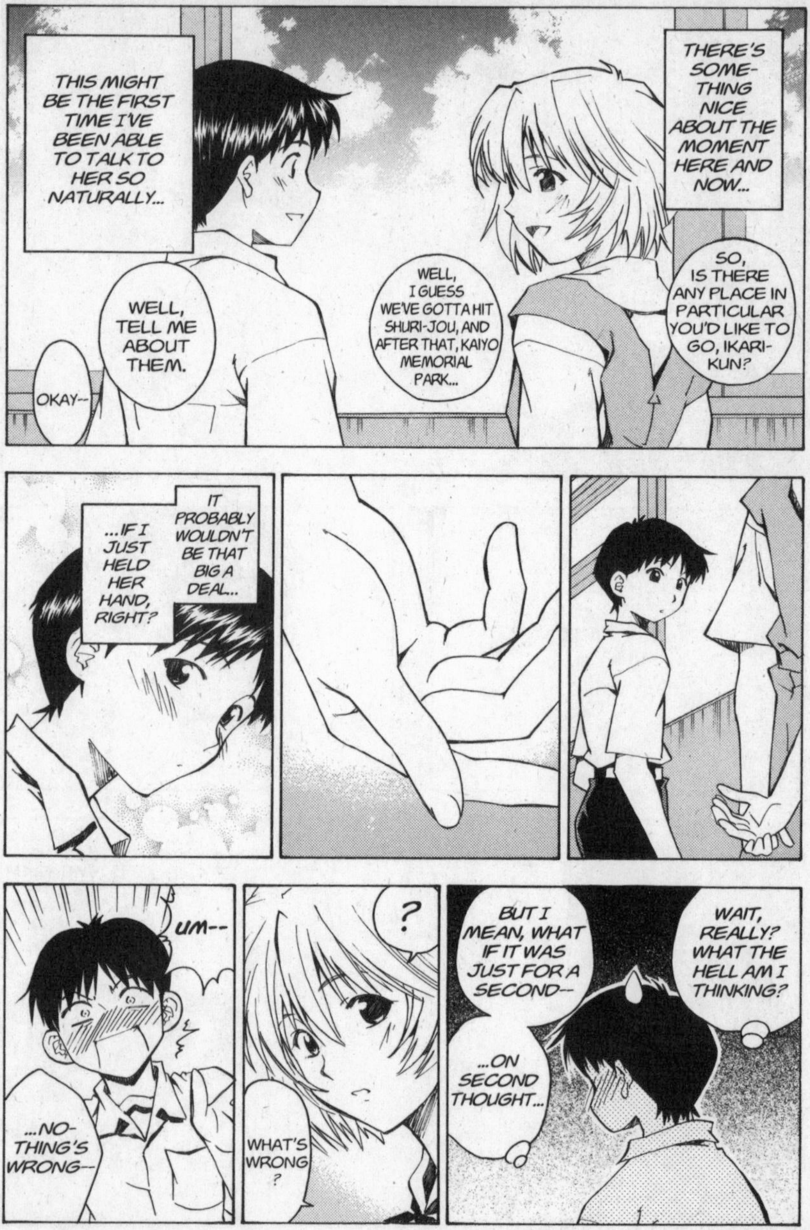
THERE'S SOMETHING NICE ABOUT THE MOMENT HERE AND NOW...
THIS MIGHT BE THE FIRST TIME I'VE BEEN ABLE TO TALK TO HER SO NATURALLY...
SO, IS THERE ANY PLACE IN PARTICULAR YOU'D LIKE TO GO, IKARI-KUN?
WELL, I GUESS WE'VE GOTTA HIT SHURI-JOU, AND AFTER THAT, KAIYO MEMORIAL PARK...
WELL, TELL ME ABOUT THEM.
OKAY--
IT PROBABLY WOULDN'T BE THAT BIG A DEAL...
...IF I JUST HELD HER HAND, RIGHT?
WAIT, REALLY? WHAT THE HELL AM I THINKING?
BUT I MEAN, WHAT IF IT WAS JUST FOR A SECOND--
...ON SECOND THOUGHT...
?
WHAT'S WRONG?
UM--
...NOTHING'S WRONG--

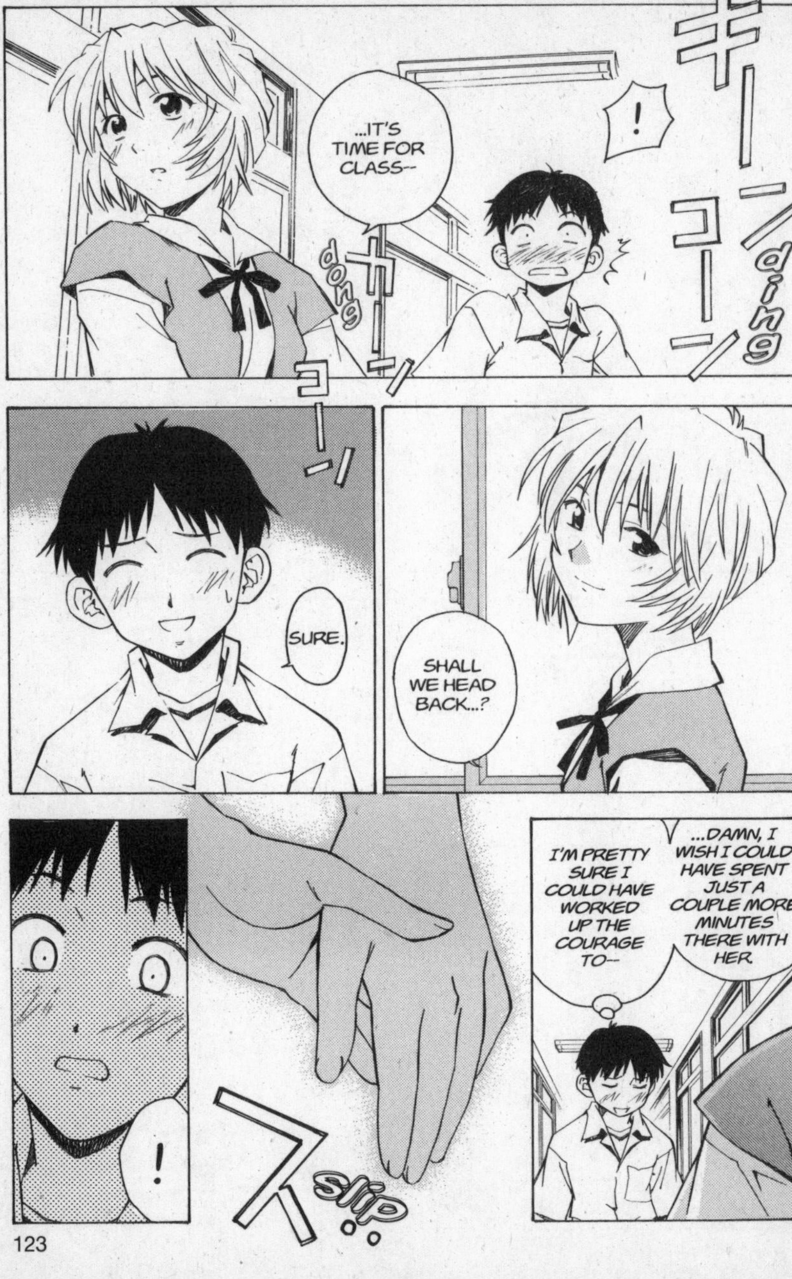
ding
!
...IT'S TIME FOR CLASS--
dong
SHALL WE HEAD BACK...?
SURE.
...DAMN, I WISH I COULD HAVE SPENT JUST A COUPLE MORE MINUTES THERE WITH HER.
I'M PRETTY SURE I COULD HAVE WORKED UP THE COURAGE TO--
slip
!

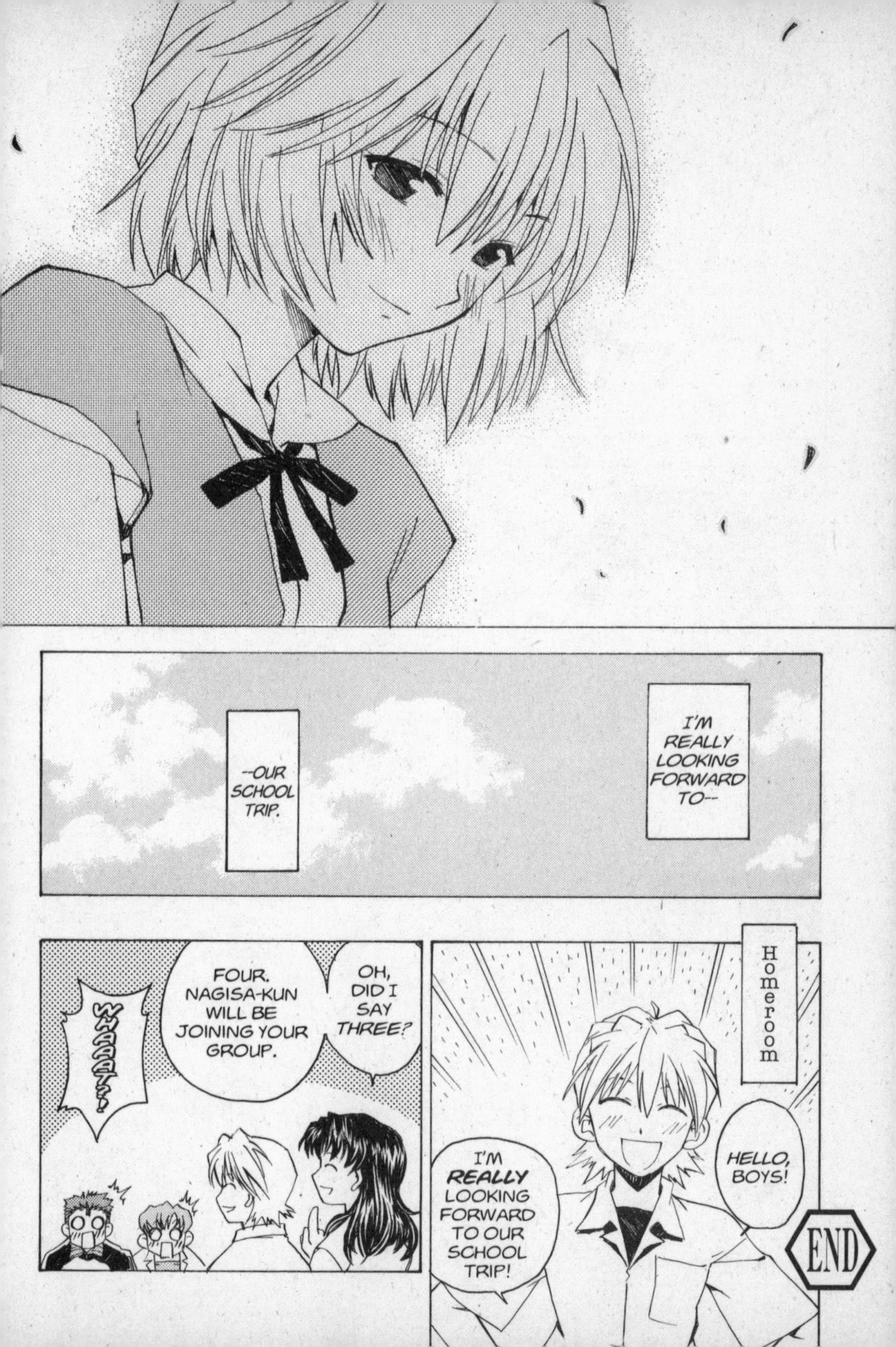
I'M REALLY LOOKING FORWARD TO--
--OUR SCHOOL TRIP.
Homeroom
HELLO, BOYS!
I'M REALLY LOOKING FORWARD TO OUR SCHOOL TRIP!
END
OH, DID I SAY THREE?
FOUR. NAGISA-KUN WILL BE JOINING YOUR GROUP.
WHAAAAT?!

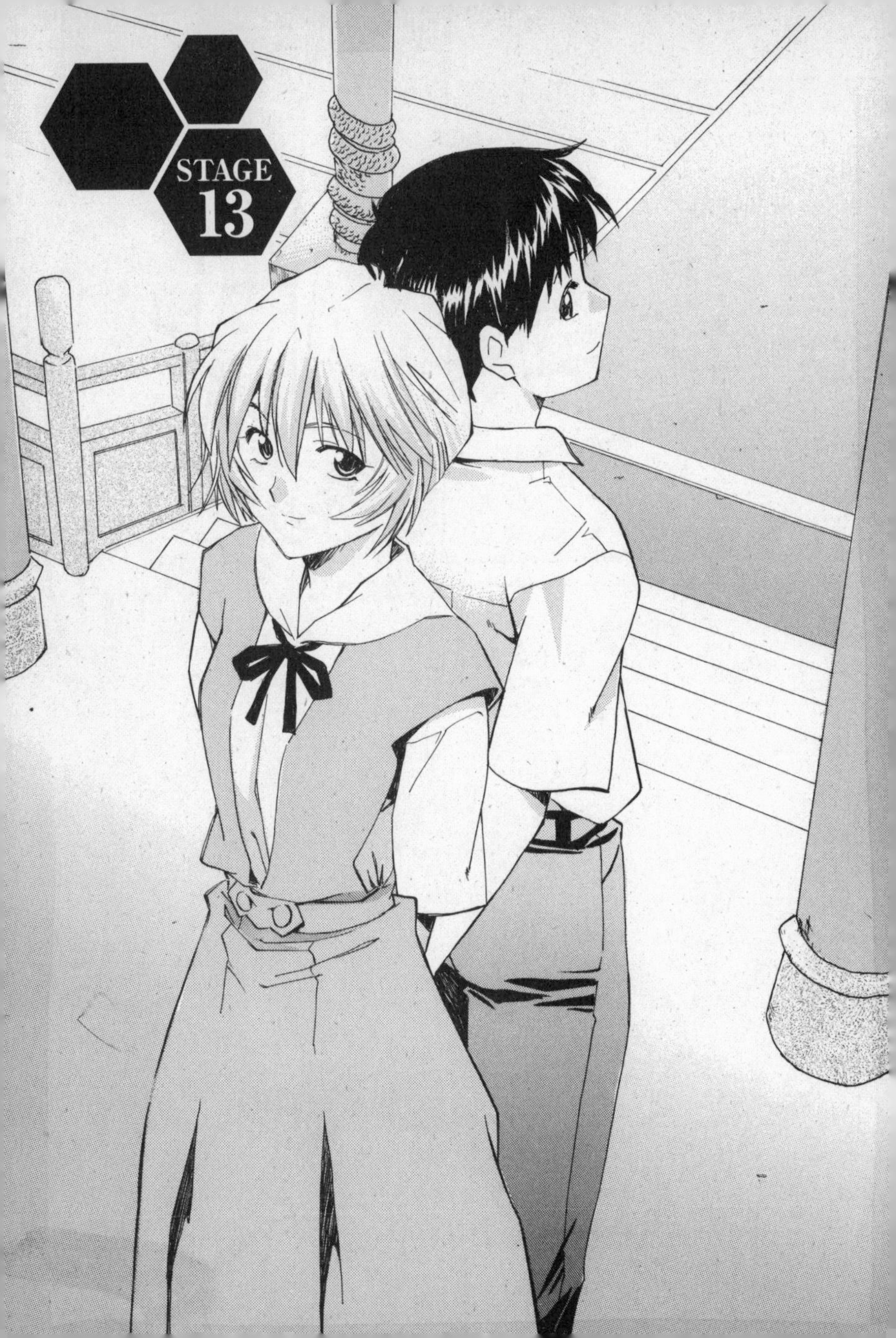
STAGE
13

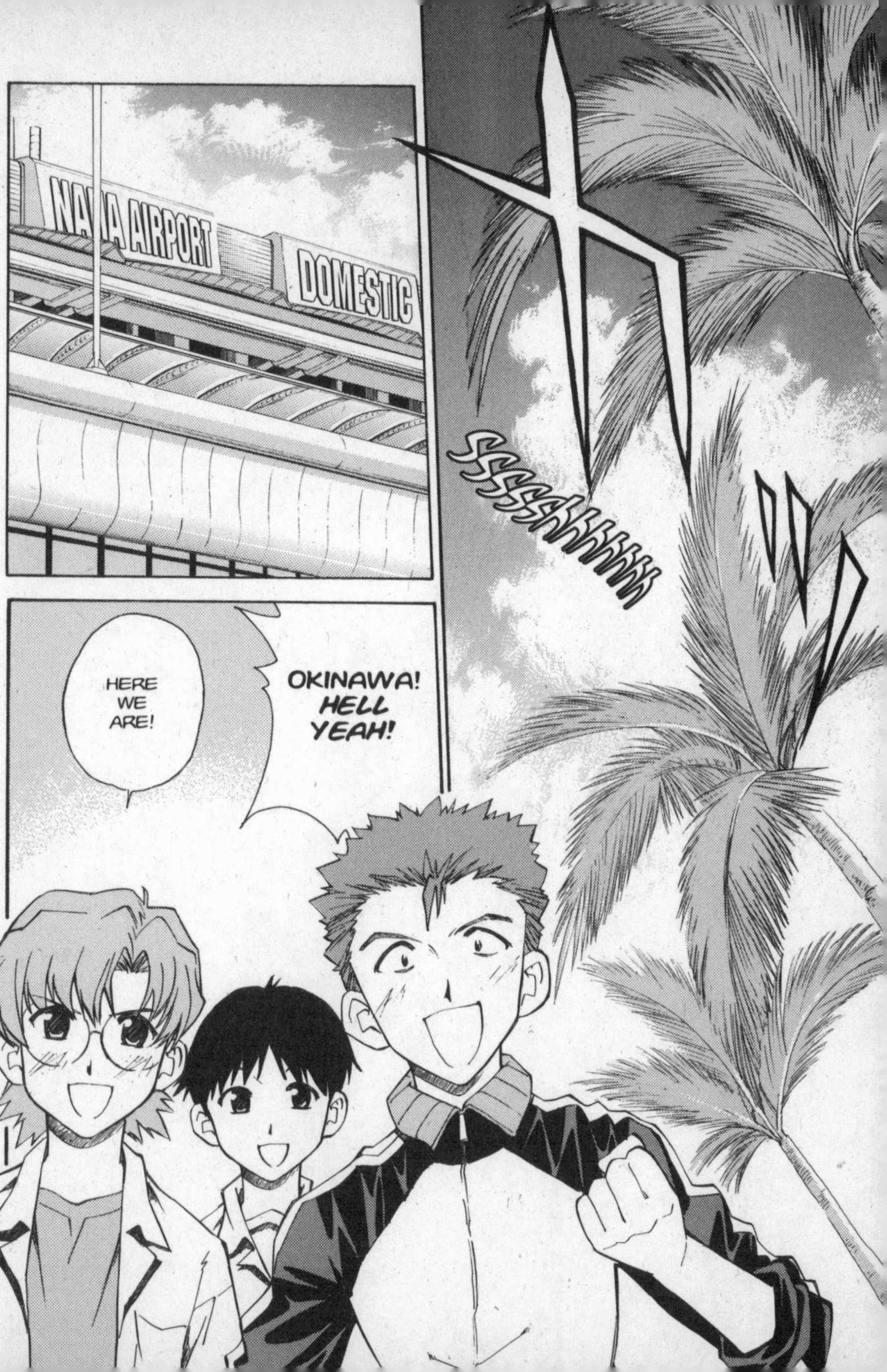
SSSSSHHHHHK
NAHA AIRPORT
DOMESTIC
HERE WE ARE!
OKINAWA! HELL YEAH!

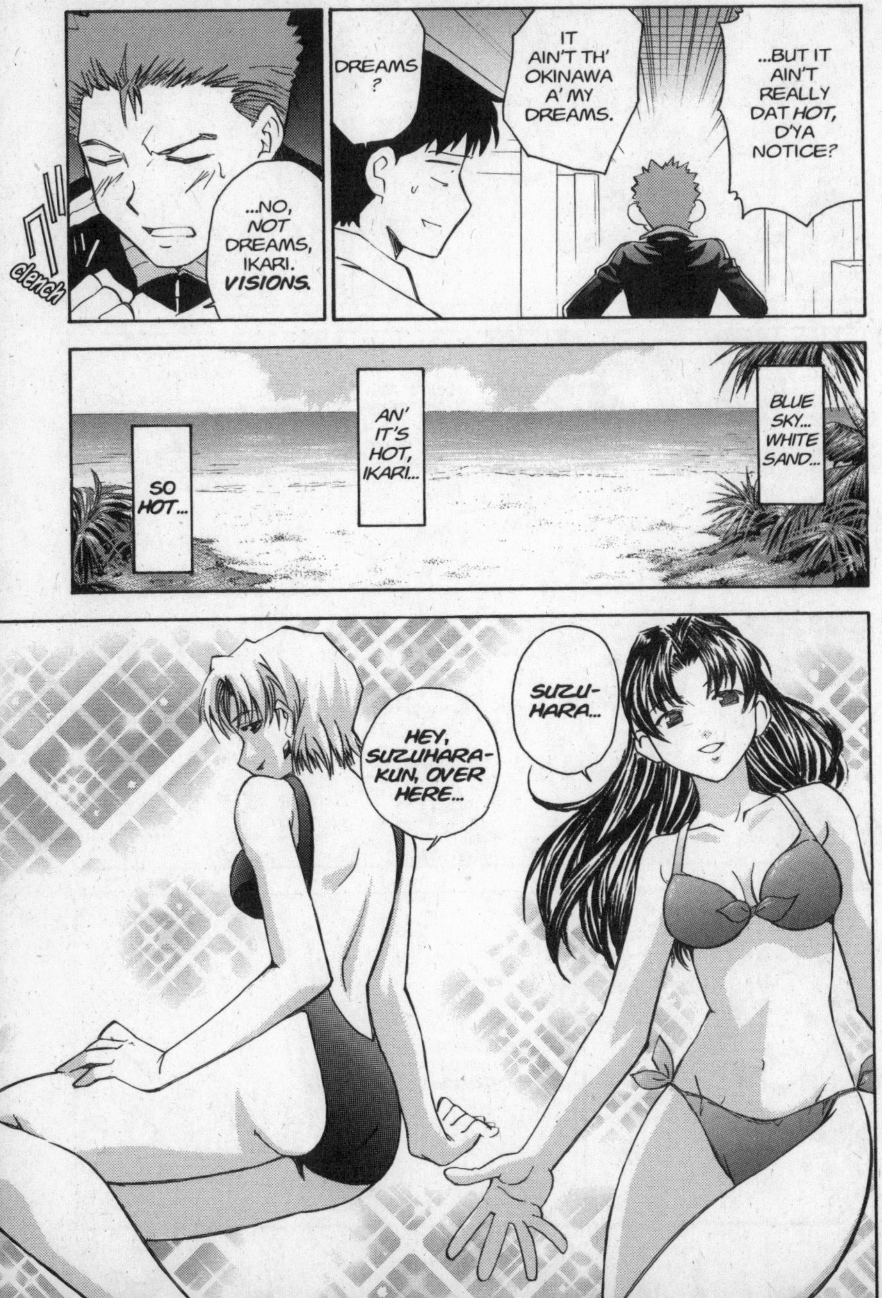
...BUT IT AIN'T REALLY DAT HOT, D'YA NOTICE?
IT AIN'T TH' OKINAWA A' MY DREAMS.
DREAMS?
...NO, NOT DREAMS, IKARI. VISIONS.
clench
BLUE SKY... WHITE SAND...
AN' IT'S HOT, IKARI...
SO HOT...
SUZU-HARA...
HEY, SUZUHARA-KUN, OVER HERE...

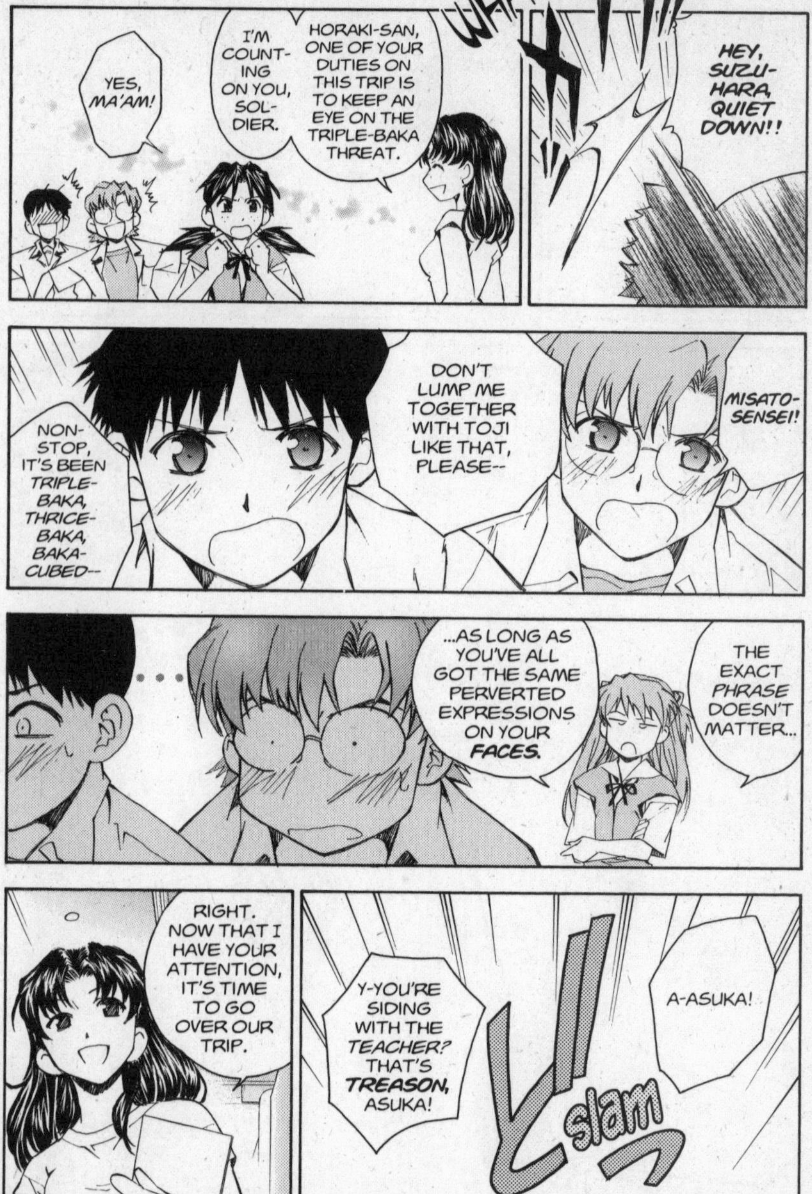
WHACK!
HEY, SUZUHARA, QUIET DOWN!!
HORAKI-SAN, ONE OF YOUR DUTIES ON THIS TRIP IS TO KEEP AN EYE ON THE TRIPLE-BAKA THREAT.
I'M COUNTING ON YOU, SOLDIER.
YES, MA'AM!
MISATO-SENSEI!
DON'T LUMP ME TOGETHER WITH TOJI LIKE THAT, PLEASE--
NON-STOP, IT'S BEEN TRIPLE-BAKA, THRICE-BAKA, BAKA-CUBED--
THE EXACT PHRASE DOESN'T MATTER...
...AS LONG AS YOU'VE ALL GOT THE SAME PERVERTED EXPRESSIONS ON YOUR FACES.
• • •
A-ASUKA!
Y-YOU'RE SIDING WITH THE TEACHER? THAT'S TREASON, ASUKA!
slam
RIGHT. NOW THAT I HAVE YOUR ATTENTION, IT'S TIME TO GO OVER OUR TRIP.

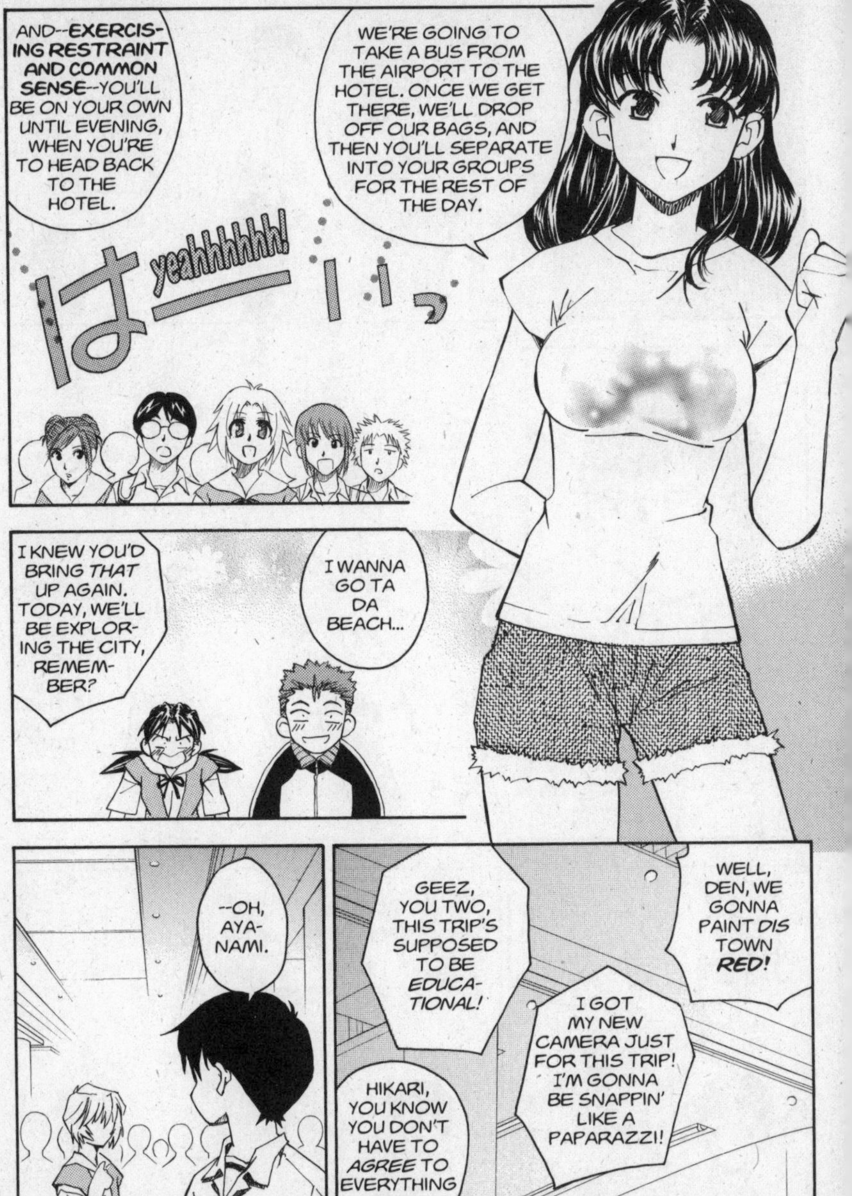
WE'RE GOING TO TAKE A BUS FROM THE AIRPORT TO THE HOTEL. ONCE WE GET THERE, WE'LL DROP OFF OUR BAGS, AND THEN YOU'LL SEPARATE INTO YOUR GROUPS FOR THE REST OF THE DAY.
AND--**EXERCISING RESTRAINT AND COMMON SENSE**--YOU'LL BE ON YOUR OWN UNTIL EVENING, WHEN YOU'RE TO HEAD BACK TO THE HOTEL.
はーいっ
yeahhhhhhh!
I WANNA GO TA DA BEACH...
I KNEW YOU'D BRING *THAT* UP AGAIN. TODAY, WE'LL BE EXPLORING THE CITY, REMEMBER?
WELL, DEN, WE GONNA PAINT *DIS* TOWN ***RED!***
I GOT MY NEW CAMERA JUST FOR THIS TRIP! I'M GONNA BE SNAPPIN' LIKE A PAPARAZZI!
GEEZ, YOU TWO, THIS TRIP'S SUPPOSED TO BE *EDUCATIONAL!*
HIKARI, YOU KNOW YOU DON'T HAVE TO *AGREE* TO EVERYTHING THEY--
--OH, AYANAMI.

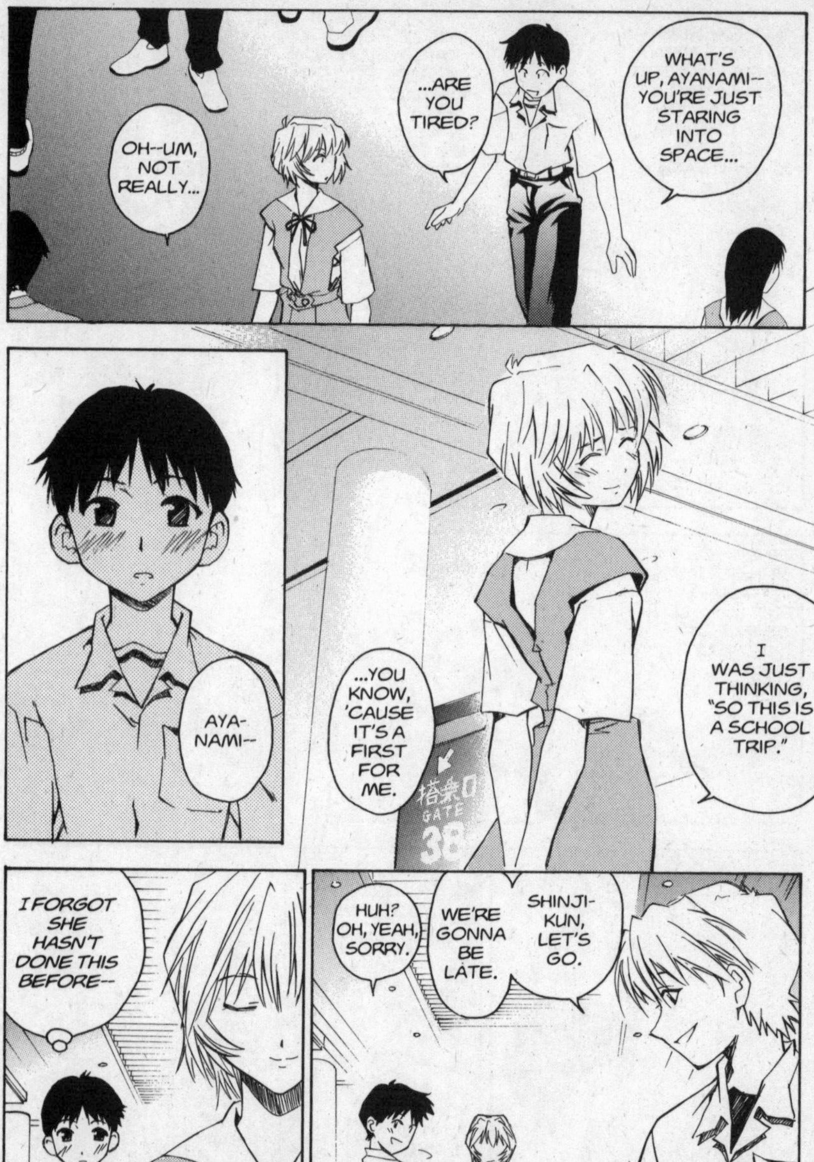
WHAT'S UP, AYANAMI-- YOU'RE JUST STARING INTO SPACE...
...ARE YOU TIRED?
OH--UM, NOT REALLY...
I WAS JUST THINKING, "SO THIS IS A SCHOOL TRIP."
...YOU KNOW, 'CAUSE IT'S A FIRST FOR ME.
搭乗口 GATE 38
AYA-NAMI--
SHINJI-KUN, LET'S GO.
WE'RE GONNA BE LATE.
HUH? OH, YEAH, SORRY.
I FORGOT SHE HASN'T DONE THIS BEFORE--

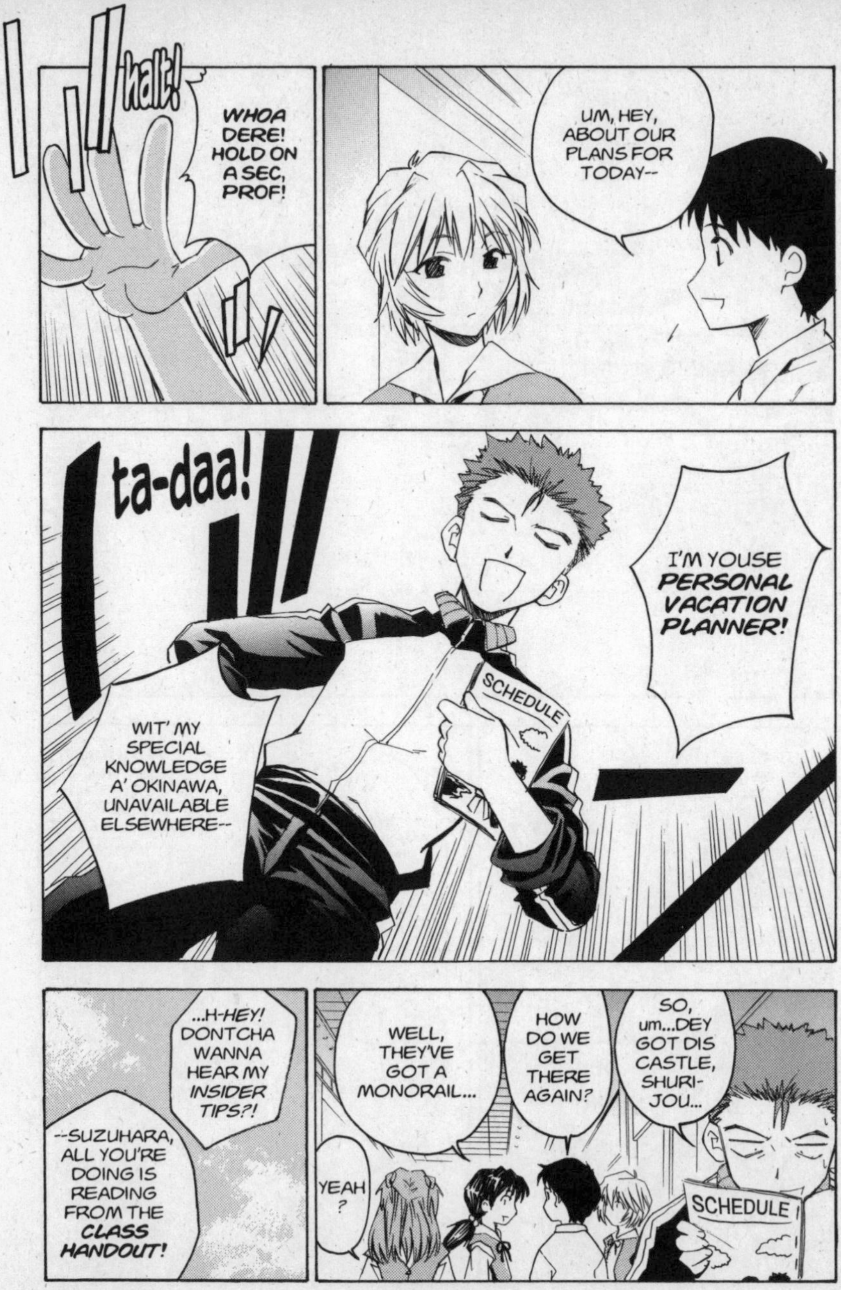
UM, HEY, ABOUT OUR PLANS FOR TODAY--
halt!
WHOA DERE! HOLD ON A SEC, PROF!
ta-daa!
I'M YOUSE PERSONAL VACATION PLANNER!
SCHEDULE
WIT' MY SPECIAL KNOWLEDGE A' OKINAWA, UNAVAILABLE ELSEWHERE--
SO, um...DEY GOT DIS CASTLE, SHURI-JOU...
HOW DO WE GET THERE AGAIN?
WELL, THEY'VE GOT A MONORAIL...
YEAH?
SCHEDULE
...H-HEY! DONTCHA WANNA HEAR MY INSIDER TIPS?!
--SUZUHARA, ALL YOU'RE DOING IS READING FROM THE CLASS HANDOUT!

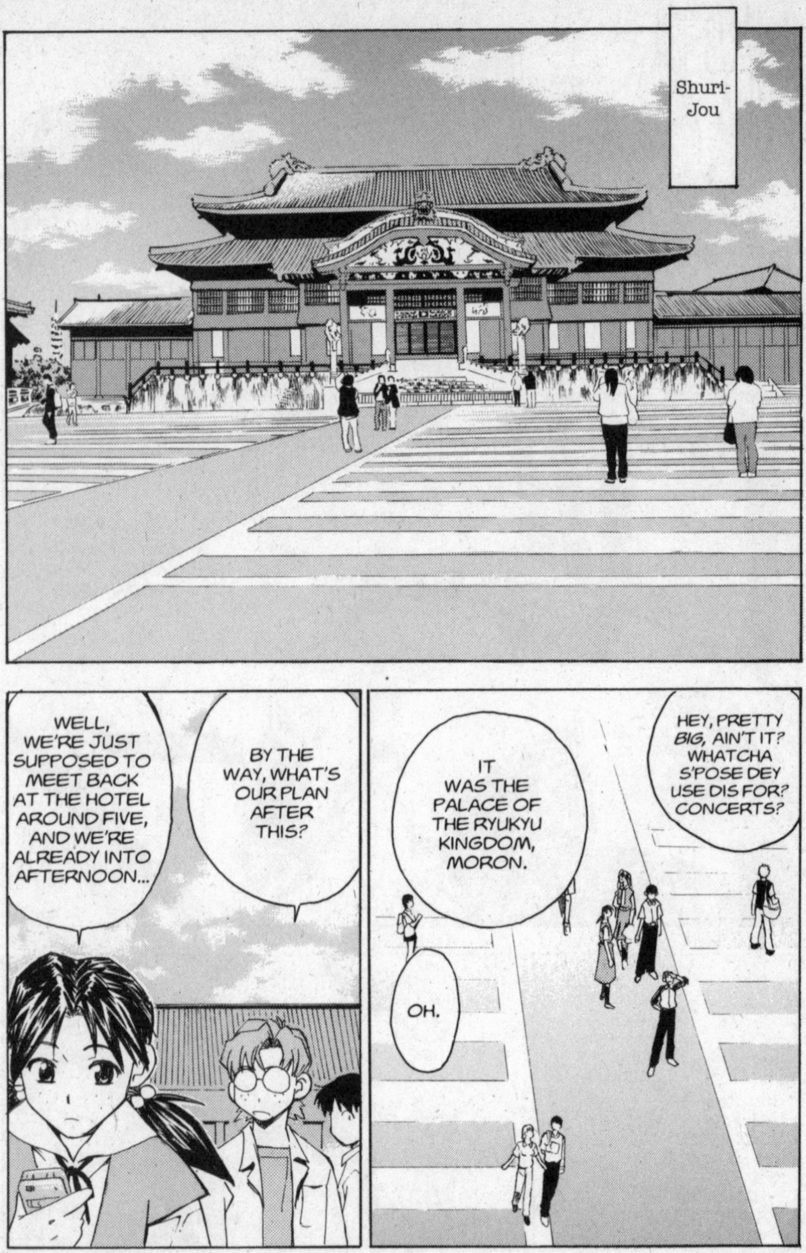
Shuri-Jou
HEY, PRETTY *BIG*, AIN'T IT? WHATCHA S'POSE DEY USE DIS FOR? CONCERTS?
IT WAS THE PALACE OF THE RYUKYU KINGDOM, MORON.
OH.
BY THE WAY, WHAT'S OUR PLAN AFTER THIS?
WELL, WE'RE JUST SUPPOSED TO MEET BACK AT THE HOTEL AROUND FIVE, AND WE'RE ALREADY INTO AFTERNOON...

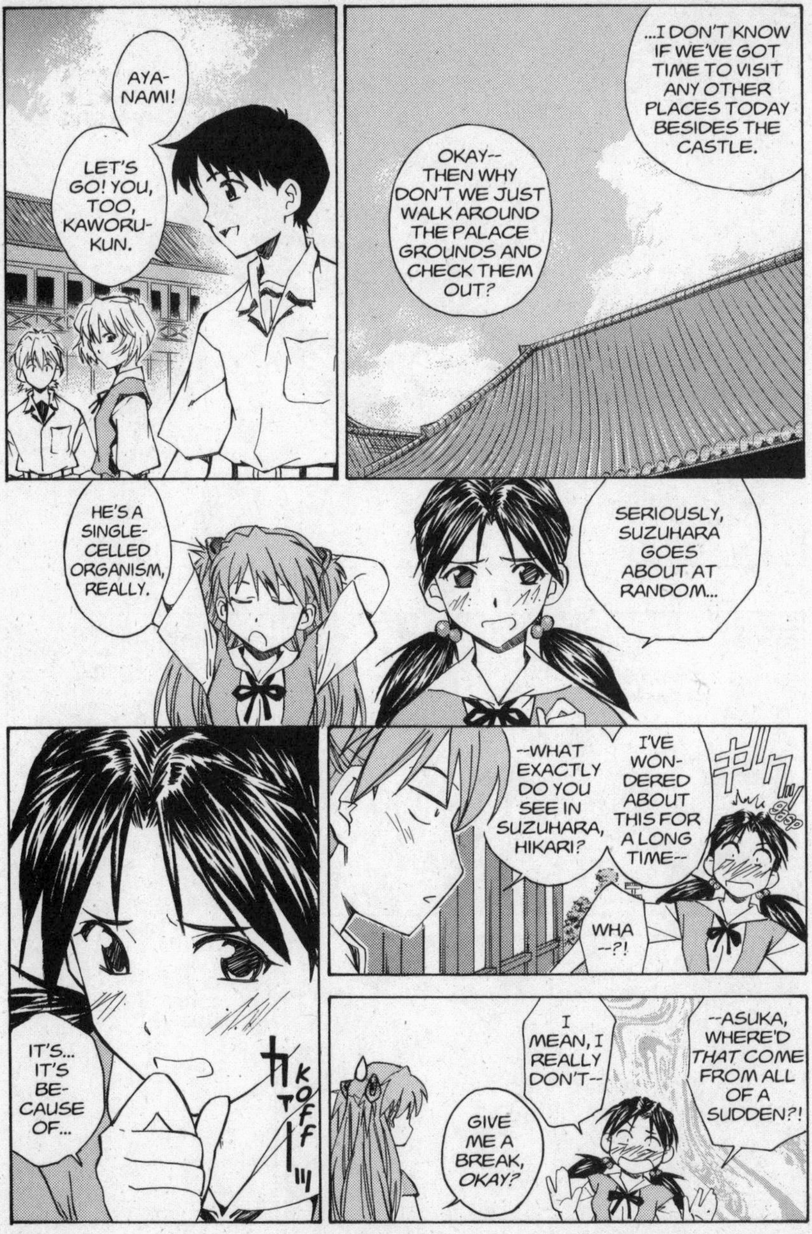
...I DON'T KNOW IF WE'VE GOT TIME TO VISIT ANY OTHER PLACES TODAY BESIDES THE CASTLE.
OKAY-- THEN WHY DON'T WE JUST WALK AROUND THE PALACE GROUNDS AND CHECK THEM OUT?
AYA-NAMI!
LET'S GO! YOU, TOO, KAWORU-KUN.
SERIOUSLY, SUZUHARA GOES ABOUT AT RANDOM...
HE'S A SINGLE-CELLED ORGANISM, REALLY.
I'VE WON-DERED ABOUT THIS FOR A LONG TIME--
--WHAT EXACTLY DO YOU SEE IN SUZUHARA, HIKARI?
gasp
WHA --?!
--ASUKA, WHERE'D THAT COME FROM ALL OF A SUDDEN?!
I MEAN, I REALLY DON'T--
GIVE ME A BREAK, OKAY?
IT'S... IT'S BE-CAUSE OF...
KOFF

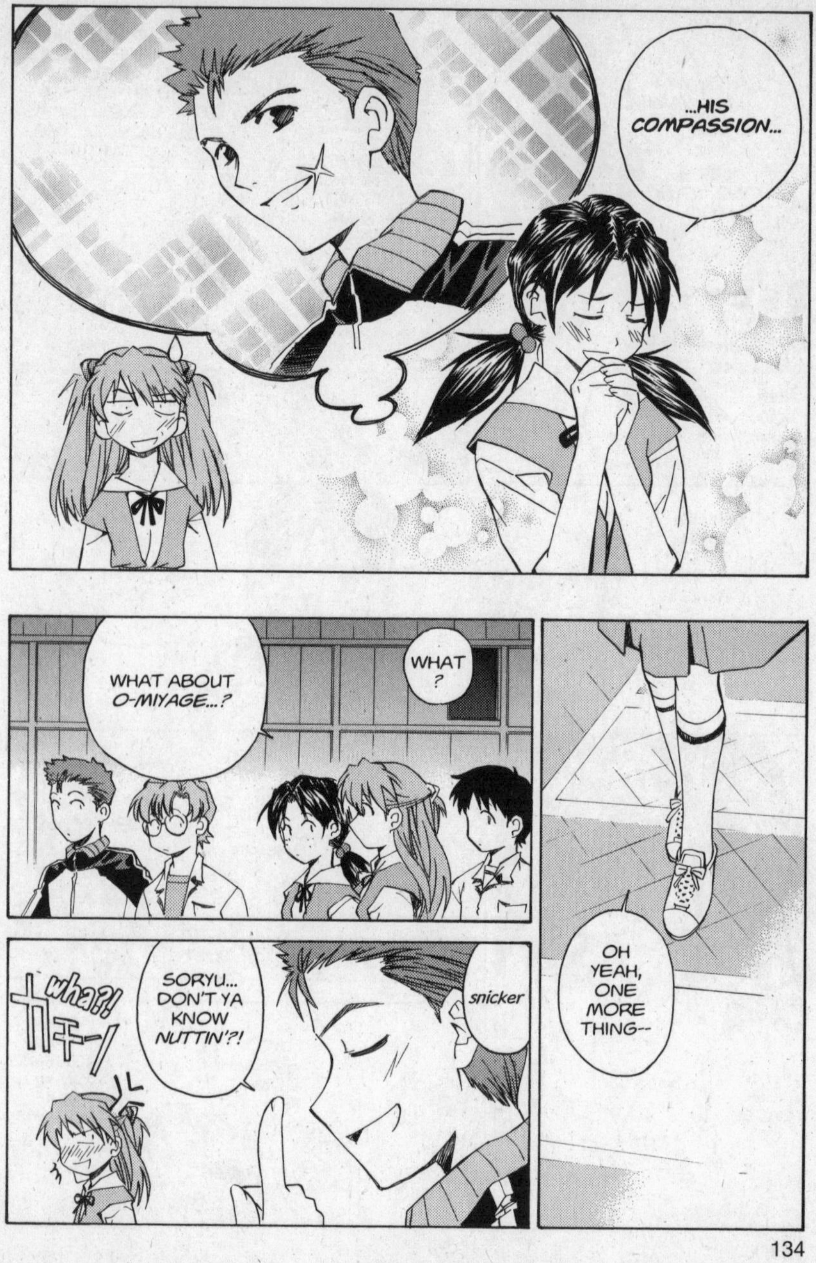
...HIS COMPASSION...
OH YEAH, ONE MORE THING--
WHAT?
WHAT ABOUT O-MIYAGE...?
snicker
SORYU... DON'T YA KNOW NUTTIN'?!
wha?!
カチーン

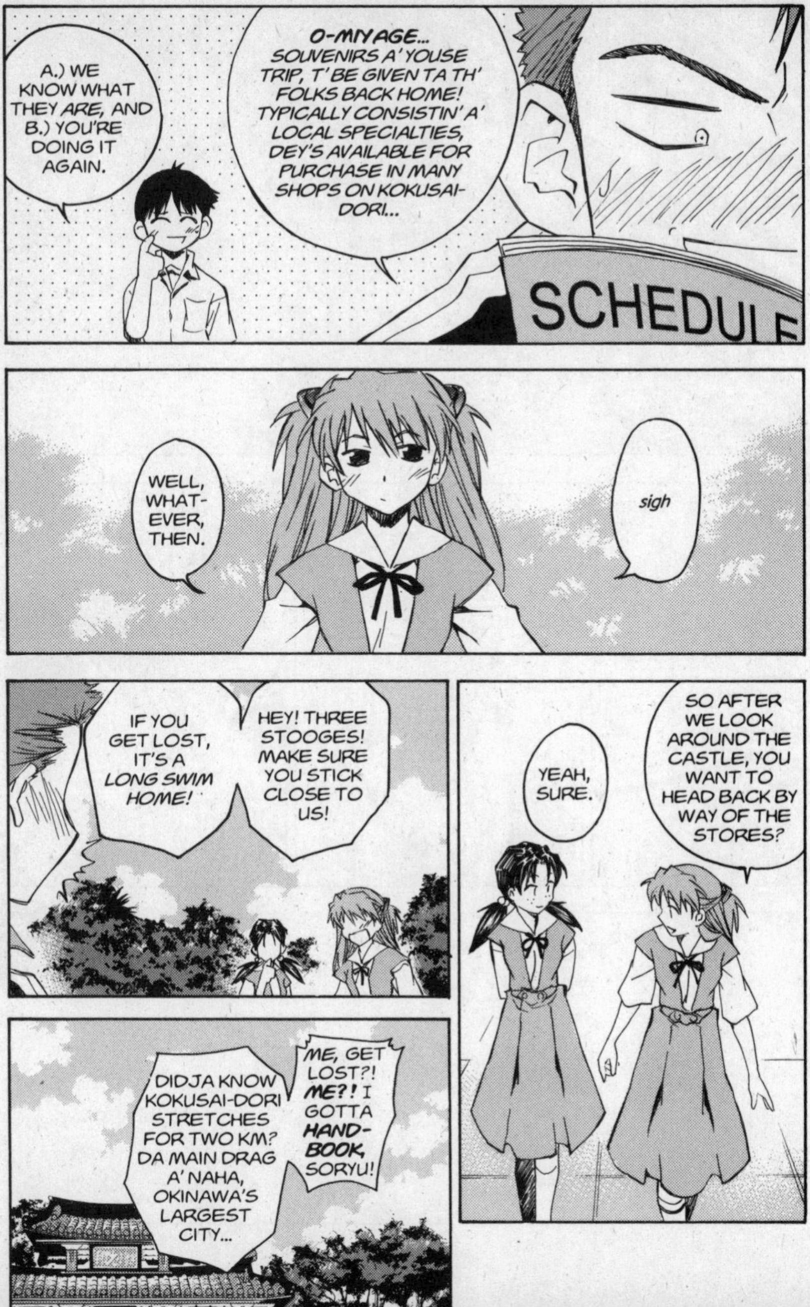
O-MIYAGE... SOUVENIRS A' YOUSE TRIP, T' BE GIVEN TA TH' FOLKS BACK HOME! TYPICALLY CONSISTIN' A' LOCAL SPECIALTIES, DEY'S AVAILABLE FOR PURCHASE IN MANY SHOPS ON KOKUSAI-DORI...
SCHEDULE
A.) WE KNOW WHAT THEY ARE, AND B.) YOU'RE DOING IT AGAIN.
sigh
WELL, WHAT-EVER, THEN.
SO AFTER WE LOOK AROUND THE CASTLE, YOU WANT TO HEAD BACK BY WAY OF THE STORES?
YEAH, SURE.
HEY! THREE STOOGES! MAKE SURE YOU STICK CLOSE TO US!
IF YOU GET LOST, IT'S A LONG SWIM HOME!
ME, GET LOST?! ME?! I GOTTA HAND-BOOK, SORYU!
DIDJA KNOW KOKUSAI-DORI STRETCHES FOR TWO KM? DA MAIN DRAG A' NAHA, OKINAWA'S LARGEST CITY...

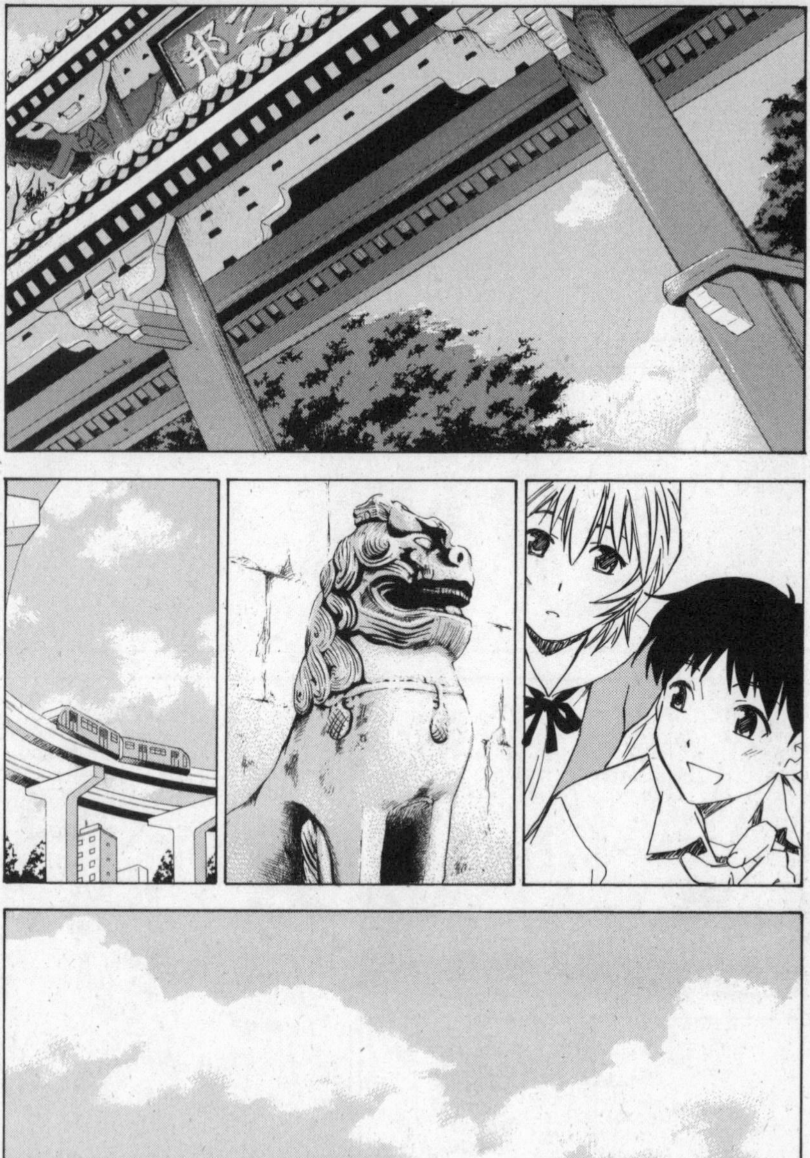

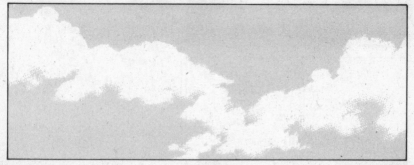

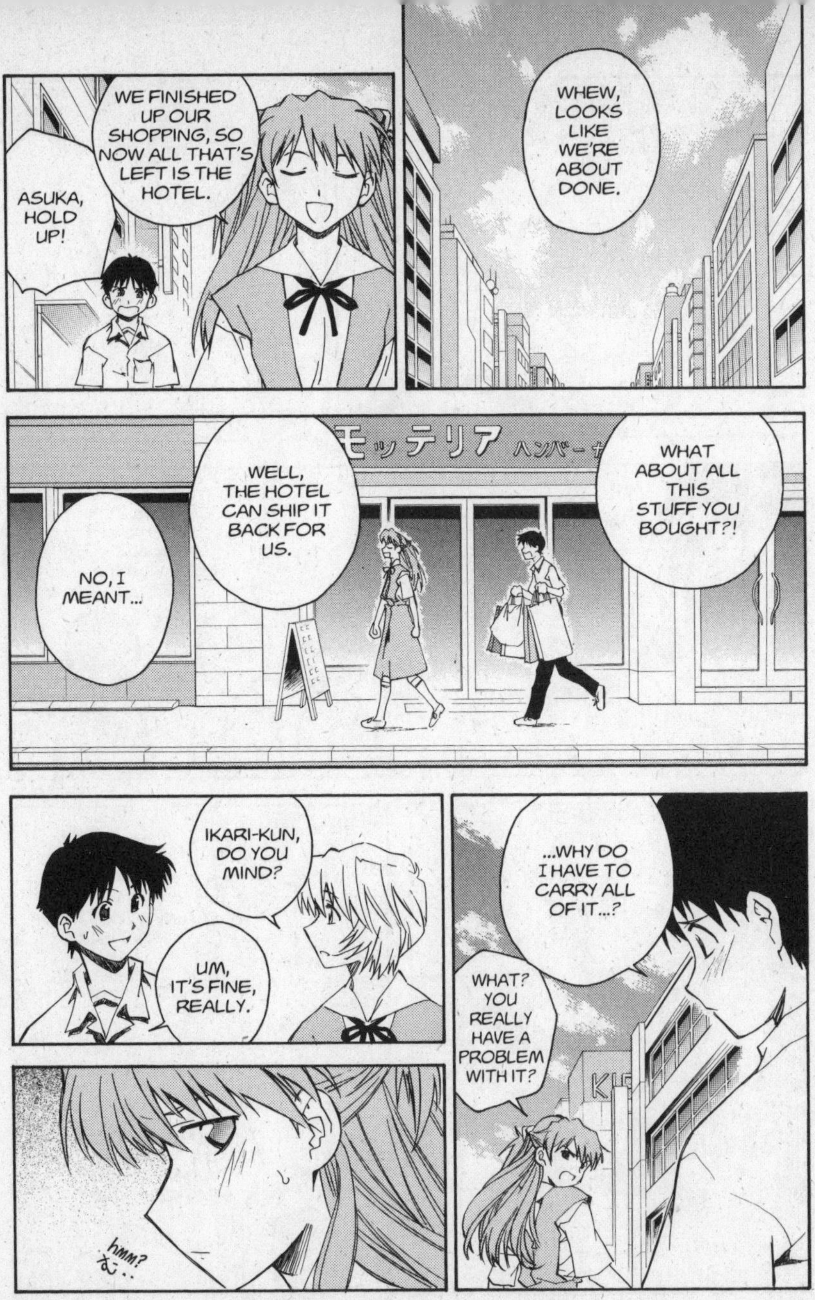
WHEW, LOOKS LIKE WE'RE ABOUT DONE.
WE FINISHED UP OUR SHOPPING, SO NOW ALL THAT'S LEFT IS THE HOTEL.
ASUKA, HOLD UP!
モッテリア ハンバー
WHAT ABOUT ALL THIS STUFF YOU BOUGHT?!
WELL, THE HOTEL CAN SHIP IT BACK FOR US.
NO, I MEANT...
...WHY DO I HAVE TO CARRY ALL OF IT...?
WHAT? YOU REALLY HAVE A PROBLEM WITH IT?
IKARI-KUN, DO YOU MIND?
UM, IT'S FINE, REALLY.
hmm?
む..

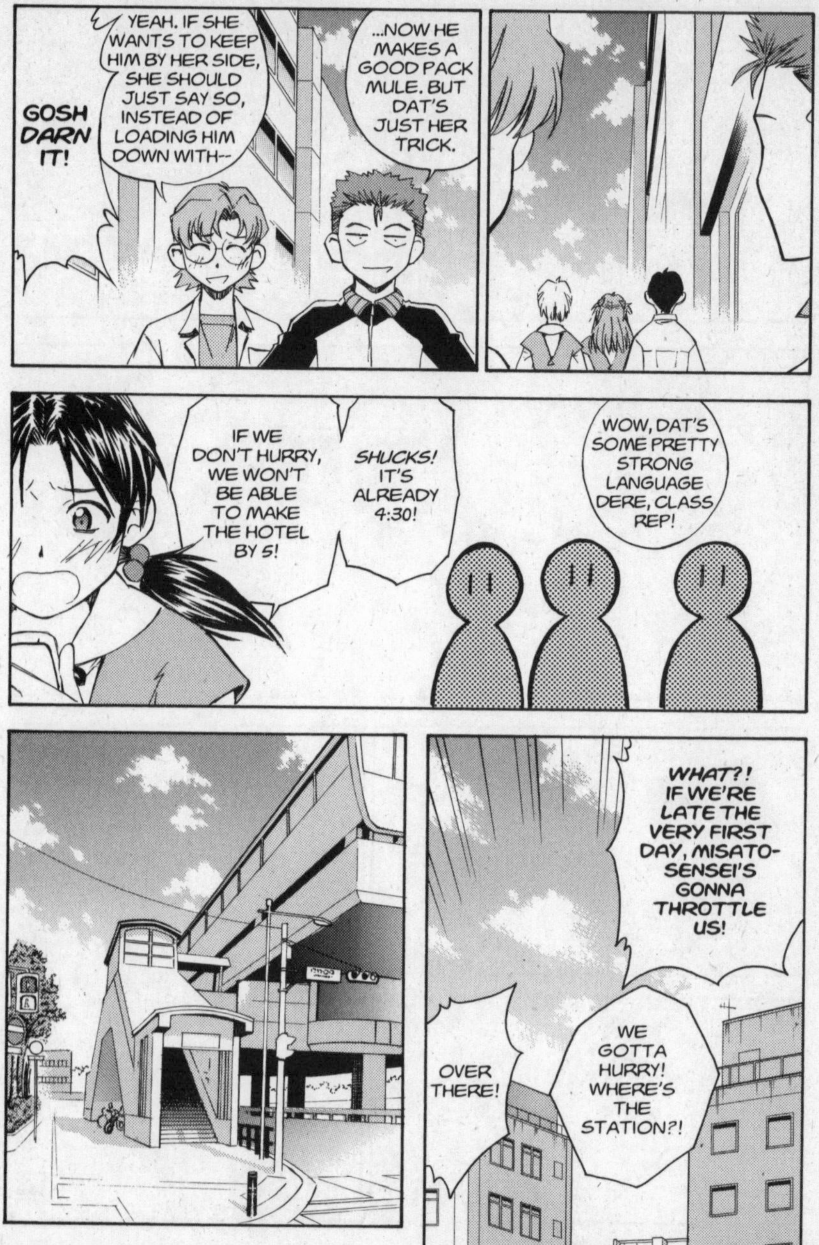
...NOW HE MAKES A GOOD PACK MULE. BUT DAT'S JUST HER TRICK.
YEAH. IF SHE WANTS TO KEEP HIM BY HER SIDE, SHE SHOULD JUST SAY SO, INSTEAD OF LOADING HIM DOWN WITH--
GOSH DARN IT!
SHUCKS! IT'S ALREADY 4:30!
IF WE DON'T HURRY, WE WON'T BE ABLE TO MAKE THE HOTEL BY 5!
WOW, DAT'S SOME PRETTY STRONG LANGUAGE DERE, CLASS REP!
WHAT?! IF WE'RE LATE THE VERY FIRST DAY, MISATO-SENSEI'S GONNA THROTTLE US!
WE GOTTA HURRY! WHERE'S THE STATION?!
OVER THERE!

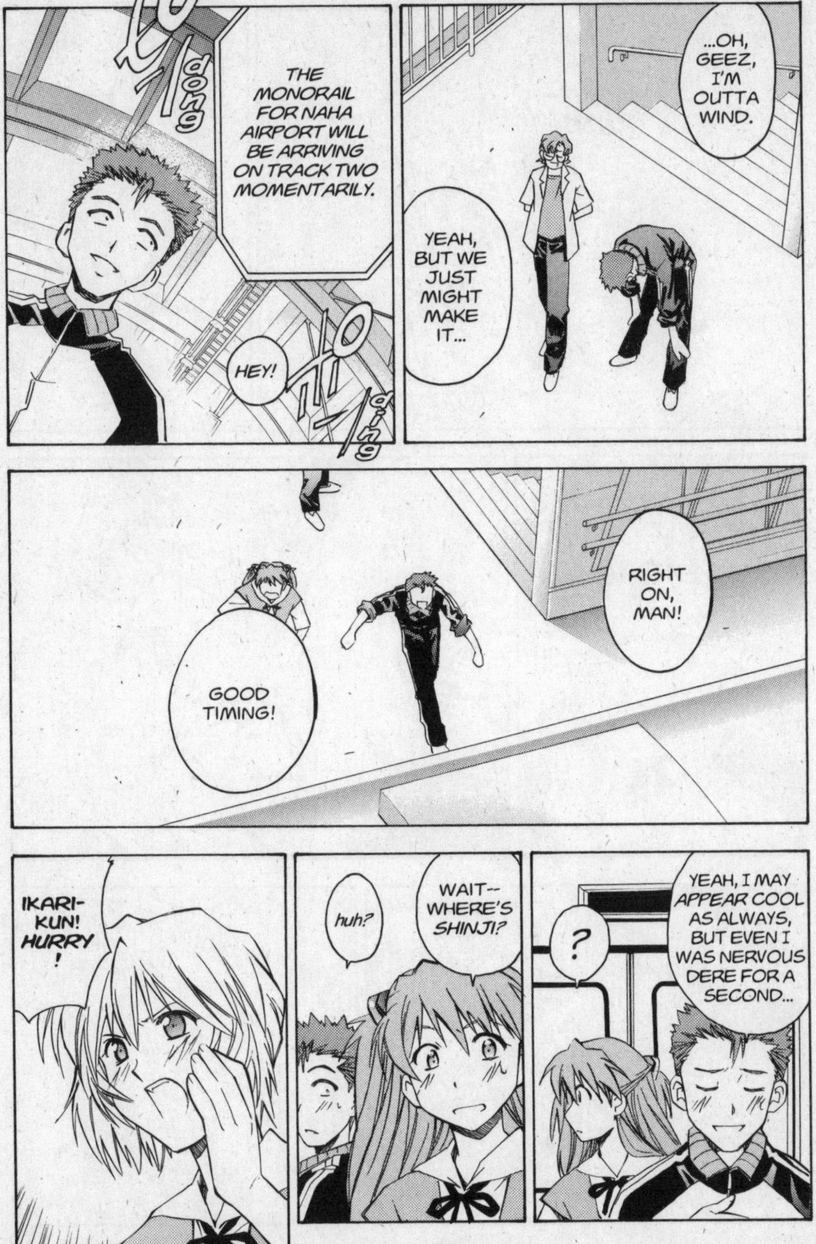
...OH, GEEZ, I'M OUTTA WIND.
YEAH, BUT WE JUST MIGHT MAKE IT...
dong
THE MONORAIL FOR NAHA AIRPORT WILL BE ARRIVING ON TRACK TWO MOMENTARILY.
HEY!
ding
RIGHT ON, MAN!
GOOD TIMING!
YEAH, I MAY APPEAR COOL AS ALWAYS, BUT EVEN I WAS NERVOUS DERE FOR A SECOND...
?
WAIT-- WHERE'S SHINJI?
huh?
IKARI-KUN! HURRY!

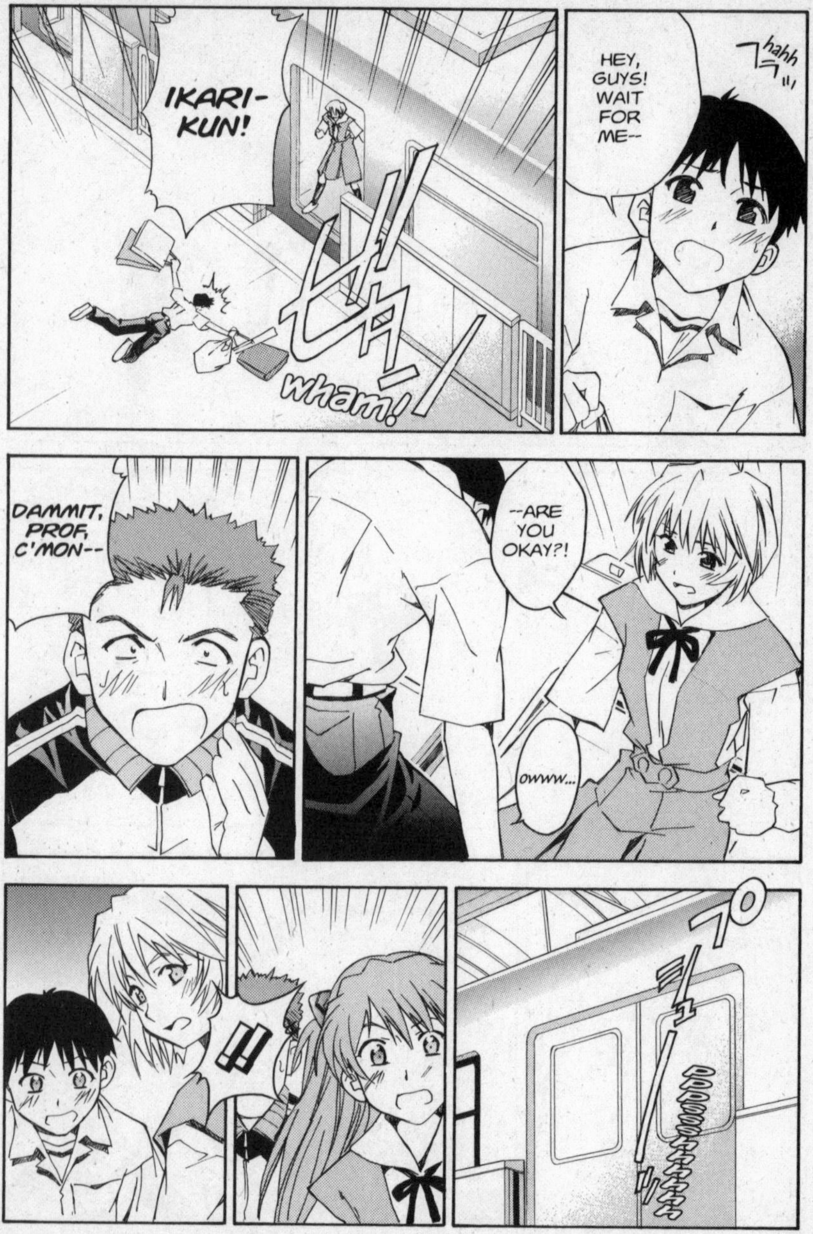
hahh
HEY, GUYS! WAIT FOR ME--
IKARI-KUN!
wham!
--ARE YOU OKAY?!
owww...
DAMMIT, PROF, C'MON--
!!

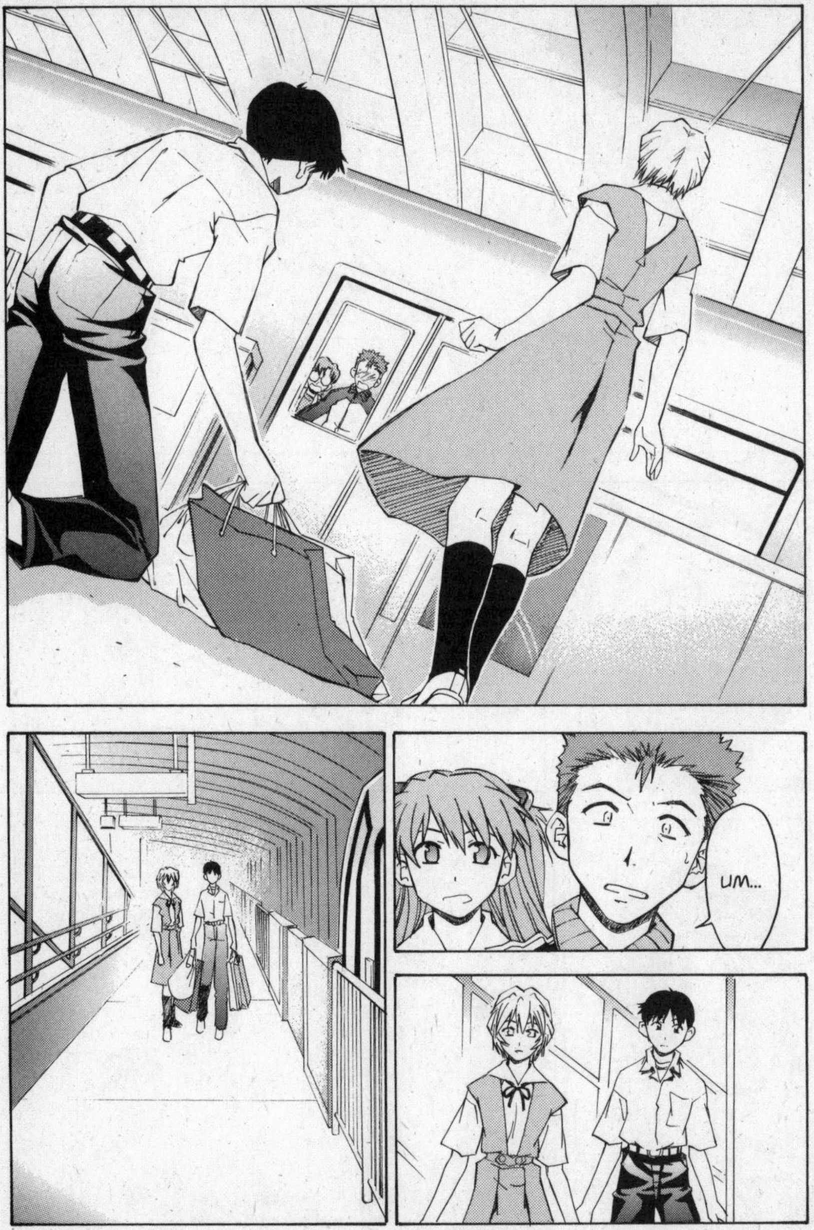
UM...

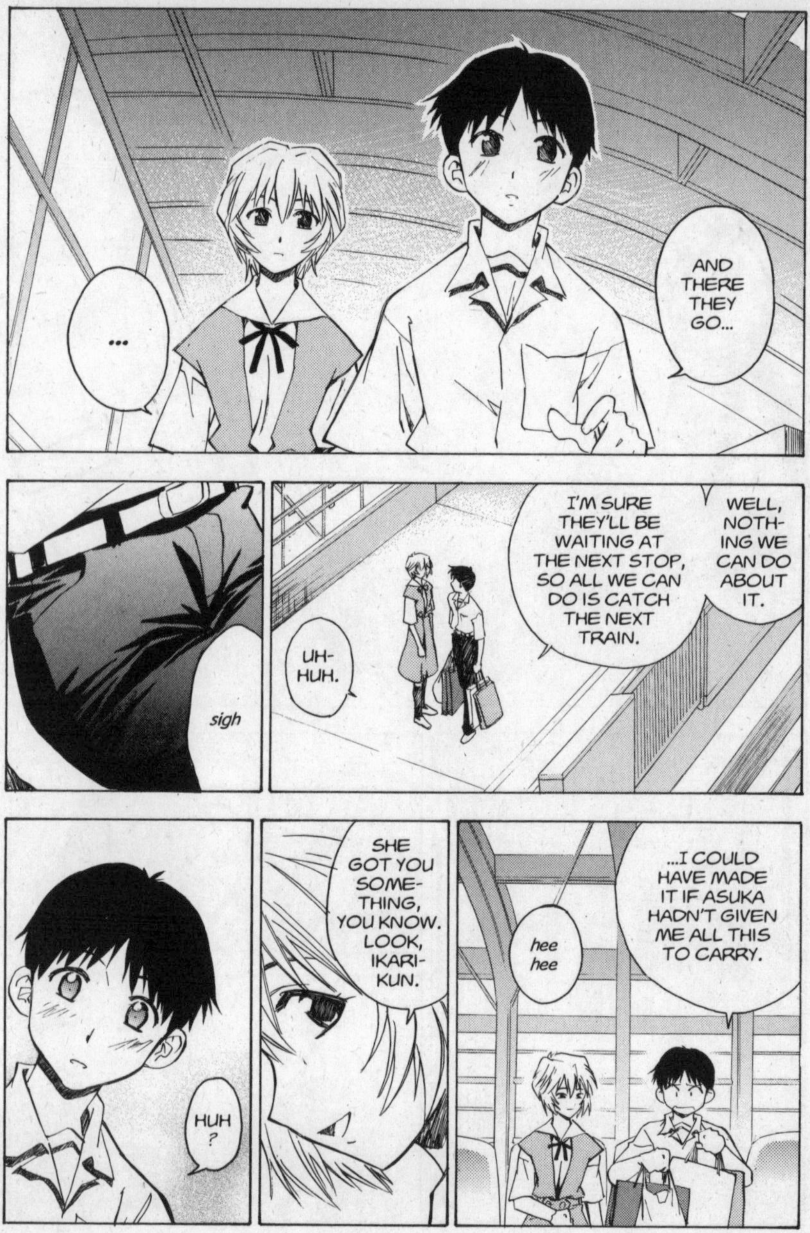
AND THERE THEY GO...
...
WELL, NOTHING WE CAN DO ABOUT IT.
I'M SURE THEY'LL BE WAITING AT THE NEXT STOP, SO ALL WE CAN DO IS CATCH THE NEXT TRAIN.
UH-HUH.
sigh
...I COULD HAVE MADE IT IF ASUKA HADN'T GIVEN ME ALL THIS TO CARRY.
hee hee
SHE GOT YOU SOMETHING, YOU KNOW. LOOK, IKARI-KUN.
HUH?

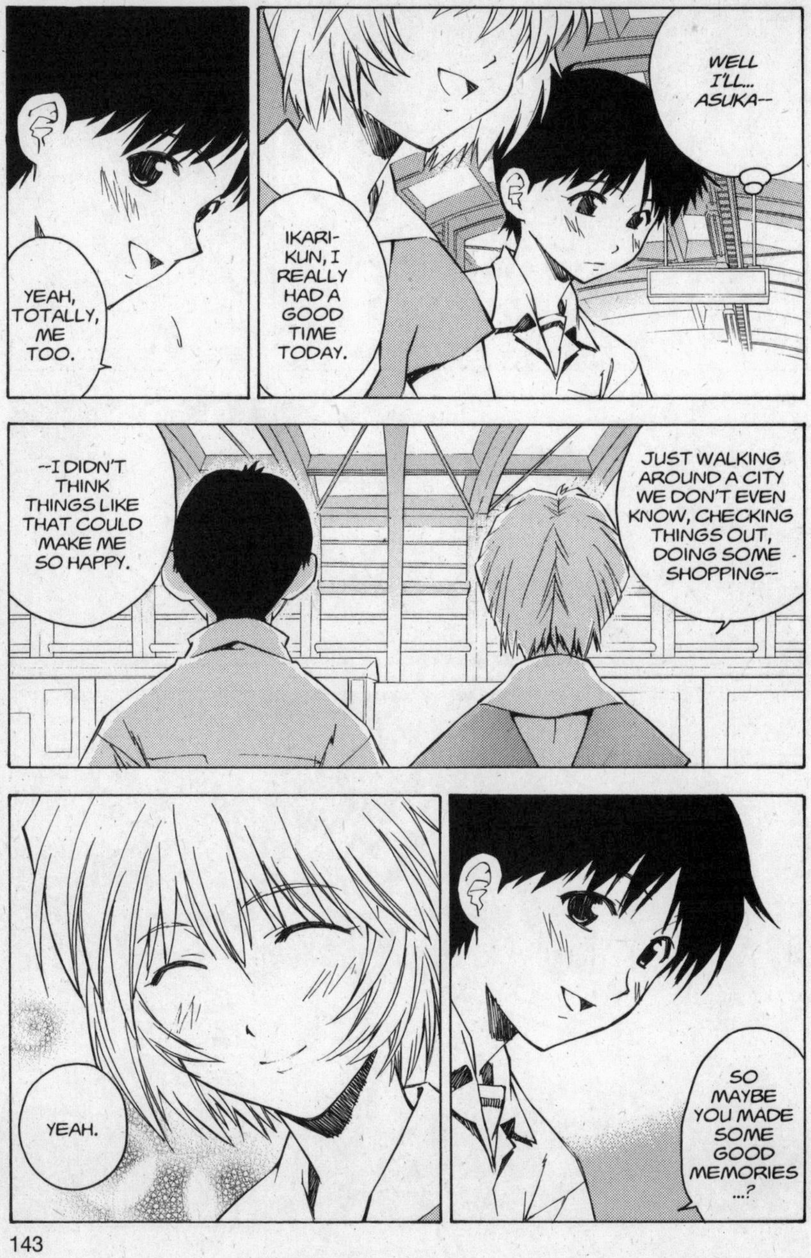
WELL I'LL... ASUKA--
IKARI-KUN, I REALLY HAD A GOOD TIME TODAY.
YEAH, TOTALLY, ME TOO.
JUST WALKING AROUND A CITY WE DON'T EVEN KNOW, CHECKING THINGS OUT, DOING SOME SHOPPING--
--I DIDN'T THINK THINGS LIKE THAT COULD MAKE ME SO HAPPY.
SO MAYBE YOU MADE SOME GOOD MEMORIES ...?
YEAH.

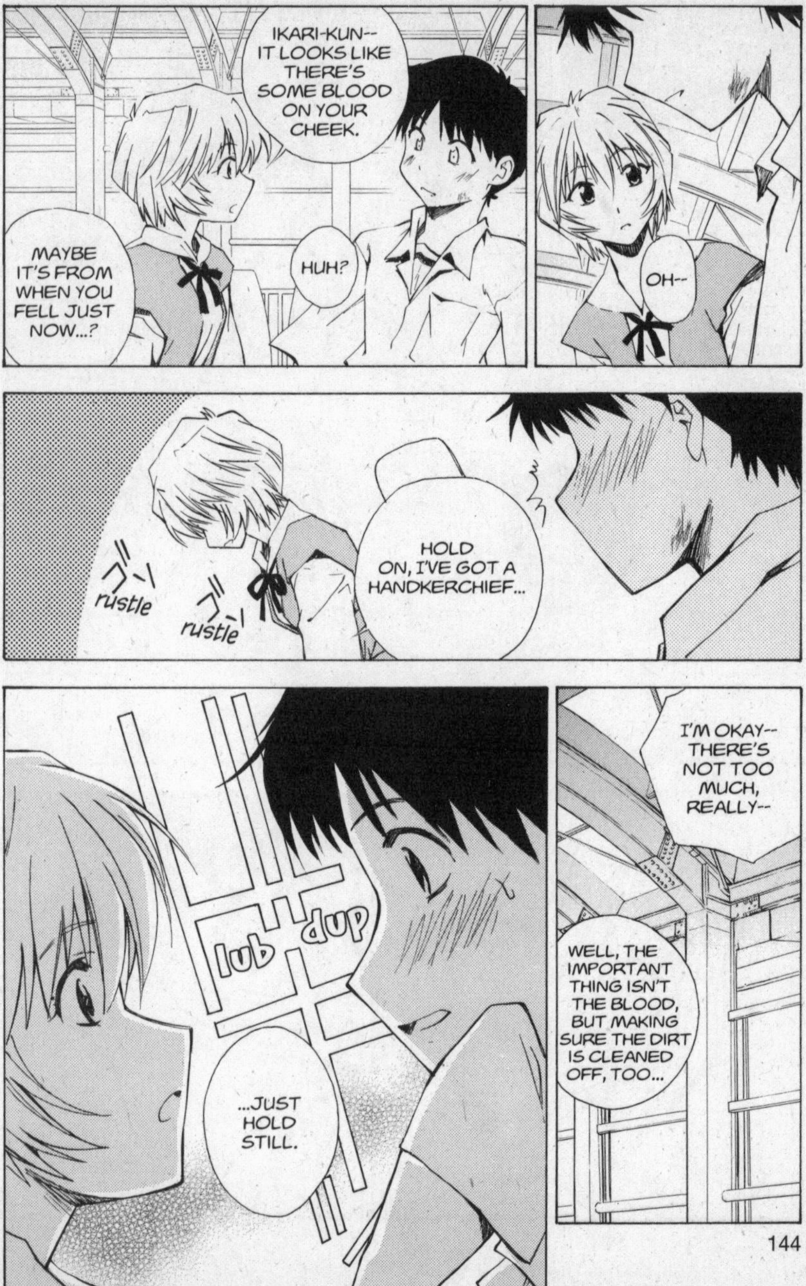
OH--
IKARI-KUN-- IT LOOKS LIKE THERE'S SOME BLOOD ON YOUR CHEEK.
HUH?
MAYBE IT'S FROM WHEN YOU FELL JUST NOW...?
HOLD ON, I'VE GOT A HANDKERCHIEF...
rustle
rustle
I'M OKAY-- THERE'S NOT TOO MUCH, REALLY--
WELL, THE IMPORTANT THING ISN'T THE BLOOD, BUT MAKING SURE THE DIRT IS CLEANED OFF, TOO...
lub dup
...JUST HOLD STILL.

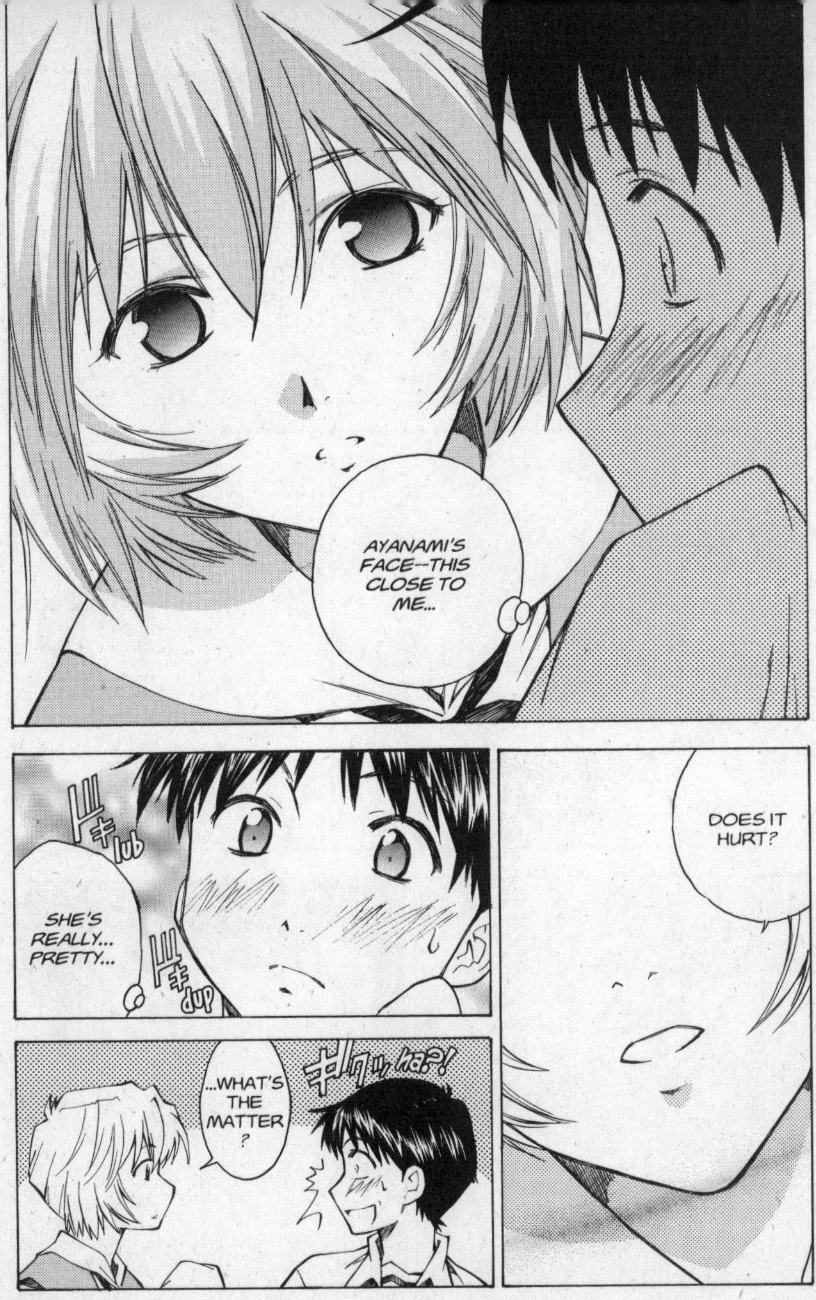
AYANAMI'S FACE--THIS CLOSE TO ME...
DOES IT HURT?
lub
SHE'S REALLY... PRETTY...
dup
...WHAT'S THE MATTER?
ha?!

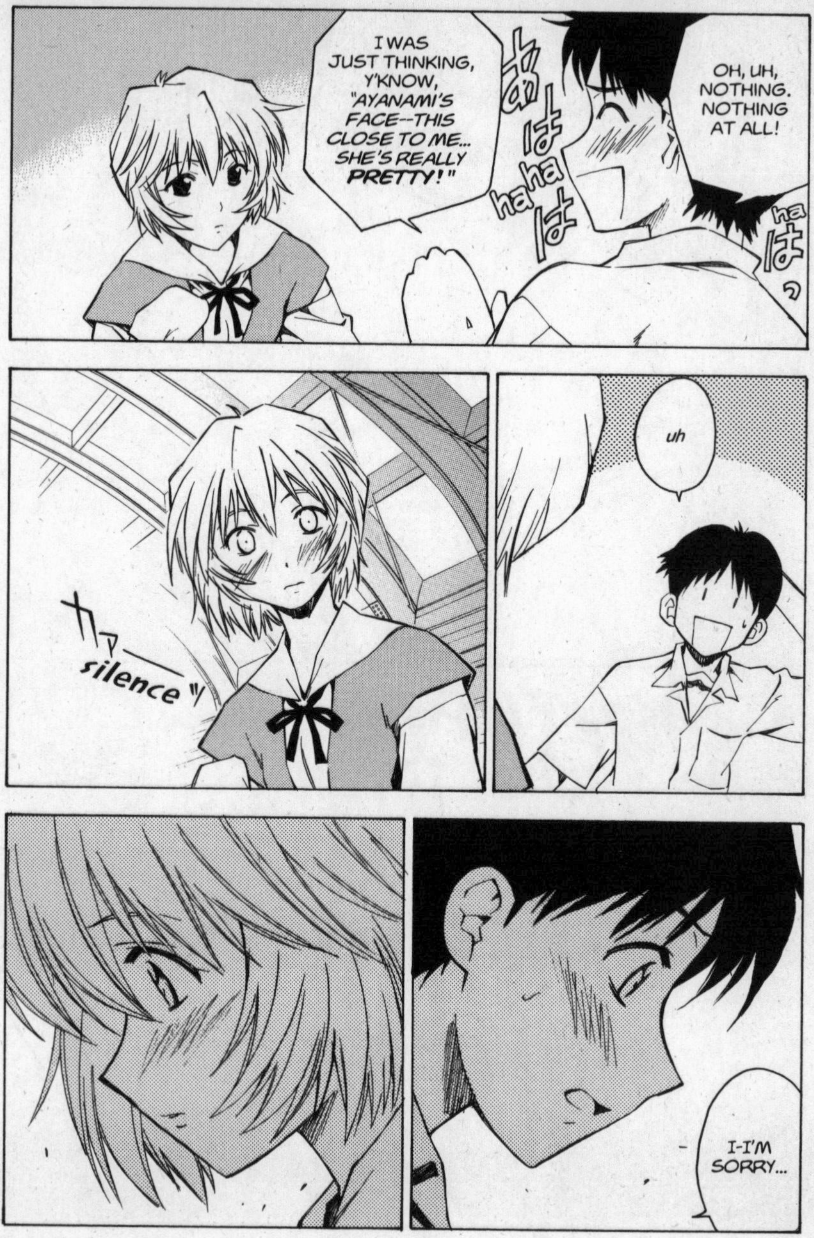
OH, UH, NOTHING. NOTHING AT ALL!
ha はっ
あはは ha ha
I WAS JUST THINKING, Y'KNOW, "AYANAMI'S FACE--THIS CLOSE TO ME... SHE'S REALLY PRETTY!"
uh
カァー silence ッ
I-I'M SORRY...

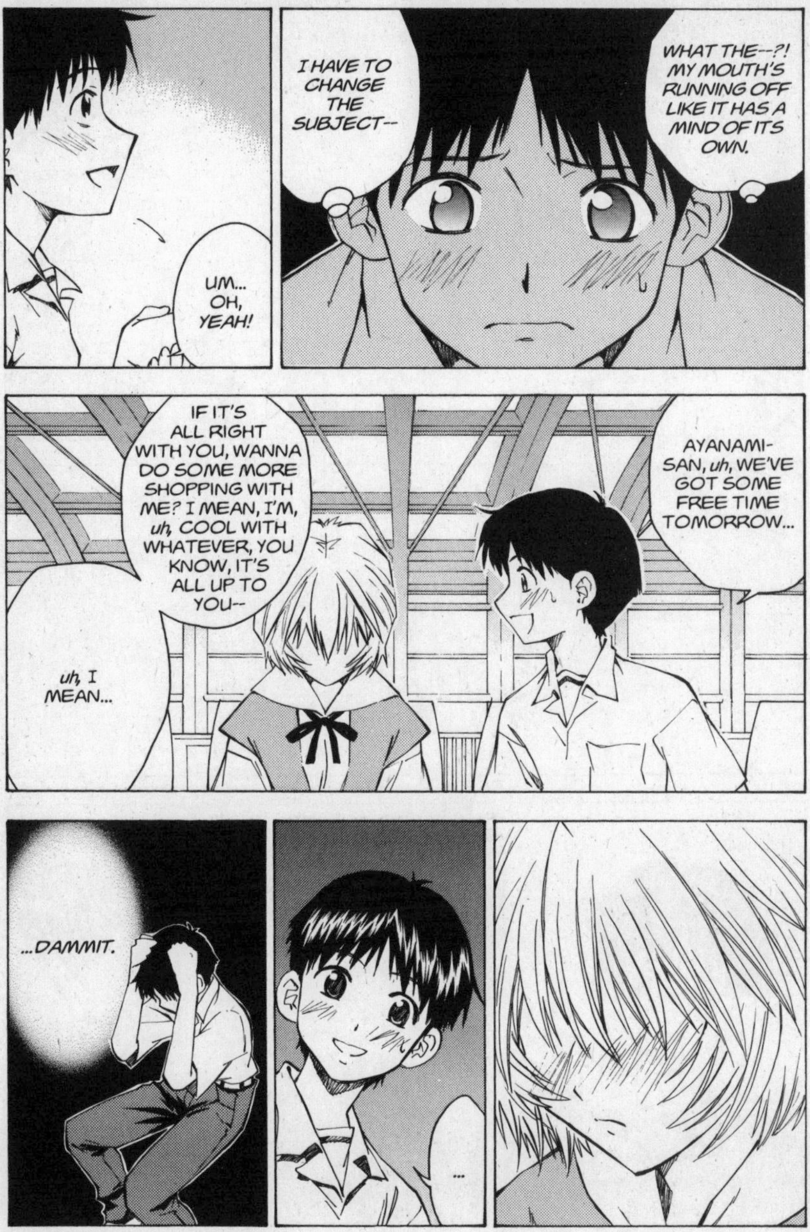
WHAT THE--?! MY MOUTH'S RUNNING OFF LIKE IT HAS A MIND OF ITS OWN.
I HAVE TO CHANGE THE SUBJECT--
UM... OH, YEAH!
AYANAMI-SAN, *uh*, WE'VE GOT SOME FREE TIME TOMORROW...
IF IT'S ALL RIGHT WITH YOU, WANNA DO SOME MORE SHOPPING WITH ME? I MEAN, I'M, *uh*, COOL WITH WHATEVER, YOU KNOW, IT'S ALL UP TO YOU--
uh, I MEAN...
...
...DAMMIT.

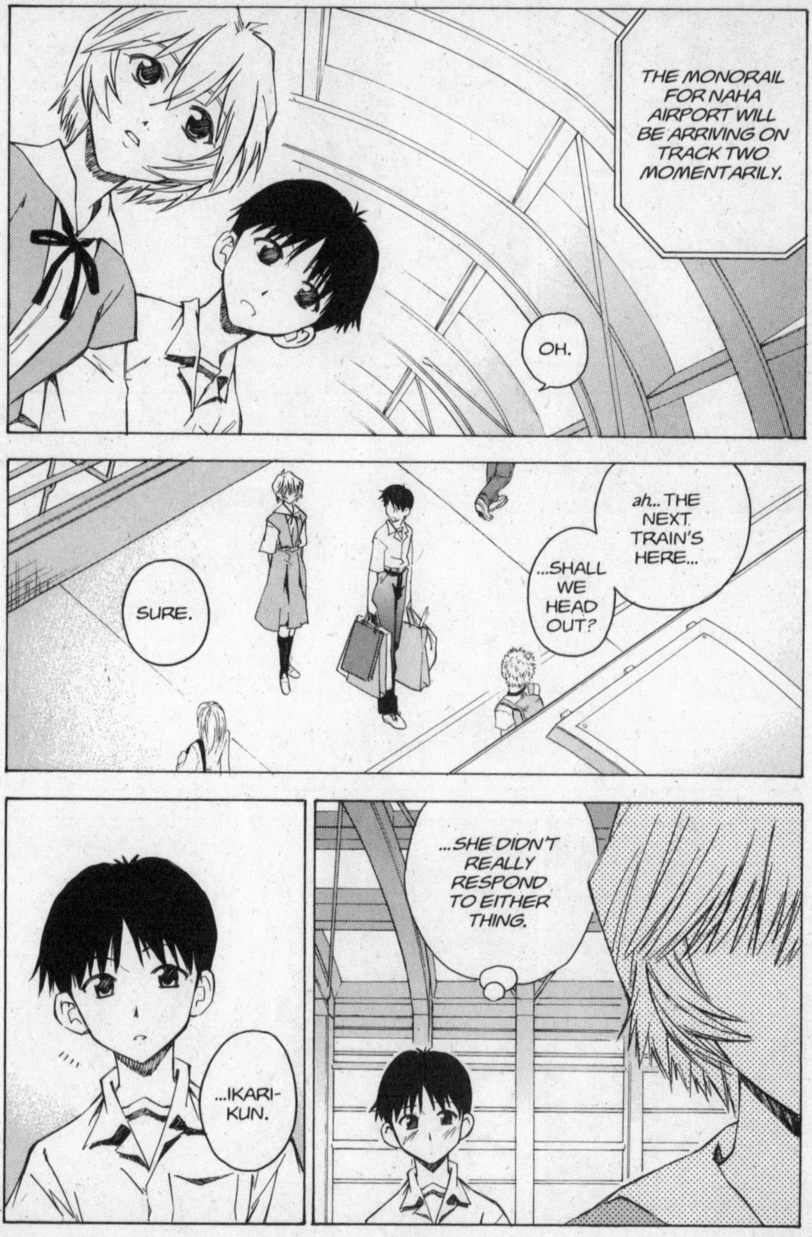
THE MONORAIL FOR NAHA AIRPORT WILL BE ARRIVING ON TRACK TWO MOMENTARILY.
OH.
ah... THE NEXT TRAIN'S HERE...
...SHALL WE HEAD OUT?
SURE.
...SHE DIDN'T REALLY RESPOND TO EITHER THING.
...IKARI-KUN.

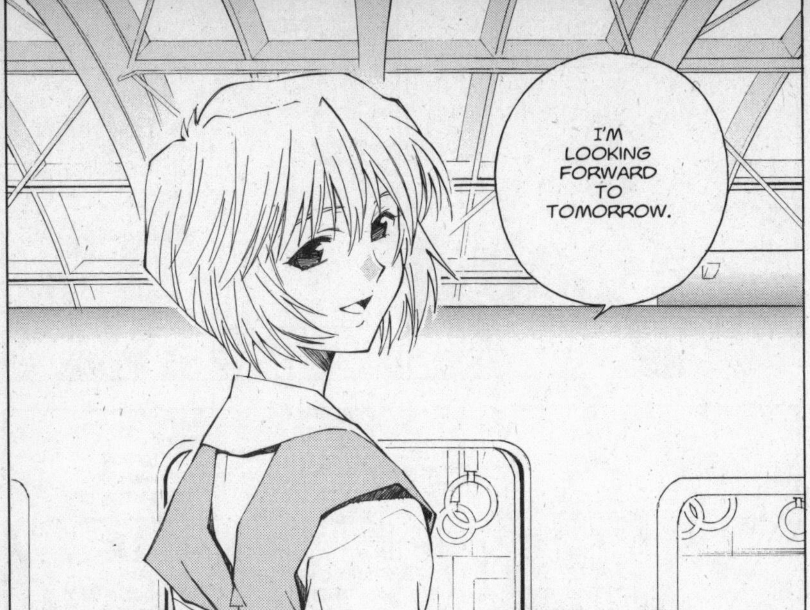
I'M LOOKING FORWARD TO TOMORROW.
乗車位置に止ま
降りる方がすんで
日産
レンタ
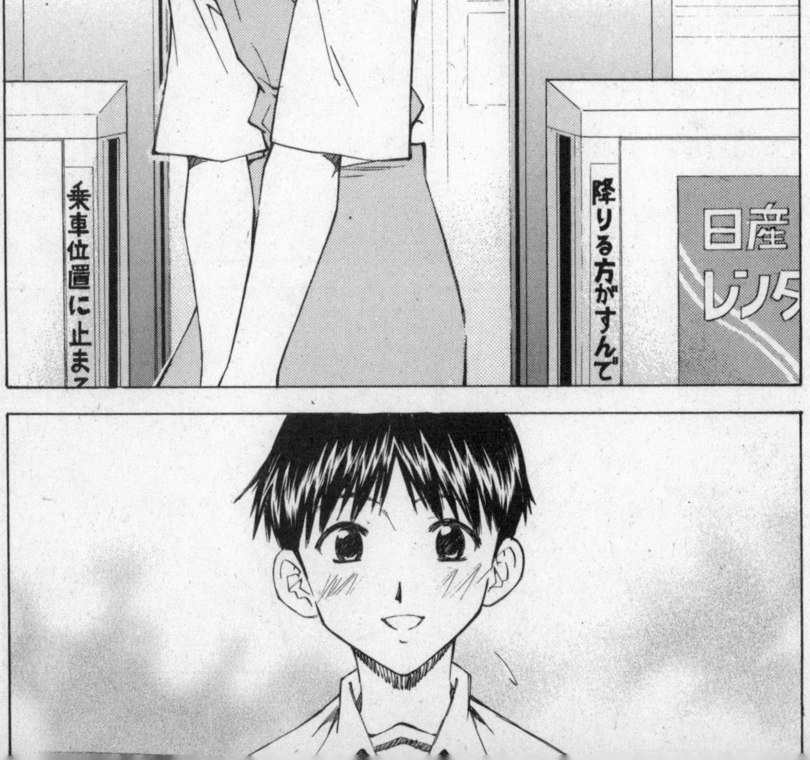

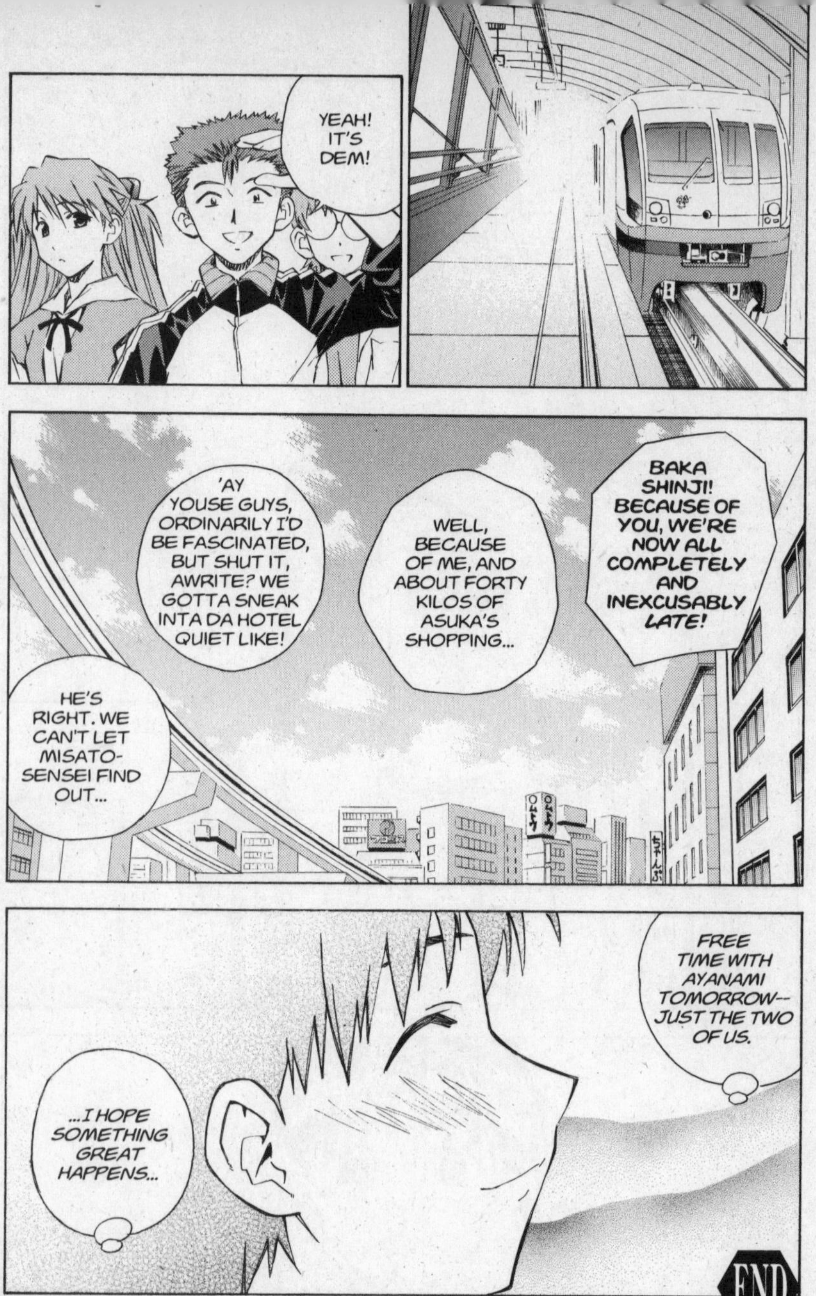
YEAH! IT'S DEM!
BAKA SHINJI! BECAUSE OF YOU, WE'RE NOW ALL COMPLETELY AND INEXCUSABLY LATE!
WELL, BECAUSE OF ME, AND ABOUT FORTY KILOS OF ASUKA'S SHOPPING...
'AY YOUSE GUYS, ORDINARILY I'D BE FASCINATED, BUT SHUT IT, AWRITE? WE GOTTA SNEAK INTA DA HOTEL QUIET LIKE!
HE'S RIGHT. WE CAN'T LET MISATO-SENSEI FIND OUT...
FREE TIME WITH AYANAMI TOMORROW-- JUST THE TWO OF US.
...I HOPE SOMETHING GREAT HAPPENS...
END

STAGE 14

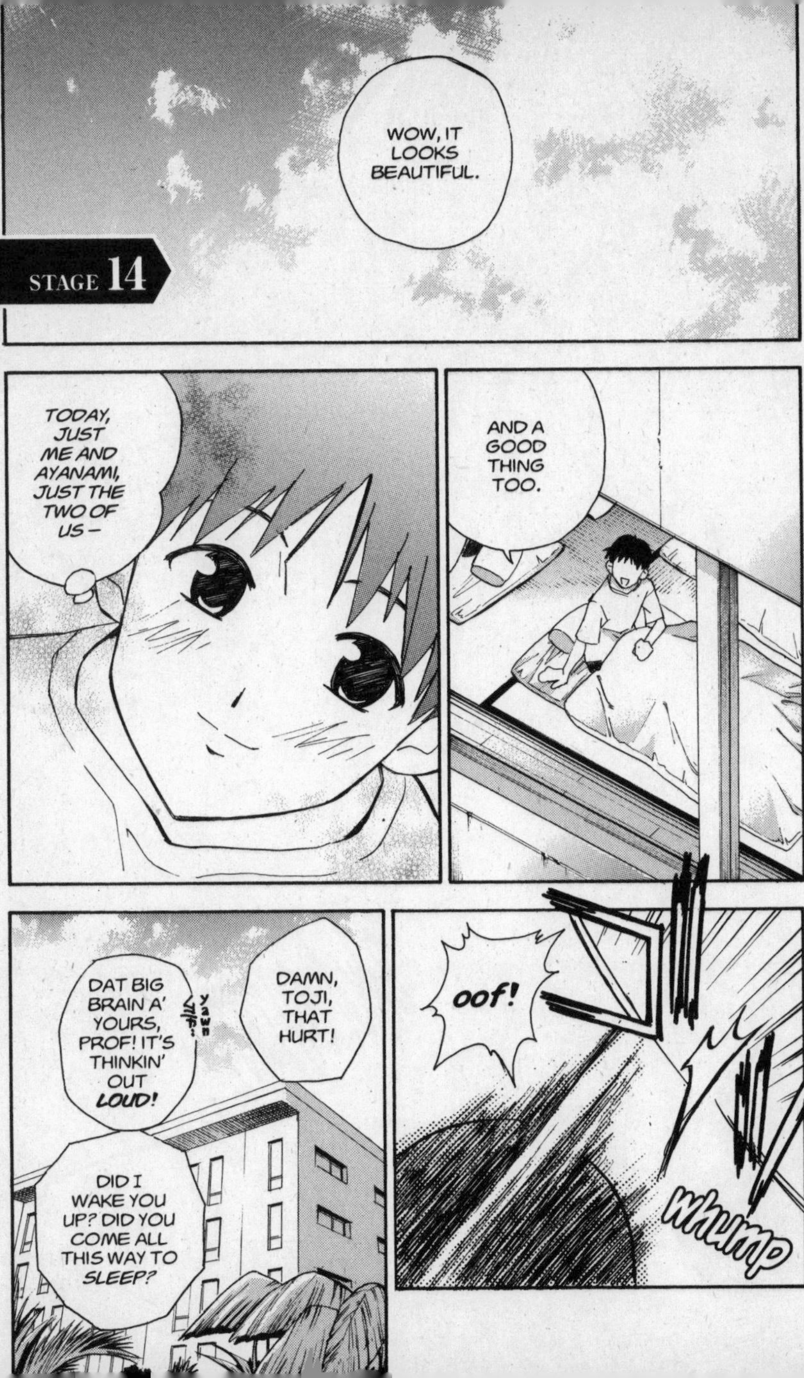

WOW, IT LOOKS BEAUTIFUL.
AND A GOOD THING TOO.
TODAY, JUST ME AND AYANAMI, JUST THE TWO OF US—
oof!
whump
DAMN, TOJI, THAT HURT!
DAT BIG BRAIN A' YOURS, PROF! IT'S THINKIN' OUT LOUD!
yawn
DID I WAKE YOU UP? DID YOU COME ALL THIS WAY TO SLEEP?

STAGE 14

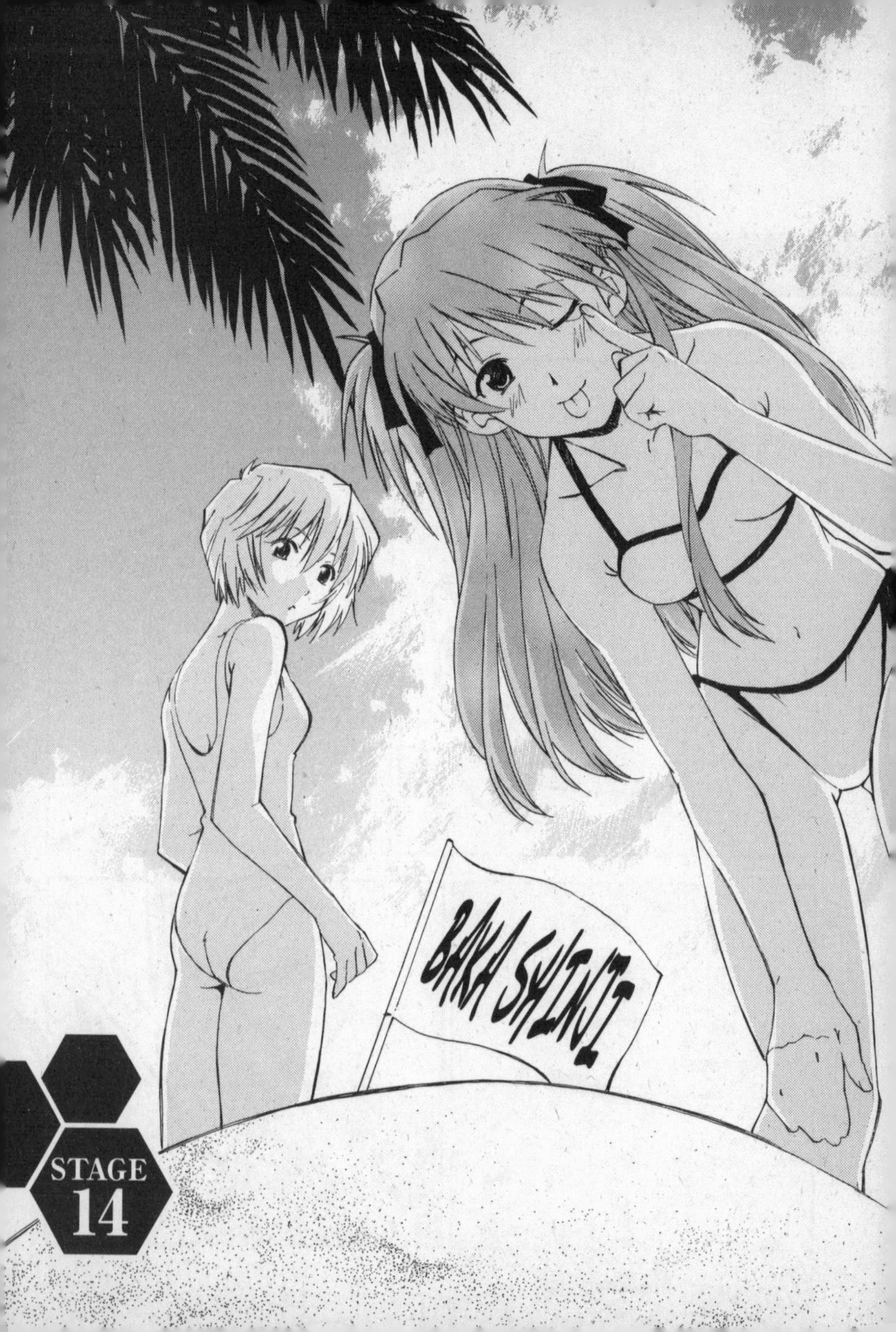
BAKA SHINJI!

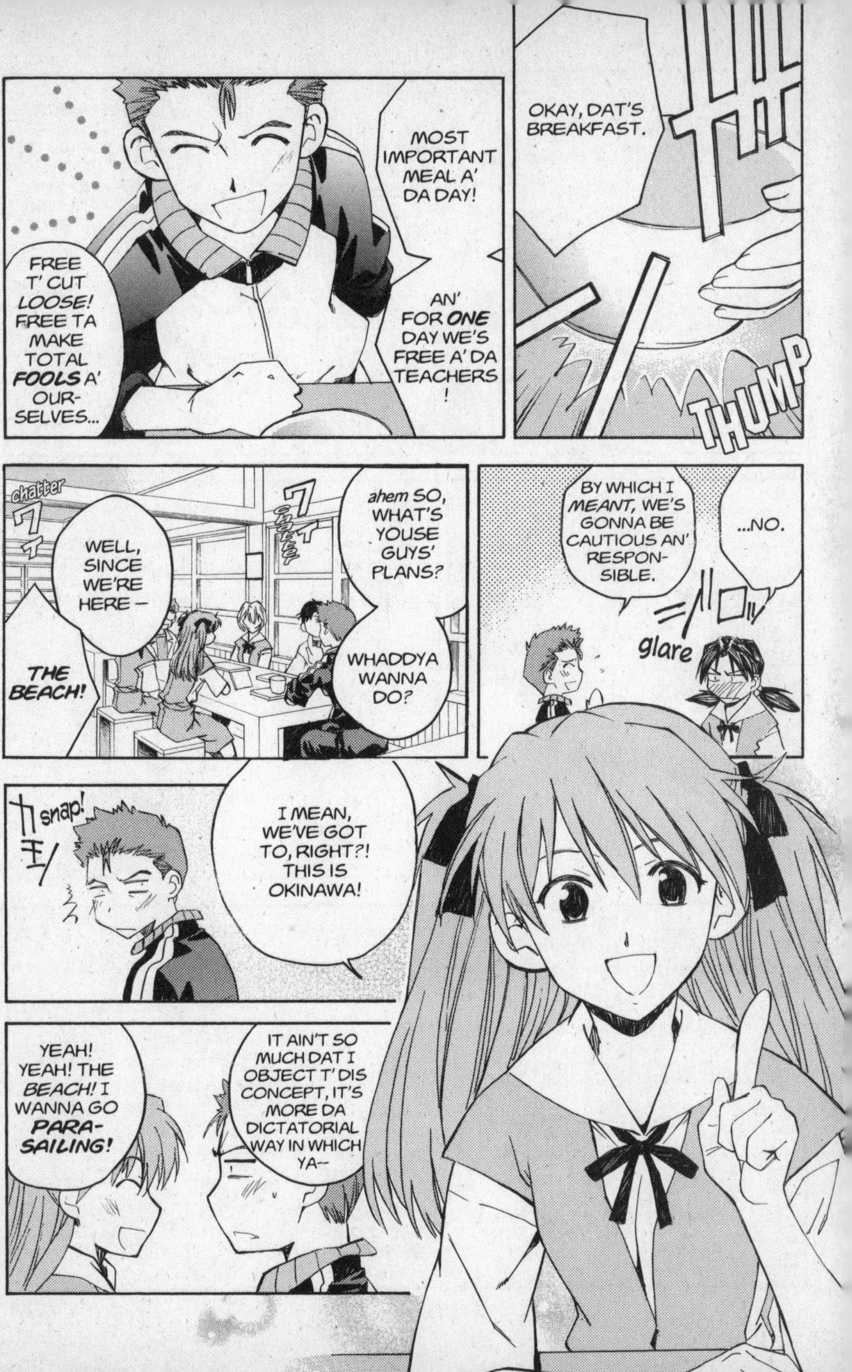
OKAY, DAT'S BREAKFAST.
THUMP
MOST IMPORTANT MEAL A' DA DAY!
AN' FOR ONE DAY WE'S FREE A' DA TEACHERS!
FREE T' CUT LOOSE! FREE TA MAKE TOTAL FOOLS A' OURSELVES...
BY WHICH I MEANT, WE'S GONNA BE CAUTIOUS AN' RESPONSIBLE.
...NO.
glare
ahem SO, WHAT'S YOUSE GUYS' PLANS?
WHADDYA WANNA DO?
chatter
chatter
WELL, SINCE WE'RE HERE —
THE BEACH!
I MEAN, WE'VE GOT TO, RIGHT?! THIS IS OKINAWA!
snap!
IT AIN'T SO MUCH DAT I OBJECT T' DIS CONCEPT, IT'S MORE DA DICTATORIAL WAY IN WHICH YA--
YEAH! YEAH! THE BEACH! I WANNA GO PARA-SAILING!

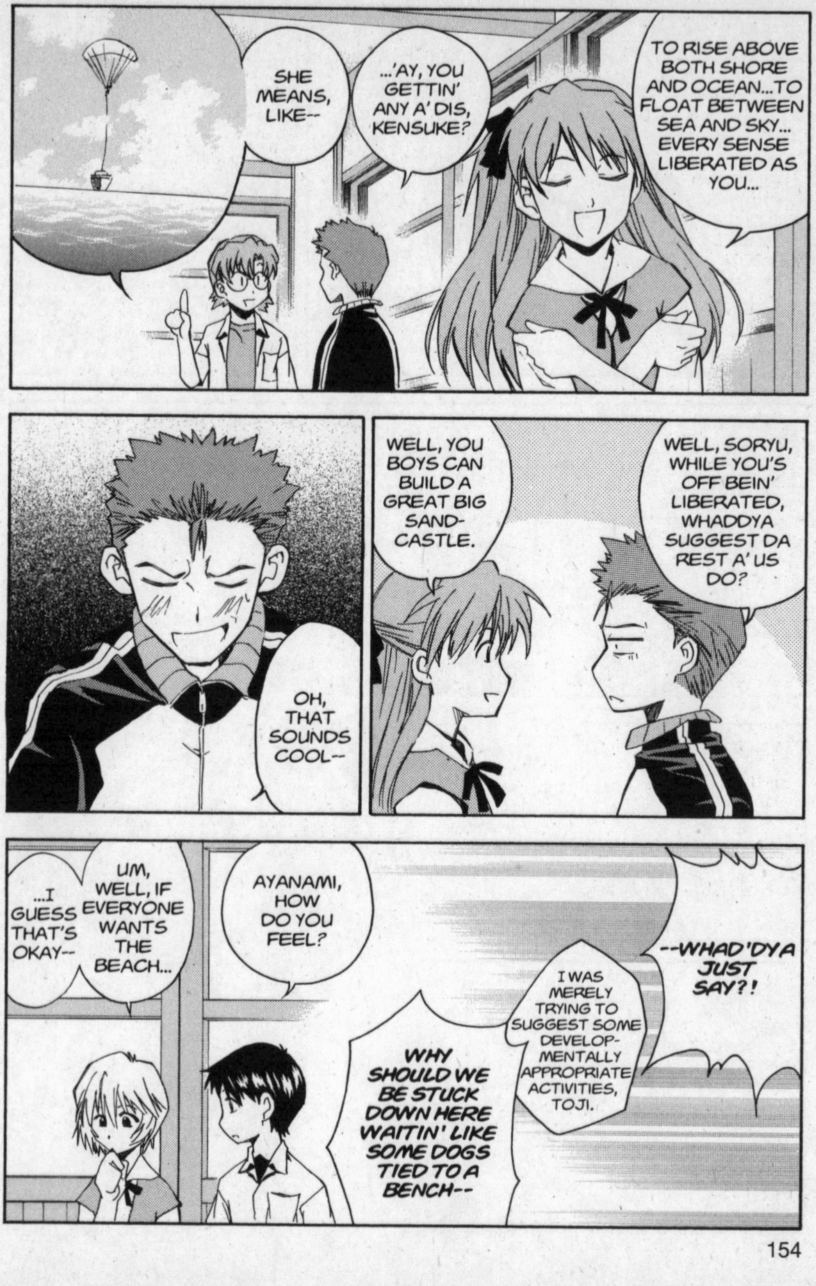
TO RISE ABOVE BOTH SHORE AND OCEAN...TO FLOAT BETWEEN SEA AND SKY... EVERY SENSE LIBERATED AS YOU...
...'AY, YOU GETTIN' ANY A' DIS, KENSUKE?
SHE MEANS, LIKE--
WELL, SORYU, WHILE YOU'S OFF BEIN' LIBERATED, WHADDYA SUGGEST DA REST A' US DO?
WELL, YOU BOYS CAN BUILD A GREAT BIG SAND-CASTLE.
OH, THAT SOUNDS COOL--
--WHAD'DYA JUST SAY?!
I WAS MERELY TRYING TO SUGGEST SOME DEVELOP-MENTALLY APPROPRIATE ACTIVITIES, TOJI.
WHY SHOULD WE BE STUCK DOWN HERE WAITIN' LIKE SOME DOGS TIED TO A BENCH--
AYANAMI, HOW DO YOU FEEL?
UM, WELL, IF EVERYONE WANTS THE BEACH...
...I GUESS THAT'S OKAY--

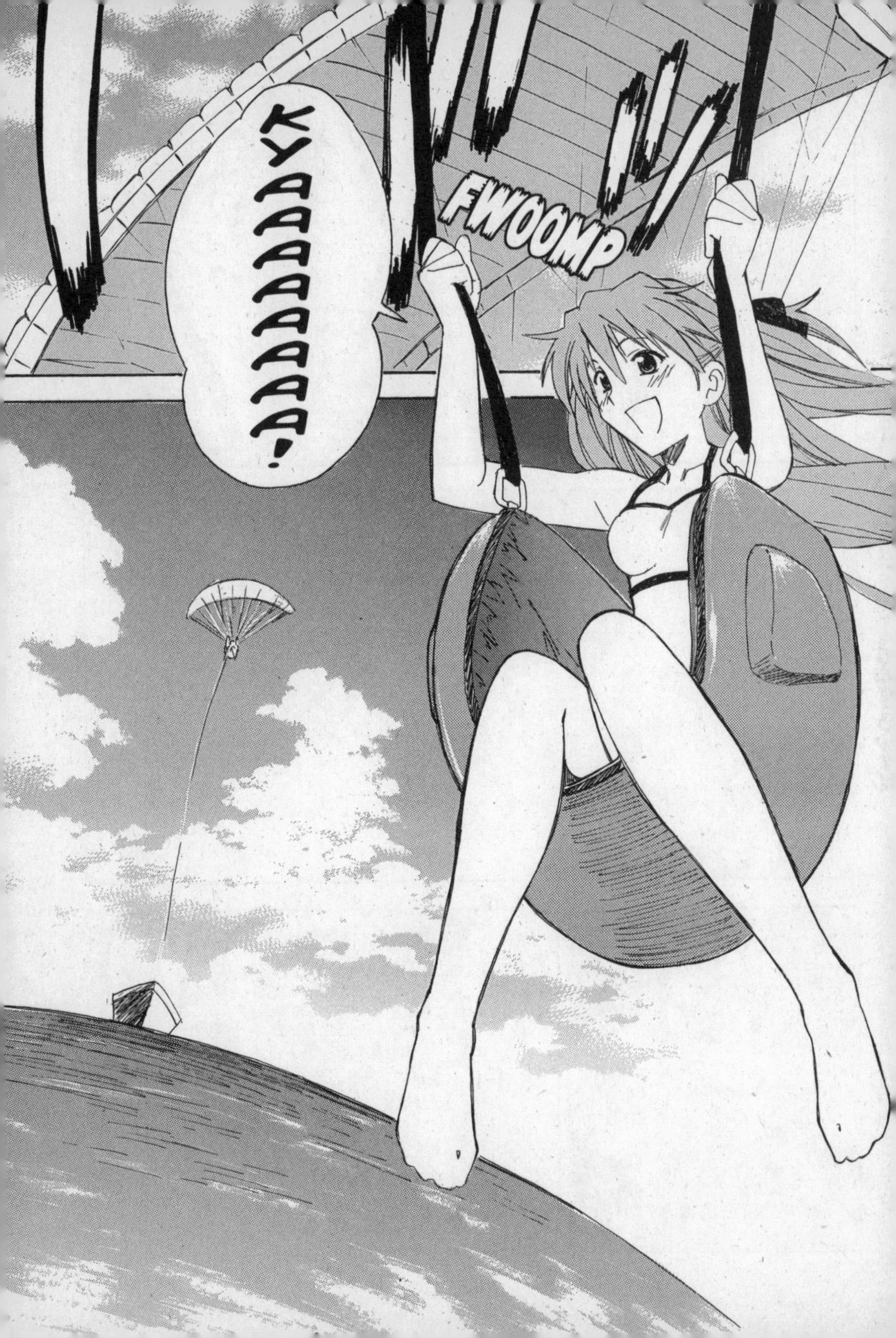
KYAAAAAAAAA!
FWOOMP

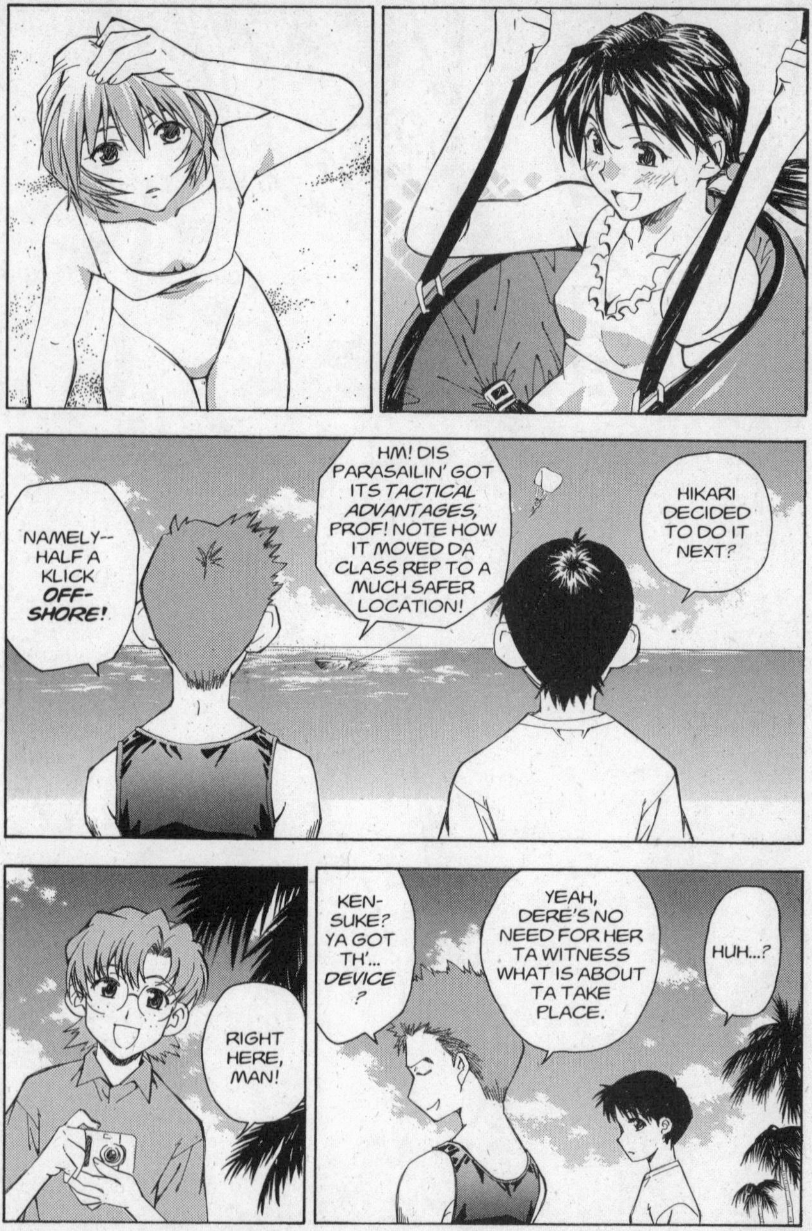
HIKARI DECIDED TO DO IT NEXT?
HM! DIS PARASAILIN' GOT ITS *TACTICAL ADVANTAGES,* PROF! NOTE HOW IT MOVED DA CLASS REP TO A MUCH SAFER LOCATION!
NAMELY-- HALF A KLICK **OFF-SHORE!**
HUH...?
YEAH, DERE'S NO NEED FOR HER TA WITNESS WHAT IS ABOUT TA TAKE PLACE.
KEN-SUKE? YA GOT TH'... *DEVICE*?
RIGHT HERE, MAN!

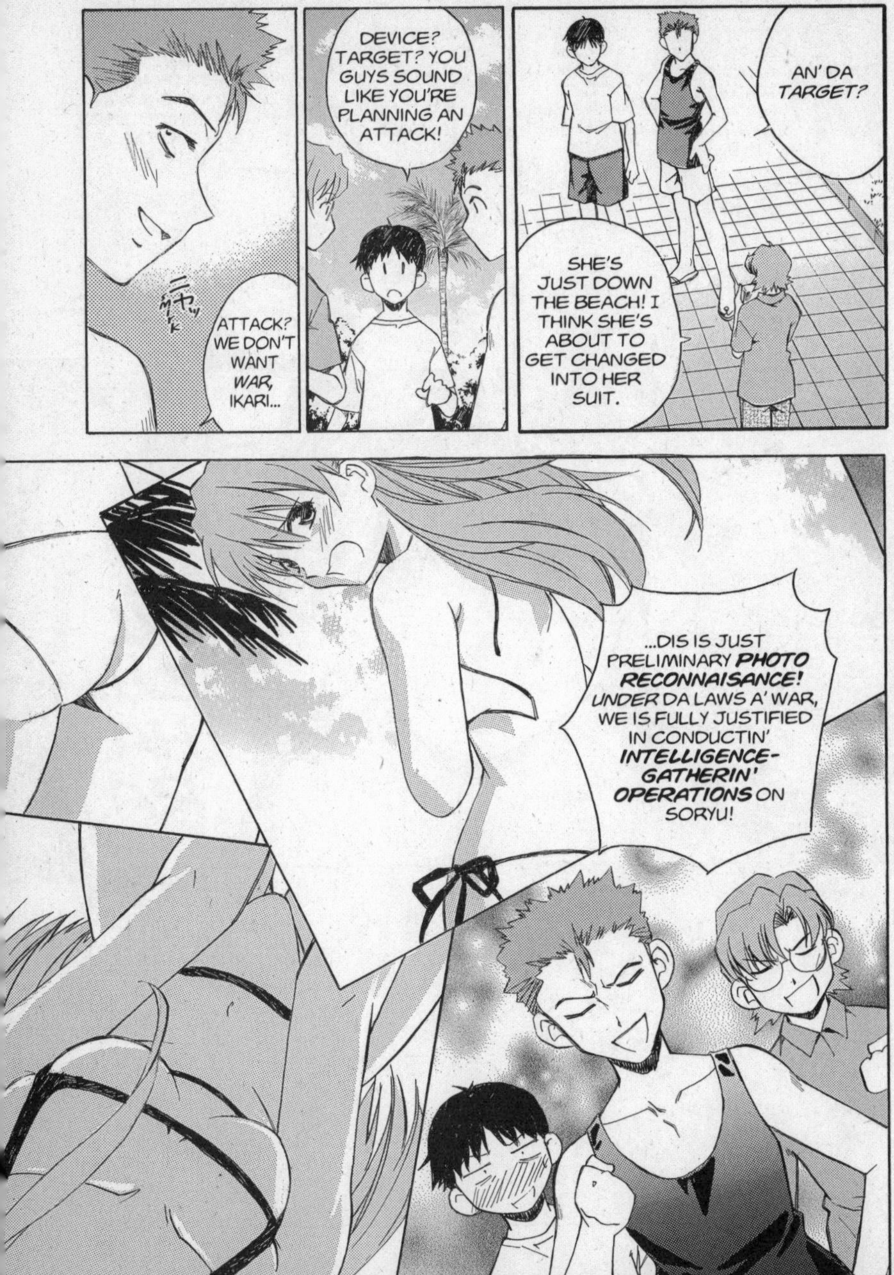
AN' DA TARGET?
SHE'S JUST DOWN THE BEACH! I THINK SHE'S ABOUT TO GET CHANGED INTO HER SUIT.
DEVICE? TARGET? YOU GUYS SOUND LIKE YOU'RE PLANNING AN ATTACK!
ニヤッ
SMIRK
ATTACK? WE DON'T WANT *WAR*, IKARI...
...DIS IS JUST PRELIMINARY ***PHOTO RECONNAISANCE!*** UNDER DA LAWS A' WAR, WE IS FULLY JUSTIFIED IN CONDUCTIN' ***INTELLIGENCE-GATHERIN' OPERATIONS*** ON SORYU!

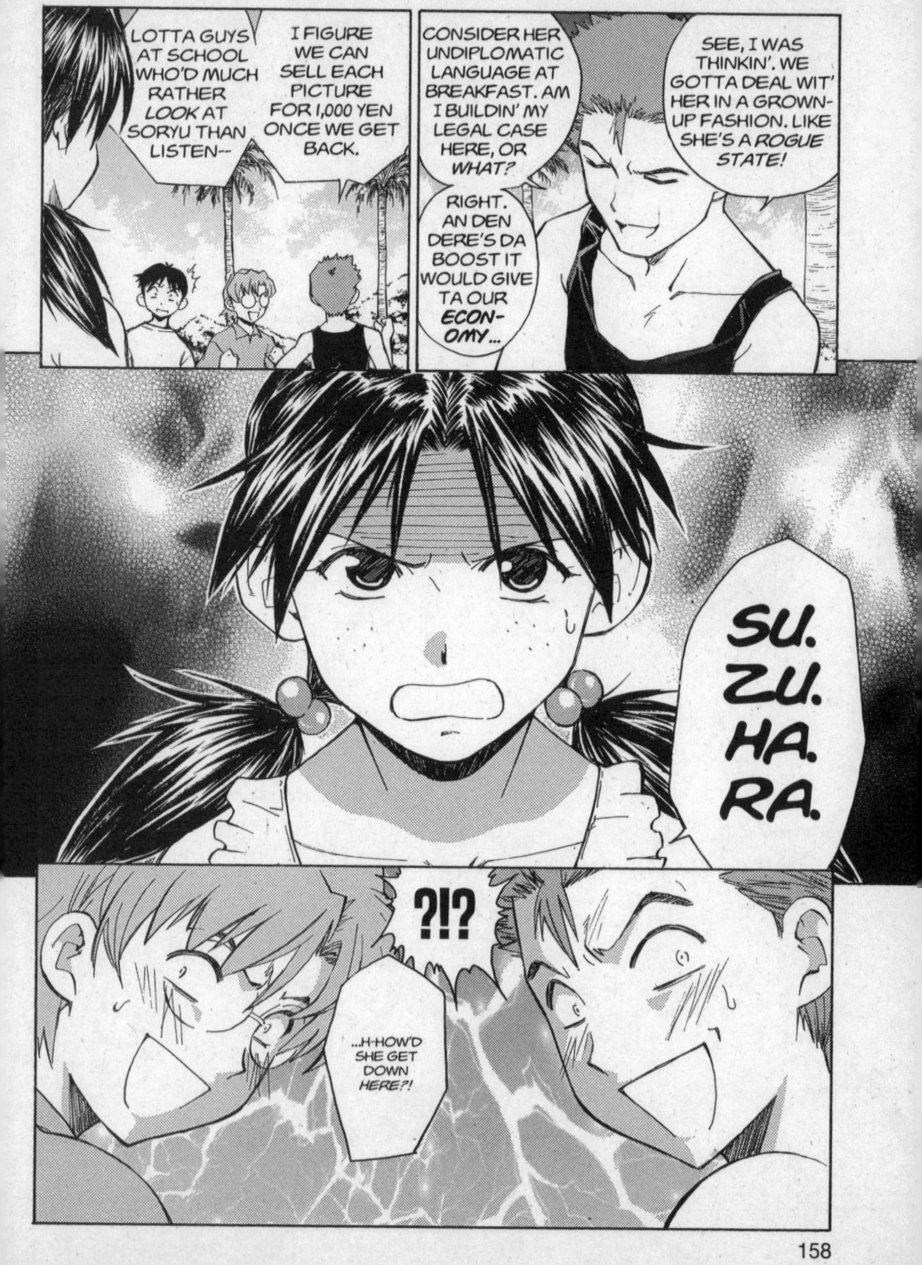
SEE, I WAS THINKIN'. WE GOTTA DEAL WIT' HER IN A GROWN-UP FASHION. LIKE SHE'S A *ROGUE STATE!*
CONSIDER HER UNDIPLOMATIC LANGUAGE AT BREAKFAST. AM I BUILDIN' MY LEGAL CASE HERE, OR *WHAT?*
RIGHT. AN DEN DERE'S DA BOOST IT WOULD GIVE TA OUR *ECONOMY*...
I FIGURE WE CAN SELL EACH PICTURE FOR 1,000 YEN ONCE WE GET BACK.
LOTTA GUYS AT SCHOOL WHO'D MUCH RATHER *LOOK* AT SORYU THAN LISTEN--
SU. ZU. HA. RA.
?!?
...H-HOW'D SHE GET DOWN *HERE?!*

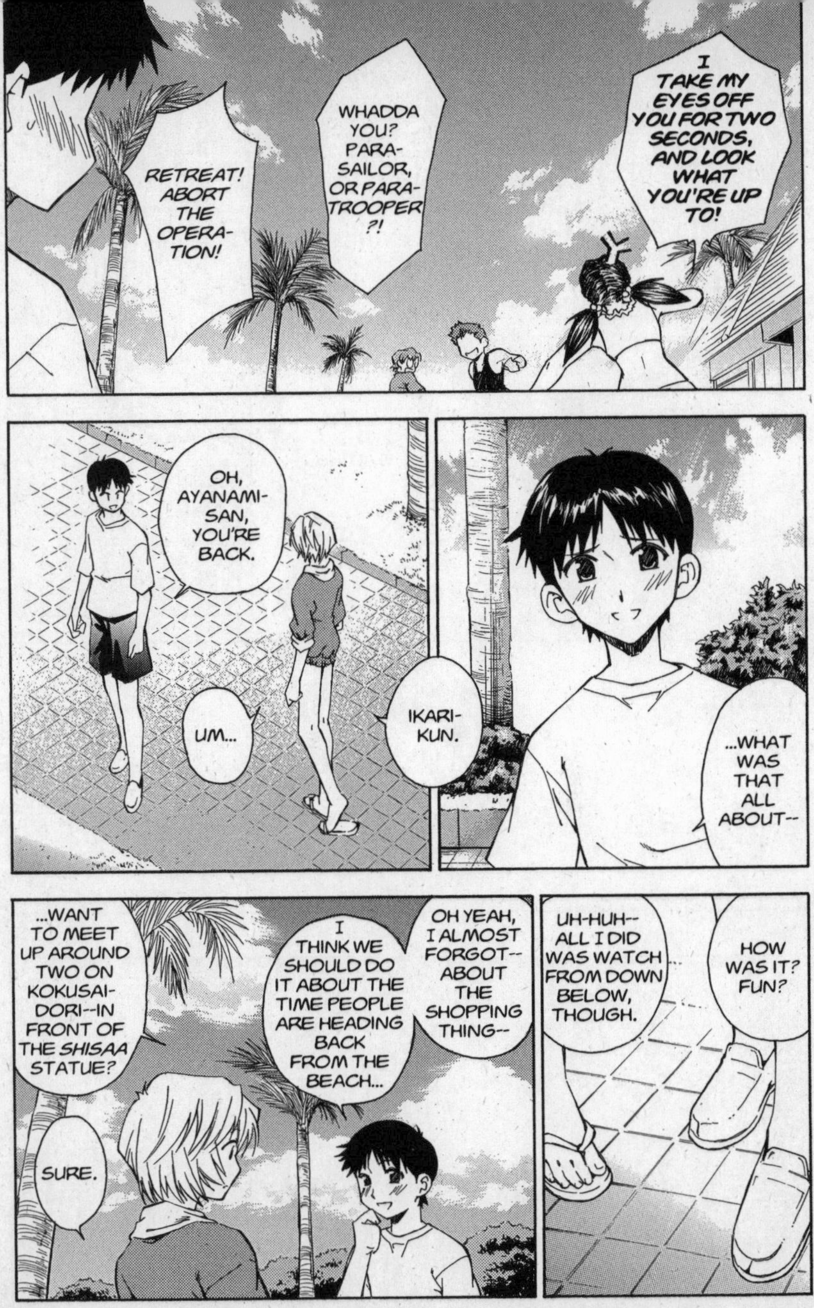
I TAKE MY EYES OFF YOU FOR TWO SECONDS, AND LOOK WHAT YOU'RE UP TO!
WHADDA YOU? PARA-SAILOR, OR PARA-TROOPER?!
RETREAT! ABORT THE OPERATION!
...WHAT WAS THAT ALL ABOUT--
OH, AYANAMI-SAN, YOU'RE BACK.
IKARI-KUN.
UM...
HOW WAS IT? FUN?
UH-HUH-- ALL I DID WAS WATCH FROM DOWN BELOW, THOUGH.
OH YEAH, I ALMOST FORGOT-- ABOUT THE SHOPPING THING--
I THINK WE SHOULD DO IT ABOUT THE TIME PEOPLE ARE HEADING BACK FROM THE BEACH...
...WANT TO MEET UP AROUND TWO ON KOKUSAI-DORI--IN FRONT OF THE *SHISAA* STATUE?
SURE.

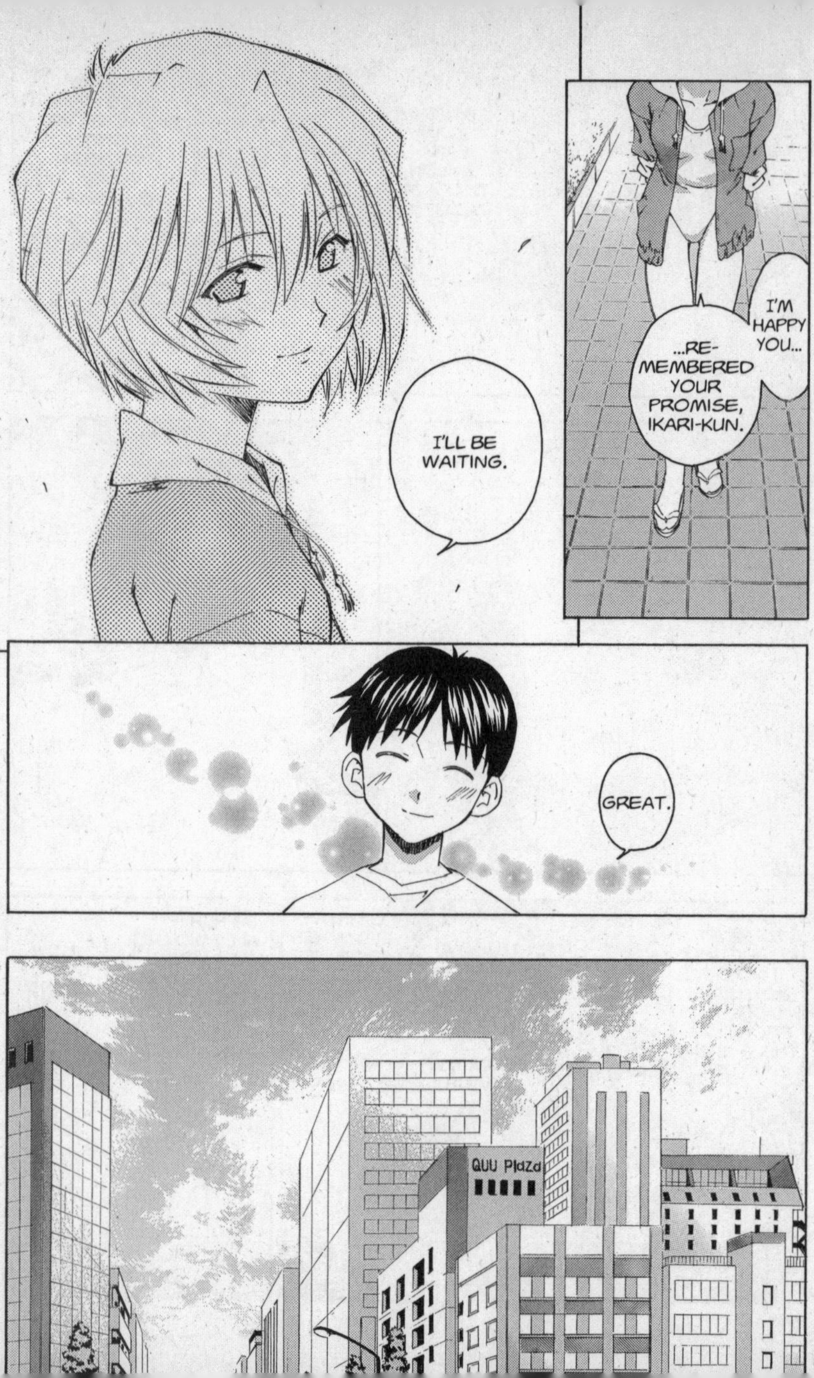
I'M HAPPY YOU...
...RE-MEMBERED YOUR PROMISE, IKARI-KUN.
I'LL BE WAITING.
GREAT.
QUU Plaza

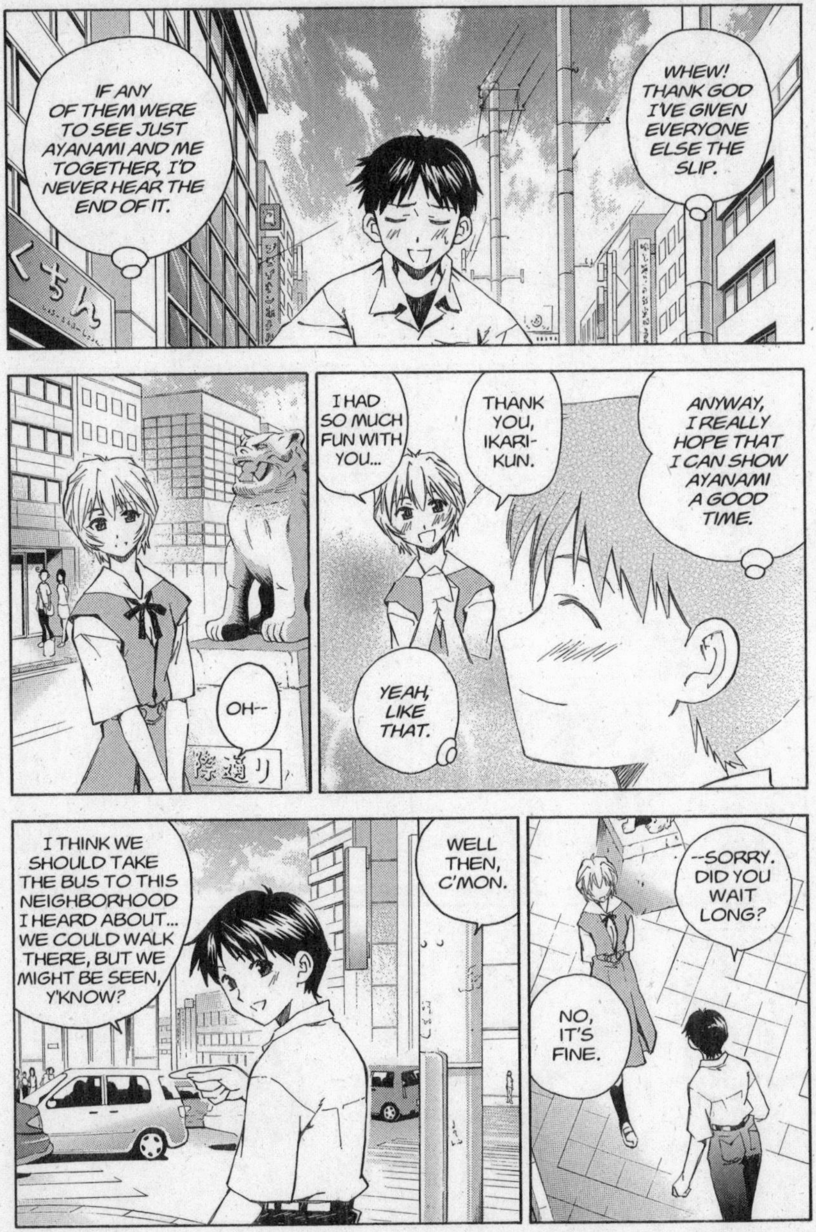
WHEW! THANK GOD I'VE GIVEN EVERYONE ELSE THE SLIP.
IF ANY OF THEM WERE TO SEE JUST AYANAMI AND ME TOGETHER, I'D NEVER HEAR THE END OF IT.
ANYWAY, I REALLY HOPE THAT I CAN SHOW AYANAMI A GOOD TIME.
THANK YOU, IKARI-KUN.
I HAD SO MUCH FUN WITH YOU...
YEAH, LIKE THAT.
OH--
--SORRY. DID YOU WAIT LONG?
NO, IT'S FINE.
WELL THEN, C'MON.
I THINK WE SHOULD TAKE THE BUS TO THIS NEIGHBORHOOD I HEARD ABOUT... WE COULD WALK THERE, BUT WE MIGHT BE SEEN, Y'KNOW?

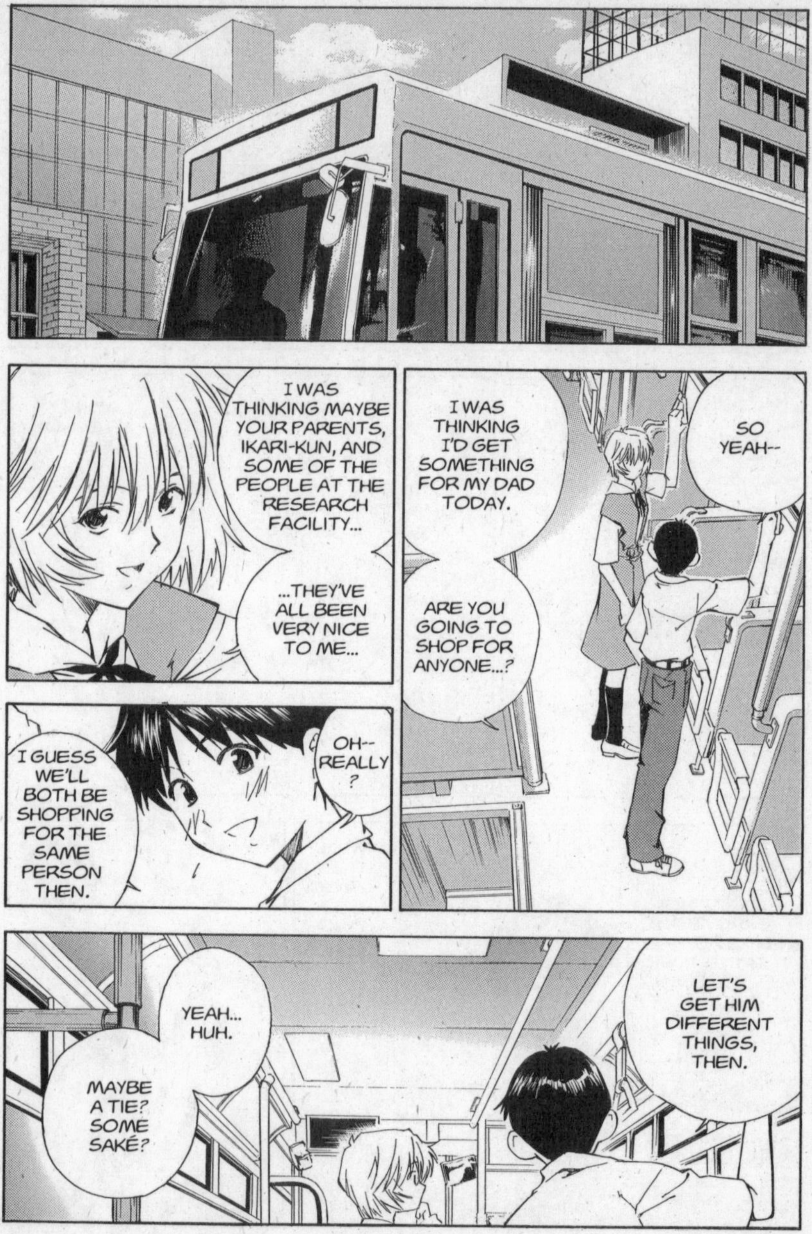
SO YEAH--
I WAS THINKING I'D GET SOMETHING FOR MY DAD TODAY.
ARE YOU GOING TO SHOP FOR ANYONE...?
I WAS THINKING MAYBE YOUR PARENTS, IKARI-KUN, AND SOME OF THE PEOPLE AT THE RESEARCH FACILITY...
...THEY'VE ALL BEEN VERY NICE TO ME...
OH--REALLY?
I GUESS WE'LL BOTH BE SHOPPING FOR THE SAME PERSON THEN.
LET'S GET HIM DIFFERENT THINGS, THEN.
YEAH... HUH.
MAYBE A TIE? SOME SAKÉ?

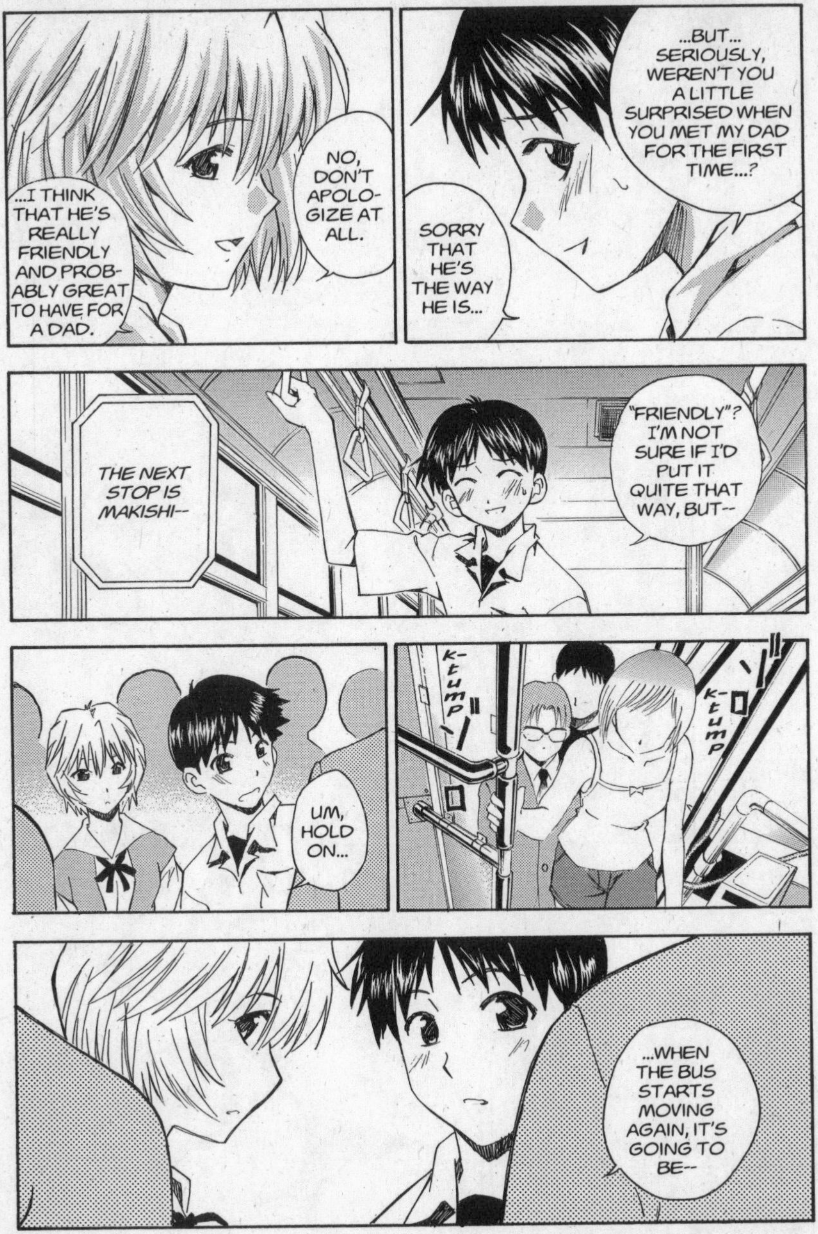
...BUT... SERIOUSLY, WEREN'T YOU A LITTLE SURPRISED WHEN YOU MET MY DAD FOR THE FIRST TIME...?
SORRY THAT HE'S THE WAY HE IS...
NO, DON'T APOLOGIZE AT ALL.
...I THINK THAT HE'S REALLY FRIENDLY AND PROBABLY GREAT TO HAVE FOR A DAD.
"FRIENDLY"? I'M NOT SURE IF I'D PUT IT QUITE THAT WAY, BUT--
THE NEXT STOP IS MAKISHI--
k-tump
k-tump
UM, HOLD ON...
...WHEN THE BUS STARTS MOVING AGAIN, IT'S GOING TO BE--

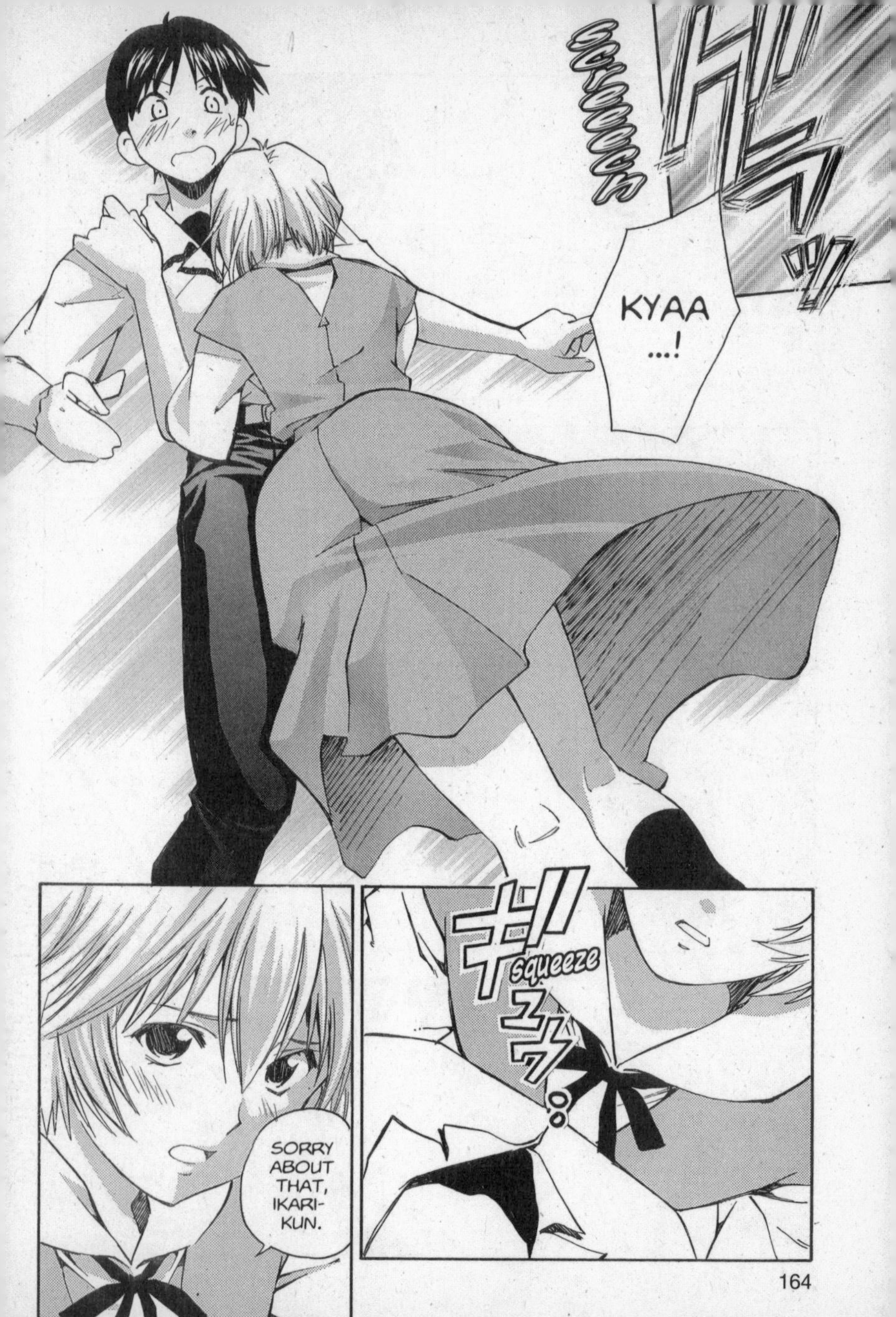
KYAA ...!
squeeze
SORRY ABOUT THAT, IKARI-KUN.

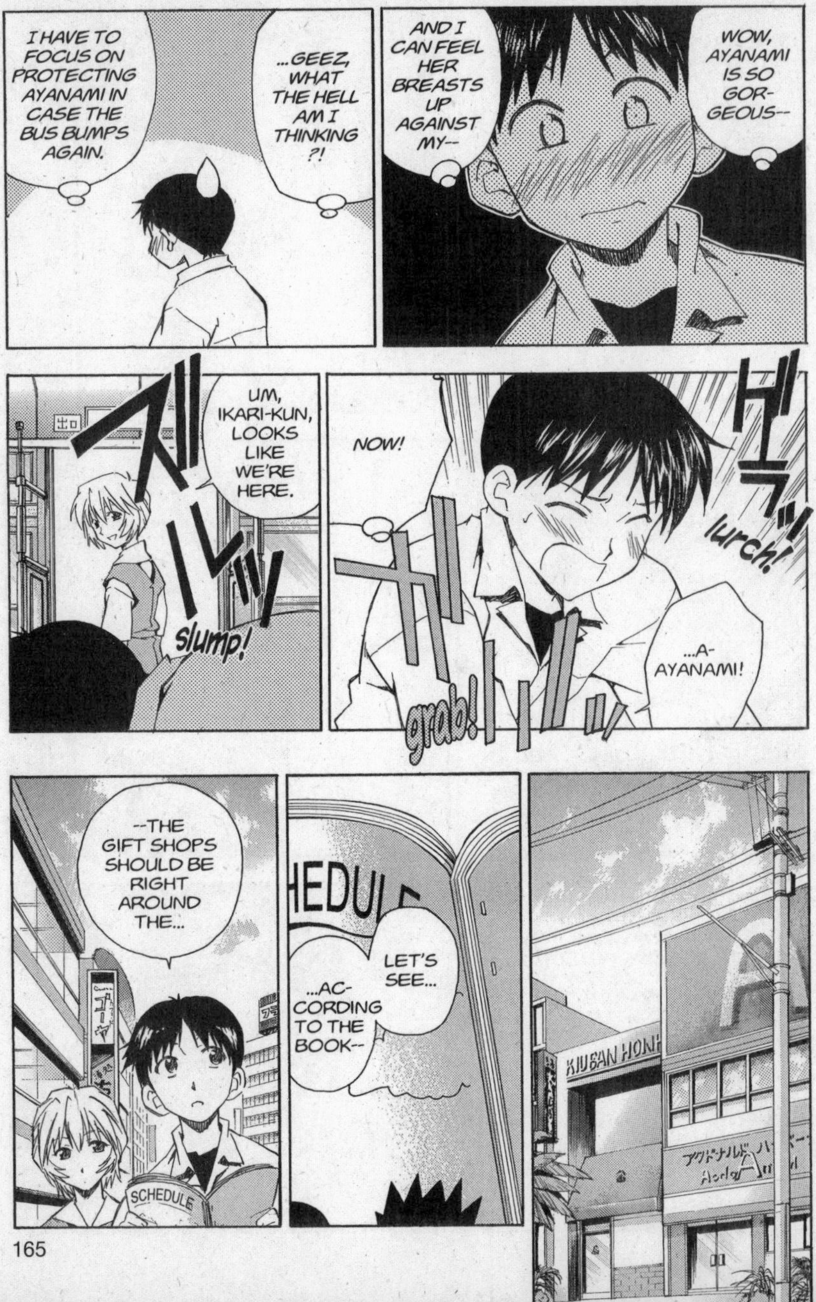
WOW, AYANAMI IS SO GORGEOUS--
AND I CAN FEEL HER BREASTS UP AGAINST MY--
...GEEZ, WHAT THE HELL AM I THINKING?!
I HAVE TO FOCUS ON PROTECTING AYANAMI IN CASE THE BUS BUMPS AGAIN.
lurch!
NOW!
...A-AYANAMI!
grab!
UM, IKARI-KUN, LOOKS LIKE WE'RE HERE.
slump!
LET'S SEE...
...ACCORDING TO THE BOOK--
--THE GIFT SHOPS SHOULD BE RIGHT AROUND THE...
SCHEDULE

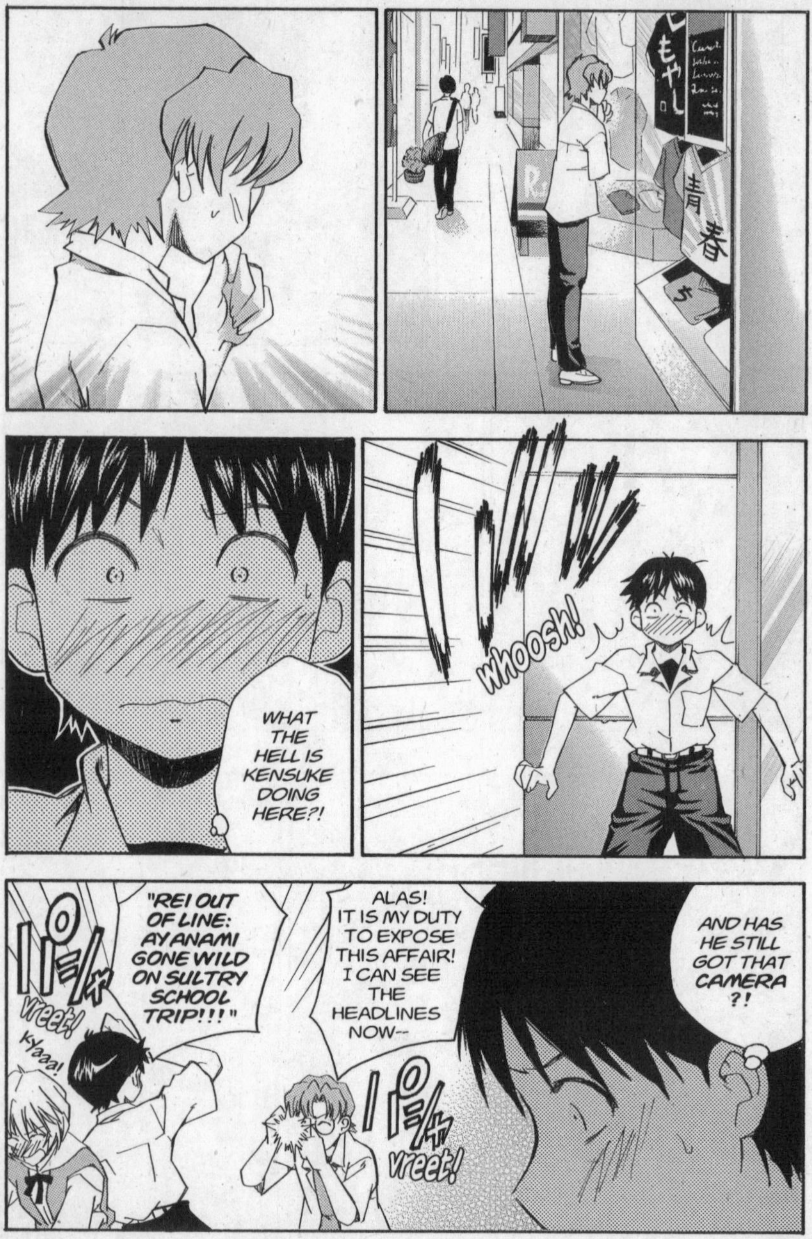
もやし
青春
whoosh!
WHAT THE HELL IS KENSUKE DOING HERE?!
AND HAS HE STILL GOT THAT CAMERA?!
ALAS! IT IS MY DUTY TO EXPOSE THIS AFFAIR! I CAN SEE THE HEADLINES NOW--
vreet!
"REI OUT OF LINE: AYANAMI GONE WILD ON SULTRY SCHOOL TRIP!!!"
vreet!
kyaaa!

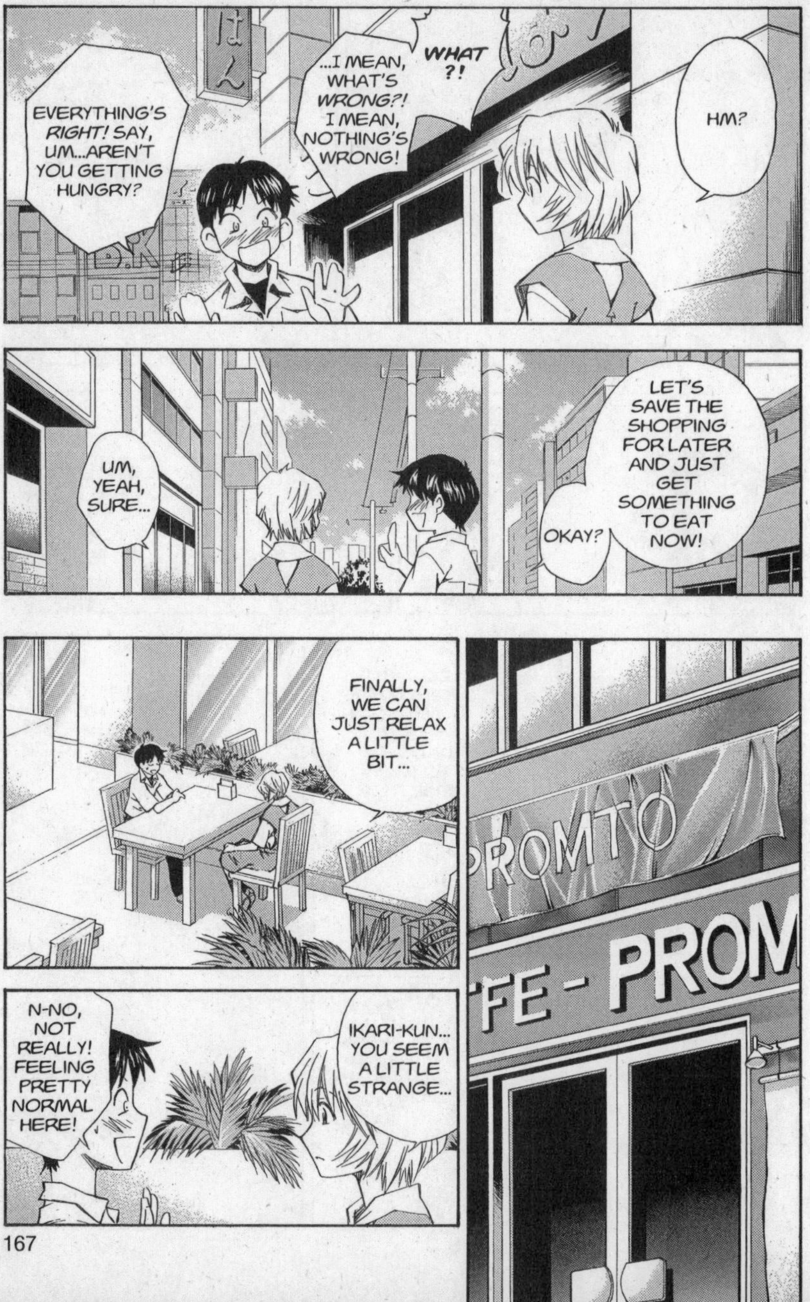
HM?
WHAT?!
...I MEAN, WHAT'S WRONG?! I MEAN, NOTHING'S WRONG!
EVERYTHING'S RIGHT! SAY, UM...AREN'T YOU GETTING HUNGRY?
LET'S SAVE THE SHOPPING FOR LATER AND JUST GET SOMETHING TO EAT NOW!
OKAY?
UM, YEAH, SURE...
PROMTO
FE - PROM
FINALLY, WE CAN JUST RELAX A LITTLE BIT...
IKARI-KUN... YOU SEEM A LITTLE STRANGE...
N-NO, NOT REALLY! FEELING PRETTY NORMAL HERE!

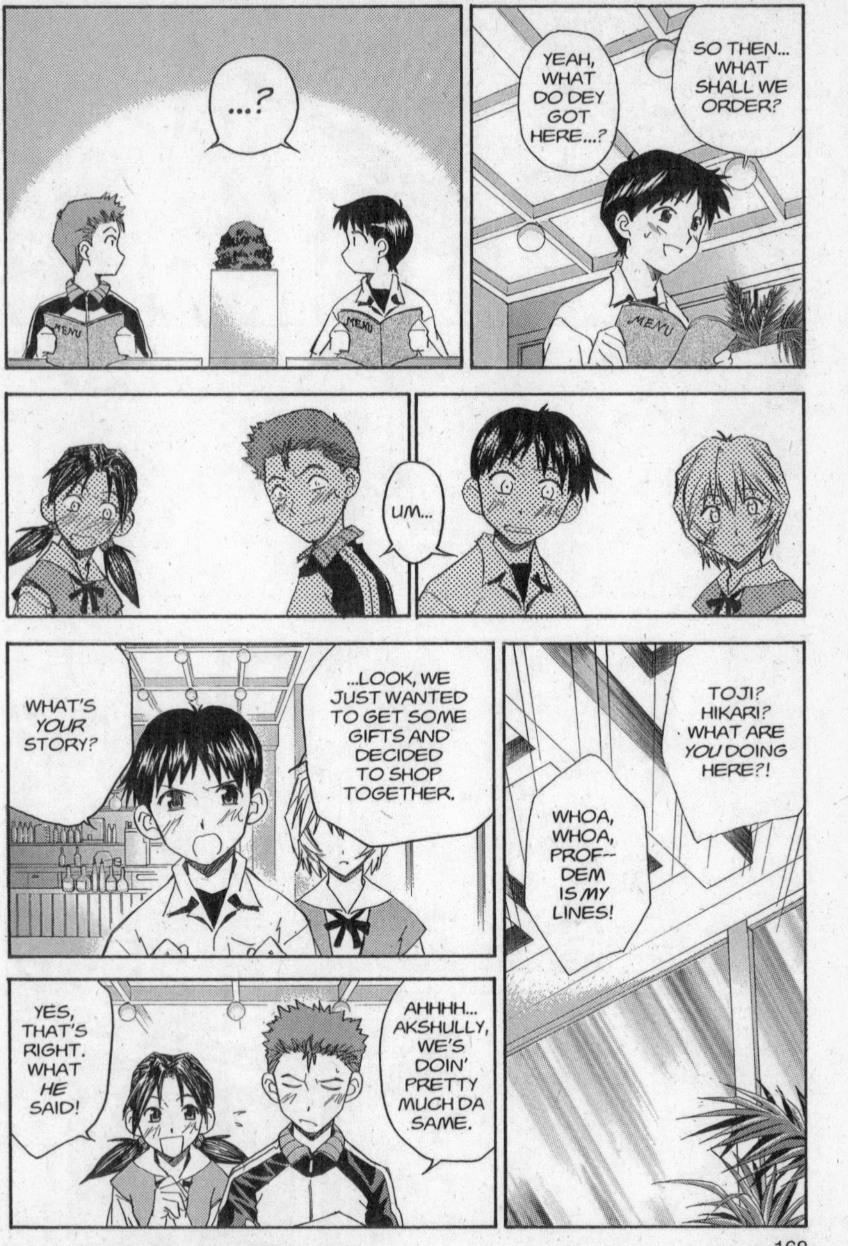
SO THEN... WHAT SHALL WE ORDER?
YEAH, WHAT DO DEY GOT HERE...?
...?
UM...
TOJI? HIKARI? WHAT ARE *YOU* DOING HERE?!
WHOA, WHOA, PROF-- DEM IS *MY* LINES!
...LOOK, WE JUST WANTED TO GET SOME GIFTS AND DECIDED TO SHOP TOGETHER.
WHAT'S *YOUR* STORY?
AHHHH... AKSHULLY, WE'S DOIN' PRETTY MUCH DA SAME.
YES, THAT'S RIGHT. WHAT *HE* SAID!

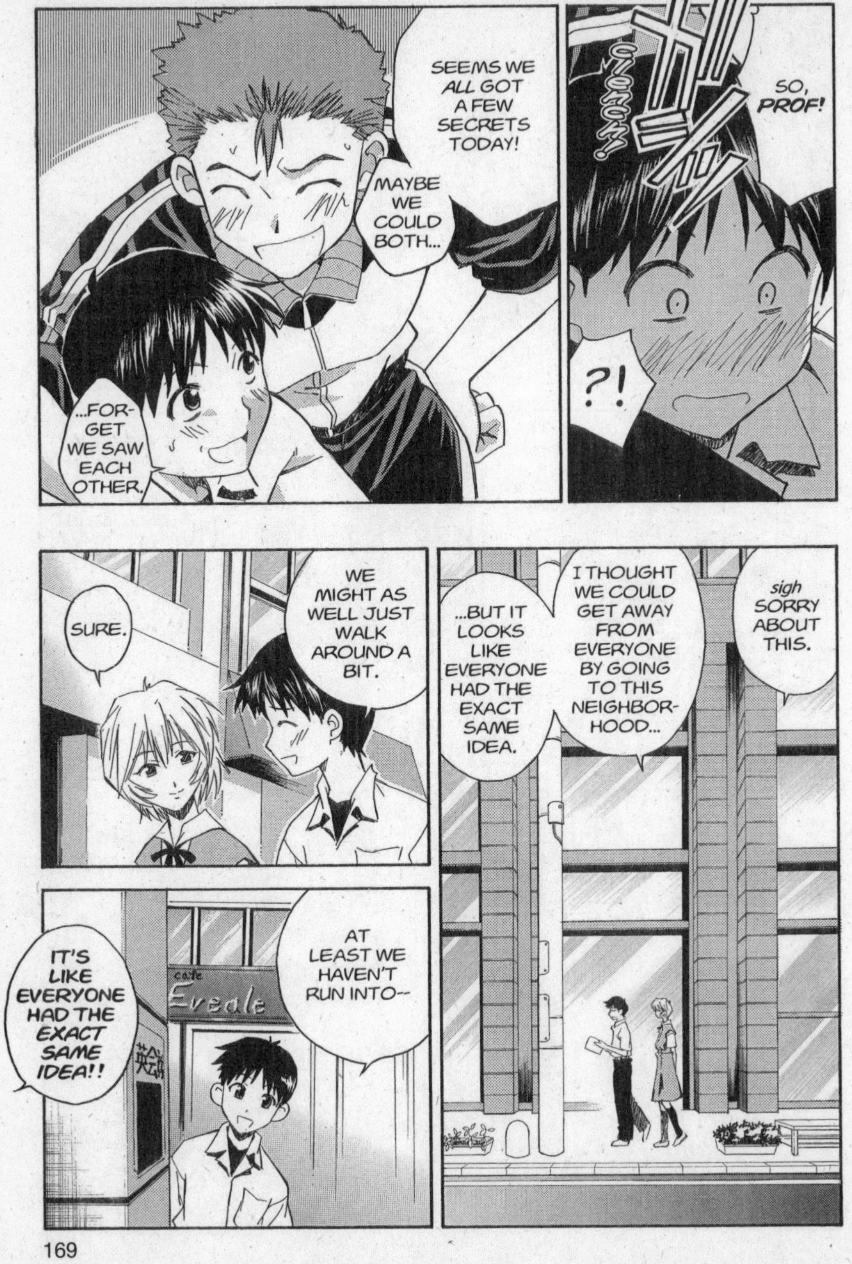
Grench!
SO, *PROF!*
?!
SEEMS WE *ALL* GOT A FEW SECRETS TODAY!
MAYBE WE COULD BOTH...
...FOR-GET WE SAW EACH OTHER.
sigh SORRY ABOUT THIS.
I THOUGHT WE COULD GET AWAY FROM EVERYONE BY GOING TO THIS NEIGHBOR-HOOD...
...BUT IT LOOKS LIKE EVERYONE HAD THE EXACT SAME IDEA.
WE MIGHT AS WELL JUST WALK AROUND A BIT.
SURE.
AT LEAST WE HAVEN'T RUN INTO--
IT'S LIKE EVERYONE HAD THE *EXACT* SAME IDEA!!

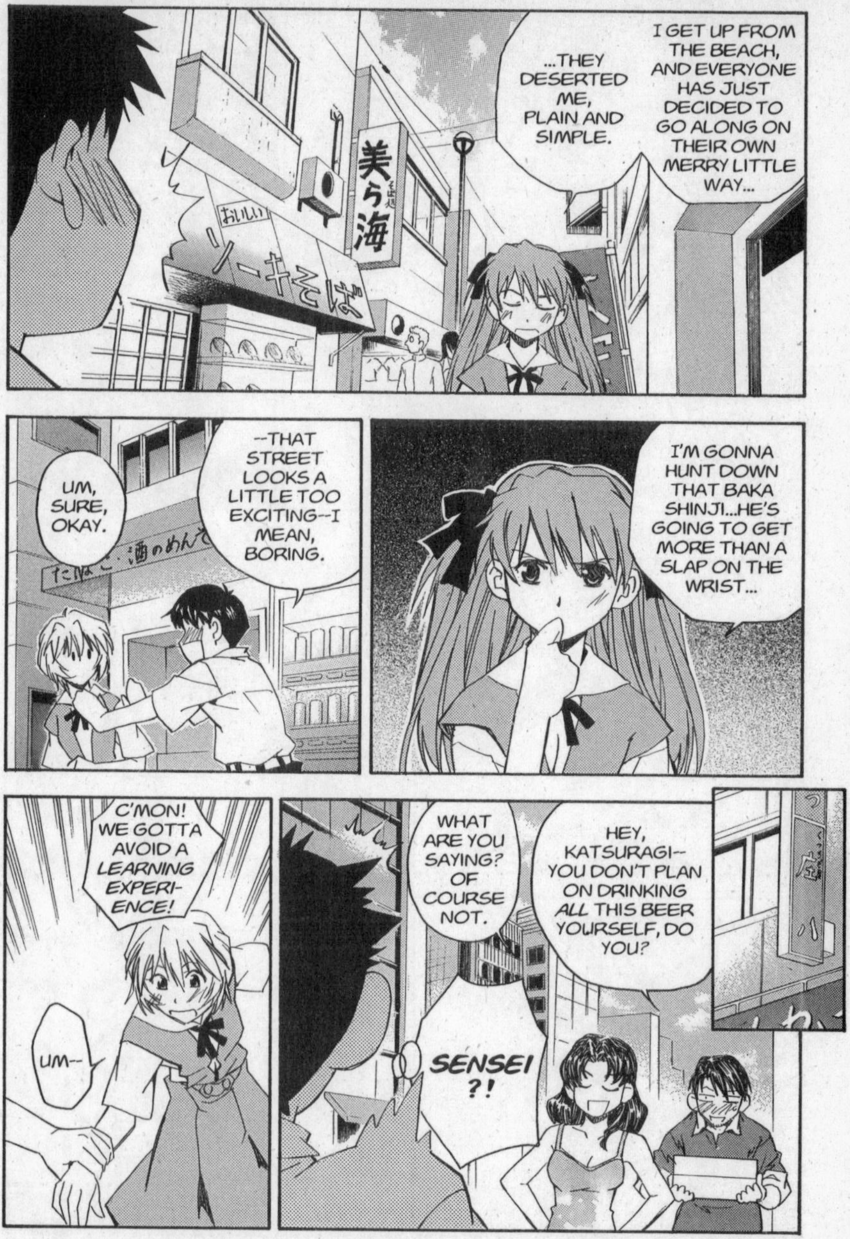
I GET UP FROM THE BEACH, AND EVERYONE HAS JUST DECIDED TO GO ALONG ON THEIR OWN MERRY LITTLE WAY...
...THEY DESERTED ME, PLAIN AND SIMPLE.
美ら海
おいしい
ソーキそば
I'M GONNA HUNT DOWN THAT BAKA SHINJI...HE'S GOING TO GET MORE THAN A SLAP ON THE WRIST...
--THAT STREET LOOKS A LITTLE TOO EXCITING--I MEAN, BORING.
UM, SURE, OKAY.
HEY, KATSURAGI--YOU DON'T PLAN ON DRINKING *ALL* THIS BEER YOURSELF, DO YOU?
WHAT ARE YOU SAYING? OF COURSE NOT.
SENSEI?!
C'MON! WE GOTTA AVOID A LEARNING EXPERI-ENCE!
UM--

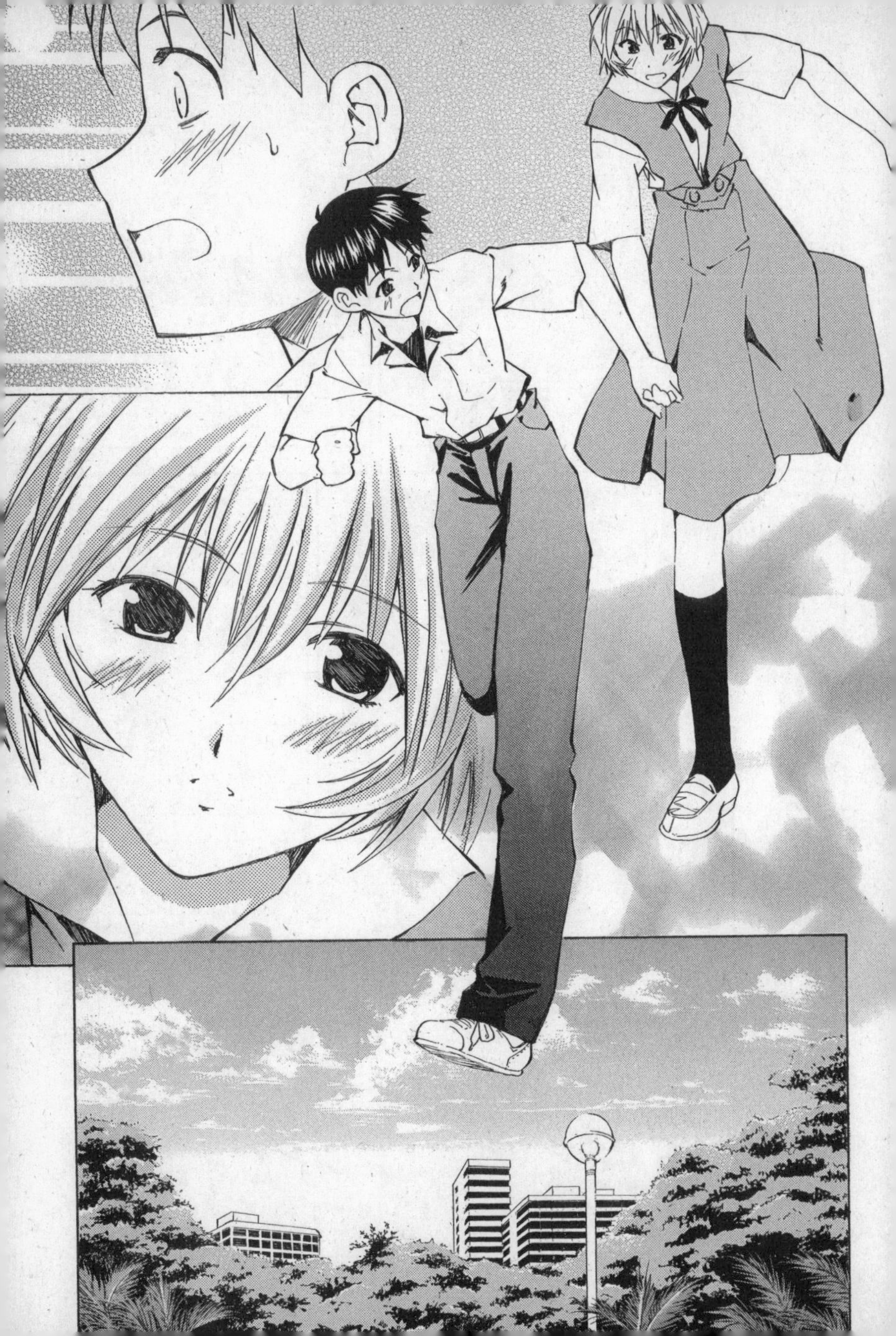

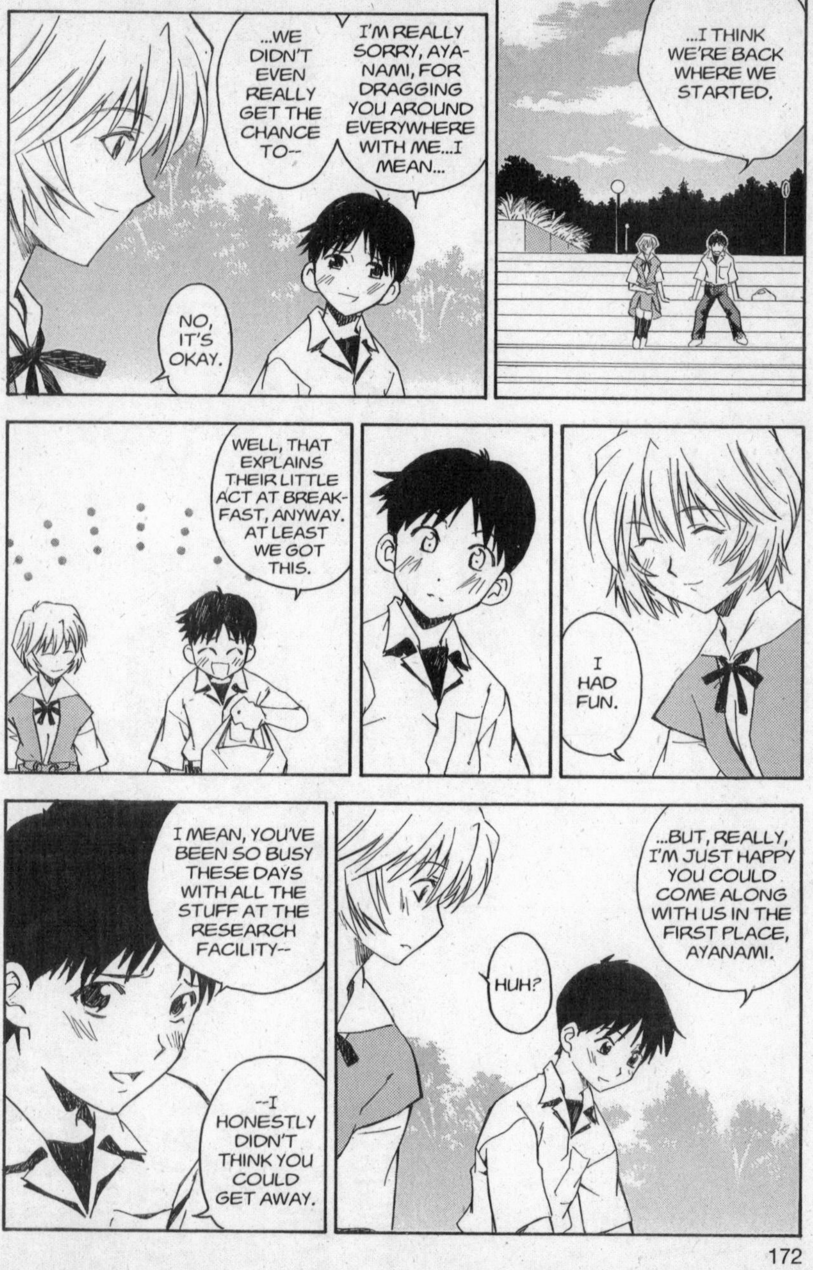
...I THINK WE'RE BACK WHERE WE STARTED.
I'M REALLY SORRY, AYA-NAMI, FOR DRAGGING YOU AROUND EVERYWHERE WITH ME...I MEAN...
...WE DIDN'T EVEN REALLY GET THE CHANCE TO--
NO, IT'S OKAY.
I HAD FUN.
WELL, THAT EXPLAINS THEIR LITTLE ACT AT BREAK-FAST, ANYWAY. AT LEAST WE GOT THIS.
...BUT, REALLY, I'M JUST HAPPY YOU COULD COME ALONG WITH US IN THE FIRST PLACE, AYANAMI.
HUH?
I MEAN, YOU'VE BEEN SO BUSY THESE DAYS WITH ALL THE STUFF AT THE RESEARCH FACILITY--
--I HONESTLY DIDN'T THINK YOU COULD GET AWAY.

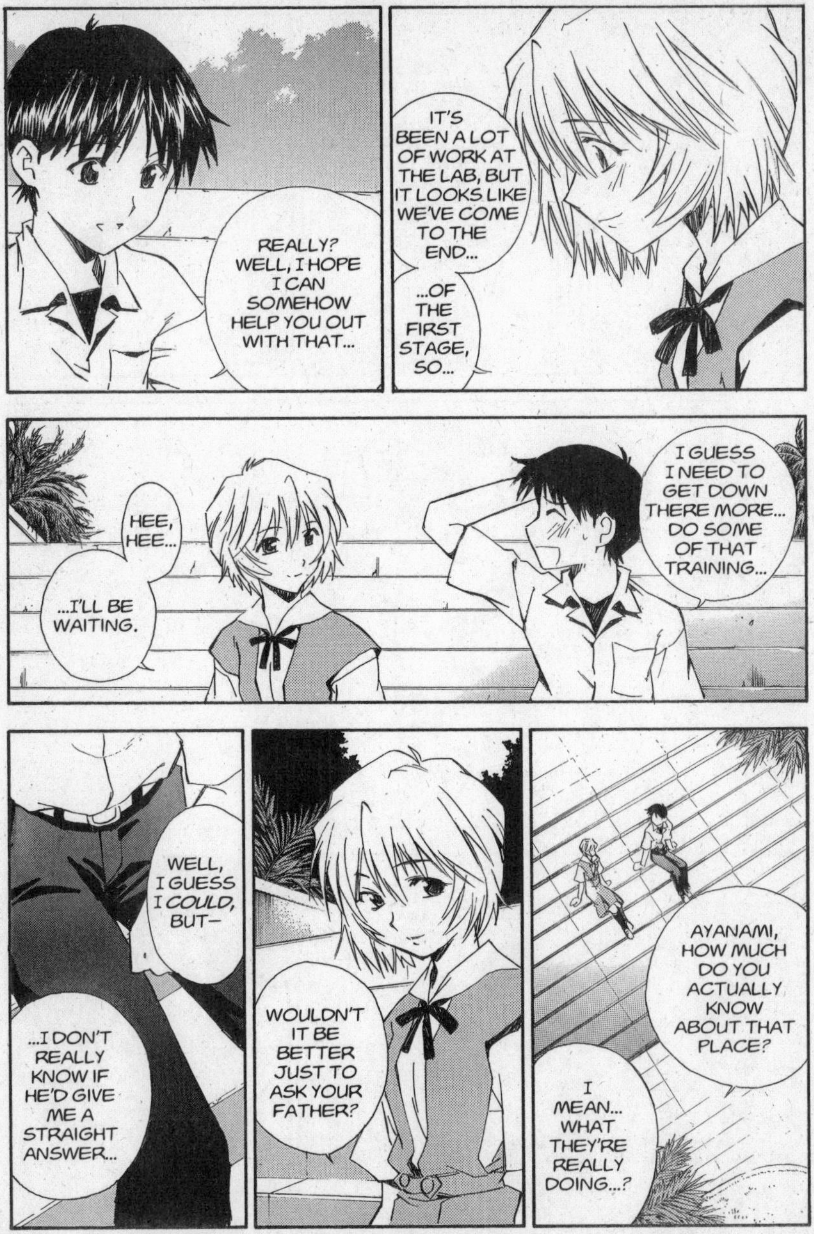
IT'S BEEN A LOT OF WORK AT THE LAB, BUT IT LOOKS LIKE WE'VE COME TO THE END...
...OF THE FIRST STAGE, SO...
REALLY? WELL, I HOPE I CAN SOMEHOW HELP YOU OUT WITH THAT...
I GUESS I NEED TO GET DOWN THERE MORE... DO SOME OF THAT TRAINING...
HEE, HEE...
...I'LL BE WAITING.
AYANAMI, HOW MUCH DO YOU ACTUALLY KNOW ABOUT THAT PLACE?
I MEAN... WHAT THEY'RE REALLY DOING...?
WOULDN'T IT BE BETTER JUST TO ASK YOUR FATHER?
WELL, I GUESS I *COULD*, BUT–
...I DON'T REALLY KNOW IF HE'D GIVE ME A STRAIGHT ANSWER...

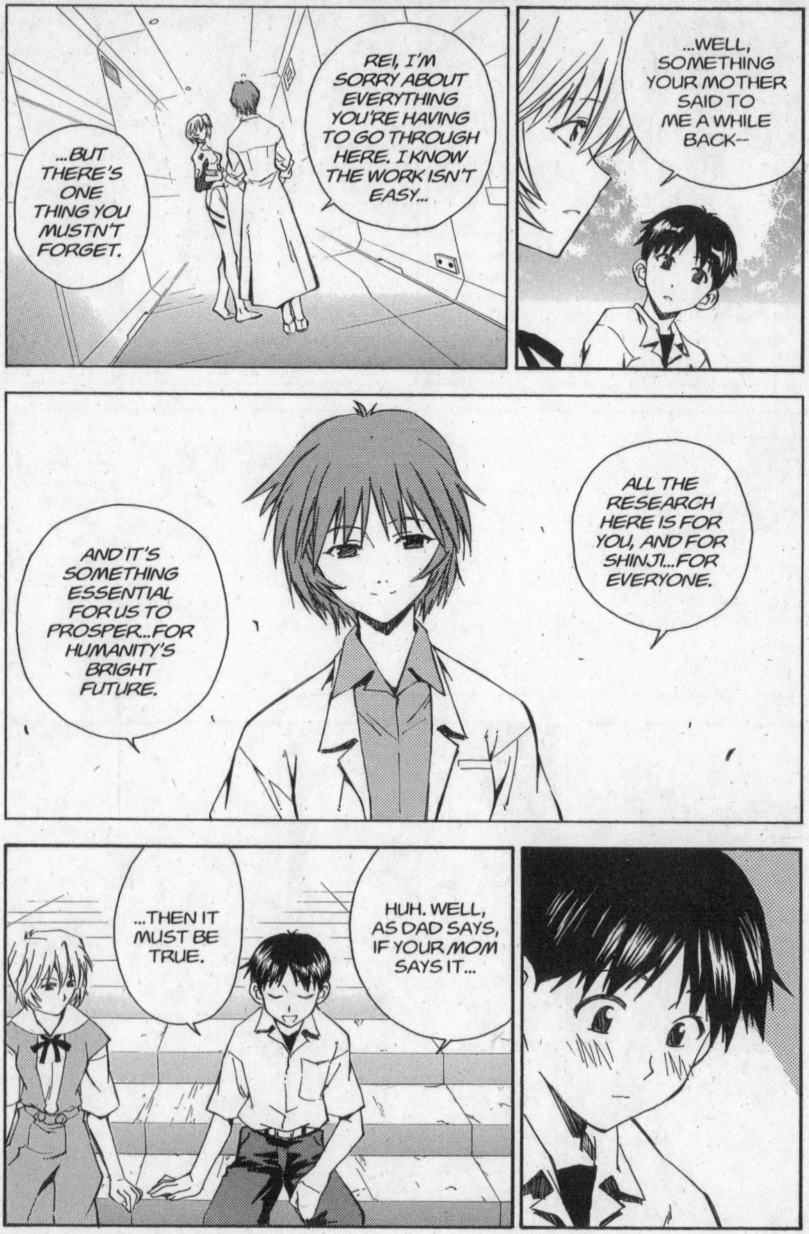
...WELL, SOMETHING YOUR MOTHER SAID TO ME A WHILE BACK--
REI, I'M SORRY ABOUT EVERYTHING YOU'RE HAVING TO GO THROUGH HERE. I KNOW THE WORK ISN'T EASY...
...BUT THERE'S ONE THING YOU MUSTN'T FORGET.
ALL THE RESEARCH HERE IS FOR YOU, AND FOR SHINJI...FOR EVERYONE.
AND IT'S SOMETHING ESSENTIAL FOR US TO PROSPER...FOR HUMANITY'S BRIGHT FUTURE.
HUH. WELL, AS DAD SAYS, IF YOUR MOM SAYS IT...
...THEN IT MUST BE TRUE.

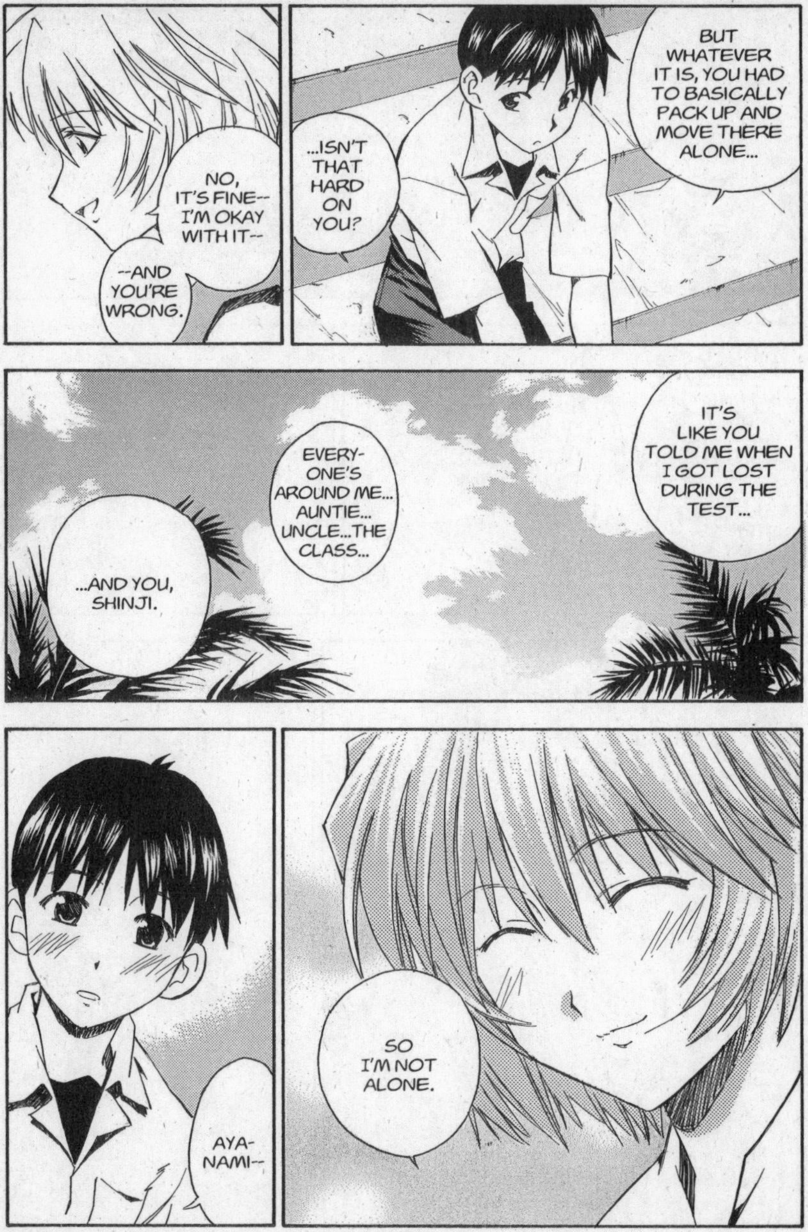
BUT WHATEVER IT IS, YOU HAD TO BASICALLY PACK UP AND MOVE THERE ALONE...
...ISN'T THAT HARD ON YOU?
NO, IT'S FINE-- I'M OKAY WITH IT--
--AND YOU'RE WRONG.
IT'S LIKE YOU TOLD ME WHEN I GOT LOST DURING THE TEST...
EVERY-ONE'S AROUND ME... AUNTIE... UNCLE...THE CLASS...
...AND YOU, SHINJI.
SO I'M NOT ALONE.
AYA-NAMI--

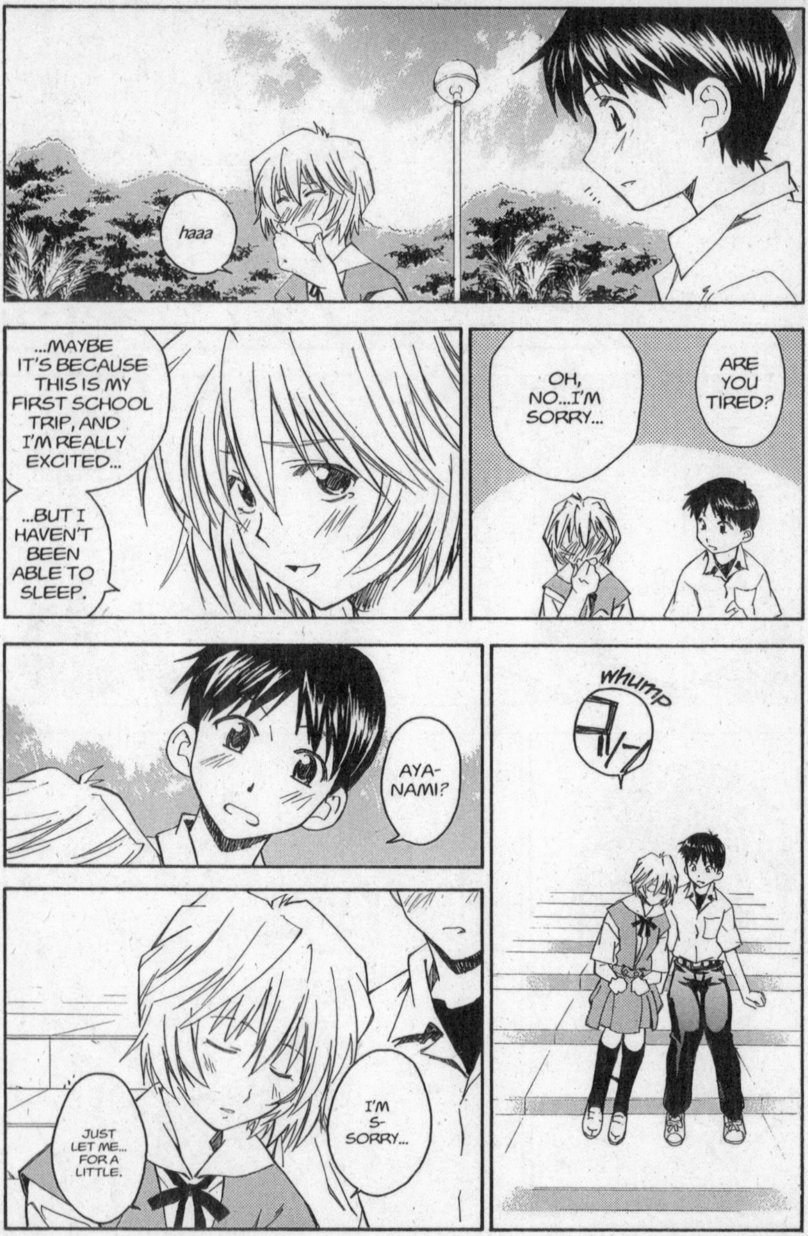
haaa
ARE YOU TIRED?
OH, NO...I'M SORRY...
...MAYBE IT'S BECAUSE THIS IS MY FIRST SCHOOL TRIP, AND I'M REALLY EXCITED...
...BUT I HAVEN'T BEEN ABLE TO SLEEP.
whump
AYA-NAMI?
I'M S-SORRY...
JUST LET ME... FOR A LITTLE.

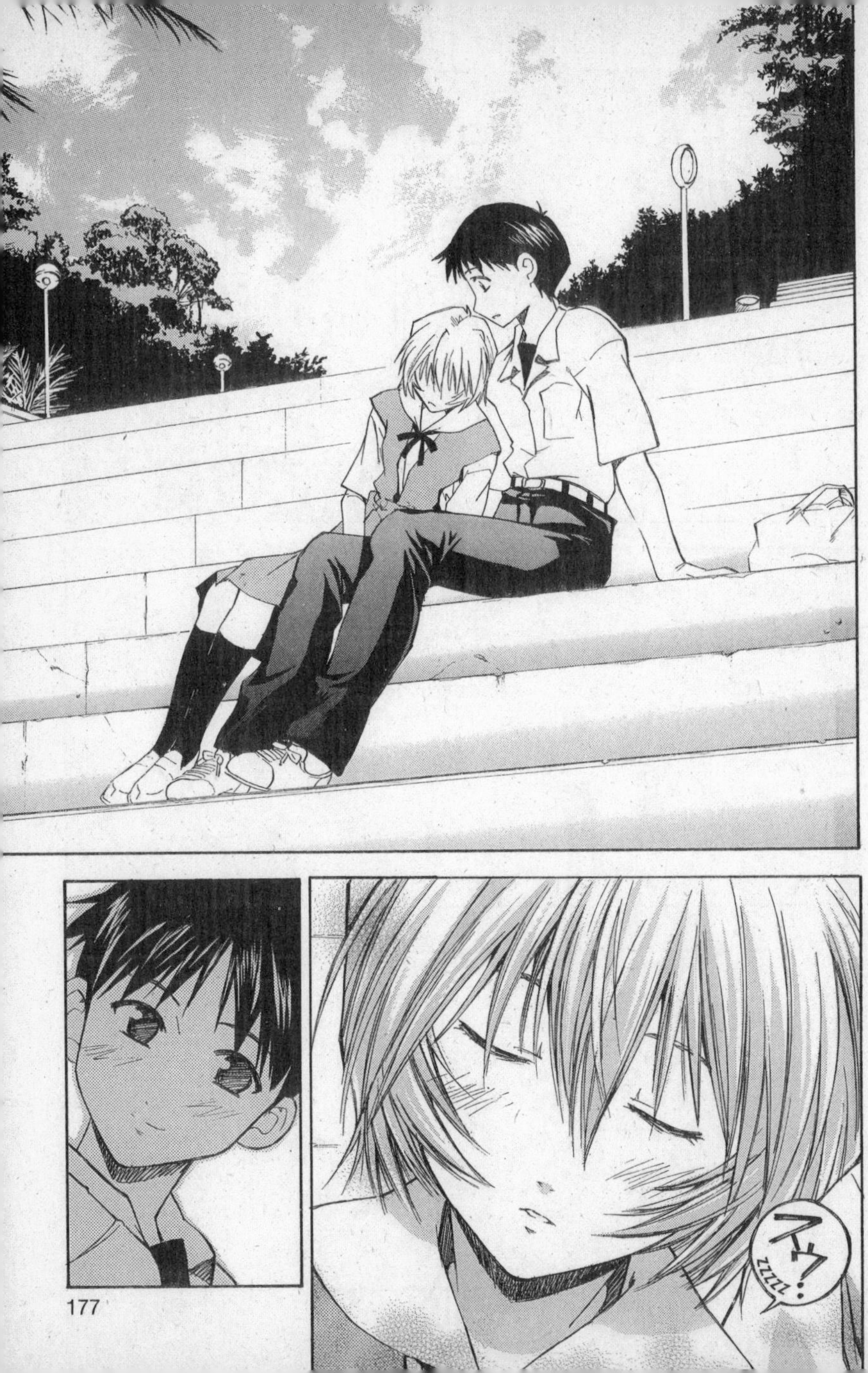
スゥ…
zzzzz

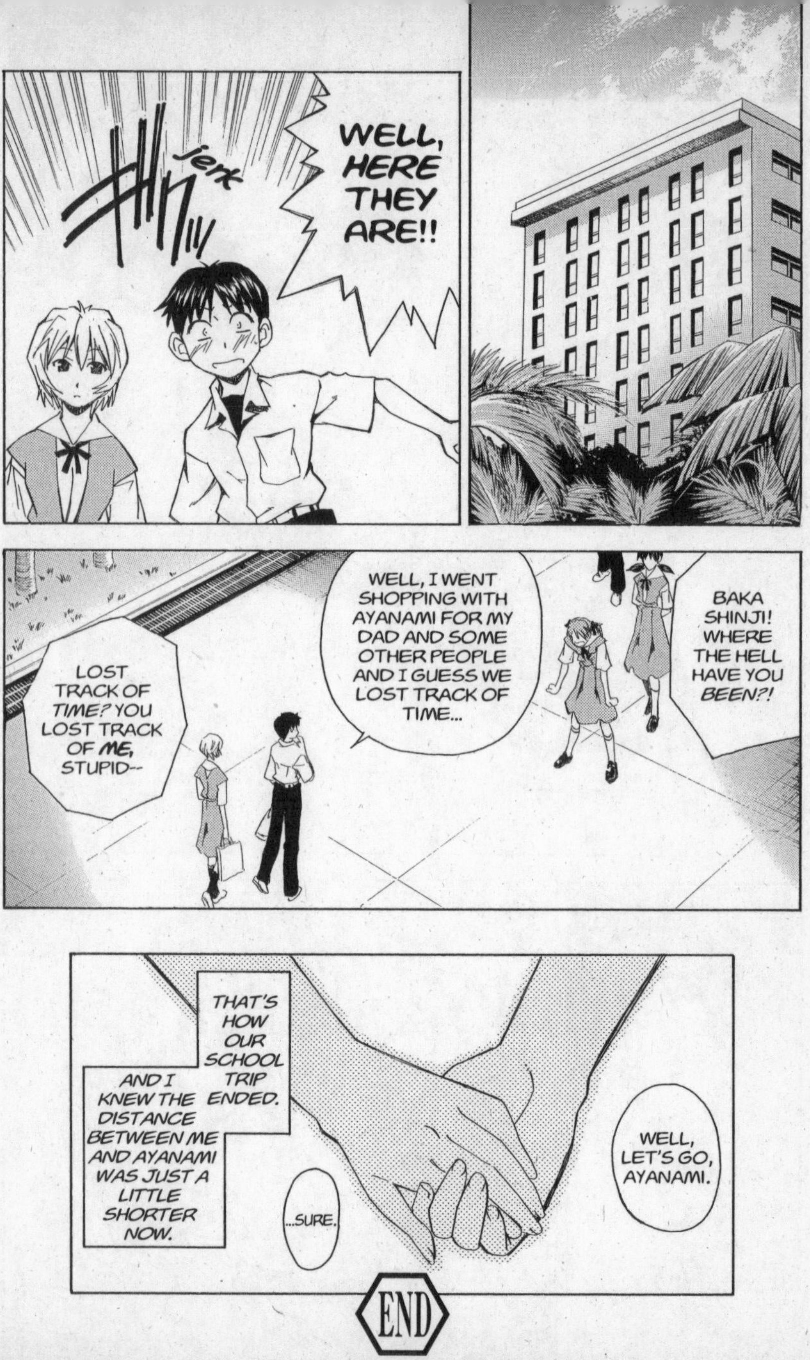
jerk
WELL, HERE THEY ARE!!
BAKA SHINJI! WHERE THE HELL HAVE YOU *BEEN?!*
WELL, I WENT SHOPPING WITH AYANAMI FOR MY DAD AND SOME OTHER PEOPLE AND I GUESS WE LOST TRACK OF TIME...
LOST TRACK OF *TIME?* YOU LOST TRACK OF **ME,** STUPID--
THAT'S HOW OUR SCHOOL TRIP ENDED.
WELL, LET'S GO, AYANAMI.
AND I KNEW THE DISTANCE BETWEEN ME AND AYANAMI WAS JUST A LITTLE SHORTER NOW.
...SURE.
END

AFTERWORD

Shinji, Rei, and Asuka are all middle-school students. So, what—about fourteen years old, I guess?

And so, when I was writing this, I'd try my best to harken back to the memories of my own middle-school days. However, my memory of that period is cloudy, at best, and I couldn't recall much . . .

Wow—was it really **that** long ago?

-Osamu Takahashi

~STAFF~

Kasumiryo

Tatsuya Kamishima

Kanna

Kiyuuki Takashi

Michio Morikawa

Mevius 9

Miki

COVER DESIGN

Seki Shindo

See you in vol. 3 . . .

EDITOR
CARL GUSTAV HORN

EDITORIAL ASSISTANT
ANNIE GULLION

DESIGNER
STEPHEN REICHERT

PUBLISHER
MIKE RICHARDSON

English-language version produced by Dark Horse Comics

Neon Genesis Evangelion: The Shinji Ikari Raising Project Vol. 2

First published in Japan as NEON GENESIS EVANGELION IKARI-SHINJI IKUSEI KEIKAKU Volume 2. © OSAMU TAKAHASHI 2006 © GAINAX • khara. First published in Japan in 2006 by KADOKAWA SHOTEN Publishing Co., Ltd., Tokyo. English translation rights arranged with KADOKAWA SHOTEN Publishing Co., Ltd., Tokyo, through TOHAN CORPORATION, Tokyo. This English-language edition © 2009 by Dark Horse Comics, Inc. All other material © 2009 by Dark Horse Comics, Inc. All rights reserved. No portion of this publication may be reproduced or transmitted, in any form or by any means, without the express written permission of the copyright holders. Names, characters, places, and incidents featured in this publication are either the product of the author's imagination or are used fictitiously. Any resemblance to actual persons (living or dead), events, institutions, or locales, without satiric intent, is coincidental. Dark Horse Manga™ is a trademark of Dark Horse Comics, Inc. All rights reserved.

Published by
Dark Horse Manga
A division of Dark Horse Comics, Inc.
10956 SE Main Street
Milwaukie, OR 97222

darkhorse.com

To find a comics shop in your area, call the Comic Shop Locator Service toll-free at 1-888-266-4226

First edition: September 2009
ISBN 978-1-59582-377-9

1 3 5 7 9 10 8 6 4 2
Printed in Canada

publisher Mike Richardson • **executive vice president** Neil Hankerson • **chief financial officer** Tom Weddle • **vice president of publishing** Randy Stradley • **vice president of business development** Michael Martens • **vice president of marketing, sales, and licensing** Anita Nelson • **vice president of product development** David Scroggy • **vice president of information technology** Dale LaFountain • **director of purchasing** Darlene Vogel • **general counsel** Ken Lizzi • **editorial director** Davey Estrada • **senior managing editor** Scott Allie • **senior books editor** Chris Warner • **executive editor** Diana Schutz • **director of design and production** Cary Grazzini • **art director** Lia Ribacchi • **director of scheduling** Cara Niece

MISATO'S FAN SERVICE CENTER

c/o Dark Horse Comics • 10956 SE Main Street • Milwaukie, OR 97222 • evangelion@darkhorse.com

Aaaaaa, he he—picture me saying that, and putting my hand behind my head like SD Noriko in the *Gunbuster* Science Lessons. That's pronounced *ahhhhhh heh heh*, of course, like it would be in Japanese. I hope when people type "he he" on boards and such they aren't trying to say "hee hee." Because somehow, that would be really irritating.

Anyway, like Noriko, I'm a little embarrassed, because it was pointed out to me by more perceptive people (99 percent of the human race would qualify) that there really *won't* be much time for people to send in their fan art and letters between the time they read our request to do so in the back of vol. 1, and the time we have to get vol. 2 (i.e., what you're reading right now) to the printer. Like *Gunbuster*, manga publishing exists in a kind of relativistic tragedy that forces you, the reader, and me, the editor, to exist in different times.

Because each volume has to go through many stages of translation, editing, design, printing, and distribution, even a book that comes out three months apart like this one is already well into work on the next volumes before the previous one even hits the stands. The upshot is that we have to start putting together "Misato's Fan Service Center" for vol. 2 in early June, several weeks before vol. 1 hits the stands. That means the flood of fan letters and art in response to vol. 1's heartfelt appeal can't appear until vol. 3. That flood *is* coming, right? This is a trip! I'm actually speaking, at this moment, to the FUTURE!!!

So, for vol. 2, we must rely, just as we did for vol. 1, on those early adopters who heard about "Misato's Fan Service Center" *even before vol. 1 came out*—spooky, isn't it. There is one such

person who made their way here after vol. 1 went to the printer—Brian Gin, whose two portraits of Rei grace these pages. I was awfully chuffed, as Bertie Wooster would say, to see that Brian goes to UC Berkeley.

Brian writes, "I'm relatively new to the manga/anime scene, and only got into it after the Tezuka exhibit they had a few years ago in the city." I also feel glad to have him say that, as I participated in that exhibit too on behalf of Dark Horse, as we are the publisher of Tezuka's *Astro Boy*, *Nextworld*, *Lost World*, and *Metropolis*.

I consider the San Francisco Bay Area to be my homeland (although I was born in the LBC) and spent years living all around it, mostly in the East Bay and Contra Costa. Everyone knows that Berkeley is famous as a place to find subcultures, but that includes gaming, comics, anime, and manga as much as radical politics. In the 1980s it was always a thrill for a kid such as myself to journey into Berkeley to score.

In other parts of the country, the place you'd get your manga, comics, or RPGs might be in a strip mall or big shopping center, but back then in Berkeley it'd be a place like the world-famous Telegraph Avenue. It's a long street, but the part people usually mean when they say "Telegraph Avenue" are the several blocks immediately south of the UC Berkeley campus. I still remember when I was eleven years old on Telegraph, and being asked for spare change for the first time (thinking, dude, you're a grownup—aren't you supposed to be giving *me* the spare change?), not to mention it being the first time someone ever made vague eye contact with me and muttered "Buds . . . ? Buds . . . ?" He was wearing a *Dawn of the Trout* T-shirt

("When There's No More Room in the RIVER . . . the TROUT Will Walk the Earth.")

These encounters were on my way to Comics & Comix on Telegraph Ave., which at the time was perhaps the greatest comics store in the United States (today that title might be held by Comic Relief, two blocks north of the downtown Berkeley BART station). Part of what made Comics & Comix so great was that they were among the first to start carrying manga—almost all of it, by necessity, untranslated imports, for manga didn't start to be published here in English on a regular basis until 1987. It was there that I bought my very first manga (and one of the very first to be in English) in 1982, *Barefoot Gen*. The person who might have sold it to me was Diana Schutz, today my fellow editor at Dark Horse (her titles include *Usagi Yojimbo*, *300*, and *Sin City*, among many others). Even at Comics & Comix, she was already editing their extensive newsletter, *The Telegraph Wire*.

Another person who worked at Comics & Comix, someone who had a tremendous influence on me, was Mike Ebert. At the store a little later in the mid-'80s, he was known for making sure it carried the latest anime magazines and art books "The" Japanese bookstore in San Francisco, Kinokuniya, carried manga then but not anime-related books—and even the manga were ordered only for their Japanese-speaking customers; the thought of catering to American fans was still years away. On the plus side, they didn't shrinkwrap their manga then, so I could read all kinds of things I wasn't supposed to, like Koike and Kano's *Brothers*. Imagine the *Color of Rage* team let loose in Reagan-era America. And yes, Reagan is in it.

Mike, who today is the lead game designer for the Activision studio Toys For Bob (he has worked on *Tony Hawk's Downhill Jam* and *Madagascar*), was my Kamina—the first really cool *aniki* I could look up to as a young fan. He would lend me his import anime videos (in those days, literally on videotapes that cost 8,000 yen and up) and soundtracks (on vinyl LP!), trusting that I would return them, even though at first I was just this kid who came into the store. I was drawing manga-inspired comics in high school just for my friends, but back then he was actually getting his published in *Dark Horse Presents* issues #13 and #15—another example of foreshadowing in retrospect. ^_^

Moreover, Mike was inspiring, because he was helping to create a new kind of English-language anime journalism. From his apartment on Milvia St. (about five blocks down from where Kerouac had lived), he was art director and production manager of *Animag*, the first North American anime and manga fan magazine that sought to emulate the quality of Japanese magazines such as *Newtype*. Years ahead of its time, as early as 1987 *Animag* wasn't just reprinting anime artwork from Japan, but commissioning original covers from Yoshiyuki Sadamoto (who needs no introduction to you) with U.S. artists such as Ebert and Schulhoff Tam making their own double-page illustrations for the magazine in a sophisticated anime cel style. *Animag* was later edited by Trish Ledoux, who would become editor of Viz's long-running *Animerica* magazine; *Animag*'s assistant editor, Toshifumi Yoshida, is, among many other things, today the translator of Dark Horse's *The Kurosagi Corpse Delivery Service*.

But perhaps Berkeley's greatest lasting legacy to English-speaking fans of anime and manga came from the city's *raison d'être*—the university, and its students. This year is the twentieth anniversary of U.C. Berkeley's anime club, Cal Animage Alpha. In the early 1990s, it was the largest club in North America, with several hundred people showing up to their weekly programs; behind the scenes, it was also a live-action version of *Genshiken*. ^_^ Cal Animage Alpha was one of the sponsors of AnimeCon '91, which itself branched off in 1992 into a little event called Anime Expo; many CAA alumni, including Mike Tatsugawa and Trulee Karahashi, continued to help shape AX down to the present year.

So Brian Gin may be new to anime and manga, but he's joined an incredible legacy by getting into Berkeley, which itself is no mean feat; what makes Cal Animage Alpha all the more remarkable is that in their spare time its students meet the academic challenges of the finest public university in the United States. Maybe Mr. Gin is wondering whether all that work will pay off. Here at "Misato's Fan Service Center," it already has—he will receive a set of stickers from the new *Evangelion: 2.0* film, *You Can (Not) Advance*, which premiered June 27 in Japan. (No word yet on its U.S. release, although the earlier movie *Evangelion: 1.0 You Are (Not) Alone* is slated for release on DVD from FUNimation on November 10.) Even better, FUNimation has it in selected North American theaters—check funimationfilms.com/events.html for details!

Don't worry, those *Evangelion* folding fans we showed you in vol. 1—they're still here, and they're safely in escrow (i.e., the massive metal flat file cabinet in my office—Scott Cook would make a certain remark at this point, were he designing *Evangelion*, but, fortunately for me, Stephen Reichert is). They'll just be given away in vol. 3 instead. By the way, I forgot to mention the keychains given away in vol. 1 were a very kind gift from Deb Aoki (manga.about.com). At least she can see they were used unselfishly. ^_^

Note the stickers contain not only the rather weak new logos for NERV and SEELE, but the dreaded new last name for Asuka, "Shikinami." That is, it's her new last name in *Evangelion: 2.0*—no one has asked us to go back and change all the times her original last name of "Soryu" is given in this manga.

CENTRAL DOGMA
FINAL GATE / UNLOCKED
CENTRAL DOGMA
FINAL GATE / LOCKED
人類補完計画
EVANGELION
MODEL
02
SHIKINAMI ASUKA LANGLEY
EVANGELION 2.0

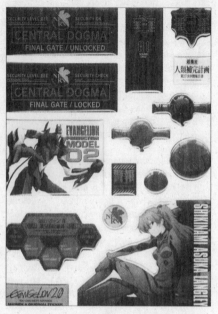

Shikinami, like *Soryu* itself (and like other *Evangelion* character names, including *Katsuragi*, *Akagi*, *Aoba*, and *Hyuga*) is presumably named after a Japanese warship of WWII. The *Soryu* was an aircraft carrier that took part in the Japanese attack on Pearl Harbor, and was sunk seven months later at the Battle of Midway; the destroyer *Shikinami*, which survived Midway (is that why Anno changed it?), was torpedoed by the USS *Growler* in the South China Sea on September 12, 1944. More than half of its crew lived, but the *Growler* itself went down with all hands less than two months later, probably hit by the Japanese destroyer *Shigure*. Which, you guessed it, was itself torpedoed ten weeks later by the USS *Blackfin*. War is not fun.

You've probably all heard about the special, *Evangelion*-themed cell phone available through Sharp—of which, on June 5 in Japan, 20,000 were sold in five hours at 90,000 yen each. That's over 18 million dollars gross—considerably more than *The End of Evangelion* made at the Japanese box office back in 1997, even though it was considered a success at the time. For being residents of a country whose economy has been in the toilet ever since anyone can remember (and not even a Western-style toilet either, but one of those Japanese squat pots), the otaku of Japan can certainly still whip out the cash when needed.

(By contrast, *we* have only asked you to fork out 1 percent of what that cell phone cost to purchase vol. 2 of *Neon Genesis Evangelion: The Shinji Ikari Raising Project* from Dark Horse, and please let me take a moment to thank you for doing so. Well, 1.094 percent, to be exact.)

Scott Cook, since he designs the English edition of *Oh My Goddess!*, would also point out that some of what follows here is a copypasta from *Oh My Goddess!* Vol. 33's letters column (called "Letters to the Enchantress"). That's because I ran into a Belldandy cosplayer at the GAINAX party at the recent FanimeCon 2009 in San Jose, so my report sort of did double duty for both manga titles.

Mention of FanimeCon takes us back to the Bay Area—South Bay instead of East Bay. And although Anime Expo, like the Raiders, moved to Los Angeles (James Hetfield voice: *"I dub thee unforgiven, whoa-oh, whoa-oh."*), the Bay Area still has a major anime and manga con—and, like the Expo, it grew out of student clubs.

San Jose, in case you don't know, is the largest city in California's famous "Silicon Valley," and is at the lower end of San Francisco Bay; consequently, it is the ideal site for northern California's largest anime and manga convention, FanimeCon, which celebrated its fifteenth anniversary this year with as many as 16,000 people in attendance over a four-day weekend. And as you might guess, its roots lie in a number of local clubs, including Foothill Anime, "America's Most Beautiful Anime Club"—which, as its name implies, is set amidst the Los Altos Hills.

Taking inspiration in part from medieval Japan, at Foothill College you will find massive cobblestone buttresses and the type of sloped, shingled roofs ninja love to run across, seventy (count them—seventy) varieties of bamboo, and an Azumaya meditation pavilion built by the students of the International College of Crafts and Arts in Toyama as a gift to the school; Foothill has been three times honored by the American Institute of Architects for its design. You can even intern from Foothill at NASA's nearby Ames Research Center, which controls the just-launched Kepler Space Telescope, the first satellite capable of detecting Earth-sized planets around different stars—you'll admit that's pretty cool.

After its first two years at Cal State Hayward (I told you students were behind this ^_^), Fanime-Con spent 1996, 1997, and 1998 at Foothill, during which time it increased its attendance almost by a factor of five, and acquired its first Japanese guest, GAINAX's executive director, Hiroyuki Yamaga. The reason FanimeCon had to leave Foothill eventually wasn't so much because it got big (19,000 people attend classes on campus), but because there's nowhere to spend the night, limiting the con to daytime events. I remember in 1998 having taken shelter from a rainstorm in the basketball court (where the dealer's room was set up!) and emerging as the clouds broke, with great beams of light coming down on the hills like the poster for Mr. Yamaga's film *The Wings of Honneamise* and saying, "I can't believe we're trading this next year for a hotel."

These days, in 2009, FanimeCon is held at the San Jose Convention Center, but Mr. Yamaga is

still its most honored guest, and he and other members of GAINAX attend every year. Sunday evening at this year's Fanime, GAINAX hosted a party at the Fairmont Hotel for the other guests, and one hundred fans that were lucky enough to win an invitation at random.

Can *you* spot the L in the first pic (bottom left) among the one hundred? Although iconic, I can't help but feel that L is kind of the quick-'n'-easy cosplay choice for guys these days, sort of the way Shinji himself used to be. Actually, it basically *is* Shinji, just with jeans and hair gel. In the second pic (above), that's not a cosplayer on the far right, but an honest-to-God butler attending to the hors d'oeuvres. The butler fetish isn't as popular among fans as the maid fetish, but in this regard at least, the party did supply it.

From right to left (but of course): Masafumi Ishikawa and Yasuhiro Akamatsu, both of whom were compositors on the first *Tengen Toppa Gurren Lagann* film, *Crimson Lotus Chapter*. They're wearing official staff polo shirts; note the Dai-Gurren Brigade logos on the back. Note also

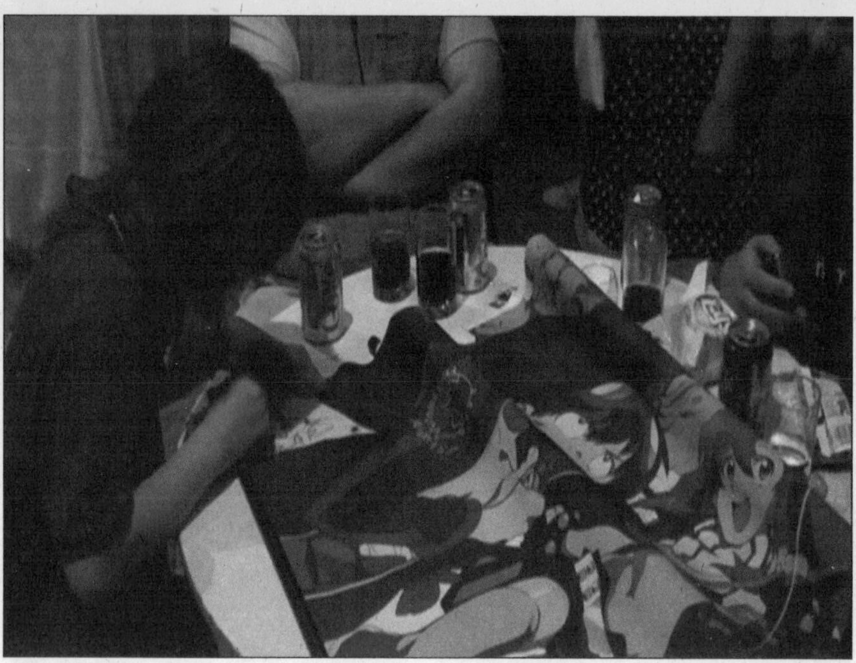

that you can't see either of their faces, because I took this image, and frankly, I'm not very bright.

Animator Megumi Kouno is drawing Nia on the same wall hanging that Ishikawa and Akamatsu adorned earlier. Again, thanks to careful planning on my part, the artist is not visible.

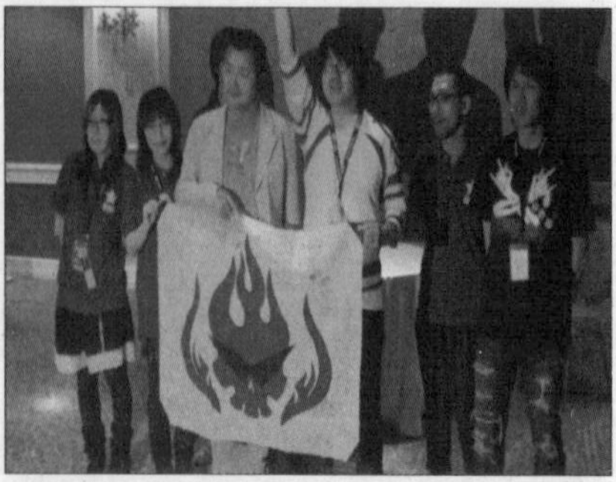

After the party: starting from right to left, Hirokazu Kojima (key animator on episode 27 and *Gurren Lagann Parallel Works*), and Masafumi Ishikawa. In white with raised fist is *Gurren Lagann*'s director, Hiroyuki Imaishi, who told the crowd at the panel earlier that he had been really touched the previous year to have met all the American *Gurren* fans when he came to Fanime 2008, and that he wanted to let everyone know he was thinking of them while working on the *Gurren Lagann* movie in Japan. To Imaishi's left, and holding the flag at its center, is GAINAX's executive director, Hiroyuki Yamaga. Behind Mr. Yamaga, I have managed to conceal Yasuhiro Akamatsu's features once again. To Yamaga's left is Megumi Kouno, and on the left end is compositor Kiko Nagase. Nagase noted that she, like a number of the GAINAX staff at Fanime this year, came onto the project only with the first *Gurren Lagann* movie, and that during the making of the TV show, she was still a fan like everyone else there.

At Fanime, GAINAX showed the aforementioned *Tengen Toppa Gurren Lagann: Crimson Lotus Chapter*, which was enjoyed by hundreds of fans, despite the fact it was in Japanese without any translation (the same way, I couldn't help but reflect, we enjoyed most anime in the 1980s. GAINAX also hosted the world premiere of a documentary about the making of *Gurren Lagann* itself, shot more than two years ago at their studio during the original series' production. Hiroyuki Yamaga spoke about their motivations in making *Gurren Lagann* in an intriguing remark with odd resonance for *Neon Genesis Evangelion*: "At the time *Gurren Lagann* was made, robot anime were becoming less mainstream. We felt we shouldn't run away from *not* making a robot anime, and then, after making *Gurren Lagann*, we can graduate, and move in a different direction."

Oh, yeah, *Neon Genesis Evangelion*. Note that Asuka's "Kimochi warui!" in 61.2 is exactly the same as her famous final line from *The End of Evangelion* (which, I suppose, until the new films end in 2013,* must also count as the final line in the *Evangelion* story itself). If you picked up on this right away, all the better, but it was left untranslated here as a sort of metajoke (we are all about the meta) over the ongoing interpretation** of that final line (*The End of Evangelion* should have perhaps done the same thing that other apocalyptic classic, *The Book of Revelation*, did, and simply end with an "Amen"). Hikari's line in 134.1 is, of course, a quote from episode 18. Then there's Kawaru's paraphrase of episode 24 in 18.3 . . .

Now would be a good time to remind everyone once again that an excellent place to discuss these ideas, and anything else *Evangelion*, is **evageeks.org**. As of June 2009, they have over 219,000 postings from 2000-plus registered users, on everything from "MAGMADIVER IS THE WORST EPISODE EVER" to "Is ANYTHING coming from Lilith's crotch? (PIC provided)" to "Reconsidering the PS(2/P) Game's Canonicity" to "Secret Life of Pen Pen" to "Spiral, Seed, Shield, and Spear." I sometimes think that whereas Japanese-speaking fans express their love of *Eva* through merchandise and doujinshi, English-speaking fans do so on a higher, spiritual plane, with threads that contain 280 replies and 15,000 views.

you say k-on-i say DMC
you say code geass-i say MAZINKAISER

you say lucky star-i say OTAKU NO VIDEO
you say anima-i say EROICA
you say oel-i say ur comics
you say comics-i say manga up your ass.
92% of teens have turned to moe and mierda
if your one the 8% who like to headbang and disturb the peace copy and paste to 3 manga letter columns

(Sorry! I don't know where *that* came from. Someone must have put it in to teach me a lesson about using copypasta.)

—Carl

* Projected end date based on the Japanese 1.0 coming out in 2007, and 2.0 in 2009. The problem is, of course, that 2013 is only two years before 2015, which no doubt will be marked by some new revival, remake, or re-release. My guess is that *Evangelion*'s creators might unveil a new service where fans can simply directly deposit their paycheck.

** If one wants the final line to best sum up both the series and the reason for it, then I think the sickness is existential, as in the title of episode 16.

the KUROSAGI corpse delivery service

黒鷺死体宅配便

If you enjoyed this book, be sure to check out *The Kurosagi Corpse Delivery Service*, a new mature-readers manga series from the creator of *Mail*!

Five young students at a Buddhist university find there's little call for their job skills in today's Tokyo . . . among the *living*, that is! But their studies give them a direct line to the dead—the dead who are still trapped in their corpses, and can't move on to the next reincarnation! Whether you died from suicide, murder, sickness, or madness, they'll carry your body anywhere it needs to go to free your soul! Written by Eiji Otsuka of the notorious *MPD-Psycho*!

Volume 1:
ISBN 978-1-59307-555-2

Volume 2:
ISBN 978-1-59307-593-4

Volume 3:
ISBN 978-1-59307-594-1

Volume 4:
ISBN 978-1-59307-595-8

Volume 5:
ISBN 978-1-59307-596-5

Volume 6:
ISBN 978-1-59307-892-8

Volume 7:
ISBN 978-1-59307-982-6

Volume 8:
ISBN 978-1-59582-235-2

Volume 9:
ISBN 978-1-59582-306-9

$10.95 each!

Kosuke Fujishima's

Dark Horse is proud to re-present *Oh My Goddess!* in the much-requested, affordable, Japanese-reading, right-to-left format, complete with color sections, informative bonus notes, and your letters!

$10.95 each!

AVAILABLE AT YOUR LOCAL COMICS SHOP OR BOOKSTORE
*To find a comics shop in your area, call 1-888-266-4226

For more information or to order direct:
•On the web: darkhorse.com •E-mail: mailorder@darkhorse.com
•Phone: 1-800-862-0052 Mon.–Fri. 9 AM to 5 PM Pacific Time.

EDEN

It's an Endless World!

Volume 1
ISBN 978-1-59307-406-7

Volume 2
ISBN 978-1-59307-454-8

Volume 3
ISBN 978-1-59307-529-3

Volume 4
ISBN 978-1-59307-544-6

Volume 5
ISBN 978-1-59307-634-4

Volume 6
ISBN 978-1-59307-702-0

Volume 7
ISBN 978-1-59307-765-5

Volume 8
ISBN 978-1-59307-787-7

Volume 9
ISBN 978-1-59307-851-5

Volume 10
ISBN 978-1-59307-957-4

Volume 11
ISBN 978-1-59582-244-4

Volume 12
ISBN 978-1-59582-296-3

$12.95 each!